THE UNIVERSITY OF OXFORD

G.R. Evans is Professor Emeritus of Medieval Theology and Intellectual History at the University of Cambridge. Her companion volume, *The University of Cambridge: A New History* (2010), is also published by I.B.Tauris.

THE UNIVERSITY OF OXFORD

A NEW HISTORY

G.R. EVANS

I.B.TAURIS
LONDON · NEW YORK

New paperback edition first published in 2013
by I.B.Tauris & Co. Ltd
London • New York
Reprinted 2016, 2014
www.ibtauris.com

First published in hardback in 2010 by I.B.Tauris & Co. Ltd

Front cover image: Radcliffe Square, Oxford. Photo by Paul Press, all rights reserved.
Back cover image: Hertford Bridge (or the Bridge of Sighs), Hertford College, Oxford. Photo by Alex Rawlings, all rights reserved.

References to websites were correct at the time of writing.

Every attempt has been made to gain permission for the use of the images in this book. Any omissions will be rectified in future editions.

ISBN: 978 1 78076 494 8
eISBN: 978 0 85773 025 1

A full CIP record for this book is available from the British Library
A full CIP record is available from the Library of Congress

Library of Congress Catalog Card Number: available

Printed and bound by CPI Group (UK) Ltd, Croydon, CR0 4YY

I wonder anybody does anything at Oxford but dream and remember the place is so beautiful. One almost expects the people to sing instead of speaking. It is all – the colleges I meen (sic) – like an opera.

– W.B. Yeats (aged 23), Letter to Katharine Tynan,
30 August 1888, *The Collected Letters*,
ed. J.Kelly and E. Domville (Oxford, 1986), Vol.I, p.93

PREFACE

> At the head of the procession comes the UNIVERSITY MARSHALL carrying a silver wand. He wears a velvet cape and a long broadcloth coat with velvet cuffs and large buttons. His hat is round and squashed with a rosette on it. ...He is a man of great charm and tact through his duty of 'assisting the relations of undergraduates with the Proctors.' Behind the University Marshall come eight BEDELS.... They carry staves. Their sole duty seems to be to announce people on official occasions. Now comes the Chancellor himself. His robe is black interspersed with twisted gold.... A perfectly ordinary undergraduate in evening-dress carries his train.... The Chancellor can only come to Oxford with the permission of the Vice-Chancellor, and then he is only invited as a guest.... Next comes the HIGH STEWARD, with the robe or hood of his degree... there is an obscure Court over which he may preside for trying undergraduates accused of treason, felony and maim. He receives five pounds a year, but looks richer. Behind the High Stewards comes the VICE-CHANCELLOR. The absence of the chief functionary in the University makes the Vice-Chancellor all-powerful.... You may see him during term-time taking his official walks abroad, preceded by a mace-bearer and attendants. The University BURGESSES follow, then the Doctors.... Now you may see the SENIOR and JUNIOR PROCTORS... to-day is an off-day for the Proctors as they, and the Vice-Chancellor... have no powers, because the Chancellor himself is present.... You may see one or other of the proctors walking about the Oxford streets of an evening attended by two or more University police... 'bulldogs' [who] – wear bowler hats and can run very fast.[1]

This is how John Betjeman describes the procession ('never will you feel more common and herded than before this ribbon of learning that will presently come winding by') which takes place at Encaenia each year in Oxford before the award of Honorary Degrees, after the peaches and champagne have been enjoyed under the provisions of the benefaction of Lord Crewe (1633–1721):

Betjeman's is an affectionate portrait. Is it a caricature? The Morse and Lewis television series have portrayed a beautiful, eccentric Oxford, but is this the real Oxford? A generation or so ago, the Inklings (C.S. Lewis, J.R.R. Tolkien and Charles Williams), met regularly in an Oxford pub to encourage one another in the writing of fictions set in fantasy worlds, Tolkien's starting from a location closely resembling the medieval English Midlands where he spent most of his youth. Oxford has remained a favoured location for the modern fantasy novel. Phillip Pullman's Gyptians live on the Oxford canal and it is from Oxford that his characters gain entry to another world.

And who is to say there is not a living fantasy in Oxford's modern life? Jan Morris described in the 1960s how:

> at George's [Café in the covered market] in June there are often a few young couples eating bacon-and-eggs after dancing all night, their long dresses crumpled, their black ties askew, their faces expressing an awful determination to keep awake and amused for just half an hour longer.[2]

The visitor walking among the golden colleges may still see students setting off for examinations dressed in black and white, with black ties for the girls and white ties for the boys, some in the raggedy wisps of black cotton gowns which pass for Commoners' gowns and some wearing the fancier gowns of Scholars. The Honorary Degree procession still goes on as Betjeman describes it. It is still *de rigeur* to wear an Oxford gown in academic processions (and not the gown of another university), over the same black-and-white ('subfusc') attire. There has never been an archive record of the correct forms of academic dress, though a set of copper-plates depicting the norms of 1770 was kept in the Convocation House to discourage innovations.[3]

It is a confident society which can maintain traditions so eccentric and so enduring while sending off a steady stream of graduates who will be running the country. Oxford has always been vigorously engaged with the 'real' world, providing a preponderance of the leading politicians of Britain and endless famous names in every field of professional and artistic activity. It is true that Oxford is a little world to itself, a village where everyone knows one another and stops in the Broad or the High to exchange local gossip. But those academic encounters in the street are as likely to be tough grapplings with active politics (local, national and international) as exchanges about a point of scholarly detail. Oxford is crowded with tourists and townspeople. It is no backwater and certainly not an ivory tower. The 'reality' of Oxford is that it is not at all a land of faery. Tolkien and Lewis had it right not with their fairy-tales but with their allegory, with its cosmic contexts, for they were placing their stories in that much larger 'world'.

The author of a book on Oxford written in the climate of the first decade of the twenty-first century enters dangerous political territory as well as a minefield of colourful expectation. Oxford divides opinion. Politicians speak of a conspiracy to keep Oxford for the 'privileged'. That has long been nonsense, but it means that 'going to Oxford' carries baggage. Again and again Oxford has protested that the stories are not true and done its best to correct the false impression. Hastings Rashdall (1858–1924), a Fellow[4] of New College, wrote his classic three-volume study of the early history of universities at the end of the nineteenth century,[5] in a climate of contemporary debate about their future remarkably similar in many respects to the one in which modern society is actively engaged. In his last volume Rashdall took a view on the contemporary debate about the future of universities. He thought the handing on of knowledge was one of the essential tasks of universities ('education ... must always be, from the necessities of the case, a tradition'). But he also believed they must adapt to meet new needs ('new needs must be met by new machinery'[6]) in an age which seemed at the end of the nineteenth century to be challenging old certainties. A century later, in 1998, the Vice-Chancellor's Oration, preoccupated with much the same questions touched on the widening of 'access':

> Whatever the crass stereotypes trotted out with such relish in some public comment, it is absurd to think that those who teach and research in Oxford do not desire to see the excellence of this university as a ladder of opportunity to talented young people whatever their background. Indeed, many of us have benefited in that way: why should we wish to deny it to others?[7]

In this decade there was also significant Oxford development in 'lifelong learning', as Continuing Education at Rewley House became the responsibility of the new Kellogg College.

So why a new book now, and what can it offer? The 'official' multi-volume *History of the University of Oxford*[8] ends with the Franks Commission, and a bare sketch of what happened after 1970 and before the 1990s. It is not easy to continue the story from then to now because it involves events whose protagonists are still alive, in many cases still in Oxford. It is difficult to get the distance the historian needs to balance the sense of engagement which is inseparable from university life. The trick is to make the distance part of the composition. To tell the recent story without setting it in the context of its long background would be to sketch only the smile of the Cheshire cat and not attempt to paint the whole elegant beast with its unpredictable tendencies to spit or to purr, to catch rats or to lie luxuriously on a window-sill in the sun.

> To judge rightly of an author, we must transport ourselves to his time, and examine what were the wants of his contemporaries, and what were his means of supplying them. That which is easy at one time was difficult at another.[9]

Samuel Johnson made this observation in his discussion of Dryden, in his *Lives of the poets*. It applies with even greater force to the story of the University.

ACKNOWLEDGEMENTS

I am grateful to the reading room staff of Duke Humfrey's Library in the Bodleian, to Catja Pafort and James Willoughby, for their help with pictures, to Alex Wright for his editorial skills and expertise, to Tim Horder and Bernard Sufrin for reading the book in draft and for their comments and to Victoria Nemeth and Anula Lydia for once again exercising copy-editing with skill and patience, and to all those friends and acquaintances in Oxford who make up its distinctive community.

ABBREVIATIONS

Aubrey's *Lives*	John Aubrey, *Brief lives,* ed. Oliver Lawson Dick (Michigan, 1957)
Cambridge History	G.R. Evans, *A concise history of the University of Cambridge* (London, 2009)
Gazette	*Gazette Oxford University* (Oxford, 1870–)
Hansard	House of Commons and House of Lords Debates, http://www.publications.parliament.uk/pa/cm/chron.htm
HC	*House of Commons*
Hearne Remains	Thomas Hearne, *Reliquiae Hearnianae,* ed. P. Bliss (Oxford, 1857)
Hearne's Collections	*Remarks and collections of Thomas Hearne,* ed. H.E. Salter, OHS, 67 (1915)
HL	*House of Lords*
OHS	*Oxford Historical Society*
Oxhist	*The history of the University of Oxford,* general editor T.H. Aston (Oxford, 1984–94), 8 vols
PL	*Patrologia Latina*
Ruskin, *Works*	John Ruskin, *The works of John Ruskin* (London, 1871–80), vols 1–
Salter, *Medieval Archives*	H.E. Salter, *Medieval archives of the University of Oxford* (Oxford, 1920–1)
Statuta Antiqua	*Statuta Antiqua universitatis Oxoniensis,* ed. A. Strickland Gibson (Oxford, 1931)
Wood, *Annals*	A. Wood, *The history and antiquities of the University of Oxford,* ed. J. Gutch, 2 vols. in 3 parts (Oxford, 1792–6), pp.124–6.
Wood, *Athenae Ox*	Anthony Wood, *Athenae Oxonienses* (London, 1691)
Wood, *Life and times*	*The life and times of Anthony Wood, Antiquary, of Oxford,* 1632–95, collected by Andrew Clark, OHS, 26 (1894).

CONTENTS

LIST OF ILLUSTRATIONS

Plate sections located between pages 110 and 111, and between pages 238 and 239

INTRODUCTION: COMING TO OXFORD

> It could not be real, he thought. It was a fragile city spun out of dreams, so small that he could have held it on the palm of his hand and blown it away into silver mist. It was not real. He had dreamed of it for so long that now, when he looked down into the valley, the mist formed itself into towards and spires that would vanish under the sun the moment he shut his eyes ... He shut his eyes, opened them, and the towers were still there.[1]

Elizabeth Goudge (1900–1984) describes in her novel *Towers in the mist* (1938), set in the late sixteenth century, the scene that still meets the newcomer who comes upon Oxford from Shotover Hill. Evelyn Waugh, writing in *Brideshead revisited* about the Oxford of the 1930s, waxes equally lyrical about the deceptively delicate-seeming beauty of Oxford:

> Oxford, in those days, was still a city of aquatint. In her spacious and quiet streets men walked and spoke as they had done in Newman's day; her autumnal mists, her grey springtime, and the rare glory of her summer days – such as that day – when the chestnut was in flower and the bells rang out high and clear over her gables and cupols, exhaled the soft airs of centuries of youth.[2]

This is the Oxford of legends, longings and aspiration, its college quadrangles opening out of one another in a succession of golden stone spaces full of honeyed architectural witticisms and little jesting gargoyles, with battered bicycles partly held together with string, resting four or five deep beside the gate to the Lodge. In the old centre one must still walk with ankle-wrenching painfulness over cobbles laid in the alleyways in times when they stank and were full of ordure, and pedestrians badly needed a hard surface. Out towards the river to the east the cobbles give way and one may choose between visiting a 300-year-old deer park on one's left in the grounds of Magdalen College, and a Botanic Garden dating from 1633 on one's right, described in the late seventeenth century by Thomas Baskerville:

> The Phisick Garden & its Rarityes of that nature ... stands on ground lately purchased from Magdalen Colledge ... prouving serviceable not only to all Physitians, Apothecaryes, and those who are more immediately concerned in the practise of Physick, [and] to persons of all qualities seruing to help ye diseased and for ye delights & pleasure of those of perfect health, containing therein 3000 severall sorts of plants for ye honor of our nation and Universitie & service of ye Common-wealth.[3]

This is the Oxford which fills the mind of even the casual visitor with lingering images of dappled shade on immaculate lawns under great trees in the college gardens, and which, for those who spend time there as students or dons, becomes a woven fabric of associations. Thomas Hardy, Evelyn Waugh, Philip Larkin, C.S. Lewis, J.R.R. Tolkien, Iris Murdoch, Philip Pullman and others to be met in these pages, all found they were 'Oxford' novelists, even those who tried to get away. When Iris Murdoch set a novel in London, she found herself peopling it with characters who are often recognizably 'Oxford types'. At the beginning of *The Book and the Brotherhood,* an Oxford summer ball is the venue for a reunion.[4]

Elizabeth Goudge was the daughter of Henry Leighton Goudge, who became Regius Professor of Divinity in Oxford when she was twenty-three and she already had strong loyalties to other places where she had grown up. So she found herself startled, smitten with Oxford when she was not much older than the typical undergraduate. She had a privileged entry to it as she and her family moved into the house in Christ Church's Great Quad. By contrast, in Philip Larkin's *Jill,* John, a boy from a working-class home, arrives on a train to become a student during the Second World War. Strong feelings of social discomfort spoil his arrival. His mother had taken him shopping to buy him the things on the list the College had sent, but his room-mates are mocking. 'That list they send you's enough to make a cat laugh. Breakfast china and tea china – do they think you're made of money?'[5] He feels himself an outsider. He eats his breakfast among a crowd of self-conscious freshman scholars, speaking to no one.[6] He has an impulse many who have arrived in Oxford as first-generation students will recognize: to run away, give up on Oxford and return to a life in which he was comfortable. He began to feel that 'he did not want to go any further with this new life. ... How much pleasanter it would be to go back, though the past was even by this time unemphatic and twilit'.[7] But few do. Oxford's 'drop-out' rate is tiny.

Today's arriving students or visitors gaze on an Oxford whose peculiar visual harmony was mainly a creation of the fourteenth to eighteenth centuries, with an area of Victorian development to the north not prominent among the 'towers in the mist' when the city is viewed from the hills. The Oxford to be seen now had a narrow escape from the ambitious notions of Nicholas Hawksmoor (1661–1736). He had a grand scheme to make Oxford look completely different, baroque, monumental, with Magdalen College demolished so as to build a great complex with colonnades. There was even a scheme to turn All Souls Gothic.[8]

Over Shotover Hill ran the road into Oxford from London which was used for centuries and which comes in through Headington. For the period from the Domesday Book till 1660 when Charles II ascended the throne (by which time it was somewhat dilapidated), it had been clad in a royal forest. But even in times when travellers came from other directions, roads for arriving in Oxford have always been limited by the geography of the place, for it is set on low land amongst a confusion of rivers and tributaries to the Thames, with large areas always unfit for building or for the construction of roads.

For road-users, there have always been really only three or four main ways to arrive. One is the road from Abingdon running up St. Aldate's, or round past what is now the railway station and the Said Business School, once allowing the visitor the choice of entering through the south or the east gate of the old city. This approach took the traveller or would-be student through the area favoured in the thirteenth century by the mendicant Orders whose members formed so substantial a proportion of the medieval University, and later by Cardinal Wolsey when he formed the plan to build the biggest and best college in the University, the venture which is now Christ Church.

The second offers a choice of the roads from Iffley, Cowley, and Headington, which join to form the High Street, after running through the industrial areas which arrived with the Industrial Revolution. John Ruskin (1819–1900) had been an erratic undergraduate at Christ Church, though he won the Newdigate Prize for poetry and eventually became Oxford's first Slade Professor of Fine Art in 1869. He deplored the effect as he observed it walking in from Iffley with its remarkable twelfth-century Romanesque church, to a central Oxford which he found to be in inner-city decline, at least in terms of the regrettable ᶠ its streets. He described his feelings in a lecture he gave on 24 February 1872:

> I walked back from Iffley to Oxford by what was once the most beautiful approach to an academical city of any in Europe. Now it is a wilderness of obscure and base buildings. You think it a fine thing to go into Iffley Church by the front door; – and you build cheap lodging-houses over all the approach to the chief university of English literature! That, foresooth, is your luminous cloister, and porch of Polygnotus to your temple of Apollo. And in the centre of that temple, at the very foot of the dome of the Radclyffe, between two principal colleges, the lane ... is left in a state as loathsome as a back-alley in the East End of London.[9]

He returned to the theme at other times with equal indignation:

> The entire charm and educational power of the city of Oxford, so far as that educational power depended on reverent associations, or on visible solemnities and serenities of architecture, have been already destroyed ... by the manufacturing suburb which heaps its ashes on one side and the cheap-lodging suburb which heaps its brickbats on the other.[10]

The later advent of the car factories in Cowley (the Morris Motor Company in 1913) encouraged the building of the Blackbird Leys estate in the 1950s and 1960s. This was to give Oxford an industrial aspect which was never quite matched in Cambridge. (Cambridge's modern 'links with industry' belong to the era of Silicon Valley.) The arrival of the car industry also created tensions for the city, a new complex of town and gown resentments taking forward the saga of battles between two rival communities in a small place which we shall trace in the chapters that follow. Civic and commercial development became important for Oxford.

Dorothy Sayers in *Gaudy Night,* published in 1935, describes the arrival from Headington into the High Street, as her heroine comes back to Oxford for a College 'Gaudy', the annual feast (so-called from the Latin *gaudium,* 'rejoicing') from:

> Headington Hill, up which one had toiled so often, pushing a decrepit bicycle. It seemed less steep now, as one made decorous descent behind four rhythmically pulsating cylinders ... then the narrow street, with its cramped, untidy shops, like the main street of a village ... Magdalen Bridge,

> Magdalen Tower ... the heartless and indifferent persistence of man's handiwork ... Long Wall St., St. Cross Road.[11]

It is from the north that the historical expansion of the University itself is most apparent. The locations of the earliest colleges, Balliol (1263), Merton (1264), University (1249) and the University Church of St. Mary which lie within it, give an indication how tiny medieval Oxford was. What may look like the northern part of the city to the modern visitor, for example, the broad space of St. Giles where St. Giles's Fair is held at the beginning of September every year, lay outside the medieval city walls. So do several of the most imposing of the early modern colleges, St. John's (1555) for example, and all those to the north which mark by stages the Victorian and twentieth-century expansion of the collegiate life of Oxford: Keble (1870), St. Anne's (starting as the Home Students in 1878), St. Hugh's (1886), Wolfson (1966, a college from 1981). The town had its walls rebuilt in the mid-thirteenth century, and the portions of those which can still be seen within New College give a sense of the smallness of the original town which lay within them.

Up the converging Woodstock and Banbury Roads which run from the north into St. Giles, the University area spread in the late nineteenth century when College Fellows were allowed to marry and needed family houses. It was this process, the Victorianization of North Oxford, which created the modern Gothic suburb of North Oxford. As Ruskin observed, Gothic was all the fashion at the time: 'It has been thought, gentlemen, that there is a fine Gothic revival on your streets of Oxford, because you have a Gothic door to your County Bank' (built 1868).[12]

In her novel *The house in Norham Gardens,* Penelope Lively describes the result, if one comes down Banbury Road into Oxford:

> Belbroughton Rd. Linton Rd. Bardwell Rd. The houses there are quite normal. They are ordinary sizes and have ordinary chimneys and roofs and gardens with Laburnum and flowering cherry. Park Town. As you go south they are growing. Getting higher and odder. By the time you get to Norham Gardens they have tottered over the edge into madness: these are not houses but flights of fancy. They are three stories high and disguise themselves as churches. They have ecclesiastical porches instead of front doors and round Norman windows or pointed gothic ones, neatly grouped in threes with flaring brick to set them off. They reek of hymns and the Empire,

> Mafeking and the Khyber Pass, Mr. Gladstone and Our Dear Queen. They have nineteen rooms and half a dozen chimneys and iron fire escapes.[13]

These new extravaganzas did not encroach on the University Parks, which occupy the area beyond the science laboratories and the Natural History Museum and stretch for seventy acres as far as Marston, across land too flooded for building. Part of the area had long been used for the University Walks, it is said by Charles II when he wanted somewhere to walk his dog in 1685. The Parks proper were purchased from Merton College by the University in 1853–4 and plans put in hand for developing them. A portion was set aside for the building of the University Museum (1855–60). Charles Dodgson (Lewis Carroll) described the Museum and the Parks at this time in *The deserted parks*:

> Museum! Loveliest building of the plain
> Where Cherwell winds towards the distant main…
> In peaceful converse with his brother Don,
> Here oft the calm Professor wandered on;
> Strange words he used – men drank with wondering ears
> The languages called 'dead', the tongues of other years.[14]

The Victorians, says Penelope Lively:

> had gone the whole way with the Natural History Museum…Here is a building dedicated to the pursuit of scientific truth built in a precise imitation of a church.…It was like entering a Victorian station, St. Pancras, or Euston: but a station furnished with fossils and pickled jellyfish and whale skeletons hung absurdly from the glass roof.…There was Prince Albert in a marble frock-coat, presiding…and there too were Galileo and Newton and Charles Darwin five steps behind and slightly smaller, like figures on an Egyptian frieze, as befitted mere scientists, and commoners at that.[15]

The small Pitt-Rivers Museum added at the back in 1884 was to house a collection of anthropologically interesting specimens as eccentric as anything on the outsides of these Victorian buildings, given to the University by the collector himself:

> Pitt Rivers…the Indian totem towering over the central well of the place…glass cases too close together and creaking floorboards…three small boys staring respectfully at the shrunken heads and a man in a dirty mac who looked as though he had strolled in from some seedy spy film.[16]

The Museum stood at first in grand isolation like a country house and gazed upon views over parkland, for which the University began to evolve plans to make parts of it into an arboretum. James Bateman had been a student at Magdalen, across the road from the Botanic Garden where he had been a frequent visitor. He had made his name as a garden designer in the 1850s at Biddulph Grange in Staffordshire and now he was asked to design the layout and planting of the Parks. His design was rejected by Oxford's Convocation[17] in 1863 because they thought it would be too expensive to implement.

Keble College was founded in 1870 in memory of the Tractarian John Keble (1792–1866), across from the Parks:

> If the Victorians can be said to have rampaged, they did so to greatest effect in the few acres of Oxford beside and immediately south of the University parks.... There is Keble College, red brick sprawling so copiously that one feels the stuff must have got out of control, unleashing some dark force upon a helpless architect. Or the houses that survive as tenacious Gothic islands amid the concrete cliffs of the new University Departments.[18]

The 'helpless architect' was William Butterfield (1814–1900), influenced by the Oxford Movement as well as the taste for medieval revival in building.

Touching on this visual excess with a light wit, Lewis Carroll includes teasing remarks in *The new belfrey of Christ Church, Oxford*[19] about the avidity of lady tourists to see it. By contrast, in 'Maggie's visit to Oxford', he describes in amiable doggerel a little girl's less affected tour, which took place in his company from 9 to 13 June 1889:

> You dear old City,
> With gardens pretty,
> And lanes and flowers
> And college-towers,
> And Tom's great Bell.[20]

Ruskin had his doubts about these developments. He mentions the idea of adding pinnacles to Christ Church,[21] but on the whole he thought the 'enlargement' of Oxford for profit 'is purely injurious to the University and to her scholars'.[22] Ruskin wrote to Harrison, who had been rhapsodizing about the walks round Magdalen, with its 'sweet landscape, with its myriad blossoms and foliage, its meadows in their golden glory', as a source of reflection about human achievements down the ages:

> Why didn't you promenade in our new street, opposite Mr. Ryman's? or under the rapturous sanctities of Keble? Or beneath the lively new zig-zag parapet of Tom Quad? – or, finally, in the name of all that's human and progressive, why not up and down the elongating suburb of the married Fellows, on the cock-horse road to Banbury?[23]

John Betjeman's Oxford was first published as *An Oxford University Chest*, illustrated by L. Moholy-Nagy, Osbert Lancaster and Edward Bradley ("Cuthbert Bede") (Oxford, 1938 and 1979). Betjeman contributes his own opinions on the visual development of the city, sketching 'the town called Jericho behind the University Press (partly built to house its workers)', and 'Christminster' which John Betjeman largely equates with the old St. Ebbe's area. The small red-brick Victorian houses there were pulled down in an act of Council vandalism in the 1960s, though a few streets of the sort he describes as 'gabled and covered with plaster washed yellow' survived.[24] He writes of 'New Inn Hall Street (in medieval days it was known as the Lane of the Seven Deadly Sins, though it now contains almost as many Nonconformist and other Protestant places of worship)',[25] 'the quiet bicycle-haunted, laburnum-shaded roads of North Oxford'[26] and St. Giles's Fair:

> about the biggest fair in England. The whole of St. Giles and even Magdalen Street by Elliston and Cavell's right up to and beyond the War memorial, at the meeting of the Woodstock and Banbury roads, is thick with freak-shows, roundabouts, cake-walks.[27]

It is of course possible to come in by water. Oxford's convenient position at a bridge allowing crossing of the complex of navigable and non-navigable waterways at the head of the Thames, and on the main road from north and south between Northampton to Winchester and beyond, was probably one of the main reasons for its medieval existence. Merchants met there and markets flourished. Water transportation modernized itself to Oxford's advantage with progressive social change. The Oxford Canal was one of the earliest in England, built between 1774 and 1790, with the intention of facilitating the transport of coal from Coventry to Oxford. It made a junction with the Thames and offered a route by water to London from the Midlands. Phillip Pullman put the residents on the Oxford Canal (the

Gyptians) into *His dark materials* (1995–2000). The Gyptians moored off Osney Island are a fiction. Close by is the Waterman Pub which has been serving real beer for 200 years and can be visited in the real world now. The waterways in were not of special interest to the University though, until it took up punting and rowing in earnest:

> I took the punt downstream without mishap…and as we drew nearer to Oxford it became apparent that this had drawn numerous pleasure-seekers to the river…the momentary glimpse of a distant spire, small boat-houses and abandoned landing-stages, narrow rills and dubiously navigable backwaters…from behind a tiny islet another punt had suddenly appeared…on the minute decked prow as Oxford, but not Cambridge, regards it[28] sat just such another youth, idly dabbling a hand in the water…but I knew how to use my pole as a rudder, heaving it in a wide arc through the sluggishly resistant stream.[29]

Coming to Oxford is not much different now.

1 TOWARDS OXFORD TODAY

Not an Inkling of the future?

The Inklings: the characters

Modern Oxford was shaped by the generation born as Victorians who broke off their studies to go and fight in the First World War, survived the carnage and lived on through another World War to become the generation of ageing dons some readers will remember from their own student years. These straddlers of change brought Oxford up to date; they are the place to begin the story of Oxford for they help to link its past centuries with a present within the reach of memory.

The 'Inklings' are a sample. The Inklings have become a public face of Oxford, a veritable tourist-attraction, part of the 'cult' which formed round C.S. Lewis (1898–1963) after his death. Along with Morse, and another 'Lewis' – fictional television detectives – and 'Harry Potter', whose 'Hogwarts' was manufactured on film partly from Oxford interiors, their names are on the lips of tourist guides, sometimes to the exclusion of the main story of the University and its buildings. It is even possible to see teachers in witches' hats taking parties of small children into the Divinity School on 'educational' visits.

The Inklings were real Oxford. Oxford was not for them the mere location of a film-set. They met on Tuesday mornings in a pub, the Eagle and Child (affectionately known as the 'Bird and Baby') in St. Giles. The 'Bird and Baby' is one of those small, dark pubs with a series of little rooms. They were also sometimes to be found in the King's Arms, opposite the Bodleian Library. These have become places almost of pilgrimage, but for the Inklings themselves they were merely convenient places for talk in their own 'village' of Oxford.

The Inklings were in many respects carried protestingly onwards by time into modern Oxford rather like the dwarves in the barn at the end of C.S. Lewis's *The last battle,* who sat 'very close together in a little circle facing one another'[1] with their backs resolutely turned to events, grumbling morosely that they were being kept out of something good while the world as we know it ended and heaven burst forth around them. The Inklings were an exclusive set. It does not seem to be recorded that casual drinkers in the pub were encouraged to join them and there would be no outsiders when on Thursday evenings they gathered in Lewis's rooms at Magdalen College. Straddlers between Victorian and modern Oxford they may have been, but not includers of a wider social world, or of women. The first part of this chapter can be read as a commentary on their attitudes. After the Second World War we shall need to turn to another 'Oxford guide book'.[2]

The chief Inklings were all born in the reign of Victoria. The central figure, C.S. Lewis (who liked his friends to call him 'Jack'), served briefly in the First World War, though he did not enlist until near the end in 1917. The still-new Oxford English School in which he chose to take his degree had from the first a strong predilection for the study of the language in its early evolution, and for English medieval texts. He liked allegory. He was drawn to the 'world system' which informs medieval English literature and which provided the foundations for the Renaissance too. C.S. Lewis remained a Fellow of Magdalen College from 1925 to 1954, but he was never the sort of Oxford don who spends his time on college or University politics; he lacked the light touch for negotiation it required. He was rumoured to be something of an intellectual bully and his students called him 'heavy'; a domineering insistence that his views should be accepted was not the Oxford way. Lewis's academic progress to one of Oxford's more prestigious Professorships, the Merton Chair of Medieval and Renaissance Literature, seems to have been blocked by an Oxford distaste for the 'evangelical' sympathies which won him such a great and continuing following in the USA. In 1954 he moved to Cambridge to be Professor of Medieval and Renaissance Literature and became a Fellow of the other Magdalene College, though he never really 'settled' there. The large battered rug on the floor of his old room at Magdalene was still to be seen at the end of the twentieth century. He wrote his seven children's books on Narnia as Christian allegories between 1950 and 1956.

One of the least-known of the Inklings today was one of the most important in the intellectual and ultimately the religious formation of C.S. Lewis. Arthur Owen Barfield (1898–1997) was passionately drawn to the philosophy of religion. He had been an undergraduate at Wadham immediately after the First World War, when Lewis was reading English at University College, and he had transferred to English too. This was a bold move for both of them. English was still a relatively new subject in which to take an Oxford degree. There had been a long period of acrimonious debate about having a degree in the subject at all. 'English' was offered only from 1894, and had largely been given its shape (not to mention its Faculty Library) under Walter Raleigh, who became the namesake of Queen Elizabeth's *Sir* Walter Raleigh when he received a knighthood for his achievements. So it was a brave and unusual move for certain of the future Inklings to choose this degree subject as young men, though it allowed them a good deal of latitude in shaping it and deciding where to concentrate their efforts.

At first the preponderance of undergraduates reading English was female, and English was known as a soft subject. That did not mean that all its female students were lightweight or unable to hold their own in a cutting exchange. J.R.R. Tolkien much later recollected:

> C.S.L.'s story of an elderly lady ... (She was a student of English in the past days of Sir Walter Raleigh.[3] At her viva[4] she was asked: What period would you have liked to live in Miss B? In the fifteenth C said she. Oh come, Miss B., wouldn't you have liked to meet the Lake poets? No, sir, I prefer the society of gentlemen. Collapse of viva.[5])

The Inklings were not all the conventional Christian believers an Oxford undergraduate was still expected to be. They shared a strong taste for religious debate, but they dabbled in the occult and the outrageous. Barfield's personal interests lay on the fringes of the philosophy of religion. In 1923 he became a disciple of Rudolf Steiner (1861–1925) whose 'anthroposophy' involved an attempt to create a 'spiritual science' with a methodology for the study of the supernatural, to set alongside natural science. Barfield read Steiner's ideas as a modern solution to problems which, he felt, the Romantic Movement of the early nineteenth century had failed to resolve satisfactorily.[6] He and C.S. Lewis were close friends long before the Inklings began to meet as a larger group and they corresponded energetically about Barfield's ideas in a 'great war' of rival opinion which seems to have been a significant factor in prompting Lewis's own 'conversion' in 1931.

J.R.R. (John Ronald Reuel) Tolkien's war service weighed much more heavily in setting his lifelong priorities. Tolkien (1892–1973) was a few years older than Lewis. The son of an English bank manager, he had been born while the family was in South Africa. When his father died, his mother went home to England and settled to the west of Birmingham. There he spent time as a boy exploring the Malvern and Clent hills, and encouraged by his mother, who was a keen botanist, drawing what he observed. His chief natural bent was for languages.

His mother was well-equipped to be his teacher and she had him learning Latin very early. She died when she was only 34 and he was 12, but she provided him with guardians from the Birmingham Oratory. She had become a Roman Catholic convert and this added another dimension to his religious life. He was sent by his guardians to King Edward's School in Birmingham.

In 1911 he went on a walking holiday to Switzerland in a party of a dozen friends, and remembered in a letter of 1968 that 'the hobbit's [Bilbo's] journey from Rivendell to the other side of the Misty Mountains, including the glissade down the slithering stones into the pine woods, is based on my adventures in 1911'.[7] That October he went to Exeter College, Oxford, to read Greats (Greek and Latin), soon changing to English, like Lewis and Barfield, with a special enthusiasm for Old English and its literature. Some of the letters he wrote to Edith Bratt, to whom he became engaged in January 1913, when he was 21, describe the intrusion of obligatory drilling in the University's Officers' Training Corps into his time for reading and his growing interest in writing stories. He was commissioned into the Lancashire Fusiliers as soon as he graduated in 1915 and complains of the miserable cold and waiting about of the training at Rugeley Camp to which he was sent. But he was still writing story-poems, one of which he sent to Edith with a letter in late November.[8] In March he told her he was putting 'touches to my nonsense fairy language'.[9]

He was sent to France as signalling officer for his battalion in 1916, and he was at the Somme by the end of June. He coped with the grim conditions and the fear by withdrawing into his fantasy life, writing stories and designing languages for elves. As he described it to his son Christopher (experiencing his own war in May 1944), he wrote:

> in grimy canteens, at lectures in cold fogs, in huts full of blasphemy and smut, or by candlelight in bell-tents, or even some down in dug-outs under shell fire.... I was not a good officer.[10]

But he learned a respect for the stolid endurance of the ordinary soldiers, on whom he later said he had modelled Sam Gamgee in *The Lord of the Rings*. He survived. He caught a fever and was sent back to England in October. But many of his close friends died and he wrote in an Introduction, when the second edition of the *Lord of the Rings* was published, that the experience of being 'caught by youth in 1914' was 'hideous'.

When war was over, Tolkien began his academic career at Leeds but he was soon back in Oxford. Like Lewis he became a member of the English Faculty and a lifelong Oxford don. From 1925 to 1945 he was Rawlinson and Bosworth Professor of Anglo-Saxon at Oxford and from 1945 (when Lewis failed to get it) to 1959, he held the Merton Chair of English Language and Literature. The fantasy-writing continued, with the support of the Inklings, to whom he read passages for 'approval'. He fashioned a world as a commentary on society and the cosmos. As he wrote to Michael Tolkien, his other son, who was at Sandhurst in June 1941:

> I have spent most of my life, since I was your age, studying Germanic matters (in the general sense that includes England and Scandinavia). There is a great deal more force (and truth) than ignorant people imagine in the 'Germanic' ideal. I was much attracted by it as an undergraduate ... in reaction against the 'Classics'. You have to understand the good in things, to detect the real evil.[11]

Charles Williams (1886–1945) was the odd one out of the trio who formed the central group of Inklings, and the last to join. He had studied at the University of London not at Oxford and he did not complete his degree. He began work in the Methodist Book Room. He lectured to adult education classes. In 1908, still based in London, he became a reader for the Oxford University Press. He too was drawn to the occult and to the theory of magic and joined the Order of the Golden Dawn in 1917, founded by A.E. Waite. His novels[12] exploit what he learned in an experimental, almost metaphysical, fiction, in which the supernatural world penetrates ordinary life and the reader glimpses the operation of cosmic forces, good and bad, in episodes of the eternal 'war of good and evil'.

It was *The Place of the Lion*, published in 1931, that attracted C.S. Lewis's attention. The book deals with medieval versions of the Platonic theory of Ideas in the context of a story about a modern medieval researcher working on Peter Abelard. At the same time Charles Williams was proof-reading C.S. Lewis's *Allegory of Love*, to be published by the Oxford University Press in 1936. They wrote to one another. They became friends. When the Second World War approached Williams was moved to Oxford with other employees of the Oxford University Press, Lewis invited him to come to meetings of the Inklings. The English Faculty was glad to make use of him as a lecturer, when many of its academics went off to war. He was rather a success, especially when he lectured on Milton in the Lent term of 1940. He wrote on Dante, too, a pioneering work, *The figure of Beatrice: a study in Dante* (London, 1943). This had a startling effect on Dorothy Sayers, who had been writing *The mind of the Maker* (published in 1941). Reading Williams's book on Dante, she perceived with a fresh intensity the theology and metaphysics of the Dantean universe and her translation of the *Divina Commedia*. Oxford gave Williams an honorary MA in 1943, but his 'belongingness' really owed much to Lewis. He died suddenly in 1945.

The Inklings: the meetings

This assorted band of friends – and from time to time a number of other acquaintances, including Neville Coghill, Jack Bennett and John Wain – came together, with C.S. Lewis always its central and dominant figure, in the 1930s. Lewis borrowed the name for the Inklings from an undergraduate society which had been founded in 1931 by one of his pupils at University College. The name was available because the society, like other student experiments, had been short-lived. Recollecting the founding of the group in a letter he wrote in 1967, Tolkien commented that the name was 'a pleasantly ingenious pun in its way, suggesting people with vague or half informed intimations and ideas plus those who dabble in ink'.[13]

The heyday of the Inklings' meetings as a group was the inter-war period, but they were still meeting after the Second World War. Despite their respectable conventional careers as academics (or in the case of Charles Williams, working for the Oxford University Press), they were brought and held together[14] by interests at the edges of contemporary intellectual respectability. The Inklings were also implicitly posing questions about the relationship between academic and creative writing, for Oxford took the view that when it came to the study of literature, criticism rather than creative writing was the primary task of scholarship.

Giving themselves a name – even such a light-hearted and self-mocking one – and agreeing to meet regularly, lent the Inklings' experiment a certain weight and it certainly meant that individuals who might not have met but for their approval by Lewis for inclusion in the meetings, were able to have an effect upon one another's work. The 'society' did not consciously aim to be yet another version of the Cambridge Apostles or of Oxford debating societies. That does not mean that Lewis at least did not quietly have a more grandiose theory about what they were doing:

> What is now the Royal Society was originally a few gentlemen meeting in their spare time to discuss things which they (and not many others) had a fancy for. What we now call

> 'the Romantic Movement' once was Mr Wordsworth and Mr Coleridge talking incessantly (at least Mr Coleridge was) about a secret vision of their own.[15]

The Inklings kept no records of their conversations and because they were meeting so often there is little by way of correspondence among them. Tolkien's letters offer some snapshots. In a letter of 6 October 1944, he describes how 'on Tuesday at noon' he 'looked in at the Bird and B':

> There to my surprise I found Jack [C.S. Lewis] and Warnie [Lewis's brother Warren] already ensconced. (For the present the beer shortage is over, and the inns are almost habitable again.) The conversation was pretty lively.[16]

Lewis married very late and for most of his creative and academic lifetime his most important friendships were with men. The Inklings, including the outer circle who attended the meetings, were all men. They chose to meet over beer in a pub in a manner which tended to exclude female attendance in the decades when they were active as a group. In his book on *The four loves,* Lewis included some distinctly misogynistic passages. If you include a woman in a conversation of male friends, he says, you will find that:

> Her presence ... has destroyed the very thing she was brought to share. She can never really enter the circle because the circle ceases to be itself when she enters it. ... Her grandmother was far happier and more realistic. ... She was at home talking real women's talk to other women. ... She may be quite as clever as the men whose evening she has spoiled, or cleverer. But she is not really interested in the same things, nor mistress of the same methods ... such women ... banish male companionship, and therefore male Friendship, from whole neighbourhoods.[17]

The picture of Oxford friendships the Inklings evoke has a flavour of its time between the wars and just after:

> our slippers are on, our feet spread out towards the blaze and our drinks at our elbows; when the whole world, and something beyond the world, opens itself to our minds as we talk; and no one has any claim on or any responsibility for one another, but all are freemen and equals as if we had first met an hour ago, while at the same time an Affection mellowed by the years enfolds us.[18]

Here in the Inklings' meetings was Oxford at its most accommodating, a comfortable place to be for Victorians and early 'moderns', able to start up the study of new subjects and shape them, able to make room for those who neglected administration, who veered off into activities not strictly scholarly at all, who had opinions and changed them, but who were consistent in the one thing that mattered to the University. They lived the life of the mind and they lived it socially. But was it modern Oxford? And there is much to question about the way they met. In theory, colleges were intellectual societies, but Lewis and the Inklings met in a pub. They pushed at the boundaries of intellectual endeavour, but in ways which were derivative of medieval culture. They were not entirely comfortable in the modern world into which the passage of time was taking them.

Riding out the First World War

The coming of war

A Keble undergraduate, Ralph Kite (1895–1916), wrote home when his family had delivered him at Keble to begin his first term just before the beginning of the First World War. 'I am sorry you cried when you left me. I felt like doing the same.' He describes how he had had to spend a surprising amount of money in equipping his room, even, it seems, with furniture. 'They supply practically nothing':[19]

> I got several pictures, which are cheap in Oxford, amongst them Sir Galahad, Napoleon on the Bellerephon coloured and Boy where's your father coloured, also two of Lawson Wood's.[20]

He was a sporting young man, a serious Rugby player. ('It is quite nice training in this weather. Early to bed, up early, cold bath, walk round Parks before breakfast'.[21]) He liked cricket too ('I have got elected to a cricket club, the Heretics, known, of course, as the 'ticks'. It is rather an honour, as it is run by the Dean'.[22]) This ordinary boy, no great intellectual, showing no evidence of outstanding promise, did not finish his degree because he went off to fight in the First World War. He was killed in 1916.

Oxford was rapidly emptied of its students as they rushed to join up in the summer of 1914. By 1918 only about 12 per cent of the numbers who had been resident as students at the outbreak of war (about 3000), were in residence. Dons enlisted too, some to fight, some to work in intelligence, some to offer medical work.

Ignore or adapt? Oxford in war time

Oxford scarcely knew whether to carry on as normal or to make major adjustments in the face of a war everyone hoped would be over by Christmas, 1914. What was an institution of immense antiquity with traditions to maintain to do in the face of unpredictable change? As it happened, the seventh centenary of the birth of Roger Bacon, one of Oxford's great medieval Franciscan scholars,[23] fell in 1914. There seemed no good reason to abandon plans to celebrate Bacon's birthday just because war loomed. On 10 June 1914, there was an Oxford celebration of the seventh centenary of his birth, including the unveiling of a statue of him at the University Museum and a lunch at Merton College, together with an exhibition at the Bodleian and a garden party at Wadham. A document with a Cambridge seal sent from the Cambridge Registrary, John Neville Keynes, authorized James Ward, Sc.D. and Professor of Mental Philosophy and Logic, to represent the University of Cambridge at the celebrations, the Senate of the University of Cambridge having met to appoint him on Friday, 1 May 1914.[24] Moreover, the Franciscans were keen to come back to Oxford at the beginning of the twentieth century. The *Oxford Magazine* describes how:

> Fr. Cuthbert ... directed his energies to refounding the Friary as a direct successor to the earlier Greyfriars. ... Fr. Cuthbert's tenure of office is sprinkled with events of Franciscan interest – the Roger Bacon celebrations of 1914, when the statue was placed in the University Museum and a memorial plaque erected in St. Ebbe's on the site of the old Greyfriars.[25]

With the wish to make an appropriate contribution to the war effort, Oxford academics were busy analysing what was happening in Europe. A good deal of intellectual effort was put into justifying Britain's participation. *Why we are at war: Great Britain's case,* was put by the members of the Oxford Faculty of History in a publication which was already in its third edition in 1914.[26] Oxford's historians said in its Preface, 'We are not politicians, and we belong to different schools of political thought ... [but] we have some experience in the handling of historic evidence'.

Being historians they saw no reason not to begin the story in the 1640s in the period leading to the execution of Charles I:

> The war in which England is now engaged with Germany is fundamentally a war between two different principles – that of *raison d'état*, and that of the rule of law. The antagonism

> between these two principles appeared in our own internal history as far back as the seventeenth century, when the Stuarts championed the theory of state-necessity and the practice of a prerogative free to act outside and above the law in order to meet the demands of state-necessity... the same antagonism now appears externally in a struggle between two nations... the one regards international covenants to which it has pledged its own word as 'scraps of paper' when they stand in the way of the *salus populi*; the other regards the maintenance of such covenants as a grave and inevitable obligation.

T.S. Eliot was among those who tried to carry on as though there were no war. He gives us a glimpse in a letter to Eleanor Hinkley, of the way Oxford appeared to this visiting American in October 1914:

> Oxford is not intellectually stimulating – but that would be a good deal to ask of a university atmosphere.... It is a dreadful climate, I know, but one seems able to eat and sleep very well, and keep very healthy.

His feelings of displacement grew stronger in a later letter:

> Oxford is very pretty, but I don't like to be dead... I am very dependent upon women (I mean female society); and feel the deprivation at Oxford.... One walks about the street with one's desires, and one's refinement rises up like a wall whenever opportunity approaches.[27]

He went for walks. 'There is a dear little village named Cumnor, which perhaps you know, with low thatched cottages, where I have walked.' He planned to 'take up a little rowing, if we can gather enough Americans and such English as are too short-sighted to be acceptable for the Training corps.'

Nevertheless, the war was pressing upon him more than he wanted to acknowledge. He notes the disappearance of two-thirds 'of the ordinary enrollment'. 'One feels the strain of the present situation even in Oxford.'[28]

It was all very unsettling in other ways too. German Rhodes scholars had been provided for in Cecil Rhodes's will, in a codicil of 1901, in which he provided for the funding of fifteen of them to study in Oxford. His belief was that this would help prevent war. The Kaiser was to choose the recipients and that meant that they tended to come from well-connected families and not be especially conspicuous for their scholarship. In *Zuleika Dobson*, Max Beerbohm describes the impact of both the American and the German Rhodes scholars. These were not the wandering scholars we shall meet in earlier centuries, turning up in Oxford at their own peripatetic whim. They threw down a multi-cultural social challenge:

> 'The President showed much deference to his guest.... To all Rhodes Scholars, indeed, his courtesy was invariable. He went out of his way to cultivate them. [But h]e found these Scholars, good fellows though they were, rather oppressive. They had not – how could they have – the undergraduate's virtue of taking Oxford as a matter of course. The Germans loved it too little, the Colonials too much'.... He held... in his enlightened way, that Americans have a perfect right to exist. But he did often find himself wishing Mr. Rhodes had not enabled them to exercise that right in Oxford. They were so awfully afraid of having their strenuous native characters undermined by their delight in the place.[29]

By 1916 it had become impossible to defer any longer the suspension of the German branch of these scholarships, and the funds began to be used to assist scholars from allied countries. This shifted the balance of Oxford's overseas friendships, with scholarships going to southern Africa, Canada, the Caribbean, Hong Kong. An attempt was made to revive the German link in the 1930s but the Second World War ended the arrangement.[30] The American links continued. In 1917, the doctorate in philosophy (DPhil) was accepted as an Oxford degree partly in order to attract American graduate students back to the University.

Oxford does its bit

From a practical point of view, Oxford did its bit. It offered hospitality to Belgian refugees, who were billeted partly in University and college accommodation. Serbians were welcomed too, and both Belgians and Serbians were admitted as students though not matriculated as members of the University.[31] The empty residential space was used for billeting soldiers and for the provision of hospitals. The women of Oxford came into their own. The 'Home Students' were young women who did not live in the early 'women's colleges' but at home. Their successors were to form St. Anne's College. Along with the other women students, they found themselves in a majority at lectures in the First World War. Some women interrupted their studies to do war work, as far as the social conventions of the time allowed. Many of the women students who remained in Oxford, in what now seemed disproportionate numbers in comparison with the male students, did voluntary work.

Catching up and maintaining standards?

At the end of the nineteenth century, Robert Sangster Rait was unhappy about proposals to shorten 'the time necessary for graduation'.[32] After the First World War, the notion of an 'emergency' two-year degree appeared in Oxford as a pragmatic means of allowing young men who had been fighting to catch up and the nation to benefit from the services of at least some of the graduates it might have expected in ordinary circumstances. The poet Robert Graves (1895–1985), who became an undergraduate at St. John's when he returned from the war, describes the way this option looked to him:

> I could take a two years' course at Oxford with a Government grant of two hundred pounds a year and be excused the intermediate examination (Mods.) on account of war-service. The preliminary examination I had already been excused because of a 'higher certificate examination' passed at Charterhouse; so there remained only the finals. The grant would be increased by a children's allowance. It seemed absurd at the time to suppose that university degrees would count for anything in a regenerated post-war England; but Oxford offered itself as a convenient place to mark time until I felt more like earning a livelihood.[33]

Oxford takes the state's penny

Fisher and the money

After war came post-war financial constraints.[34] Oxford has always been heavily involved in politics, but it prefers it if politicians are not eager to interfere with the University in return. In May 1919, at the insistence of the Hebdomadal Council (the weekly meeting of a working 'executive' since 1854), the *University Gazette,* now the official published record of the University's business for nearly half a century since it began publication in 1870, took an unusual step. It published in full the correspondence between the Vice-Chancellor and the President of the Board of Education.[35] The correspondence was about money.

Publication of an exchange of letters with the Government was so unusual that a defensive note needed to be struck, or the dons would have been indignant. They were acutely aware that they still held the reins of the University. It was carefully explained that the Vice-Chancellor, currently Herbert Blakiston (1862–1942),[36] was fully aware that he had been acting without the consent of Convocation, the University's governing body of all its graduates. He had been approached in July 1918 by the Vice-Chancellor of Birmingham University, Sir Oliver Lodge, who wanted to organize a deputation 'for the purpose of applying to the Government for greatly increased financial support'. Oxford's Vice-Chancellor could not at that time of year consult the University's Hebdomadal Council or Convocation and he was anxious not to associate Oxford too closely with universities 'already in receipt of the Treasury grant'. He knew opinion in the University was much too sharply divided for him to have authority to commit Oxford to any application 'for State-aid'.

H.A.L. Fisher as President of the Board of Education was sensitive on this point and in a letter of 6 November he wrote to Blakiston to say that 'it would be a convenience to the Government to have a conspectus of the likely requirements of Higher Education all over the country', in order to get a sense of the 'need for a larger measure of State financial assistance to the Universities after the war', so it would be helpful if Oxford and Cambridge would come, although of course he wished to apply no 'pressure'. Oxford and Cambridge consulted one another and decided to join in. Memoranda were prepared.

Oxford used its best cunning to apply for State aid on terms which would not compromise its independence. It drew attention to the long history of 'Royal benefactions' to Oxford, 'usually assigned to special purposes but not saddled with onerous conditions'. If the Government could see its way to budgeting for capital expenditures, not necessarily to be used, then if, say, Oxford found it needed new Chemistry laboratories, it 'could apply for a draft on this sum'.

But the scientists scented money. This was a different Oxford from the one of a mere generation earlier when uncertainties about the lasting value of scientific work and its potential to attract students were still being expressed. In the 1880s, the University had proved reluctant to vote the money to improve expensive laboratories.[37] It had still to be agreed whether 'science' was appropriate matter for student study, whether its importance would last, whether it belonged in the realms of the higher, more abstract studies of universities, or in mechanics' institutes where men learned how to make things work, where the 'discoveries' were more likely to take the form of practical 'inventions'.

Now the scientists wrote collectively from the University Museum directly to Fisher, to draw attention to additional – and by no means hypothetical – needs. They wanted money for salaries adequate to pay Demonstrators, who would now be able to command four or five times their pre-war Oxford salaries in commissions in the armed forces or in other employments. 'Under these conditions no first-class men (unless they have private means) can be expected to remain in Oxford as Demonstrators.' The Colleges must also be encouraged to 'give a larger number of scholarships in science and mathematics' and then there are the 'salaries and pensions' of head of department which 'should be adequate to command the services of men who have reached the head of their profession'.[38] The very future of science was at stake, they cried. Those:

> on comparatively small salaries are likely to engage in research with a practical and remunerative end in view.... Unless purely scientific research receives support real progress cannot be expected even in industrial and other practical applications; for useful inventions have mostly had their origin in research carried on without any interest other than that of advancement of knowledge.

Here already are two of the great policy-driving arguments of the twentieth century, first that academics must be attracted and retained by being paid salaries which will prevent their being captured by industry and the professions; and second, that blue-skies research must be protected aggressively against the tendency of funders to want results which can be turned to industrial and manufacturing profit.

This letter and others like it prompted a clarification from Fisher in a letter of 16 April 1919, which was to prove of the utmost importance to higher education funding for the century to come. Oxford had been assuming that 'all grants would be applied for and received with the permission of Convocation, and only on behalf of separate Departments'; in other words, they would be specific and targeted. No, explained Fisher:

> each University which receives aid from the State will receive it in the form of a single inclusive grant, for the expenditure of which the University, as distinguished from any particular Department, will be responsible.[39]

Here was the 'block grant', a device which has shaped the funding of higher education throughout the following century, with its insistence that the state should hand a lump sum to each university for it to use as it saw fit and not try to direct the spending by detailed State control.

But here, too, was the end of Oxford's hope of not compromising the financial independence of the University as a whole, and keeping to a series of on-off and specific requests for funding.

Moreover, in this letter, Fisher pointed out that if Oxford wanted money it would have to submit like other universities to investigation of its 'revenue and expenditure' and allow the Government to ascertain 'with some exactness the material facts of [its] finances and organisation':

> The Government will ... be prepared, as soon as the comprehensive inquiry above mentioned has been completed, to consider in conjunction with the University, if it so desires, the conditions under which a grant designed to meet the permanent requirements of the University might be made.

There is a nod to academic autonomy, 'the vital importance of preserving the liberty and autonomy of the Universities', for 'the State is, in my opinion, not competent to direct the work of education and disinterested research which is carried on by Universities':

> I do not believe that any of the Universities which have received state grants have ever found any reason to think the receipt of such grants has involved State interference in matters for which they are themselves properly responsible.

Oxford was alarmed. It wrote back on 22 May to say that the University of Oxford had not made an application for 'a single inclusive grant'. There were precedents for asking for one-off grants for Departments. This is something new. Convocation has not been asked about this new idea. It will need to consider whether it will sanction an inspection of its finances. And it cannot speak for the colleges. 'There is no procedure for obtaining the collective consent of the Colleges.'[40]

Asquith and a challenge to independence

One of the consequences of these exchanges was the setting up of a Royal Commission to look into the finances, the financial viability, and the general conduct of the affairs of both Oxford and Cambridge. Both Universities gave evidence. For example, Bertha Johnson gave evidence before the Asquith Commission just before her resignation from running the Home Students in March 1921,[41] describing some of the helpers and supporters of the enterprise.[42] The fragility of the scant surviving record of the hearings (a few carbon copies) may say something about the lack of will to preserve them in either Oxford or Cambridge.

Indeed, one would scarcely know from the *Oxford University Gazette* that a Commission had been at work. The official historical record as preserved in the *Gazette* suggests that Oxford was perhaps more concerned to report on these matters to its own governing body and to the colleges than to any outsiders. For instance, the *Gazette*, of 26 November,[43] published 'Accounts presented by Board of Finance, including from Colleges,' but emphasizing that these are not typical, because of the war there had been diminished income *from* students and diminished expenditure *on* students, with some extra income for the colleges coming from revenues connected with Cadet Companies under Military Instruction.

The final result was new Statutes, made by Commissioners under the Oxford and Cambridge Act of 1923. One of the running grumbles of the first decades of the twentieth century had been the fact that members of Convocation, the Masters of Arts of the University, could still participate in its decision-making, even though they might be out of touch with Oxford, living far away, and some decades beyond their graduation. This was a legacy of the medieval governance structure which it was felt timely to adjust. The Statutes of 1926 put into the hands of a new-style Congregation of those actually teaching in the University, all the principal decision-making powers. They did not abolish Convocation, though that had been proposed, but left it with only a few powers. It could elect the Chancellor and the High Steward and the Professor of Poetry. It could confer honorary degrees. It could send letters on behalf of the University. The changes were, overall, not of a sort to capsize Oxford's 'boat', but they did include an acceptance of State funding which had a capacity to rock it not fully foreseen at the beginning of the century.

The Senior Proctor takes stock

> The business of the University has once again survived the intrusion into its inner machinery of two College Tutors, as eager as inexperienced.... Especially I would mention the Registrar who, as you have so often seen him enter this House, follows the two proctors as the sage ploughman follows his plough-team.

In 1927 the Oration of the Senior Proctor on demitting office was published in the *Gazette* of 25 March.[44] He asked – as the convention was – for permission to speak English not Latin, lest he 'stumble among false quantities, obscuring my meaning in the profundity of a learned tongue'. He spoke consciously in the wake of the work of the

Asquith Royal Commission and the ensuing Oxford and Cambridge Act of 1923 and the appointment and actions of the Commissioners:

> We have found ourselves in the Counsels of the University at a time when, as it has seemed to us, the University, released from the Commission (as an arrow from the bow), is moving forward with a new vigour to new duties and a fuller implementing of its traditional obligations, both in the world of learning and in the national life.

He mentions the advent of the University Lecturer, 'that admirable misnomer' for he 'need not lecture (at least not more than most of us)', and the freeing of the College Tutors 'from excessive burdens of teaching' so that they may have 'leisure for research'.

He includes, by convention, the disciplinary events of the year, deriving as part of the proctorial office 'from the lively imagination of the Middle Ages':

> In the last twelve months we have met with all sorts and conditions of men, with evil-doers and with the police, with parents and with landladies, with keepers of hotels and coffee-stalls, with managers of cinemas, teachers of dancing and station-masters, with officers of undergraduate clubs, with undergraduate editors, and last but not least, with the disciplinary officers of colleges.

Letting the women in: 1920 and after

> There has been no greater mistake made in Oxford than the abolition of compulsory chapel, except of course the admission of women and the abolition of compulsory Greek.[45]

The story so far

Bertha Johnson (1846–1927), writing in 'The Oxford Souvenir' in 1925, gave an account of some of the earliest attempts to bring women into the intellectual life of Oxford. First came a bid in 1866, when permission was obtained for women to attend some of the University's lectures and classes were organized for women. Mrs. Humphrey Ward and a group of friends, including Bertha Johnson herself, had tried again in 1873:

> Prominent University men took much interest in it; the University lent us rooms in the Clarendon Building for lectures and classes, and gave us orders to read in the Bodleian

> Library ... but it was slightly discouraging to hear ... from one of our lecturers, Mr Laing, of Corpus Christi College ... that he saw all the evil effects of examination upon women and feared that our lectures had not improved them, for that there used to be feminine character and originality about their writing, and now they tried to be manly and were only the ordinary man![46]

During Benjamin Jowett's term as Vice-Chancellor (1882–6), a petition was laid before the Hebdomadal Council by Oxford MAs 'to lay before the University a scheme by which women may be admitted to at least some of the Honour Examinations'. It carried 120 signatures.[47]

Among the schemes of this period was the idea of establishing two 'residence halls', one 'Lady Margaret Hall representing the Church of England' and the other 'Somerville Hall, which was purely undenominational'. 'A third body of students was also provided for, those who preferred family life to College life, or for whom, for various circumstances, College life was impossible.'[48] This constituency was to be provided for by the 'Home Students', who eventually became St. Anne's College.

Some of the male dons supported these efforts or gave encouragement to individual girls who took no notice of society's expectations and sought to learn as their brothers did. Charles Dodgson (Lewis Carroll) wrote on 8 March to Mrs. F.S. Rix about the educational ambitions of her daughter. He fears the girl '*does* [italic in the original] work too hard, and is in danger of defeating her own object':

> The amount of work you tell me she went through in 5 months is simply absurd ... if there is one subject less adapted than another to be got up by 'cram' it is Mathematics. ... That she 'passed' an examination in those subjects is no real criterion of her having mastered them.[49]

Dodgson adds a comment on patterns of study which are clearly not intended to apply only to girls. 'That she should be "insatiable in work" is an excellent thing.' But he fears the girl will burn herself out. She must learn 'how to be idle *too*, at fitting times'.

> I am no great advocate for regular work – i.e. so many hours a day all the year round. I believe in periods of intense work followed by periods of perfect idleness: I think your daughter needs to be driven to the latter more than the former![50]

Dodgson writes disparagingly of Girton and only slightly more encouragingly of Newnham because he wants the girl to come to

Oxford where he can 'befriend' her himself. But he continues with reflections which underline the limited career possibilities open to such girls:

> I had a talk with Miss Wordsworth, principal of Lady Margaret Hall, about some young friends of mine who wish to earn money by teaching, and took the opportunity of naming your daughter.[51]

The advice he received, together with some papers to send on to the girl, was that 'she should offer herself for the 'First Examination' on 8 June. (This was a 'university' not a 'school' examination.) He reassures the mother that the teaching her daughter would receive at Lady Margaret Hall would be that of a 'Christ Church man' and so (by implication) of good academic quality but also that he would be a 'gentlemanly fellow', so, from that point of view, not a danger to the girl.[52] He mentions that '"Exhibitions" are to be had, for students whose means are limited'.[53]

Another passage of correspondence survives in which Charles Dodgson gave advice for an academically inclined girl. This time it was a different family he sought to help; he wrote to Isabel Standen and interviewed the Principal of Somerville to ask about the options:

> She thought that a better opening for teachers, than under-mistresses in High Schools, was to be found (specially for those not possessing certificates of high Honours) in head-mistress-ships of "Board Schools" (i.e. schools for girls of the lower classes, under the management of the School-Board). For these are very glad to get ladies.[54]

Dodgson perceived paradoxes in these limited career expectations for educated women, for the same, or nearly the same, education opened different doors for the sexes. It meant that a modest qualification, which would not take a boy very far, might place a girl higher on her shorter ladder of lifetime professional opportunity. 'Why should a certificate, which would fit a boy for a clerkship, be supposed to fit a girl for high educational work?'[55] He was rather exercised about the plan of adding 'to the army of *un*trained and *un*educated teachers'.

> Girls of refinement, and well-trained, would have an enormous advantage over others if they would only see that their refinement will not do by itself... 'prepare them by correspondence for the Cambridge Women's Examination', and let them only take at one time the number of subjects in

> which they can get distinction in the First Class. Nothing else is the smallest good.[56]

There were few other possibilities beyond teaching and work as a governess to which an intellectually able girl might aspire. One further avenue of respectable work for a 'lady' offered itself if she felt called to be a deaconess. Among the Rules of the London Diocesan Deaconess Institution in 1869 was a requirement that 'except under special circumstances, each Sister is expected to contribute £50 per annum for maintenance and Sister's dress'. That ruled out the impecunious, except where the committee might allow a Sister to be maintained 'on the funds of the Society'. In that case, she would have to provide a medical certificate to warrant her good health. A form of lay sistership was allowed. 'Women also of humbler social position, accustomed to work with their hands' could join in order to 'minister to the sick and suffering'. 'Wages are not offered to them, but they will be supplied with all that is necessary for health and comfort.' If they become disabled the Society will do its best to maintain them, but it insists that they are fit on arrival. For ladies, it was possible to come for 'one year's training' for the office of Deaconess, without becoming Sisters. They could then 'act' in their chosen profession on a bishop's licence. For all these categories the expectation is that they will live lives of labour and 'self-denial' in 'devoted toil'.[57]

War changes things

At the end of the First World War, in Oxford as in Cambridge, women were again knocking to be let in to full membership of the University. Women had been trying to gain acceptance as Oxford students since the end of the nineteenth century. They had won the right to take the same examinations. Now they wanted degrees on the same terms as the men. In Cambridge the battle was to continue until after the Second World War. Oxford gave women membership and degrees much sooner.

A student becomes a member of Oxford or Cambridge by 'matriculation', a word derived from *matricula*, 'register'. This involves a ceremony at which each individual undertakes to obey the Statutes and the subordinate domestic legislation made under the Statutes, and becomes (for life), a member of the ancient corporation of the University. The first question was whether women could be allowed to matriculate, for then they would be members of the University just like men. In the *Oxford University Gazette* of 22 October 1919 were published legal opinions 'on the proposed admission of women to membership of the University and to degrees in the University'. There were some who wanted women to be able to receive degrees without becoming members of the University. The question was whether the university's Statutes could allow this to happen. Nowhere did the existing Statutes define what was meant by 'membership of the university',[58] nor was it even clear whether that 'membership' extended to both undergraduates and graduates (a disputed point which had arisen in the Middle Ages too).

Counsel's opinion, published in the *Oxford University Gazette*, was that only the matriculated had ever been allowed degrees 'in the ordinary course':[59]

> The only qualification for the status of corporator being the position of scholar, any person who is qualified to be scholar is qualified to be corporator: that the one qualification for the position of scholar is ability to learn what the University has to teach, and that of this the University is sole judge: that women are not less able to learn than men: that consequently the University is entitled, if it thinks fit, to admit women to be scholars: that if it does, they are ipso facto corporators.[60]

But it was pointed out that muddle had been allowed to occur in the procedures which applied to male candidates. Matriculation requirements did not appear to have been strictly enforced, so even some male graduates appeared to be of uncertain standing. However, precedent seemed to show that 'the University had the power of entering in its matriculation registers persons who are not at any rate in the full sense of the word members of the University'.[61]

Straddling the war and coming back to a new Oxford

For some of the women now pressing for membership and proper degrees the war had meant at least a temporary break with Oxford. Vera Brittain (1893–1970), later to be the mother of the politician Shirley Williams, had arrived in Oxford as a consequence of attending a series of University Extension lectures provided by Oxford in Buxton in 1912 and 1913. The lecturer, John Marriott, saw her ability and encouraged her to try for Oxford. With some coaching, she won an exhibition to Somerville where she spent a first year in 1914–15 reading English like many other girls. She broke off to do war service as a nursing assistant, nursing wounded soldiers at the local hospital in Buxton and then in London at Camberwell. She was sent to nurse in Malta in the autumn of 1916. These proved her most formative years. She lost four male friends in close succession, one of them the man she had hoped to marry. Vera Brittain's *Testament of youth* was largely based on her First World War diary.

When the war ended, Vera Brittain went back to Oxford, but now to read Modern History not English. She had become interested in politics. She wanted to take a broad view of what had happened in its historical context, 'to understand how the whole calamity [of the war] had happened, to know why it had been possible for me and my contemporaries, through our own ignorance and others' ingenuity, to be used, hypnotised and slaughtered'.[62] She wrote a letter in 1923 in which she notes how different Oxford seemed with the perspective of her years away:

> Students came up fresh from school, inexperienced, keen, idealistic often enough, but accustomed to direction.... They come up to college and are told by the dons from the moment they come to the moment they go down, that the only thing that matters is intellectual success.... When I was at college there was not a soul to whom one could go to ask for advice about a knotty point, or even who held up any sort of suggestion about behaviour – only about brains.[63]

She describes the transformation brought about by the granting of degrees to women:

> After the first Degree-giving in the Sheldonian Theatre, when honorary M.A. degrees were granted to the five Principals of the women's foundations, Oxford became suddenly filled with unfamiliar feminine figures cycling up and down the High Street in scholars' and commoners' gowns.[64]

A recollection of Bertha Johnson in 1920 by 'K.R' (an American and one of the Home Students) describes her:

> little sharp enquiring gaze...so that spiritually you stood at salute...She never told me to work, but I did...because she assumed, as a matter not requiring discussion among ladies...that Oxford was a place designed for work....The first impression was typical of the universal contrast between the impersonal mass treatment of students in the American college and the instant personal relationship in which each of us found herself, with her tutor, her hostess, and that family the Society [of Home Students] from whom soon came unfamiliar invitations to 'tea' and 'games'.[65]

K.R. conveys the seriousness with which the women students characteristically worked at becoming academics in their own right, in pursuit of that 'intellectual success' mentioned by Vera Brittain:

> Nowhere else, nowhere but in Oxford, do [books] seem to be so thoroughly natives of the place, so natural and inevitable and withal so entrancing; from the moment when one first visits Blackwell, which is the initiation of the neophyte, to that when first the book-boy at the Bodleian staggers to one's desk with his piled folios.[66]

The changes, such as dropping compulsory Greek and the widening range of courses including English, were likely to assist the women whose secondary education disadvantaged them in Greats, but some looked askance at anything which tried patronizingly to make things easier for them.[67]

Vera Brittain became a close friend of the novelist Winifred Holtby, for she too had returned to Somerville in October 1919 after a period of war service with the Women's Army Auxiliary Corps. As they came to the end of their time and took their degrees, both Winifred Holtby and Vera Brittain were strongly encouraged by the dons to become professional academics. Posts were offered. But 'Winifred, like myself, had no real doubt where her dearest ambitions lay,' comments Vera Brittain. 'We both pictured a vague but wholly alluring existence of novel-writing and journalism, financially sustained by the barest minimum of part-time teaching, and varied with occasional excursions into lecturing and public-speaking.'[68]

So when they left Oxford in 1921 they set up house together and embarked on parallel careers as writers. Winifred Holtby wrote of Joanna, heroine of her novel *The land of Green Ginger* in terms which say a good deal about the equivocal position of ambitious girls even after 1920:

> In the summer of 1914, misfortune came upon Joanna ... she failed to matriculate in Mathematics and Latin ...
>
> 'All you have to do is want enough,' said Rachel ... 'Look how I fought my parents to get them to let me try for Somerville. People will always give way to you if you really mean to do something, and all getting on in life is making people give way.' ... 'It's the indolent people, pleasant and popular like yourself, who make things so hard for the fighters. We're never so nice as you are because we see beyond our noses and try to get there.' ...

> 'My lamb,' comforted Agnes. 'Rachel went to a Suffragette meeting in the Town Hall last night, and it went to her head a little.'[69]

Women settle down in the University

These two were unusual. Women were, for several generations, going to remain by and large more earnest than the men, and conspicuous in the University not only by reason of their sex. Betjeman's observation of the 1930s was that women dons did not really fit in even then. They were not 'welcomed in either professional or tutorial circles'. 'A pretty undergraduette can be excused: but a pretty woman don seems an anomaly.' It is claimed that women 'over-emphasise the necessity for reading and learning and sitting up night after night... learning lists and arguments and references'. 'Women dons, say the anti-feminists, discountenance genius at the expense of hard work... Those men who have been examined *viva voce* by a woman don will remember... the negation of any chance of covering up the lack of knowledge with abundance of wits'.[70]

Dorothy Sayers offers her readers several of this sort in her novel *Gaudy Night*. Mildred Pope is thought to have been the real Somerville don who was the model for Miss Lydgate in *Gaudy Night* and once Dorothy Sayers's tutor. She left Oxford in 1934 to become Professor of Romance Philology at Manchester. Dorothy Sayers sketched her in her speech proposing a toast to the University at the Somerville Gaudy that year:

> the integrity of judgement that gain cannot corrupt, the humility in the face of facts that self-esteem cannot blind, the generosity of a great mind that is eager to give praise to others, the singleness of purpose that pursues knowledge as some men pursue glory.[71]

Women students might see these anxious dons more affectionately. Nina Bawden speaks of 'the small, warm, dignified person of Helen Darbishire',[72] Helen Darbishire, Principal of Somerville 1931–9, was a leading scholar in English literature, and had been English tutor at Somerville since 1908 when she became Principal. She was born and educated in Oxford (at the High School) and rarely spent much time away. The perception of her as the insider's insider and the academic's academic created controversy when she was elected, for others wanted someone who could take the College out to compete in a wider world. This is an early example of a dilemma repeatedly faced by the colleges in succeeding centuries, some keeping to scholars as leaders, some going for businessmen or civil servants or judges or politicians, even 'celebrities', with mixed results. Helen Darbishire tightened things up at Somerville. She continued to teach and to spend her time with Milton but she would have urgent college business brought to her where she regularly worked in the Bodleian.[73]

Some women who made their mark as scholars on equal terms with their male colleagues also became activists in politics. Jenifer Hart (1914–2005) was one of the brightest Oxford history students of the 1930s. She won a First Class degree in 1935, before coming third in the Civil Service Examination, the highest place then attained by a woman candidate. She married Herbert Hart, who worked for MI5. After the War she went back to Oxford and by 1952 she was a History and Politics don at St. Anne's, as the Home Students had now become. When the Cambridge spies were unmasked in 1983, and their stories told, rumours circulated about her too.[74] Peter Wright, in *Spycatcher*,[75] names several Oxford figures, including Jenifer Hart, and also the brothers Bernard and Peter Floud.

It would be a mistake to see the settling in of the women and their colleges as all of a piece. There was some tension between the traditional women's colleges and the Home Students, whose arrangements did not require the funding of residential places.[76] In the mid-1930s Somerville was beginning to get bequests from successful former students and to earn money from conferences, especially through the American summer schools run jointly by the women's colleges.[77] When war loomed once more there was again the question whether the University would be able to continue its normal activities and whether space would need to be requisitioned. Heads of House were called to a meeting with the Vice-Chancellor in February 1939 and it was agreed that the University should coordinate the colleges' responses to call upon their resources. Somerville had had a request for use of its premises as a first-aid station already.[78]

It would also be a mistake to assume that the sometimes extreme, even eccentric, qualities of the first women were aped by succeeding generations. The 'professional' jobs to which these women students found their way were largely in teaching, just as they had been in the late nineteenth century, and many married and ceased to work at all.[79] In *Jane and Prudence*, published in 1953, the two principal characters, a tutor and her former student, meet at a Gaudy. Those who have attended Gaudies, will remember their peculiar sweet-and-sour flavour, nostalgic of a golden youth, but uncomfortably evocative of opportunities wasted. However, the novelist Barbara Pym (1913–80) was a graduate of St. Hilda's and a woman without illusions:

> Jane and Prudence were walking in the college garden before dinner. Their conversation came in excited little bursts, for Oxford is very lovely in midsummer, and the glimpses of grey towers through the trees and the river at their side moved them to reminiscences of earlier days.[80]

But then the student is brought up against a realization:

> 'Here we are all gathered round you,' said Jane, 'and none of us has really fulfilled her early promise.' For a moment she almost regretted her own stillborn 'research' – 'the influence of somebody upon somebody' hadn't Virginia Woolf called it? – to which her early marriage had put an end.[81]

Between the Wars

A mortar board in a brown paper bag

In his anthology *An Oxford University Chest* (1938), John Betjeman included recollections of a student called Ernest Marsh, which he entitled 'An industrial worker at Oxford'. March went to Oxford on an Extra-Mural Scholarship, after attending a special tutorial class for industrial workers run by the University. Here are the observations of one of the next generation of students, for some of whom 'access' was 'widened'. 'At the age of fourteen I handed in my school books for the last time' and went to work; 'many of us who were schoolboys one day became railwaymen the next.' He comments that as an undergraduate he could get up an hour later and still have time to read and study before his first lecture.

Did these worker-students feel out of place? Not for long, he says:

> The discovery that academic dress in Oxford attracts no more attention than blue overalls in an industrial town soon rids one of any feeling of self-consciousness. That I was not, at the outset, alone in this respect, I found when a friend who had been a miner called on me in my rooms the day we were matriculated with his mortar board in a brown paper bag.[82]

He took the opportunity to study seriously, but not uncritically. 'Whether attendance at lectures be regarded as work or recreation depends largely upon the lecturer. At all events I usually come away with fewer notes for future reference from those lectures which have been most enjoyable and stimulating':

> The lecturer appears.... The lecturer pauses hopefully.... He coughs apologetically, as though reluctant to interrupt. A dead silence follows.
>
> He is in good form this morning, and makes a gallant effort to infuse life into his subject. Only a few of his witticisms at the expense of previous commentators on the text with which he is dealing fall flat. He talks steadily for an hour accompanied by the furious scratching of pens. At twelve o'clock he ceases as abruptly as he had begun, and sweeps out of the room with such rapidity that he appears to be uttering his last words as he disappears through the doorway.

He wonders whether the students might appreciate lectures more if there was a charge for admission.

Betjeman's Dons

Ernest Marsh spoke rather well of the dons he encountered as an anomalous undergraduate:

> I soon discovered that dons... were not only quite human, but very friendly, and that passing through the College porch was not like taking up one's ticket at the factory gate. No undergraduate is made to feel that he is merely a cog in a vast machine.[83]

Betjeman himself was more critical. He gives a series of opinions 'of a don regarding the duties of other dons'. 'There are the research dons... Some great brains, they say, should never be allowed the hampering necessity of meeting and teaching undergraduates at all.' Each rates his own field the most important. And if a 'rich man' comes to dinner at high table 'and if it is thought that he may endow a chair of something, or a Research Fellowship of a few hundred a year to the college, the scramble, the plotting and the back-biting flourish'. 'On only one matter are the Research enthusiasts agreed and that is on the uselessness of the dons who confine their activities to teaching. They describe them as mere hacks.' 'The teaching dons have equally weighty arguments against research.... Specialization... has turned... English Literature into a collection of the texts of mediaeval allegoric poets and the study of mutations in Anglo-Saxon.'[84] 'The research virus, say the teaching dons, infects a man who is slightly priggish and turns him into a pedant while he is still in his early twenties.'[85]

Brideshead and the Christian Union

Evelyn Waugh's *Brideshead revisited* begins in the inter-war period, but it was published in 1945, and written in times of post-war austerity when, as he later admitted, the recollection of a more elegant past still alive in the 1930s was particularly piquant. *Brideshead* comes close to caricaturing an age of Oxford privilege so as to contrast it with an unwelcome accommodation of twentieth-century expectations. Here is an examination candidate from the first of those 'worlds':

> Jasper's subfusc suit and white tie proclaimed him still in the thick of it; he had, too, the exhausted but resentful air of one who fears he has failed to do himself full justice on the subject of Pindar's Orphism.[86]

Yet the social choices to be made by students were beginning to involve social duty as well as social status and they could determine future careers as well as the flavour of the student's time at the University. As Sebastian tells Charles:

> I got in with some thoroughly objectionable O.S.C.U. [Oxford Student Christian Union] men who ran a mission to hop-pickers during the long vac. But you, my dear Charles, whether you realize it or not, have gone straight, hook, line and sinker, into the very worst set in the University.[87]

Peter Osmund, who matriculated in 1933, was a real undergraduate of Keble, and another whose letters home survive; he was a serious boy who became a School Inspector, and one who seems to have been influenced in the long term by the Evangelical movement as he encountered it in the University. He tasted numerous clubs in the spirit of a modern Freshman. He wrote about 'japes' and horseplay and his personal friends. 'Barsley has some wizard records & a super gramaphone [*sic*]. One of the records is of Edith Sitwell reciting her poems to weird and exotic music.'[88]

He was a pious youth who went to Student Christian Movement meetings to discuss the ethics of gambling and the nature of patriotism (and whether it might involve civil disobedience); he was sceptical about the religious sincerity of some of the members of this College founded with such high church pretensions:

> Some of the people who think they are going 'into the Church' would amaze you. It's very distressing.... Quite a percentage of these baptised and confirmed people are confirmed atheists.... The people here are very patchy: there are some

> nests of very good men. The fresher ordinands nearly all seem perfectly wet.[89]

It is possible to see here the beginnings of a changing social mix which was going to have a different effect from the minglings of poor students and wealthy young gentlemen in earlier centuries. The presumption of the past had been that poor students would rise socially as a consequence of their studies and we shall see many examples of that happening. The new pattern was to be the creation of a human stew in which all ingredients simmered together.

Morris Motors and Nuffield College

The move to a world in which the car factories on the outskirts of Oxford stood in a new relationship to the University was marked at the end of the 1930s by the benefactions of Lord Nuffield (1877–1963). He had been the William Morris who established Morris Motors at Cowley. He was an Oxford boy, who began his career by repairing bicycles and progressed to the manufacture of the Morris Oxford motor car, and onwards to offering largesse to the University.

The *Gazette* of 17 November 1937 sets out the terms on which Nuffield College was to be founded as part of a benefaction including money for Radcliffe Infirmary buildings (to be opened as new wards). The money was also to be targeted with what Nuffield considered a socially beneficial intention:

> to encourage research, especially but not exclusively in the field of social studies, and especially by making easier the cooperation of academic and non-academic persons.[90]

Relation between these two sides of Oxford, the academic and the commercial, industrial, manufacturing, duly grew closer, though perhaps not in ways Nuffield had anticipated. By the 1970s, J.I.M. Stewart (1906–1994), who also wrote as Michael Innes, Student of Christ Church[91] from 1949 to 1973, and author of *A staircase in Surrey*, a quintet of Oxford novels, was depicting an Oxford society conscious of the proximity of the car factories at Cowley and in routine contact with the priorities of the rest of the world:

> Around us at High Table, men had been conversing rationally about their cars and television sets.[92]

The New Bodleian

There has never been enough space in the Bodleian Library. The Copyright Act of 1911 had named the Bodleian as one of the libraries entitled to receive legal deposit copies of books published in Great Britain. Partly to accommodate these, an underground bookstore was built between 1909 and 1912 between the Radcliffe Camera and the main Bodleian building.

This problem of space entered one of its acute phases in the 1930s; a Commission of Inquiry was set up by a Decree of Congregation in March 1930, reporting in March 1931. The Commission of Inquiry could not agree with itself and Roy Harrod, who was one of its members, added a dissenting note. The dispute concerned the implications of building what became the New Bodleian across the road from the Old Library, and joining it to the Old Library by a tunnel. Harrod warned that this would not meet future needs for long. And there was the question whether to keep readers out of it or use valuable storage space for reader's desks. Younger dons thought the whole question of needs to be met by libraries was changing radically; older ones wanted things to stay the same. Everyone wanted maximum open-shelf access.

Cambridge resolved a similar problem about space by building itself a whole new library away from the centre, on a site big enough to allow for considerable expansion.[93] Oxford decided in a decree published in the *Gazette* on 28 May 1931[94] to allocate and re-allocate parts of the Old Bodleian in various ways, with 'the concentration of storage in a special building on the Broad Street site, capable of holding about 5,000,000 books', with 'preservation of the amenities of Broad Street by a front section screening the stack and containing ... rooms for the reception, handling and cataloguing of books, and for the housing of special collections' with 'a considerable amount of further free space at the Librarian's disposal'. 'The maintenance of a rapid service of books by mechanical means' was to be achieved 'through a tunnel between the Bodleian and Broad Street'. Other central libraries were to be enlarged, there was to be a new catalogue and salaries for the Bodleian staff were to be improved.[95] The New Bodleian Library was designed by Gilbert Scott and finished in 1940.

The Second World War and its aftermath

> In the autumn of 1943, Oxford slept in a strange and timeless silence. No bells rang in wartime, from clock tower or steeple, and there was almost no traffic; the uncluttered curve of the High, the spires of the colleges, slept in the clean, mist, quiet air as in some old don's dream of peace.[96]

The first *Gazette* of the War, published on 8 September 1939, made no grand announcement; it merely cancelled the lecture-list, and suspended routine arrangements for the payment of lecturers and regular requirements for lecturers to lecture, in recognition of the mass exodus to join the armed forces. There were to be no competitions for prizes or scholarships, in fairness to those students who were going to be absent to fight. It was provided[97] that the University would make up the pay of its staff who 'undertake some form of national service in the War' to the level they would have received if they had stayed in Oxford.

So wartime Oxford was as deserted by its usual academic population in the Second World War as it had been in the First. Nina Bawden, who wrote the description above of Oxford in its silent wartime sleep was a girl from the Welsh Marches who first experienced it in this unusual state, and with a distinct sense of having to find her place as an outsider, a girl, and a 'first generation student' in her family. She describes her interview by Helen Darbishire which was to secure her admission to Somerville at the end of the war:

> The tone of my interview with her still sang sweetly in my head; a note of courteous respect for callow opinions followed by a gentle suggestion that I might, perhaps, think again.[98]

Nina Bawden felt 'out of it' when she began at Somerville, as she had at school, but for quite different reasons. She discovered 'that the ideas my schoolfriends had found so extraordinary were almost distressingly common at Oxford'.[99] She goes on to describe a University still unsure how to teach its women students, but conscientious about their intellectual and pastoral care:

> I had gone up to read French – for reasons which are now obscure to me since I had no gift for languages. My tutor was Enid Starkie, a small, sharp woman, reputed to be a lesbian, who wore splendid clothes in startlingly flamboyant colours; purple, pink and orange.[100]

Bawden changed subjects in order to learn something new and was sent to the Master of Balliol for tutorials in philosophy. He had not taught a girl or a student from a state grammar school before 'and could not believe I had never learned Greek'. 'He seemed convinced (although he was far too polite ever to say so) that I must be concealing this simple and fundamental skill out of some mysterious modesty.' He gave her hot milky drinks and treated her kindly but 'what was so simple to him, the flowing order and clarity' of Berkeley's arguments, 'became, as it dripped through the sieve of my incomprehension, bewilderingly muddled and murky'. She was sent to MacKinnon of Keble to see whether he could be more helpful to her:

> A large, untidy engaging man who rolled on the hearth rug and played with the coal in the scuttle, sometimes chewing a lump... while I read him my essays.

She felt that she 'stood on the threshold of a brightly lit room but a locked door barred' her entry. She told him so. He gave her a sardine sandwich 'with his coaly fingers' and sent her to a pupil of his who was 'a young don from Glasgow living in a bed-sitting room in north Oxford'. He taught her slowly and patiently 'the basic words, the first principles; coaxing me into the sea of philosophical method'.[101]

Her encounters with tutors continued to be colourful. One 'read Hobbes aloud in a Viennese accent, or flirted with me, saying I reminded him of a squirrel'. Another 'tried to persuade me that darning his socks would be a more suitable occupation for a young woman than learning statistics. He was also interested in the sort of man I would like to father my children'. 'And there was a small, gallant Englishman who had been parachuted into France to join the Resistance' and who 'occupied our tutorial hours very pleasantly' by describing his experiences.[102]

But she joined energetically enough in the war work done by undergraduates. She describes how she invited American soldiers two at a time to tea at Somerville from the camps outside Oxford and did two stints a week as a waitress at the Red Cross Club in Beaumont St.:

> Although I knew other girls who did more (it was clear that one Somervillian, who changed from her drab working clothes into butterfly garments... when she left college at six every evening, was not merely setting forth to cut sandwiches).[103]

In 1963 the poet Philip Larkin (1922–85) wrote an introduction to his undergraduate novel *Jill,* originally published at the end of the war. Because his bad eyesight excluded him from war service he was one of the relatively small number who came to St. John's in the usual way at the usual age. He too had come up to Oxford as a working-class boy, but not on his own. He had an old school fellow from King Henry VIII School in Coventry as a room-mate, but that did not shield him from the culture-shock of encountering boys who had quite different ideas of life:

> I shared rooms with Noel Hughes, with whom I had just spent two disrespectful years with the Modern Sixth,[104] but

> my tutorial-mate was a large pallid-faced stranger with a rich Bristolian accent...Norman at once set about roughing up my general character and assumptions. Any action or even word implying respect for qualities such as punctuality, prudence, thrift or respectability called forth a snarling roar like that of the Metro-Goldwyn-Mayer lion and the accusation of Bourgeoisisme.

On his first day, after breakfast, John, the hero of *Jill*, 'handed in his ration book at the Bursary'.[105] John goes to see his tutor as instructed at 11.00 on that first morning and encounters a 'character' much like the real ones Nina Bawden describes:

> He was a tall cadaverous man, very slow in his movements and shy to make a definite suggestion; it was by a series of these suggestions that he brought the conversation round to literature....The Tutor opened a tiny notebook, but just then a telephone buzzed on his desk, and with a weary movement he went to answer it....He replaced the receiver and came back to them. 'I'm afraid it is impossible for me to take you separately at the moment.'

'So John is to have his tutorials with a partner, Christopher Warner', a man 'whose self-confidence seemed to increase with every admission of ignorance' and whose 'manner suggested that the Tutor was a personal friend who insisted upon talking tediously about literature'.[106] John is greatly impressed by this confident upper-class approach to life and admires him immensely.

Maurice Bowra and the 'bring your own Widmerpool' party

But the admirableness of a confident 'upper-class' Oxford was being brought into question. Larkin himself went off as gloomily as A.A. Milne's Eeyore to be an academic librarian at Hull. Among the more vivid examples of those who aspired to a particularly Oxford form of 'celebrity' is Maurice Bowra (1898–71),[107] Warden of Wadham from 1938 to 1970. He had served in the First World War before going to Oxford, and the experience cut deep. He once attacked a group of RAF officers during the Second World War, 'asking them if they knew what it had been like to live in mud, shit and decomposing corpses' in the first.[108]

In 1919 he became an undergraduate at New College, where the Warden at the time was William Spooner (1844–1930), of the famous 'Spoonerisms'. Bowra arrived in Oxford perceiving himself no longer a child but an adult. He graduated and won a Fellowship at Wadham in 1922 and stayed there for the rest of his life. He encouraged his pupils to live, at least in their minds, an idealized form of the life of ancient Greece, a mode of life and a pattern of teaching which became an expression of his own striving to be a poet and to mend the damage his war experiences had done him. Cyril Connolly once commented that he 'saw human life as a tragedy in which great poets were the heroes who fought back and tried to give life a meaning'.[109] This was the sort of don encountered with some bewilderment by the likes of Nina Bawden and Philip Larkin coming from working class homes in the Second World War and after.

Yet Bowra was in some ways a disappointed man. He began his academic life insecure and apparently remained so, finding almost more than he could bear his failure in 1936 to win the Regius Chair of Greek which had been held by Gilbert Murray (1866–1957), his friend and active patron, and which he had expected would come to him next. Gilbert Murray's bookplate, showing a view of Athens above his name and one of Oxford below it, is stuck, a little askew, into a copy of Bowra's Andrew Lang Lecture on 'Homer and his Forerunners', which he gave at St. Andrews in February 1955. The copy is now in the Sackler Library in Oxford, removed there from the classics library in the Ashmolean. The old tie held. Bowra's work on Greek and Greek poetry continued. The Chair went to E.R. Dodds.

Bowra looked about him for other sources of personal fulfilment once the Greek Chair evaded his grasp. He was to become Professor of Poetry at Oxford but not until 1946–51. His energies went instead into influencing people and cutting a figure. The latter was not easy for someone of his physical appearance. He was short and rather squat and very sensitive about it. He harboured homosexual proclivities which made his lack of attractiveness a special grief to him, and a further source of a sense of inadequacy. These are characteristics which can make a man a clown but in Oxford the need to 'perform' and to 'shine' took Bowra another way. He became an adopter of protégés rather than a cultivator of friends; he preferred to 'cultivate' the famous, and so he made himself a famous host in order to attract them. His protégés were often men of distinction, such as Isaiah Berlin (1909–97). He was always an Oxford man though he made himself so widely known in social circles outside it – and not only in Britain – and his standing remained that of a notorious don; he would have been less famous, less notorious without the protection and support of that context.

He adopted a 'role-model' already hopelessly dated but still attractive to his sophisticated guests. He sought to be – in terms of wit and style – an Oscar Wilde for his times. He tried, almost too hard, to out-Wilde Oscar with pithy 'shocker' paradoxes. He became, self-consciously, a wit, deliberately outrageous ('Buggery was invented to fill that awkward hour between evensong and cocktails.'). So successful was he in these endeavours that he became an Oxford archetype, with stories which used to be told about Benjamin Jowett being told about him in their turn.[110] He appeared in novels as characters thinly disguised; for example, he is Mr. Samgrass in *Brideshead revisited*.[111] Elizabeth Bowen put him into *To the North* in 1932 as Markie, with sharp observation of a wit 'incisive, spectacular, mordant' in a man who when he came into a room was 'delighted to see himself'. He loved this fictional immortality. It was said that he had even held a 'bring your own Widmerpool' party as a stylish acknowledgement of the debt he thought Anthony Powell's novel-sequence *A dance to the music of time* (published between 1951 and 1975) owed him, though he was mistaken if he thought he was Widmerpool as well as Samgrass. He knew a great many people whom he amused hugely and who regarded him with affection.

Bowra was a left-over Victorian who vociferously regretted the modernization of Oxford, gave amusement, became a cynosure. He made himself famous, but as a caricature of an Oxford whose passing he regretted. Oxford, with its growing intake of 'first-time' students and its widening class-base, was beginning to look towards a new future and adjusting its 'style' accordingly.

Oxford science and the war

Nowhere was the movement of change so evident as in the development of Oxford science. Scientific teaching and research were much affected by the war, as individuals left to join the armed forces and whole research teams went off to provide specialist service for their country. The Professor of Engineering Science 'advised' the Ministry of Supply.[112] E.B. Moullin, Reader in Electrical Engineering, took all his research students with him as a group to the Admiralty. His personal attractiveness and stylish approach to life is nicely caught in a recollection by Brigadier Douglas Henchley, who had been one of the students who attended his lectures before the war:

> He was referred to as the most attractive bachelor in Oxford. He had a very fast car – Alfa Romeo I think – and a powerful motorbike, a Harley Davidson. He lectured on mechanics. I saw him briefly when I dined at BNC [Brasenose College] in 1943 when the College had been taken over by the Royal Armoured Corps – and I was invited to give a lecture about

> my corps – the Royal Electrical & Mechanical Engineers which was founded in October 1942.[113]

The graduates of Henchley's year (1933) were only nine, with six postgraduate students, and he notes in the same reminiscence that the status of some of the scientist lecturers, especially the engineers, was precarious and they were not always invited to become Fellows of Colleges. The lack of a Fellowship was one of the marks of remaining an outsider in Oxford:

> In those days there were also some external tutors – mainly for men at colleges who did not have an engineer on their staff. For example my own college – Keble – only had one Science fellow and he was a chemist but he had to keep an eye on any student who was reading a Science subject. None of the lecturers were Fellows of colleges – that status came along later. The head of the School was RV (later Sir Richard) Southwell. All the tutors were Cambridge graduates. Southwell had graduated I think early in the First World War. I was told that he was on the design staff of one of the early airships – R34 I think – which crashed on its maiden voyage. I was told that this blighted his career for a bit but he was elected to the Oxford professorship I think in 1929 and attached to BNC.

The call the scientists had made at the end of the First World War for adequate salaries for Demonstrators had not succeeded in establishing a secure career path for university teachers in the sciences; the problems of the later twentieth century which were to arise from offering only what amounted to a lifelong series of short-term contracts for scientists were already to be glimpsed here.

Now, with national war-time needs to be met, Oxford's expertise was harnessed. Research into nuclear weapons (involving separating the 235 isotope of uranium by gaseous diffusion) disguised by the title 'tube alloys', was conducted in the Clarendon Laboratory by F.E. Simon, himself a German-Jewish refugee who had come to England in the 1930s.[114] There was work designed to improve the science of defences against germ and chemical warfare and to make a more effective charcoal for respirators.[115] The investment in knowledge and facilities involved put Oxford – like other universities – in a stronger position to expand its science teaching after the war, during the period when the practical benefits of scientific research had become apparent.

New buildings and a great deal more equipment were needed if Oxford was going to stay at the forefront in this new 'bigger' science. The University showed a determination not to lag behind in new fields. A Computing Laboratory was set up in Parks Road as early as 1957. The Radcliffe Science Library was expanded to accommodate the increasing numbers of science students who needed to use it, by the excavation of the Lankester Room reaching under the forecourt of the University Museum, running beneath the lawn across which a dinosaur's footprints are now marked for the amusement of children visiting the Museum. A new system of funding had to be developed, in which state 'project' funding took the lead, through such bodies as the Medical Research Council, the Science Research Council, and the Agricultural Research Council. Oxford scientists learned to win such funding.

Chemistry remained in the forefront in both numbers and reputation, but all the sciences grew in student numbers and ambition. One of the important impacts on the University as a whole was going to be the pattern of teaching the scientists evolved as student interest in their fields expanded. This began to be fundamentally different from the tutorial system of the arts and humanities in that it tended to be organized through Faculties and Departments and not by the Colleges. This also created a balance in which the professoriate was disproportionately powerful, and controlled access to bench space and approval for planned research projects, by a junior workforce of academics whose contracts were easily terminated and whose continuation in their careers might depend heavily upon the patronage of their seniors.

The job of University Demonstrator had grown up to meet a need. 'A demonstratorship is the principal teaching appointment in nearly all the science subjects,' commented *The Oxford Magazine,* the unofficial complement to the *Gazette*, in 1957.[116] It is explained that a Demonstrator requires the skill to make an experiment work when a student gets stuck, and to devise experiments for the students to carry out which will be sufficiently interesting and worthwhile. But the most important work consists in the supervision of research students:

> Postgraduate research is now an essential part in the training of a first-rate scientist, and a man is not really fully qualified as a research scientist until he has spent about three years in this way.

It was realized that research supervision in science involved much more time and close attention than for those doing research in the arts subjects. The fledgling scientist could not make do with 'an hour's discussion now and then'; he might 'need advice daily, if not hourly'. But then the supervisor would be able to regard himself as a collaborator and results would be published jointly to the benefit of the demonstrator's own research. Thus emerged the modern system of research teams and shared projects.[117]

Janet Vaughan, Principal of Somerville (1945–67), was the College's first scientist to be a Head of House, and moreover, one of those who most conspicuously entered public life in a quite different way from that chosen by Maurice Bowra. She was a woman of wide experience of the 'real' world and of running things, an experienced committee-woman. She was also a political activist, a strong supporter of the Labour Party (until much later she was drawn into the Liberal Democrats by Shirley Williams). She had run the blood transfusion service for London during the war. Like Helen Darbishire she saw her Principalship of Somerville as no reason to stop work as a scholar and she continued active research in haematology. However, she expected things to be more business-like than they had been up to then. She thought the Principal ought to have a telephone at least, and she had opened her post every morning well before 9.00.[118]

A Symposium at Worcester: the 1950s to the 1980s

Gamesmanship and the direction of reform

Plato's *Symposium* is a dinner-party conversation. J.C. Masterman (1891–1977), Provost of Worcester, borrowed the conceit to provide himself with a setting for a conversation about Oxford and its direction of change in *To teach the Senators wisdom or an Oxford guide-book* (1952),[119] our second Oxford 'guide book' to the century.[120] Like some of the Inklings, he had had his First World War experiences. When war broke out he was working as an 'exchange' lecturer in Freiburg and he spent the next four years in a prisoner-of-war camp, where he was sent as an 'enemy alien'. His subsequent career was spent at Oxford, but while the Inklings continued to drink beer and talk of fantasy worlds and Maurice Bowra postured and strutted on the world's social stage, Masterman played games, from cricket to espionage. He is mentioned by Stephen Potter in *Gamesmanship*[121] but he was involved in a more serious game. Between the wars he belonged to MI5 and actively recruited students as agents. In the

Second World War he chaired the Double Cross (XX) Committee.[122] None of this prevented his becoming Provost of Worcester College from 1946 to 1961 and serving his turn as Vice-Chancellor of Oxford from 1957 to 1958. When such a figure surveys Oxford life as he has known it and considers its future, he must be taken seriously.

One of the conceits tried out in his 'guide book' is to wonder what might have happened if either Oxford or Cambridge had been bombed in the Second World War. The rebuilding would have required some modernization:

> Kitchens would be built contiguous to Halls, and with modern machinery to convey the food and crockery to and fro; every man would have an adequate number of cubic feet of space allotted to him for his living quarters; there would be labour-saving devices in every College, and running water in every bedroom and bathrooms on every staircase.

But if the other University had remained intact, future students would be able to choose. Some 'would rather live in a fourteenth-century room and walk a quarter of a mile to the nearest bathroom than be housed in the most luxurious of modern apartments'. Others would prefer the less costly and more convenient new alternative. 'Which University would be the gainer in thirty years?'[123]

There was no such wholesale destruction of either of the ancient universities, but the move to modernity and the changing expectations of students were to have their effect nonetheless. The contrast a generation could effect was evident to Masterman's fictional symposium, who reminisce about their own undergraduate experiences at the end of the nineteenth century:

> Let me see, we used to go with a can in the afternoons to a tap by the kitchen and get boiling water from there. In some Colleges they had big stone or earthenware jars which used to stand by the fire and get boiling hot – but we went to the tap. Yes – and then I used to pour the water into a tin hip-bath in front of my sitting-room fire...I used to have my tea down on the floor beside me. Very sybaritic, Prendergast, but highly agreeable. Muffins and crumpets and chocolate cake by the side of the hip-bath – dear me, that was really luxury. But of course that was in the afternoon after rowing or games; in the morning we had a cold tub. No gentleman would think of missing his cold bath in the morning, winter or summer.[124]

In many ways this was a simpler student life as was apparent to this post-war gathering:

> We had a very…plain luncheon. My recollection is that most men used to have a commons of bread and cheese, a pint of beer, and a lot of marmalade.…Of course directly after lunch we hurried off to the river…[in the evening] we used to collect in someone's rooms and sing songs and play cards and so on, and I can remember going to the theatre and to the Union, and, much better, going to one or other of our literary clubs. That's the clearest recollection of all – we used to read papers and discuss things and talk and talk.[125]

Student unrest

The Oxford Magazine (22 October 1953, p.30)[126] reported a fictional conversation between two undergraduates about their tutor, who did not seem to understand the way their lives worked:

> He…asked what work I had done in the vacation. When I said waiting in a hotel in Torquay he went up in smoke.
>
> Now that is odd. He made a terrible scene when I told him I had worked in a hotel in Bournemouth all July and August…
>
> He asked what I had done in September, and when I said a holiday in the Julian Alps, he seemed peeved. Odd, for, I mean to say, what would be the point of working all July and August if you don't go abroad in September?…
>
> 'I wonder what he really expects us to do in the vacation? I often wonder about that.'

New kinds of post-war student were arriving with changed expectations, less awestruck by Oxford than Nina Bawden and Philip Larkin, and with less respect for authority. Keble's student magazine, *The Clocktower,* made a survey of student experience in 1952. Asked why they had chosen Keble, one in four said they were there because they could not get a place at another college. There did not seem to be a high level of strong loyalty among the respondents, or the feeling of belonging many Oxford graduates continued – and continue – to feel towards their colleges; part of the reason was reported to lie in the poor quality of tutor–student relationships. This may or may not have betokened an impending threat to collegiate Oxford. (Respondents did not think much of the food either.[127])

Their seniors were concerned about the future of the collegiate system too. The *Oxford Magazine* of 28 November 1957,[128] carried a stock-taking editorial on 'the economy of the University'. The

University had, it said, received 'large sums' since 1945. 'Money has flowed in, often in embarrassing amounts, and led to expansion in activities which now have to be sustained in face of needs more central to the work of the University.' One of the challenges this was creating was to the continuing viability of the colleges:

> Some time in the near future the educational rulers of the country will have to make up their minds about the college system: whether to treat it as an untidy relic of the past, an administrative nuisance, or as an institution to be cherished, providing not only the best form of those halls of residence which they are so anxious to create elsewhere, but independent scholarship ... with individuals answerable, not to faculty or professor, but to their own conscience.

For students a financial golden era followed the 1944 Education Act, when tuition was free and maintenance grants available, and bright students from working class families who had been educated at grammar or Direct Grant schools were comparatively numerous in the University. Oxford was beginning to look different, too. Buildings which had turned from golden stone to black, were cleaned after the 1957 Oxford Historic Buildings Appeal. New modern comforts were provided in the colleges. The Keble College Record of 1958–9 records that baths were installed to ensure that no one had to walk across a quadrangle to find one. None of this prevented discontent and protest. The faintly discontented students of Keble in 1952 were followed by others throughout the University who got ideas from the mounting tide of student protest in Europe. The adolescent sense of being misunderstood by an older generation was nothing new, but now it began to be expressed in novel terms through student protest. The traditional town and gown disputes were to be replaced by student-and-university battles.

Until the 1960's students were rusticated (sent home), or even sent down (expelled) for good, if they were found overnight in the rooms of members of the opposite sex. A new era of sexual freedom was beginning to make that seem a disproportionate response. Students openly did things and said things students in Oxford had not felt so free to do before. *Isis,* a student magazine, began to carry reviews of lectures, until the Proctors banned the practice.[129] There were other attempts at Proctorial censorship, which caused such anger that students began a campaign of harassing the Proctors by telephoning them at home. The University set about dealing with such disturbing new patterns of behaviour by creating a Student Representative Council in early 1961. There were complaints that this was 'unrepresentative', but it allowed room for a number of matters to be raised and debated which were causing trouble elsewhere in British universities too – the syllabus and other academic issues, student freedoms and student behaviour and what should be a disciplinary offence.

The Senior Proctor's Oration in March 1961[130] touched delicately on the issue of proctorial censorship:

> It is ... our belief that the ordinary teaching procedures of and in the University, tutorials, discussion and practical classes, and lectures, are private occasions, at which both teacher and taught are privileged. The bond of confidence between these two is destroyed and this privilege abused, if either makes public his comments on the professional performance of the other.[131]

The speech continued with a reference to the new Representative Council, on which the Proctors said they did not look 'unkindly':

> Its aims are to afford a recognised means of communication between junior members of the University and University authorities; and to collect information and make recommendations to the University authorities on matters of general University interest.[132]

The Senior Proctor had formerly been Chairman of the 'Undergraduate Representative Council of the War years' so he was sympathetic to the needs to be met.

Meanwhile, the Senior Proctor's Oration in March 1962[133] was couched in language which seems to be bursting with feeling about much more traditional experiences of student misbehaviour. There was still trouble on Bonfire Night:

> It would not be amiss to thank junior members of the University for their cooperation on the nights of the Fourth and Fifth of November 1961.

This was one of the traditional moments in the year when noise and disturbance regularly occurred. On 12 November 1953, the Oxford Magazine had even suggested that it might be conducive to peace and quiet if the Proctors did not put in an appearance since 'to be "progged" is to raise one's social status'.[134] The Senior Proctor of that year considered that the proctorial presence had been helpful:

> The instructions which went out over your signature, Sir, and ours, were most satisfactorily followed. We started from the assumption that junior members of Oxford University are men and women of intelligence and good faith and amenable

> to reason.... The great majority of senior members of the University do not assume that newspaper accounts of proctorial intentions or proceedings have necessarily any authority.[135]

But what was happening reflected a new 'us-and-them' attitude among students, a collective student view that the University authorities were the 'opposition', and mounting anger sometimes verging on violence. The Proctors faced an angry mob of students in June 1968. From 24 February to 1 March 1970 there was a student sit-in at the Clarendon Building, then the offices of the central administration, with students (who did not realize that admissions were done by the colleges), conducting searches for incriminating files on students. Not all undergraduates approved of these tactics. After the demonstration of June 1968, a petition was got up with 1211 signatures in which junior members petitioned the Proctors (*Isis,* 12 June 1968), maintaining that the activists were unrepresentative, at least of themselves as students. The Hart Committee was set up in 1968 to look into relations with junior members.[136] One of the great pressures of the 1960s following these stirrings of rebellion was to get student representation on committees in the University.

The contrast with the sense of a tacit 'collusion of gentlemen' between Proctors and students in these matters of proper behaviour is neatly put in Masterman's reminiscent novel-guide-book. There was:

> the old East Oxford Theatre on the Cowley Road, but men only went there on Saturday nights, and I'm afraid that they only went there to rag the show, very reprehensible.... One Saturday night [the Proctor] saw an undergraduate hurrying eastward over Magdalen Bridge and clasping a large parcel to his body under his greatcoat. The proctor... asked the young man to unfold his parcel and show him what he was carrying... he disclosed a large fish. ...'Why,' he said, in his sternest tone of voice, 'why are you carrying this fish?' 'Oh, Sir,' replied the undergraduate, 'I thought it was a sound thing to have about me.' Now that was a very good answer, especially to a proctor who was also a philosopher. It would be difficult for a philosopher to decide, without adequate argumentation, that a large hake was not a sound thing to have about you at ten p.m. on a Saturday evening.[137]

Presenting the right face to the world

There was an emerging sensitivity in Oxford to potentially destructive public opinion. This would lead a few decades later to the establishment of a Press Office and an attempt at reputation-management.[138] Oxford had been in the headlines as long as there had been headlines, but usually over the squabbles of its senior members. Junior behaviour was only now becoming a regular source of potential national embarrassment. The BBC made a stilted television programme about Oxford which was the subject of criticism in *The Oxford Magazine*:

> Nor is this something we can afford to ignore; a University dependent on public funds is dependent on public opinion; T.V., we are told, is the great maker of opinion; as far as the University is concerned, the impression made must have been a deplorable one of a series of boring trivialities.

The programme, it noted disparagingly, had included a staged tea party in a studio in London 'with the object of permitting a would-be photogenic undergraduette to make some banal observations about "student life"'.

The problem with the high profile of the University was that it meant Oxford had its enemies, and plenty willing to be persuaded to be its enemies. A letter had been written to the *Manchester Guardian* 'by an irate American who has had cause to resent the insultingly simplified lectures of visiting English dons in the United States':

> in Academic intercourse, whether private or public, there is no greater solecism than the imputation of ignorance.... If a medieval historian wants to talk about his own subject to a Lecturer in inorganic chemistry, it is good form to begin, 'You know of course Pollard's absurd argument about the members of the Commons in the fourteenth century...' A short pause will then give the chemist a chance modestly to disclaim such knowledge or even to indicate that he might welcome a change of subject.[139]

The University began to make an effort to present itself acceptably to the nation and the world, to make provision which would meet criticism of its ways. Oxford provision for 'continuing education' had begun in the nineteenth century. Vera Brittain and Ernest Marsh were among those who had benefited. It was now becoming important as a part of the 'accessibility' of the face Oxford presented to the world and its social conscience about bringing what it had to offer within reach of the general public. Extra-mural studies and the changing subject-matter thought appropriate for courses for the general public was the subject of discussion in the *Oxford Magazine,* 15 May 1958.[140] One question was whether such courses should cater to general interests and try to keep up with demand, or seek to provide serious instruction so as to 'inform' public enthusiasms and even guide them. It was suggested that 'the public's sudden interest in 1927 in lecture courses on Astronomy' is less surprising if 'it is remembered that there was a total eclipse of the sun in June of that year, the first in this country since 1724'. The most consistent observation concerns 'the preponderance of courses' on 'modern International Relations' (1938–9) with a post-war boom in courses on rebuilding towns, including one in which John Betjeman participated. Then there was a switch to keenness on science subjects in the post-war period. But this was always against a strong background of concern with International Affairs, History and Economics, the traditional areas of the political and economic emphasis of the Workers Educational Association.

Waking a sleeping Congregation

It began to be noticed after the Second World War that attendance at meetings of Congregation was often very thin.[141] The *Oxford Magazine* routinely gave a report of a debate, for example, on 5 November 1953: 'In Congregation this week members of Council played to a very poor House their accustomed comedy of "enlightening the University" as to the reasons for legislation.'[142]

There was a poll in 1968 which established that only 1 per cent of those with the vote said they were regularly present at meetings of Congregation, with 63 per cent turning up only 'rarely' and 11 per cent never.[143] Was the ancient democracy losing its powers by neglect?

It was different when an argument broke out about a matter where academics felt their interests to be affected. Congregation could wake up and 'frighten the horses' in the executive. *The Oxford Magazine* (now often the forum for debate where meetings of Congregation turned out not to be) could bring a matter to everyone's attention. Its editor remarked how 'members of Congregation, stimulated by the roads controversy' (always a topic sure to generated indignation), showed a revival of interest – though not always sustained – in 'University business'.[144] But then as now, *The Oxford Magazine* ran 'on a minimum of organization and a maximum of cooperation'.[145] In the late 1950s, the *Magazine* faced one of the not-infrequent occasions when it seemed that it might have to cease publication. Both symptoms of the neglect of the importance of active academic participation in the governance of the University were warning signs.

In 1957, the Editor tried to stimulate thought about the adequacy of the machinery for conducting the democratic process by comparing

Oxford with Cambridge:

> A considerable debate has been going on at Cambridge since last term concerning a proposal to establish a new mixed science and arts school. This has been discussed at lengths unknown in Oxford save in connection with the design of roads.[146]

The Oxford Magazine on 5 December 1957 described the way such discussions were conducted in Cambridge:

> The proposal was first set out in the form of a long report from the General Board, reproduced in full in the Cambridge Reporter, the ampler Cambridge version of the Gazette. A week or two later this was followed by the verbatim report of the debate in the Senate. At the same time the suggestions have evoked a considerable number of articles, letters and editorial comment in the *Cambridge Review*. In contrast to all this machinery of debate, both official and unofficial, one recalls the resent establishment of a new school at Oxford, which most people had never heard of until it turned up quite casually one day in Congregation as an established item of expenditure.[147]

The hope of prompting active interest in Oxford in making comparisons between the two, and seeking improvements, was not realized.

'Colleges needed' for holders of University-only posts and graduate students

There were, however, matters to which Congregation urgently needed to give its attention. Oxford had the same problem as Cambridge in the 1960s in the threatened breakdown of the symbiosis of colleges and University which had become a settled thing in recent generations; now those who taught for the University did not always hold a Fellowship in a College. The arrangements about employment of those simultaneously lecturing for the University and teaching for a college were different in the two universities but Oxford and Cambridge shared a conviction that this overlapping of loyalties to College and University was essential to the well-being of the 'collegiate University'. *The Oxford Magazine* had already noted the Cambridge plan to 'build a university club at the bottom of Mill Lane ... to provide a common meeting ground and common facilities for all members of the graduate staff of the university and other persons closely connected with its work'.[148] Oxford was in due course to provide something similar in its University Club.

One significant group of the disadvantaged was formed of the scientists-without-Fellowships. But a number of lecturers of all disciplines were not entitled to College Fellowships; the colleges could not be forced to provide them, and this problem of non-entitlement became a prominent issue in the 1960s. Oxford became actively concerned when it was suggested that 'every time the University appoints a [joint-appointment?] lecturer for whom there is no college Fellowship it commits a breach of contract and the breach continues for as long as no college association can be arranged'.[149]

The *Report of the Committee on the long-term problem of entitlement* (Oxford 1970), chaired by J.E.H. Griffiths, had set about addressing the problem, but imaginative independent solutions were already emerging. Wolfson College (1965), whose first President (from 1966) was the philosopher Isaiah Berlin, was able to meet some of the need as a result of large benefactions from the Ford Foundation in 1966 and the gift from the Wolfson Foundation which made it possible to build a white concrete, unapologetically modern, building for it beside the Cherwell in north Oxford. Wolfson began with the name Iffley College, but took its new name in recognition of the generosity of its benefactor.

Graduate students, too, would not always find it easy to enjoy the dual affiliation with College and Faculty or Department which would allow them to enjoy the fullness of Oxford life. The Wolfson experiment was designed to meet this need as well as the need of uncolleged lecturers. Isaiah Berlin, who had been one of Maurice Bowra's dearest protégés, was a sociable man. He had been a Fellow of All Souls since 1932 and also a lecturer in philosophy at New College (1938–50). He found New College dull, though he met Virginia Woolf there socially and also the novelist Elizabeth Bowen, herself a friend of David Cecil and Maurice Bowra. As President of Wolfson he had ambitions to make the community 'free' and 'untrammelled', and as a graduate college it was bound to need to establish a different atmosphere from the traditional undergraduate colleges because the distance of age and academic experience between Fellows and other members was likely to be less.

Linacre House was founded in 1962 as a non-residential society to meet the social needs of graduate students. It was first housed at the bottom of St. Aldate's, and then moved to Cherwell Edge in 1977, where a community of Anglican nuns had formerly resided. It was not to be a College yet, but the University provided an endowment, money was raised, and in 1986 Linacre attained collegiate status.

Besse and the rebels of St. Anthony's

New 'experimental' colleges such as St. Anthony's College were proposed, so the University had to wrestle with the principles on which it was prepared to recognize them as colleges of the University when a prospective benefactor put forward an unusual idea:

> I well remember...going round huge country houses which at that time were up for sale in the hope that they would be suitable for the 'school for rebels' which Mr. Besse first had in mind.[150]

Besse was a French merchant trading in Aden who came to the view that the best place for his 'rebels' was likely to be Oxford and who offered it the opportunity to establish a college. The politics proved complex. There were existing colleges which were short of funding. There were needs to be met, for example, colleges for postgraduate students, which this proposed college could not easily fulfil. But the same political instincts which put considerations in the way of the straightforward acceptance of a gift also recommended checking up on Besse with the Foreign Office. It gave a hard-headed summary of his personality but it said 'he is in no sense disreputable and no taint attaches to his money'. Discussions proceeded.

Besse became impatient to see his college emerge. He had ambitious ideas which the University could not possibly have countenanced, for they would have restricted to activities of the College to make them fit the founder's notions, for example, that prospective student should be vetted for 'the essential qualities of heart and brain and a clear grasp of the aim we are pursuing – international understanding and cooperation'.[151] Besse had failed to understand that he must leave the management of the College to its Fellows and even the interim arrangements to set up a Council of Management of the company which would be needed to deal with the acquisition of a site annoyed him, because it was done without consulting him.[152] Besse died in 1951 and (not without legal difficulties) it proved possible to complete the task of creating the new College. It was tiny at first, with seven graduate students, who included John Bayley. (Bayley first saw the philosopher and novelist Iris Murdoch [1919–1999], who was to become his wife in 1956, cycling along Woodstock Rd. Iris Murdoch, who had been at Somerville [and joined the Communist Party in 1938], had become a postgraduate at Newnham College, Cambridge. She became a Fellow of St. Anne's in 1948 and remained there until she left to be a full-time novelist.)

Colleges go mixed: the decade from 1974

In 1959 the women's 'Societies' made an application to the University to be admitted as full Colleges of the University. This was agreed, and the change in status was effected by a supplemental charter and amended statutes for each in 1961. Paradoxically, many women academics, although they had Fellowships in the women's colleges, still found themselves on the fringes of University affairs. Was it from choice or were they being 'excluded'?

> Our women dons include many fine scholars, energetic tutors and devoted college fellows, but with a few exceptions they play little part in University affairs ... they presumably exclude themselves by choice, apathy or defeatism. How else can one explain their complete absence from some University bodies ... and the relatively few women on other University bodies ... partly, of course, women do not get drawn much into University life because they are insufficiently known: a university club could perform a most useful function here. But there also seems to be a reluctance to push themselves forward,[153] commented the *Oxford Magazine* in 1958.

One solution proposed was to make colleges mixed-sex. As this began to happen in the 1970s, there were worries about disadvantaging the women's colleges if all the bright girls applied to the former men's colleges. And indeed, as the men's colleges went mixed, competition for able girls became fierce. Instead of being able to choose from the cream of women in a University where there were ten places for men to every one for a woman, Somerville[154] and the other women's Colleges had to compete with the attractions of New College, Balliol or Christ Church. It was not just the architectural disadvantage. They were also too poor to tempt their students with the sort of financial support which was on offer from wealthier colleges. Yet the trend proved hard to resist. By 1994, St. Hilda's was the only remaining women's college in the University.[155] The rest had 'gone mixed', with New College in the lead.[156]

The women students in mixed colleges sometimes continued to see themselves as a group apart. Trinity College admitted women in 1979. The Trinity College first 'term card' of the Women's Group as late as the end of the 1980s offered the following themes for meetings:[157]

1st week Chocolate Party
2nd week Introduction to Holistic Massage

3rd week 'Why would anyone want to be a nun?' with Sister Andrea
4th week Video: Victoria Wood live
5th week Outing to the Body Shop
6th week Discussion
7th week 'Women in Academia' with Dinah Birch
8th week End of term Party

The balance of the sexes among the academics was much slower to change than that of students, since it had to await the occurrence of vacancies in the Fellowships; women would have to compete with male applicants and in the nature of things, they would not always get the jobs thus made available.[158]

The Franks Commission

The Report of the Robbins Committee on Higher Education (1963) was the fruit of the first Government-commissioned attempt to review higher education at large. Its terms of reference were

> to review the pattern of full-time education in Great Britain and in the light of national needs and resources to advise Her Majesty's Government on what principles its long-term development should be based. In particular, to advise, in the light of these principles, whether any new types of institution are desirable and whether any modifications should be made in the present arrangements for planning and co-ordinating the development of the various types of institution.[159]

Robbins was not much concerned with Oxford or Cambridge but it left both universities wondering uneasily whether it might not be wise to be seen to define and defend their positions. Oxford was fearful that the alternative might be to find itself subject to another Royal Commission. It set up an Inquiry into itself, to be chaired by Lord Franks, with 'internal' members making up the rest of the Commission.

Oliver Franks (1905–92) began as a philosopher and became a public servant, in much the spirit of a latter-day Cicero in reverse. A Quaker by upbringing, a Liberal in politics, he remained an idealist through a career spent in the thick of twentieth-century public life. He had been a student at Queen's from 1923 to 1927, though a relatively poor one. On Sundays he worshipped at Mansfield College, among the Congregationalists. He graduated with a First and became a don. As a tutor he was influential in bringing credibility to the novel combination of Philosophy, Politics and Economics which made up

'Modern Greats'. He was drawn into public life during the Second World War in Whitehall at the Ministry of Supply, but from 1946 to 1948 he was back in Oxford as Provost of Queen's. The Oxford Inquiry was only one of several which he chaired or in which he took a major part.

It was, as it turned out, badly timed because it left out of account several problem areas not foreseen or not fully foreseen in 1970, for example, the consequences of 'mixing' the colleges by allowing the admission of women students to the men's colleges and the appointment of women Fellows. Nevertheless, a number of significant proposals were put forward by a deceptively bland 'Franks'. The balance to be struck, as Franks perceived it, was between preserving the ancient democratic structure and ensuring that the University was able to take decisions and function with reasonable speed and efficiency. It was only a generation or so since Convocation had lost most of its powers to Congregation. Were those powers now to be diminished further? Fewer matters were to be required to be put to Congregation for its decision and it moved increasingly to a position where it gave its consent by default and retained mainly a power of veto. Franks:

> proposed that Congregation should elect members of Council and the other main administrative bodies; make, amend or repeal statutes; debate resolutions submitted by Council and the floor; ask questions; and resolve disputes between major bodies in the administration. It was also to elect 18 members of Hebdomadal Council in order to give it some influence on that body.[160]

Hebdomadal Council was to become the chief executive body, and the Vice-Chancellorship was to become a four-year rotation, which might go to someone who was not the head of a college. The integration of the university's administrative offices was planned. The poorest colleges were to be helped financially. The idea of creating the 'super-faculties' now known as Divisions did not succeed, but its time was to come. Similarly the idea of setting up a Council of Colleges to enable the colleges to make a better fist of working together did not succeed but its time too was to come. Convocation survived but it could now elect only the Chancellor and the Professor of Poetry, unless Congregation chose subsequently to add to its powers. The Franks Report was considered by Council between May and October 1966 and resulting new statutes were approved by Congregation and the Privy Council in 1967.

From student protest to the battle for academic freedom

Margaret Thatcher is refused an honorary degree

In 1985 Margaret Thatcher was causing indignation among teachers in universities because of major cuts in education funding and funding for scientific research. When she was proposed as recipient of the Honorary Degree of Doctor of Civil Law in Oxford, students and academics alike protested that it would be inappropriate to honour her. Five thousand students signed a petition and the academics voted against by 2 to 1.

Nina Bawden was at Somerville with Margaret Thatcher, whom she describes as 'a plump, neat, solemn girl with rosy cheeks and fairish hair curled flat to her head who spoke as if she had just emerged from an elocution lesson'. Bawden reported an argument with her about her decision to join the Conservative Party. 'She and I, with our lower middle-class backgrounds, had been lucky to get into Oxford. It would be despicable to use our good fortune simply to join the ranks of the privileged.' 'Margaret smiled, her pretty china doll's smile. Of course, she admitted, the Labour Club was, just at the moment, more *fashionable*.' But she was going into Parliament and she thought she would be noticed more in the Conservative Club.[161]

Daphne Park took over as Principal of Somerville (1980–9), in this period of financial tightness for higher education and with experience in the diplomatic service (and in intelligence) which had accustomed her to a variety of dangers in postings in Moscow, Leopoldville, Lusaka, Hanoi and Ulan Bator but not to the precise sophistications she would need to display in Oxford. Diplomacy in Oxford proved to be a different matter from diplomacy among the nations, and an Establishment position had new intricacies there. As Principal of Mrs Thatcher's old college, Daphne Park naïvely supported her nomination. She said, 'You don't stop someone becoming a fellow of an academic body because you dislike them'.[162] On this occasion, Oxford did exactly that.

Academic freedom is challenged again

> However good the lectures, we didn't ask for our tutorials to be driven by then and we didn't expect our exam questions to be lecture-driven either. The whole field of zoology was fair game for the examiners.... The examiners when setting the papers, and our tutors when handing out essay topics, neither knew nor cared which subjects had been covered in lectures.[163]

Thus Richard Dawkins (b.1941), who became an aggressively atheist popular writer on science and religion, describes student expectations when he was at Oxford. This chimes with the description of another rebel and radical of the 1960s, Tariq Ali (b.1943):

> Before I went to Oxford, I went to a university in Pakistan ... within the college the atmosphere was very enlightened, and there were study circles discussing Marxism, discussing Islam, discussing anything you care to think of. So that, already, was a good training. ... But they basically pushed me out. ... So I arrived at Oxford. And here, books – which weren't available in Pakistan or had been removed from the libraries – were suddenly available again. The atmosphere was very open, and I got engaged with the Left groups on the Oxford University campus very, very early on, and became very active. The Vietnam War was then beginning, and I was pretty obsessed by that war. It was my continent which was under attack.[164]

The battle to protect these and other aspects of academic freedom in Oxford hovered in the background of the student unrest of the 1960s.

By the 1970s the students had other preoccupations:

> Apart from a few long-haired left-overs from the heady revolutionary days of 1968, the students were not very politically engaged. One or two put on lapel badges in support of the two big miners' strikes of the early 1970s and when Jim Callahan (as Home Secretary) came to visit there was some loose talk about throwing him in the pond but it was all theory, no praxis.[165]

But in the 1980s, the concern awoke again and this time it was to concern the academics too, when their own freedoms were threatened by legislation which would remove old-fashioned academic tenure.

The Education Reform Act of 1988 was not passed without a struggle, because it was perceived that the implications were enormous and overlapped with questions of academic autonomy in teaching as well as in research, an institutional as well as a personal matter. The Robbins Report's quadripartite account of the essentials of academic autonomy was becoming relevant to the questions what constitutes academic freedom and whether and how it should be protected.[166] In the debate on the Queen's Speech on 30 June 1987, Lord Beloff (1913–99), formerly a student at Corpus Christi, said he had been reading two Government papers setting out the Government's ideas (*Universities Funding Council* and *Contracts between the Funding Bodies and Higher Education Institutions*), and he was 'enormously depressed'. 'The only analogy I can think of is a treatise on oceanic navigation written by someone who had never been nearer the sea than a half-day excursion to Southend'.[167] Jack Straw was concerned too. 'From beginning to end the Bill is based upon a deception... it should be called the "Education (State Control) Bill"'.[168]

In the end a compromise was reached. Academic tenure came to an end but a clause was inserted in the Education Reform Act at s.202 designed to protect academic staff from danger of dismissal or the loss of privileges if they 'questioned or tested' received opinion. Commissioners were set up to create a Model Statute, with each University to adopt a version of it, as Oxford duly did.

The 1990s and the beginning of another Oxford century

Drawing conclusions

In modern times, the Vice-Chancellor's Annual Oration at the beginning of October usually takes stock of the past year, but in 1993 Professor Sir Richard Southwood took a longer view in his valedictory 'State of the Union Address':

> In the decade after World War Two the universities were seen as an important component of the new and better world that was being built. They were appropriate recipients of public money which had for so long been devoted to winning the war and recovering from its immediate aftermath.

He observed that 'this attitude was reflected in the description "public money" which contrasts with that currently favoured by many politicians, "tax-payers' money"', for it seemed to him that

> this latter phrase is often used to suggest that the recipients have someone else's money to which they are not entitled and may well squander. Forty years ago increases in university provision were headline news and a credit to the government of the day. Now universities have lost that public esteem and world-wide are subject to harsh criticism and almost contempt. This change of attitude has been followed by a steep decline in public funding as a proportion of university income, and a concomitant but paradoxical acceleration in the rate of State intervention.

Moreover, he suggested:

> Traditional 'buffers' between governments and institutions, such as the UGC and the research councils, have disappeared or have been so transformed as to become the very channels by which the government's interventions are effected.[169]

Oxford could not stand above all this. It was going to be subject to the same funding régime as everyone else and therefore the same danger of interference. It would be included in the new Research Assessment Exercise and the quality assurance of teaching. It shortly found itself one of two universities in Oxford, Oxford and Oxford Brookes, when the former polytechnic became a university. Even in Oxford tendencies became noticeable: to move from the old 'civil service' approach of the administrators who had grown in number from the 1920s, taking over much of the administrative work hitherto done by academics in rotation, and introducing top-down management; to be 'businesslike' and form new kinds of relationship with commerce and industry. The results have produced less in the way of colourful anecdote but they must be touched on, for they presage much.

'Oxford University Library Services'

> Mr Vice-Chancellor, debate about Oxford's libraries is probably as old as the University itself, and inevitably so, since they underpin the whole of our academic activity. The debate has often in the past been, to say the least, heated; and history suggests that the debate has not always been productive. I was reminded recently of the wise advice given a century ago by the then Bodley's Librarian, Edward Nicholson – advice which, it has to be said, he never followed himself. 'Before doing anything new' in Oxford, Nicholson warned his successors, they must try to 'realise and give full weight to all objections to it'.[170]

The recurring difficulties about space and funding for the libraries, which had repeatedly sparked debate in Oxford, were heard more than once from the 1960s. Committees sat and reported. The Shackleton Report appeared in 1966[171] and the Nicholas Report[172] in 1987. Growing worries led in the 1990s to a scheme to revolutionize the future organization of the university's libraries. The Chairman of the General Board made the remarks just quoted in a speech in a debate in 1996.

The new idea was to unify the libraries under a single management. This was not popular with the librarians who had responsibility for individual specialist and faculty libraries.[173] The Chairman of the Modern Languages Faculty, expressed concerns:

> We very much fear that, once the Director of Library Services is appointed and makes his or her proposals for the creation of an integrated library service, we are going to be faced with the prospect of a huge, unwieldy, and unresponsive library system run by managers who are removed from their readers and staffed by librarians who are not specialists in the area of study to which their books pertain.

Another speaker echoed his anxiety:

> We must beware of following in the footsteps of the National Health Service, with reading-rooms being closed, readers' seats empty, and library assistants being made redundant for the sake of this battalion of managers – our bureaucratic 'tail'.[174]

Despite these worries, the plan to unify the libraries was taken forward and Oxford University Library Services emerged, with the Bodleian Library incorporated into it.

In 2003 there was a brief stock-taking of how well the scheme was working out. It was admitted that 'a degree of staff resistance has been encountered.' It was also becoming clear that the new 'resource allocation mechanism' adopted for the University as a whole was introducing a degree of competitiveness among subject areas in departments and faculties, with some scientists demanding that the lion's share of funding should go to laboratories instead of library resources, and an increasing pressure in some quarters for electronic rather than paper copies of journals, again especially among the scientists. Nevertheless, it was decided to recommend proceeding with the integration rather than pulling back.[175]

The upset over the destruction of the specialist Faculty libraries did not quickly die down. The spring and summer of 2005 brought forth protests about the future of the Taylor Institution Library (Slavonic and Greek Section), with submissions to the Inquiry into the Library Resource requirements to support Slavonic and East European Studies in the University of Oxford. Gradually there was, as had been foreseen, a shift from academic librarianship of the sort Bodley had insisted on to a more remote 'management' style and a shift towards the priorities of the early twenty-first century; for example, there were moves to create more 'social space', for students deemed to want armchairs and screens rather than books and bookshelves.

Oxford University Library Services became the section of the University with the largest number of employees. In March 2005 an *Establishment Review* was published internally to the University 'intranet', in which radical proposals were put forward for staffing cuts. This entered new territory in the way it understood the librarianship needs of Oxford. It began to undermine the traditional concept of academic librarianship. Bodley's and Radcliffe's noble buildings also began to pose problems. There was repeated concern about the intrusion of tourism into the central Bodleian buildings. The notion of turning the Radcliffe Camera into a Visitor Centre for tourists was mooted, then scotched.[176]

The New Bodleian of the 1930s proved to be in need of major refurbishment; the underground bookstacks had leaks and inadequate 'climate' protection for the manuscripts and rare books stored there. A controversial plan had been evolving for some years, to build a vast new Depository at Osney Mead to hold the overflowing collections and provide a respite space for the special collections while the bookstacks were brought up to the necessary standard; but concerns were expressed about lodging the books in the most flood-prone area of the city. The administration of Oxford University Library Services was also to move Osney Mead, retaining the Clarendon Building for the senior Library managers, who were soon to describe themselves as a Cabinet.[177]

The 'Depository' saga went on until 2008. Planning applications were put in, then withdrawn in 2006 when the University learned that they were not likely to be accepted because the profile of the building would be considered to interfere with the historic views of the city from the surrounding hills. There was redesign, resubmission, acceptance by the relevant planning committee on a single vote with many abstentions. The decision was 'called in' to the City Council, which rejected the application in November 2007. A full public Inquiry lasted two weeks in the summer of 2008, and the proposed building was finally refused permission on the ground that it would seriously harm the historic views of Oxford's skyline. In 2009 it was announced that a site had been purchased at Swindon. The University was able to acquire the historic site of the Radcliffe Infirmary and there were schemes to build a new humanities library there, again at vast and rising projected cost.[178]

A business-facing Oxford

Isis Innovation Ltd was the technology transfer company of the University of Oxford, established in 1988. So Oxford found itself ahead of the game when it came to participating in the 'technology transfer' in which Governments actively wanted to see universities engaging from the 1990s. The Vice-Chancellor's Oration of 1993 put elegantly the arguments for Oxford moving in this direction, pointing out that the:

> University has always recognised, from the time of its Bidding Prayer, its role in the propagation of useful learning. Our science (including Social Science), engineering and medical departments have achieved, with the help of our Research Support Office, an extremely high level of funding from industry, charities, and research councils: at £73 million this year the largest for any UK university.

And:

> We have taken bold steps into the marketplace, setting up our own company to develop and exploit our intellectual property – Isis Innovation – and can legitimately point to a number of high-technology spin-off companies derived from research work in this University.[179]

From Isis Innovation, sprang Isis Enterprise, established in 2004, to offer 'consulting expertise and advice in technology transfer to clients from the public and private sectors, in the UK and internationally. Technology transfer includes the management of intellectual property and its transfer from university or corporate research to commercialisation'.[180]

This was not without its worrying implications for Oxford's academics, whose old freedom to let curiosity take them where it would and to keep the financial rewards of their intellectual endeavours – should their work generate any – was now circumscribed. New rules about intellectual property were created for Oxford, and even students could be required to give up their ownership of their ideas. (The University did not automatically own them for they were not employees.) The implications of this change were still unfolding in 2005, when 'letters' were sent out indicating that staff who were not found to be doing approved research on topics in keeping with a departmental or university research strategy might find themselves subjected to disciplinary processes. That prompted huge anger and a Debate of Congregation in May 2005.[181] In 2009, a Task Force, set up in the wake of the resounding vote for academic freedom taken that day, was still working towards changes in the terms and conditions of academic staff, with the now traditional anxieties about the need to protect academic freedom raised in a Discussion on a Topic of Concern held in the Sheldonian.[182]

Management Studies and the question of donor control of academic activity

In the mid-1990s Oxford began to grapple with the idea of opening a Business School. These were the coming thing and they could be lucrative additions to a university. But there were mixed feelings. Some said 'business' was not a fit subject for academic study. And a serious mistake was made in proposing a site, on Merton playing field, which had been promised for indefinite use for sporting purposes. Moreover, this happened in the middle of the Long Vacation, a time it was suggested had been chosen so that Congregation would not notice. Congregation did notice; it had a right under the Statutes to determine the use its 'estates' were put to. In November the proposal was rejected after a debate.

The donor, Wafic Said, was persuaded not to take his benefaction elsewhere, a new site was found, and a new debate held:[183]

> Council wishes to express its warm gratitude to Mr Said for his continuing commitment to the project of a Business School in Oxford in the months following last November's vote.

The proposed new site was controversial in a different way. It would involve removing the old railway station, currently in use as a tyre-replacement outlet, for which many discovered a nostalgic affection, perhaps connected for some with arrival in Oxford for the interview which got them their place. The career diplomat Sir Crispin Tickell, subsequently Warden of Green College, spoke of:

> the LMS site, the old station that was there. Many of us in our childhood remember it actually being quite an active station, but it is now a Grade II listed building which is scarcely adorned by the tyres and other things surrounding it. People have been anxious about the fate of this building, and I think it is important to know that those fears have been recognised: something will be done about the LMS station.

There was, however, another looming difficulty, academically much more important, and that was the proposal that the benefactor should be represented on the Committee for the School. That went to the heart of an Oxford anxiety, 'that in a more polarised and commercial society, rich benefactors may come to control universities or exercise some malign, self-interested influence upon them,' as Tickell put it in his speech. Alexander Murray spoke strongly on the same subject. He had consulted lawyer-friends. They had been struck by how well the text of the proposed agreement protected the interests of the benefactor and how imperfectly it protected the interests of the University. 'Here we are, preparing to teach the whole world how to do business and we cannot, apparently, even draft a decent school statute.' 'Not a promising start,' he exploded. (This was not a new problem for the University. R. Lane Poole had commented in 1912 how in Oxford 'statutes have been amended by persons who did not take the trouble of understanding the statutes which they were revising'.[184])

Speaking on the theme of donor control of appointments, the Oxford lawyer J.M. Finnis described his satisfaction about instances where that had been prevented, and expressed his concern at what he read before him now:

> I ask myself what this decree before you this afternoon says to such donors; and it appears to me that it says some donors have the right not only to be counted among the electors but to arrange that the University itself will have only a minority voice in approving the final selection for the directorship, which is a thoroughly academic as well as managerial position.

Tickell also touched on 'the academic work of the school', the question whether business studies was really an appropriate subject for Oxford. 'This is clearly of prime importance, and I think that we need to underline its interdisciplinary character.' ... 'The school is not about teaching people how to make money; it is rather about the study of the character and functioning of the engines of modern society.' 'It ... covers and is linked with questions of law, environment, economics, psychology, and sociology, and probably other things as well.' Finnis was not entirely confident about the academic respectability of business studies:

> Either Business Studies are something different, perhaps a mock academic subject, a sort of sham academic affair, and so the normal principles of academic independence and autonomy do not apply to Business Studies, which run in a kind of dim half-light on the margins of the University. ... The alternative is that this University does no longer uphold the principles and practices of academic autonomy [and] we will surrender those well-understood principles to any donor who pushes hard enough on something that we at that time regard

> as urgent enough.... I believe the dilemma remains. Either Business Studies are publicly branded today as inherently sub-academic, marginal, second-rate, or this University's concern for its own autonomy is to be sharply demoted to the second-rate.

The proposal got through. The Said Business School building opened in 2001 next to the modern railway station.[185]

The compass points North

These developments were taking place against a background of radical change in the way the University was run and enormous change in the position and expectations of all the universities in Britain. Although Oxford had played little part in 'Robbins', it made its submission to 'Dearing', the National Committee of Inquiry into Higher Education, also reporting in 1997. This was review chaired by Lord Dearing who had a Government remit to conduct a national review of higher education and its future.

Just as it had set up the Franks Commission after the Robbins Report, so about the time when the Dearing Report was afoot, Oxford established a Commission of Inquiry into itself, this time chaired by Peter North, reporting in 1997.[186] As Oxford's Vice-Chancellor he wrote a covering letter to the Dearing submissions, stressing that:

> Consideration of the future of higher education should start from a recognition that education is not an economic or industrial process.... The purpose of higher education is much more subtle. It enables the best minds to develop to their highest level so that they can identify, analyse and solve large and abstract problems. It involves the advancement of knowledge and the general development of the intellect. It involves the search for truth. If those in higher education are not engaged in the pursuit of ideals, others are unlikely to be so.[187]

Oxford feared it would now reap adverse consequences of taking the state's penny after the Second World War. It was Dearing's view that the extra fee income per student Oxford and Cambridge colleges were granted should have to be justified in terms of demonstrable value for money:

> the college fees in Oxford and Cambridge represent a substantial addition to the standard funding for institutions of higher education. We propose that the Government

> reviews them against the two principles we have proposed (Recommendation 74).

So there were fears for the future of the collegiate system. Oxford's own Commission of Inquiry, quoting this passage, concluded that 'the clear message from all this uncertainty is that, for the future, Oxford must be in a position to react flexibly to changing funding arrangements'.

The Inquiry's Chairman was anxious to emphasize in his foreword that Oxford had had this idea by itself:

> It was, in our view, right that, some thirty years after the work of the Commission of Inquiry under the chairmanship of Lord Franks, Oxford should initiate a process of re-examination of its activities and organisation.[188]

though the Committee took time to pause and consider what Dearing said.

The Commission of Inquiry was followed by detailed work to create proposals for a revised governance structure, which had to be laid before Congregation for approval, since Congregation was still the legislative body of the University. The Working Party put forward first one report then a second.[189] The *News summary* published at the time listed 'principles' for approval by Congregation.[190] One of the most significant changes was the abolition of the old General Board, which had been a legacy of the 1923–6 changes. There would now be a unicameral system with only a Council. This got a surprising amount of support, perhaps because the General Board, in Oxford as in Cambridge, had become very powerful and was consequently resented.[191] The new Council was to be 'representative' in a mixture of ways. There was to be direct election to some places, representation for the colleges (though many 'colleges took the view that the level of representation of the colleges on Council and its committees was not adequate'), and there were to be *ex officio* seats for individuals holding certain offices:

> The working party has discussed this issue at some length, noting the arguments on both sides. It is not convinced that the notion of 'representation' is in fact an appropriate one in this context. The role of the members of the central bodies is not to promote narrow interests, but rather to provide a range of knowledge and expertise so that informed decisions can be taken collectively in recognition of the general context and the range of concerns of the collegiate University as a whole.[192]

Another major change was to be the extension of the term of office of the Vice-Chancellor, to a possible seven years, though this was opposed by some 'on the grounds that this would in practice reduce the likelihood of Heads of House being able to serve'.[193]

It will readily be seen that the tug and tension inherent in all this was going greatly to alter the balance of power. When the North Committee's Report was ready to be debated two March afternoons were set aside for debates, and it was announced that these would not be 'formal debates, but free discussions, structured by key themes'. There would also be consultation in departments and faculties and colleges and anyone who wished was invited to write to the Vice-Chancellor to express 'initial views'.[194] This was a departure from convention in recognition of the enormous scope and import of what was proposed.

The modern method of conducting a democratic discussion evolved differently in Oxford from its Cambridge form. In Cambridge Discussions are regular, unstructured and any student or graduate may speak, as well as any member of the Regent House, the actual voters. Other staff of the University may ask for permission to speak, which has usually been granted in recent years. The voting process is now postal not live, which means that attendance may be thin, with voters waiting to read the published speeches and then mark their ballot papers at leisure if a vote is called. All those who want to have their say must be allowed to do so, and sometimes that has meant that a Discussion has had to be adjourned and continued the following week. In Oxford, Debates have been rare, and conducted in a manner much closer to a parliamentary debate. The Vice-Chancellor presides and calls speakers rather like the Speaker of the House of Commons, who must endeavour to ensure a balance. To achieve that balance, those intending to speak are asked to send in their names with an indication which side they favour. This can mean that not everyone gets a chance to speak. In any case only members of Congregation may speak (and students with permission).

The debates and consultations were generally positive about the new ideas, but as the meetings and the speeches went on there were indications that the community was not finding it easy to see its way forward. In the debate of 29 April 1998, speeches were few, short and generally supportive, if a little bewildered:

> I fear that the sheer volume of problems, and the babble of contentious voices to which the Commission had to respond, has resulted in the neglect of what I believe to be one of the

> most worrying questions concerning Oxford's future. Will it be able to retain its status as a leading international university? ... In that respect, in my opinion, Mr Vice-Chancellor, Oxford's compass does not point North.[195]

'Running the place': the governance of Oxford and the 'Eight Questions'

After further debate and proposal and debate and voting, it turned out that it did. For the first time since Archbishop Laud, the Statutes of the University of Oxford were not merely thoroughly overhauled but comprehensively rewritten, by Derek Wook, then St. Hugh's College's Principal, with the intention of making their import clear to the intelligent general reader. The idea had been to reduce the domestic legislation to two levels only, Statutes and Regulations, but it was to prove very difficult to prevent the familiar proliferation of 'guidelines' and 'codes' and other sets of rules of uncertain provenance and authority. The nice clean new structure quickly became complicated again. The power-structures changed and a more managerial style emerged in Wellington Square.

Meanwhile, the colleges continued to choose the Proctors in rotation and proctorial orations did not grown less witty or challenging. In 2004 the outgoing Senior Proctor asked as usual for permission to speak English and became confidently wry about the expectations of classical scholarship which seemed to go with the office, for Oxford still knew how to tease itself:

> Professor Womersley's demitting speech started off by requiring of his audience a knowledge of the Greek word for buttock, and he spent some time developing alternative etymologies for the word 'Proctor'. As I said shortly afterwards when I met my colleague to be, this was all too much for someone who was a habitual reader only of Motor Cycle Monthly, and I realised I must have been elected principally on the 'Broadening Access' ticket.[196]

The point of such self-deprecation is to be convincingly serious. He described the steepness of the learning curve the office entailed:

> Proctors are generally extraordinarily naïve: they volunteer to do the job without really knowing what the balance of duties are: I have already mentioned ceremonial and examination matters. Then there are all manner of squabbles and disputes which come to our attention. ... But how, more widely, do we really 'Uphold the Statutes', in 2004? Well, we join the Great and Good, including those my predecessor referred to as 'the

> men in suits, of Wellington Square', at the full panoply of university committees, from Council to (in principle at least) the Committee for Ornithology; we make a cautious input, for fear of appearing precocious and forgetting our roots, but no one can deny our altruism.

The undertaking given when the new governance arrangements were eventually launched in 2000 was that five years on there should be a formal stocktaking, to pick up any problems which were emerging. The review was 'to pay especial attention to [the] transparency, efficiency and democracy of the new governance structure, by a body consisting of members directly elected by Congregation for this purpose (two from each constituency), to be chaired by a retiring or recent Proctor'.[197] In the event, with the arrival of a new Vice-Chancellor, the first from outside Oxford, the plan was changed.

A reformulated committee never reviewed the strengths and weaknesses of 'North' at all. It set about making proposals for further and still more radical change, which would have brought Oxford into the 'sector norm' governance framework and given it a governing body which was its Council not its Congregation, with a majority of external members, and a *modus operandi* which echoed that of a business corporation. In the summer of 2005, alongside the row about the libraries and the row about the 'letters' sent to academics, a row loomed about what were becoming governance proposals. The new Vice-Chancellor, a New Zealander used to a very different style of university governance, had planned to get the changes agreed that summer but he had not at all understood what would happen if the sleeping Congregation awoke, as it did. Growling, it insisted that time should be taken for proper discussion of any proposals.[198] This was a very different atmosphere from that of courteous goodwill which had surrounded the endeavours of the North Commission and the development of its proposals within the University.

On 1 November 2005, Congregation met to debate 'proposals for changes in governance'.[199] In November 2006, a final version of the proposal came before Congregation for debate. It was known that the sticking point was likely to be the 'majority of externals' the Higher Education Funding Council for England (HEFCE) wanted to see on the Council. Sir Robin Butler, who had been head of the Civil Service before coming to University College as head of house, made a bid to outwit the opposition by proposing an amendment to provide for the possibility of a bare majority the other way under certain circumstances.

A debate had to be held on this amendment before the main motions could be debated and voted on.[200] On 14 November 2006, Don Fraser, subsequently to be Senior Proctor for 2008–9, began a speech which brought the house down. 'In the words of my old colleague, James Campbell, 'It *does* seem like the thin end of Pandora's can of worms' ... 'How did we get here?' he asked. 'How is it that so much goodwill and trust in this University has been squandered?':

> The issue of governance is quite simple. It was summed up for me by a quietly-spoken colleague. He said there are two issues: (1) it is dangerous to concentrate too much power in the hands of too few individuals; (2) why should we give up something good, merely to conform to some sector norm? He is right.

He pointed up the problem of the shift of power. 'An effect of the North Reforms is that they have concentrated power in a very small number of hands.' He called the voters to one of the traditional rallying points, with 'one of the key reasons why Oxford academics are so committed to the University is that they have real independence and a genuine personal stake in the system. Oxford is a democratic partnership, not a top-down, managerial structure.'

In a packed Sheldonian Theatre, with overflow rooms having to be provided with the debate shown on screens and a packed press gallery, things became heated. Minds were changed in the course of the debate. One speaker had sent in his name proposing to make a speech in favour of the amendment. 'I am still tempted,' he said. But he spoke against. The vote was decisive. The amendment fell. With the amendment out of the way, Congregation returned to its debating two weeks later, on 28 November, again to a packed house.[201] It voted down the proposals and preserved the medieval democracy which has served it for more than eight centuries.

Fund-raising: the Campaign for Oxford

John Hood decided not to seek the extension of his period as Vice-Chancellor from five years to seven, but in his last year there was an effort, unfortunately coinciding with a sudden global recession, to outdo Cambridge, then in its eighth centenary year, in the raising of money. The Oxford Press Office had evolved into a Public Affairs Directorate, with responsibility for Media relations, University publications (but not the *Oxford Magazine*), prospectuses, *Oxford Today* (the University alumni magazine), the *Annual Review*, *Blueprint* (the University's staff newsletter) and the *Gazette*. It also spoke on behalf of the University when press comment was required, coordinated major public events and provided:

> Strategic communications advice to constituent elements of the collegiate University, including drafting and management of strategies on key University projects.

It dealt with the modern counterparts of old 'town and gown' problems ('community relations') and relations with Government and permission to film-makers to make films set in Oxford University buildings.

Here was polish; here was spin. But the capacity of the University to grab the headlines was much bigger than could be 'managed', let alone spun.

Chancellor and Vice-Chancellor: a tribute

At the Memorial Service held in 2003 for the former Chancellor of the University, Roy Jenkins, the Vice-Chancellor, the historian Colin Lucas, reviewed the trajectory of a life begun in South Wales, where 'his father was a South Wales trade union official and local Labour politician'. 'It was his father who insisted that he follow the classic path of the time as a grammar school boy headed to Oxford, where he entered Balliol in 1938.' 'Going to Balliol put him onto a different stage' and he graduated with a First in Politics, Philosophy and Economics'.

> It would be an exaggeration to suggest that he single-handedly changed Britain, but he certainly captured decisively the desire of so many of us for renovation.... One is struck not simply by his command of the House [of Commons] through oratory at difficult moments (he wrote his speeches himself), but also by his industry and his sheer toughness.[202]

Here was an Oxford Chancellor without a privileged background, who had no trouble with 'access', went on to run the country, and came back to enjoy late summer of his life in Oxford.

2 OXFORD'S MIDDLE AGES

Oxford from the inside: inventing a University

How did it all begin? For before Oxford had a university, nowhere else had one either, with the possible exception of Paris. Oxford was there at the very beginning of the European invention of a 'university' at the end of the twelfth century. Why did one of the first of these new institutions arise in little Oxford in the English Midlands?

From a remote distance across Europe, the growing demand for professional civil servants for secular and spiritual lords, kings and bishops, emperor and pope, was beginning to create new professional requirements. Secretaries were needed who could write a useful business letter. A bureaucracy was developing with the busy exchange of diplomatic correspondence. One indicator of this trend is the emergence of the formal 'art of letter-writing' (*ars dictaminis*) at the end of the eleventh century. This relied for its sense of the proprieties on the structure of a speech as taught in classical oratory, but it included new elements, such as a protocol for 'salutations' which respected the respective standings of the correspondents in contemporary society, and the use of 'cadences' providing endings to sentences pleasing to the ear by reason of their variety and balance.

So there was already a growing demand for schools to produce civil servants ('clerks') who could write to this standard as well as ordained ministers ('clergy') to serve the future Church. As to law, Irnerius (c.1050 to d. after 1125) was a Bolognese lawyer who was apparently teaching Roman law at Bologna from the 1070s. Bologna's school was not a real *universitas* yet, merely a superior vocational college. How did scruffy little Oxford emerge at the forefront of this European movement almost as soon as it began?

Oxford[1] is mentioned in the Anglo-Saxon Chronicle for 912, but Roman and prehistoric remains indicate that it was settled much earlier. It was well-placed as a crossing for the headwaters of the river Thames which inconveniently interrupted the roads from north to south. Eleventh-century Oxford was not an entirely insignificant town;

it was comparable with Winchester or Lincoln. It had a watchtower at the old north gate of the city and a castle built just after the Norman Conquest. Grandpont, now the nineteenth-century Folly Bridge, was built in the same period. Royal visits to the palace at Beaumont, just north of the north gate, gave Oxford the status of intermittent royal favour (Richard I and King John were both born there). There are indications that it was beginning to flourish in the twelfth century: great churches, abbeys and abbey churches built or enlarged at Oseney (for the Augustinians), St. Peter in the East, Iffley Church, and the Priory Church of St. Frideswide. This last became the basis of the 'chapel' of Cardinal Wolsey's new college of Christ Church, which became the cathedral church of the new diocese of Oxford in the sixteenth century.

But this was no home of beautiful buildings and fine streets, or not yet. It was a town of alleyways built within a square of roads which intersected at what is now Carfax (a corruption of its older name of 'Quatervoys' or 'four ways'). Like Cambridge, Oxford changed the layout of its streets over the centuries. One led north to St. Michael at the North Gate, which now stands at the end of the Cornmarket. One led south down Fish Street, called after the fish market there, now St. Aldate's. One led east down the High Street 'the fairest and largest wee have', as Anthony Wood (1632–95), the invaluable antiquarian and seeker-out of colourful trifles concerning Oxford, says in his survey of the antiquities of the city in the 1660s.[2] The last, Queen Street, was once the Great Baylly and Castle Street, and went west, towards what from the nineteenth century would be the railway station.

Anthony Wood explored the name-changes with assiduous satisfaction, plunging energetically into the earliest medieval versions. From the North Gate to 'Turl Gate and Exeter College and other Colleges thereabouts' ran a route he first identifies in the reign of Henry I, but by John's reign he thinks it was called 'D'ewey's Lane; because the name of such a family who were burgesses of Oxon had their residence therein'. Later it seems to have been known as Burewald's Lane 'because such a woman with some of that name lived there'. In Edward I's reign, 'it was called Somnore's Lane', again after the residents. Then in Henry VIII's time it was Laurence Hall Lane because a student Hall stood there, but it went back to being called Somnor's Lane which became corrupted to Summer Lane.[3] This shifting of streets and street names continued beyond the Middle Ages. Logic Lane, off the High Street leading down to Merton St. was called Horseman Lane in the thirteenth century, or sometimes Horsemull Lane because there was a mill turned by horsepower in the vicinity. It had a school at the northern end where disputations were held and by the end of the seventeenth century that had given it the name Logic Lane.

In these narrow smelly streets, which carried the open drains and were always full of decaying rubbish, things were quite hectic enough without the addition of students. A vivid life went on as in any medieval town, among a population already living crowded close together, with brawls spilling out of taverns, knives drawn by quick-tempered townsmen, revengeful friends and relatives seeking to make things even. There were plentiful opportunities for disputes between householders since, until the thirteenth century, the streets had to be maintained by the adjacent residents. The household pig from next door, foraging in the street, could annoy a neighbour who might kill it to stop the nuisance, and a family feud could start over the lost bacon. So great was the need to keep the peace that the use of the local churches as places of sanctuary for someone running from justice was a practical necessity.

The arrival of a community of 'scholars', with quarrels of their own and a shifting population of the very young, was bound to spark trouble, with students living in lodging houses kept by the townsfolk. The drunkenness of students seems to have been legendary from an early stage. In the fifteenth century the boys of Magdalen College school practised their Latin translation on such stock English texts as 'bousynge and drynkynge ... late into the nyght'.[4] There would follow centuries of wrangling about who was in charge of the few square yards of the centre, 'town' or 'gown', with the University insisting on keeping 'order' within its own jurisdiction. So Oxford was not seeking the addition of a student population.

Throughout the twelfth century, the provision of higher level 'schooling' remained informal. It depended on the ambition of individual 'Masters' (*magistri*), who simply set up where they pleased and hoped to attract fee-paying students. Naturally it was easier to do this successfully where students were already known to congregate, so cathedral schools such as those at Chartres, and especially Paris, were an attraction to would-be teachers as well as to would-be students.

English scholars could and did get a taste of what was happening in Europe in these formative years of proto-university teaching. The ambitious Englishman John of Salisbury (c.1120–80) spent a dozen years in the schools of northern France from about 1136, before becoming a papal civil servant and then a civil servant in England and finally a bishop at Chartres. He retained a sense of intellectual superiority all his life and wrote scathingly in his *Metalogicon* of the failings of certain unnamed scholars in the teaching of logic. Some of the modern characteristics of an academic community, it seems, were already manifesting themselves – the intellectual arrogance, the sense of 'us and them', the rivalry and the battles. Peter of Blois, who served as another of the civil servants of the King of England for a time, speaks of being called 'from the scholarly army' (*a scholari militia*).[5]

Oxford did not have a cathedral until the sixteenth century, when Oxford became a diocese in its own right; moreover, it was a very long way from Lincoln, in whose diocese it then lay. Lincoln cathedral had its own school, with a good reputation, so it did not need a cluster of Masters at Oxford to meet the diocese's 'higher education' needs. In fact some resentment at Oxford's pretensions may be glimpsed. A letter written in 1177–9[6] by Peter of Blois (c.1135–1203), when he was a royal civil servant to the English King, criticizes Robert Blund for gadding about – he mentions Paris, Bologna and Oxford – instead of attending on the Bishop of Lincoln as is his duty. We shall see when we come to Robert Grosseteste (c.1170–1253), enthusiastic scholar, Chancellor of the University and then Bishop of Lincoln, how intimate and sometimes strained this relationship between Lincoln and Oxford continued to be.[7]

The truth is probably that Oxford built itself a reputation on the quality of its first teachers. Twelfth-century students would come to study with a famous Master (*magister*) or teacher, rather than in a particular place; if the Master moved on, they would follow. Other Masters astutely took advantage of the presence of a good cluster of students and would arrive to teach nearby. Theobald of Étampes (c.1060–c.1125) is one of the earliest scholars to describe himself as a 'Master' at Oxford. Robert Pullen (d.1147) is another. Master Vacarius (c.1115/20–1200) seems to have been a lawyer teaching in Oxford in the middle of the century. Edmund of Abingdon (1175–1240), after whom St. Edmund Hall is named, was another of the first-known Oxford Masters.[8] There is no evidence yet of a continuous history or an institutionalized school, however, despite Gerald of Wales's account of his public readings.

Gerald of Wales describes in his autobiography 'On the things he did' (*De rebus a se gestis*), how he gave three days of readings from his travel book on Ireland, *Topographia Hibernica*. He chose to do this in Oxford, probably in 1187–8, for he says this was where clerisy flourished best in England and it was the leading place for learning.[9] On the first day he read to the poor and needy. On the second he read to the doctors of the different 'faculties' and the better-known and most noteworthy students,[10] and on the third, to the rest of the scholars (*reliquos scolares*) and the townspeople of all classes. If Gerald's reading really took place a decade before the end of the twelfth century, his claim that he addressed the *facultates* is of considerable interest, for 'faculties' were not to emerge as the subject-based categories of specialist Masters until universities had formed themselves as institutions. The Masters of Arts and the Masters in the 'higher degree' faculties of theology law and medicine could scarcely be said to exist until there were real universities and they were granting 'degrees', for these became the titles which were awarded for satisfactory completion of the requirements for a degree. Oxford had not arrived at that stage at the end of the twelfth century.

Not long after Gerald held his readings, in 1197 according to the chronicler Jocelin of Brakelond, a meeting was held in Oxford in connection with the resolution of a lawsuit involving the monks of Coventry. The monks, fourteen of them, sat at a table on one side of the lodgings provided and on the other side the invited Masters of the Schools (*et ex alia parte magistris scolarum*), which suggests that there were in some loose sense, 'schools' and 'Masters'.[11] In 1201 John Grim is called *Magister scholarum Oxoniae* in a papal letter.[12]

It is likely that the consolidation of these promising 'schools' at Oxford into a 'university' owes something to the difficulties of travel to Paris during the period of the Interdict, when the Pope excommunicated King John of England (d.1216). The King had been disobliging about the choice of the next Archbishop of Canterbury, and the Pope had strong preferences of his own. The Interdict, imposed in 1207, was lifted in 1214. It meant that no one in England could celebrate the Eucharist or any other sacrament; it was a powerful weapon for bringing secular authorities to heel, for it made the population restless and uneasy about their eternal prospects if they died during such a period.

During these first two decades of the thirteenth century, an indignant exodus of scholars left in 1209, after a town-and-gown quarrel which had inflamed feeling more than the usual quarrel. This was not a mere decamping of the students. The Masters must have left too. Their protest created the future University of Cambridge, but it could also have ended the history of Oxford.[13] A comprehensive 'settlement' was proposed by the Pope's 'Legate', with the objective of creating a working basis for the future relations of town and gown, and with the further purpose of attempting to ensure that the University properly understood that it was under the jurisdiction of the Bishop of Lincoln. In token of the town's repentance for the killing of two scholars after a quarrel, the episode which had sent the scholars off in indignation, there was to be an annual payment of fifty-two shillings a year to support poor scholars and an annual dinner on 6 December (St. Nicholas' Day). Oxford had thus had at its very beginning its first taste of the likelihood that the University would be subject to outside interference, and it made its first judicious compromises with external authority.[14] It accordingly began to form its 'identity' and assert its autonomy. It was this more than any other single factor perhaps which turned a loose conglomeration of opportunist teachers into an enduring institution.

Creating a constitution

In the last decade of the twelfth century and the first decade of the thirteenth, about seventy 'Masters' can be placed at Oxford (though not all at the same time), engaged in teaching an unascertainable number of students. We have been calling them 'Masters', but what made them Masters (*magistri*)? In the first university generations there was no straightforward answer to that question. *Magister* and *discipulus* were reciprocal terms, and at first they were not technical terms at all. They simply described a teacher and a pupil. The controversial Frenchman Peter Abelard could set himself up as a 'Master' in various places, Paris among them, and his right to do so consisted in nothing more than the fact that he could attract 'pupils', and manifestly rather successfully. He had no academic 'employer', no membership of a regulatory body to obtain and maintain, no 'fitness to practise' regulations to satisfy or code of professional conduct to keep him in order. The freedom with which he could go around teaching what he liked where he liked, and his growing notoriety as a demagogue and a 'heretic', led to two attempts by the ecclesiastical authorities to silence him by putting him on trial. There were several other examples of dangerous academics encouraging 'heresy' in the twelfth century. Gilbert of Poitiers also faced trial by the ecclesiastical authorities for allegedly misleading the faithful with his advanced views on the nature of God. But no condemnation could prevent even the most troublesome from calling themselves Masters.

By the end of the twelfth century a degree of specialization was beginning to add to the majority of Masters, who provided a grounding in the 'seven liberal arts' (grammar, logic, rhetoric and the four 'mathematical' subjects of the *quadrivium*), a much smaller number of specialist older teachers of the 'advanced' or 'graduate' subjects of law and medicine as well as of theology. However, a teacher could still call himself a Magister just because he felt like it. The title implied neither qualification nor the holding of a post. Change came with the realization that there would need to be some 'quality-assurance' beyond the simple control of reputation, in the form of students feeling they had had their money's worth and the consequent power to attract more students to come and study. The additional need was to ensure that teaching did not mislead the faithful; and that preaching – essentially another mode of teaching, hortatory, homiletic, but still instructive – did not do so either.

One evolutionary change towards creating a supervisory structure can be documented with fair confidence, for Oxford had a parallel at St. Paul's Cathedral. St. Paul's provided for centuries one of the most influential pulpits in London, not only for preaching but also for lecturing. We shall hear Oxford figures from that pulpit throughout this book. St. Paul's had a Chancellor of the cathedral, and cathedrals throughout Europe had been encouraged since the days of Charlemagne to provide schools, so as to try to ensure that the canons were adequately educated theologically speaking. The granting of a licence to teach on behalf of the bishop had to be monitored and the Chancellor's office provided a mechanism for the purpose. The head of a cathedral school was in some places known as the *scholasticus,* but at St. Paul's he had been called *magister scholarum* for much of the twelfth century. The same title was possibly used for the 'head' of the schools in Oxford until in 1214 the title of 'Chancellor' was formally adopted.

There was a further need, and that was to ensure that those who were approved as competent scholars passed some form of review or test of their academic knowledge. The word *universitas* simply meant a guild, a corporate body of a type familiar in the Middle Ages and paralleled in every craft guild. A qualified fishmonger or goldsmith belonged to a guild which took him through an apprenticeship, followed by a period as a journeyman, so that he could eventually aspire to become a Master of the craft if he could satisfy the body of its existing Masters of his mastery of the skills of the trade; so a student began as an undergraduate-apprentice, became a bachelor-journeyman giving practice lectures, and then a Master of Arts, a full member of the Guild, who 'incepted' as such in a formal ceremony once he had passed his final examination to ensure that he was up to standard. Edward Gibbon (1737–94) understood this quite clearly as he describes it in his *Autobiography*:

> The use of academical degrees, as old as the thirteenth century, is visibly borrowed from the mechanic corporations: in which

> an apprentice, after serving his time, obtains a testimonial of his skill, and a licence to practise his trade and mystery.[15]

So it is appropriate that when 'universities' practising the academic craft took institutional form it was usually as 'corporate persons'. Such guilds were autonomous, democratic among themselves, strongly protective of standards, exclusive of those who were not their own members, and usually with a local attachment which kept out craftsmen from other (rival) guilds. The question is how the loose group associated with Oxford formed itself into a *universitas* which could award a form of certification, or official approval of a student as having reached a certain level (*gradus*) or 'degree'. The notion that the 'degrees' have 'steps' is touched on by Mark Pattison, who understood in the mid-nineteenth century not only the medieval notion of the *gradus*, but also how long it would take to get as far as a doctorate in the Middle Ages: 'To pass through the whole of this course ... whose successive steps were called degrees (gradus), required at least twenty years.'[16]

An Oxford *universitas* would automatically have a monopoly of degree-awarding powers in Oxford. No one could legitimately call himself an Oxford Master until he had 'incepted' as a member of the guild. But alongside this process ran the licensing power of the bishop which did not depend upon such certification by the guild. Only the University could grant degrees and it decided how they were to be earned. Only an external authority could grant a *licentia docendi*, a 'licence' to use the degree in professional practice as a teacher in the world, or some stated part of the world. The modern dilemma of the relationship between taking a course in a university and gaining 'professional body recognition', now familiar in most professions, had an early origin.

Recognition of the *universitas* by the state or the Church was useful, for the Church could confer a *licentia docendi* to graduates, and both could offer 'privileges' in the form of grants of exceptions from taxation requirements or one sort or another. Royal grants of privilege for Oxford began in 1231. The episcopal control exercised by the See of Lincoln probably discouraged Oxford from approaching the Pope for privileges directly with any degree of urgency. Robert Grosseteste was a vigilant and sometimes domineering authority figure in his years as bishop, having an insider's knowledge as a former Chancellor of Oxford himself.

The guild of 'ruling' or Regent Masters (*universitas regentium*) at Oxford ran their affairs through meetings of the community, just as we have seen the members of Congregation doing in debates up to the present day. It became a problem that the Regent Masters, those actually teaching, had a growing band of older graduates looking over their shoulders, still members, still with a passionate sense of ownership of the University's business, but some of them remote from the daily business of the community in parishes or dioceses or at court, or otherwise getting on with their lives and careers. We shall see this become a problem in later centuries. It was not fully resolved until after the First World War, when the powers of the Convocation of all graduates were greatly reduced and most of the powers were restricted to a Congregation of those actually teaching in the University.

Part of the requirement for the completion of the degree was a period of teaching immediately after graduation, so the Regent Masters of Arts were young. In some cases a Master of Arts returned in later life to take a 'higher' degree in theology, law or medicine and became a Master again at a new 'level' where he could be called a 'Doctor', but these were comparatively few in number. The Masters of Arts always considerably outnumbered the other Regents, though total numbers remained modest enough for centuries to allow of an Athenian mode of conducting affairs by direct democracy. The Masters were thus in due course grouped by 'Faculty', although, despite Gerald of Wales's tantalizing mention of the word, it is not easy to establish the existence of 'faculties' in these first years. Paris had Faculties squabbling from the early thirteenth century, particularly Arts and Theology, so there is no reason to suppose things were much different in Oxford.

The Congregation of teaching (Regent) Masters met regularly three times a year. Meetings of Congregation were formal; the Masters were required to come to them in appropriate dress and a clerical haircut (or tonsure). Less regularly in the thirteenth century, the whole body of Masters would meet in an 'extraordinary' Congregation, the ancestor of the modern Convocation, though terminology in the Middle Ages and beyond does not seem to have been used consistently to distinguish the two bodies. They were summoned by the Chancellor or the Proctors (rules on this point seem somewhat contradictory).

Proctors (*procuratores*) were the University's legal officers. They were essentially representatives, acting on behalf of the members of the guild. In Paris and in Oxford they seem to have emerged in the course of the thirteenth century as representatives of the 'nations', which in England meant just student Northerners and student Southerners, broadly defined from a geographical point of view. (At the University of Paris there were several student 'Nations'.) But their duties became essential to the orderly conduct of affairs. They were to attend and supervise the formal 'acts' of the University, the meetings of the Masters in Congregation, the granting of degrees, and they were to act on its behalf in any litigation which arose. They held office for a year at a time, in recognition both that this was an onerous responsibility and that Proctors were also scholars who would wish to return to their normal activities. They were, however, allowed to generate an income for themselves from fines and fees and selling confiscated weapons, so there were compensations.[17]

This organizational structure, the collegial guild of Masters, each with a vote, deciding things together by discussion, and the Chancellor as the appointed 'head', created an enduring tension, some of whose modern ramifications we saw in the previous chapter.

The religious orders arrive

The Masters who had spontaneously formed the University were independents with careers in view. Many of the first students apparently saw their studies as forming a 'vocational course' leading to a life as a 'cleric' or a 'clerk'. These would later be known as 'seculars' because they did not belong to religious orders. But the monastic orders soon perceived advantages in having somewhere to send young monks for an education which could go beyond what could be offered in the monastic school of an individual house. At the time when the University at Oxford began, most members of religious orders, including the Cistercians, still followed the sixth-century Benedictine Rule. 'Canons' were the attached clergy of the cathedrals, or members of the various orders of 'regular canons' established in the twelfth century. These were called 'regular' because they followed the Augustinian 'Rule'.

A pragmatic but complex arrangement – which had parallels in Cambridge – was devised by making provision to ensure that students who were monks, but whose Orders had not set up independent halls, had somewhere to live other than the lodging houses in the town, where proper supervision might be uncertain. Such a 'hall' could be a 'shared facility'. Gloucester College, on the site where Worcester College now stands, was founded in 1283 and it evolved into a cluster of rooms (*camerae*) apportioned to different religious houses which were based within the province of Canterbury. To each of these was allocated a piece of land on the site, where it built to meet its own needs. Centuries later 'the row of camerae on the south side of the quadrangle [at Worcester], patched and changed and repaired and weather-beaten, [were] still essentially what they were at the time of their first construction'.[18] From the fourteenth century this particular facility was extended to houses in the province of York too. The participating monasteries shared the cost of maintaining a common hall and chapel. A 'Prior of Students' (*Prior studentium*), presided. Nevertheless, as yet the complex did not form a single 'college community'; it was merely an arrangement for supervised residence for the young monastic students.

Among the religious orders, by far the most important in the story of Oxford are the friars. They represented a new concept in the religious life which gained approval at the beginning of the thirteenth century. These 'mendicant' Orders won papal approval at the Fourth Lateran Council of 1215. Dominicans and the Franciscans were both orders of preachers, though with contrasting visions, and it was consequently essential that their recruits became competent to preach. That meant ensuring that young friars were adequately educated, the Dominicans as travelling preachers against the heretics (needing a high level of theological expertise), the Franciscans as latter-day apostles, wandering from town to town 'simply' preaching the Gospel, as Jesus had taught his disciples to do. Mendicants arrived in Oxford in the 1220s, the Dominicans in 1221 and the Franciscans in 1224. The chronicler Nicholas Trivet describes how thirteen of the Friars Preachers were sent into England only five years after the Order had received papal approval, having impressed the Archbishop of Canterbury by preaching a sermon before him on their way through Kent.[19] These Orders set up their own *studia* or 'study-centres' wherever they established houses for their members.

Both Orders had to come to an accommodation not only with the existing ecclesiastical framework, which was initially suspicious of 'wandering preachers', but also with the University. The Dominicans were able to become 'members' of the University only when Robert Bacon, who was already a Regent Master, became a Dominican. The Franciscans, although during the thirteenth century they became serious contenders against the Dominicans, and just as academically ambitious, had a different heritage; Francis had discouraged too much study for friars who were illiterate, if it got in the way of their spiritual endeavours. Rivalry with the Dominicans throughout Europe changed all that. After 1254, the Franciscans expected every friary to have its Doctor of Theology.

Robert Grosseteste

The potential complexities of the relationship of secular Masters to friars, and of both to the outside world where they might come to hold powerful positions, are well exemplified in the lives of

Robert Grosseteste (an Oxford Franciscan) and Robert Kilwardby (an Oxford Dominican). The career of Robert Grosseteste (c.1170–1253), illustrates how unstructured an academic life could still be. As a boy, he seems to have gone to school in Lincoln. He may have been lucky enough to have a patron, Adam de Wigford the Mayor of Lincoln, who was something of a philanthropist and may have paid for the boy's schooling. He may then have gone to school in Cambridge, which would have been well before the University there began, though there are thought to have been some quite advanced schools in the town at the time.

After that Grosseteste (it is not known how he came by the name of 'Big-Head') probably began his career in the clerical civil service at Lincoln, in hopes of a benefice. The search for this sort of position dogged the lives of would-be scholars in the Middle Ages unless they belonged to religious orders; the only source of long-term income was usually a well-paid post in the Church hierarchy, which would enable them to leave the work to be done by a 'curate' or ignore it altogether and get on with their studies. He was probably unsuccessful for he also spent a period up to about 1225 at Hereford in service to the bishop there. This time spent at Hereford may be important for the development of Grosseteste's 'scientific' interests. This was a part of England in which there had been a vast amount of intellectual activity for some generations, especially in the sciences and cosmology and mathematics.[20] Grosseteste wrote on such subjects and was already an established scholar without benefit of a university education when he first came into contact with Oxford. Grosseteste's ambitious *Commentary* on Aristotle's famously difficult *Posterior Analytics* (c.1220) may belong to this period. (It was not long since John of Salisbury had been writing scathingly about the lily-livered logicians of his day, who shrank from attempting it.)

But here too he was unlucky, for his bishop died in 1198 and a new bishop would bring his own entourage of young hopefuls who were busy earning his approval and patronage. Grosseteste seems to have lingered in Hereford, working for Hugh Foliot, who was to become bishop of Hereford in his turn in 1219. This meant that his early prime was spent in that part of England, working his way up an uncertain ladder. In the company of Hugh Foliot he became a joint papal delegate, so he rose quite high. He also undoubtedly had a chance to visit France during the reign of King John when England languished under papal disapproval and the Interdict,[21] for he recalled that he had heard preaching against the heretics in the South of France at this time.

In 1225, Grosseteste returned to the diocese of Lincoln when he was offered a living there, at Abbotsley in Huntingdonshire. Lincoln was another cathedral which was an intellectual centre. Yet it was at Oxford that Grosseteste now began to lecture. He was made Archdeacon of Leicester in 1229, another preferment, but he continued to be busily involved in Oxford's affairs. He must have been a welcome addition, senior, experienced, able to play politics with the great of the land as well as discuss the latest scientific ideas with fellow-scholars. Oxford's constitution had been more formally established in 1214 when the University reopened at the end of the Interdict of 1210 and it was stated that the Chancellor was to be an annual appointment of the Bishop of Lincoln. The Masters, accustomed to run their own affairs democratically, tried to insist that they must make the actual choice, with the Bishop merely approving their selection. In 1228–30 they said they wanted Robert Grosseteste. The Bishop of Lincoln was annoyed but he allowed Grosseteste to hold the office of *Magister scholarum* for a year.

In this senior position in the University, Grosseteste now found himself drawn to the Franciscan life and to new fields for lecturing. He gave up his ecclesiastical benefices and positions and became *Lector* to the Oxford Franciscans, a position he held from 1231 to 1235. It has been suggested that he may have been influenced in this direction by hearing the preaching of the Franciscan Jordan of Saxony who visited Oxford in November 1229, and preached to the Masters, calling for more spiritual commitment and less intellectual arrogance on their part. Although he himself had chosen to become a Franciscan, Grosseteste seems even-handedly to have 'encouraged' scholars of both the great mendicant Orders.

Grosseteste's interest now turned to theology. He is the first notable Oxford theologian of whose life and work there is good evidence. If he had lived a generation or so later, he would have had to spend a considerable number of required years in theological studies and gain a higher degree before he could be taken seriously as a theologian. In Oxford as in Paris the Arts graduates tangled at their peril with their seniors, even though many of the topics they studied were the same, for philosophy as studied in the Arts course overlapped with the new 'systematic' theology. This was the age when Peter Lombard's *Sentences* were establishing themselves – after a rocky start when they were nearly condemned for heresy – as the standard theological textbook which was going to be used throughout Europe for the whole of the Middle Ages. The *Sentences* consisted of a topical arrangement of *sententiae* or 'opinions' drawn from respected early Christian writers

('Fathers' is the terminology of the sixteenth century). Peter Lombard wrote in the mid-twelfth century but his arrangement of themes provided a row of pegs on which the scholars of the later Middle Ages were going to hang philosophical and scientific questions.

The 'invention' of universities coincided with the arrival in Western Europe early in the thirteenth century of Latin translations of Aristotle's scientific and philosophical writings, and that led to the addition to the arts syllabus of texts dealing with the beginnings of subjects on the boundary between philosophy and the natural sciences. These were the subjects which would eventually develop into the modern sciences. We can see how this happened in the work of Johannes Blund (d.1248), who lectured at Oxford soon after 1200 and influenced Alexander Nequam (d.1217). Blund wrote a book *On the soul* (*De Anima*), in which he discusses the ideas of some Arabic authors and also scientific issues such as the nature of light and the mechanisms of sight.[22] Richard Rufus of Cornwall lectured on Aristotle's *Physics* (*In Physicam Aristotelis*).[23] He taught in Paris and Oxford between 1230 and 1255, becoming a Franciscan in the 1230s. His commentary on the *Physics* includes reference to Averroes's Commentary. Like Grosseteste he was interested in projectile motion – an important theme in Aristotle's *Physics* – wondering whether it came from some property of the projectiles or from momentum imparted to, for example, thrown stones, by some external force or something in the medium in which they travel.[24] To list motion, chance, transition, progress, time, distance is to make it obvious at once how these proto-scientific explorations were also philosophical. And those giving the lectures were consciously feeling their way. There is a pattern of 'it is doubted' (*dubitatur*) and 'it is asked' (*quaeritur*) and 'I think'.

Grosseteste's writings were conventional enough as 'theology' in that they were biblical commentaries. Theology was still usually called 'the study of Holy Scripture' (*studium sacrae scripturae*). He certainly thought the study of the Bible in the University important. He wanted to see lectures on Scripture in the mornings in Oxford. But his own commentaries were full of material and ideas which broke new ground for their time. The first of those which survive was probably the *Proemium* to a Commentary on the first part of Genesis, describing the six days of creation; it was this passage of Scripture which traditionally provided medieval students with a convenient peg on which to hand scientific inquiries. For example, without stretching the relevance too much, optics could be discussed at the point when Genesis says light is separated from darkness (Genesis 1.5). The flavour of the way this could be handled from a 'scientific' point of view can be glimpsed in Grosseteste's comment:

> that light went right round the earth...and made the day by its presence, and on the opposite side of the earth, its shadow made the night. And in this way it divided the light and the darkness, just as the sun now divides them. But as Bede and Jerome say, the light of the earth was not as bright as it is now....That light also differed from the light of the sun in this, that it had no power to warm or heat.[25]

He cites Basil and John Damascene on these 'light and darkness' questions too, lending an unusually strong Greek patristic aspect to the analysis. (He had already probably learned enough Greek to attempt to translate the Ps-Dionysian *Hierarchies*.) His *Hexaëmeron* ('On the six days of creation') was duly completed. He also wrote *De decem mandatis* ('On the ten commandments'), *De cessatione legalium* ('On the end of the Old Testament law'), and a commentary on the Epistle to the Galatians.

There is also evidence that he lectured imaginatively on the Psalms in the same spirit, seeking to show his students how the Bible could be relevant to scientific enquiry as well as a stimulus to good behaviour and a starting point for their pastoral studies for those who were to go on to become clergy. This was a more startling achievement that it might appear for there was already a huge body of respected commentary and most masters taught by selecting key passages from this material to dictate to their students as an aid to understanding of the text before them.

From Chancellor to Bishop

In 1235 Grosseteste was unanimously elected Bishop of Lincoln by the canons there. This altered Grosseteste's relationship to Oxford, over which he now had to exercise episcopal oversight, in ways which sometimes annoyed the University – perhaps the more because the scholars had come to regard him as one of themselves.

An example of the style of his involvement from this new distance is the episode of the 'special terms' for friars. Friars spurned the requirement to climb the ladder of *gradus* or degrees. For some time the friars had been able to allow their students to proceed to the study of theology and leapfrog to graduation without first 'incepting'[26] as Masters of Arts as other students were required to do. A new statute of 1253 put an end to that practice. Adam Marsh (1200–59), an active correspondent with Grosseteste after he became bishop of Lincoln, and head of the teaching body at the Franciscan *studium* in Oxford at the time, wrote to another correspondent about the controversy which had arisen about admitting Thomas of York to be Regent Master in theology without incepting in Arts. The Masters of Arts were indignant and of course they formed a majority. The debate raged so fiercely that it had to be held over to the next day, Sunday, when the *altercationes* were still so heated that the matter had to be adjourned once more. Marsh pointed out that it was not in question that the Chancellor and the *universitas* had the *potestatem dispensandi,* the power to dispense from the requirements of their statutes which would normally require inception in Arts first.[27] It just took the will to do it. This was not the end of the matter. In 1360–5, new statutes had to be created to prevent friars going straight to theological study without incepting first in Arts, especially very young ones under 18.

Robert Kilwardby

Once they were involved with the universities, the Dominicans and Franciscans soon began to compete with one another for students, and their Masters jostled for supremacy as candidates for the best 'lecturing' posts. They were capturing one another's students so outrageously by making false representations about the purposes of one another's Orders, that in 1267–8 Pope Clement IV felt it necessary to make an attempt to stop this kind of thing. Since the death of Francis of Assisi in 1226, the Franciscans had been torn by internal dissent about the vocation to poverty which had been central to his mission. For his view of the proper priorities of his friars had the disadvantage that it made it difficult to build a substantial Order, with houses and endowments. The 'poverty controversy' spread throughout the Church, with an alarmed 'Establishment' using much intellectual skill to argue that Jesus could not really have meant his disciples to go out into the world without possessions and simply preach the Gospel.

The Dominicans in Oxford saw their opportunity. They began to taunt the Franciscans with the claim that they were misrepresenting themselves and their Order to prospective students. Theirs was not a higher and more Christ-like way of life as they claimed. They were as disputatious and greedy as anyone else. Solomon of Ingham went so far as to say that the Franciscans were destined for hell because they broke their vows by owning property.

Robert Kilwardby (c.1215–79) was regarded by the Dominicans as one of their leading intellectuals in an age when they especially prized such abilities. He had been an Oxford lecturer himself.

From 1262 he was the English 'Provincial', or head of the Order in England, and one of his first duties was to bring into force the degree of the Dominican General Chapter in 1261 that Oxford should be a *studium generale* for the whole Dominican order. There was therefore a good deal at stake for the Dominicans in this crisis. Kilwardby declared himself unwilling to remove Solomon from Oxford or to condemn his arguments as false. The University skilfully framed a compromise.

In October 1272, Kilwardby was made Archbishop of Canterbury. He did not cease to be interested in Oxford. He presided personally at the inception of Thomas of Hereford as a Doctor of Theology in 1273. When the King gave orders that students should not carry weapons in Oxford he endorsed the instruction, in the hope that Oxford might become a more peaceful place of learning. He took an active interest in the foundation of Merton College by his friend Walter Merton. He used his archiepiscopal authority to confirm the Statutes of Merton in 1275. So Kilwardby proved an important long-term ally for Oxford, but also uncomfortably interventionist. He was active not only in its practical but also its intellectual affairs. In 1271 Giovanni of Vercelli, then Dominican Master, asked Robert Kilwardby, Albertus Magnus and Thomas Aquinas for their views on 43 'undesirable questions' which were circulating as a consequence of someone's too-stimulating lecturing. These were the kind of things regularly arising from commentary on the set books and usually held over to be considered (for and against) in formal 'disputations' with the presiding Master hearing the arguments and then 'determining' or deciding the question. Albert and Thomas did as they were asked but were not disposed to take the questions seriously; they thought many of them rather foolish. Kilwardby was more judicious and seems to have found some of them very interesting.

But he could be fiercely condemnatory. This was not an age which understood the notion of 'academic freedom' except as a freedom to be defended against institutional control by state or Church. Kilwardby intervened in Oxford in March 1277 by publishing 30 propositions in the Arts which were not to be taught, with a penalty for offenders of loss of the right to teach. Condemning opinions was rather in vogue in universities at the time, and it is possible that Kilwardby was anxious to ensure that Oxford was not left out in the 'orthodoxy' stakes. A similar condemnation had been made less than two weeks earlier in Paris, though 219 unacceptable views were identified in Oxford's rival university, and there is not a great deal of overlap. For the Dominicans the most important aspect was the need to ensure that the views of Thomas Aquinas were being respected. The Order had invested much reputational capital in getting him to provide standard manuals of instruction such as the *Summa Theologiae*. Doubts about some of his arguments among the Oxford Dominicans were not welcome, particularly as supported by Kilwardby's condemnatory list. Alarmed Dominicans were sent by the General Chapter of 1278 to restore Oxford to compliance. Kilwardby received a stern letter. The power politics of the mendicant Orders were threatening to extend to the academic work of the University.

The mendicant Orders, often in the news like this, exciting, attractive, controversial, found themselves overwhelmed with students and began to acquire substantial sites to build on, the Franciscans in St. Ebbe's and the Dominicans towards the bottom of St. Aldate's, below the present Town Hall.[28] The Dominicans soon found themselves in a dispute with the canons of St. Frideswide's who claimed that their permission had not been asked and appealed to the Pope. Honorius III approved the Dominicans' activities because the theological teaching to which they were contributing at Oxford was highly valued, but the canons remained obdurate and it took still more papal pressure, this time by Gregory IX, to get the dispute resolved. It was necessary to compensate the canons but the Dominicans built and ran their school until they were forced to move to larger premises still, towards the West, near Speedwell St.

This period of growth and ambition left its physical marks on the appearance of Oxford, the names and even the positions of its streets. There seems to have been an economic collapse of Oxford's commercial activities in the fourteenth century, when the Cotswolds became prosperous. The University, however, flourished and began to develop as established physical presence in its buildings and those of the emerging colleges.

Designing a syllabus

It is time to look in more detail at what was being taught, especially in the Arts course.[29] Oxford 'began' in competition with Paris and continued in hot competition with other universities as these began to emerge across Europe. It was natural that they should provide comparable courses so as to be in a strong position to compete for students, at least in the foundation studies of the Arts, although they did not all aspire the same reputation in all the higher degree subjects, with Paris taking the lead in theology, Salerno and Montpellier in medicine, and Bologna (especially a graduate university) in law.

The Arts consisted of seven subjects, which had emerged from the collapse of the education of the ancient world in a limited number of textbooks. These subjects were the *trivium* ('three ways') of grammar, logic and rhetoric and the *quadrivium* ('four ways') of arithmetic, geometry, music and astronomy. Of these the first two were by far the most important and thoroughly studied in the earlier Middle Ages, which makes the emergence of a group of distinguished Oxford 'mathematicians' in the fourteenth century the more notable. Robert Kilwardby's *De ortu scientiarum,*[30] which he was asked to write after he became a Dominican,[31] tried to answer the question where all these sources of knowledge had come from. To the textbooks from the ancient world the early universities were adding study aids and study guides and dictionaries of theological terms, and taking some of the ideas forward into new areas, particularly in logic. Kilwardby's own strong pedagogical instincts manifest themselves in his careful summaries of key texts, and his attempt to make them more searchable by dividing them into sections to be summarized, providing alphabetical indexes to help students find discussion of particular themes in certain books. He also attempted concordances.

Latin as the common scholarly language

> [Scholars] shall commonly speak Latin. Anyone who habitually does otherwise shall be admonished by the Principal. And if, having been admonished twice or thrice, he does not mend his ways, he shall be banned from the common table, and eat alone, being served last of all.[32]

That was the rule at Balliol in 1282. Speaking Latin fluently was taken seriously, though it was by now medieval not classical Latin. Latin remained a live and growing language throughout the scholastic Middle Ages, though usually it was treated as a work-horse rather than a vehicle of graceful or elegant expression.

It had gradually ceased to be a vernacular from late antiquity, as what were to become the 'romance' languages evolved away from it in various directions, so no one learnt it at a mother's knee by the time universities came into existence. It remained in use mainly as the official language of the Church and the working language of scholarship. But that does not mean it was not a fully operational vehicle of discourse.

Scholarly Western Europe, from the end of antiquity to the seventeenth century and beyond, had the advantage of sharing this single 'academic' language. Those who wrote on serious subjects of wider interest to European readers could still rely on their being able and willing to read a book in Latin. Milton wrote poetry in English and politics in Latin (though sometimes the other way round). Scholars such as Newton still wrote to one another in Latin if they did not share a vernacular, and sometimes if they did, for to publish in Latin was to write for the whole of Europe. Those who have been modern delegates at international conferences, struggling to discuss complex ideas in polyglot conversations, with English of varying quality likely to be the only common ground, will appreciate how convenient it would be if everyone could still launch into chattering in fluent Latin.

Students can sometimes be seen to be moving in and out of the vernacular in joky macaronic pieces in the late Middle Ages, but in essence what they studied they studied in Latin. Latin was hard to budge as the language in which all scholars felt most comfortable and which remained appropriate for liturgical use. It was perhaps, ironically, probably the fault of Latin's most eager protagonists, those like Erasmus at the beginning of the sixteenth century who wanted to raise it to 'classical' standards once more, that it ceased to be the straightforward instrument of scholarly communication to which it had adapted itself in the later medieval centuries. It had been growing to meet the technical demands made upon it; now it became overweight, stuffed with a redundant vocabulary and ultimately toppled over to lie disused. Nevertheless, Latin continued in use in the Roman Catholic Church and as a literary and technical language for several centuries after it had finally 'died' as a widely spoken language even in universities. University students, who continued to be expected to take examinations by holding disputations in Latin, grew more halting and more awkward as Oxford moved into the modern world, until in the nineteenth century examinations changed at last and took their modern written form.

It is to be assumed that medieval students already had a working knowledge of the language before they began at Oxford, for all teaching was in Latin and they would have needed to be able to understand and to speak the language to follow the course. They were expected to know a solecism and a barbarism when they saw or heard one. The evidence of surviving texts is that Latin was a living and developing clerical language, capable of conveying stylishly a range of moods and meanings. There was still something for even the most proficient speaker to learn, however, of a type considered more appropriate to advanced study. That was the theory of language, what would now be called 'linguistics', and the relationship between the use of language grammatically and its deployment in logical argument.

What was missing for most of the Middle Ages was the comparative study of languages. There was no study of the vernaculars of Europe, the languages students spoke at home (though most of Oxford's medieval students were probably English and we do not know in what language they spoke to one another in taverns and lodging-houses). Greek had dropped below the horizon of Western Europe with the fall of the Roman Empire and the break-up of the great bipolar Graeco-Latin world of late antiquity.

Robert Grosseteste took up the study of Greek and thus indirectly helped to put Oxford in the forefront of a revival of the study of Greek in England in the Middle Ages, though that was only temporary. His practical plans for the reform of study included the provision of translations of the writings of the ancient world. He set high standards in terms of command of the relevant area of knowledge itself, and of the languages needed in making a translation. He composed a Greek grammar, and parts of a Hebrew grammar by him survive.

Grosseteste may have got this idea from meeting John of Basingstoke.[33] Grosseteste certainly knew him because soon after he became Bishop of Lincoln he made John Archdeacon of Leicester. John of Basingstoke had lived in Athens for some years and had brought books in Greek back to England. Perhaps he taught the language to Grosseteste, but Grosseteste also actively sought out 'Greeks' for his episcopal household, including Robert the Greek and Nicholas the Greek (who was probably from Sicily). He also tried, with some success, to obtain more Greek books. This was, however, to be the end of the matter until the end of the fifteenth century when the revival of Greek studies helped prompt the Renaissance.[34]

Rhetoric, logic, the *quadrivium* and the Oxford mathematicians

Rhetoric tended to be the Cinderella subject of the *trivium* in the Middle Ages, for its ancient usefulness in political oratory and legal advocacy had little place in medieval society. Although no doubt medieval monarchs enjoyed flattery, few would have been able to appreciate the elegance of an *encomium* in Latin. The 'Art of letter-writing', the 'Art of poetry' and the 'Art of preaching' formed the medieval contributions to rhetoric and manuals were produced explaining how to master them. Of these, preaching was to be the most significant for Oxford.

There were, however, elements in the teaching of rhetoric such as the 'finding of arguments' and 'topics' which overlapped with logic. In this area, the main contribution of the Middle Ages to the study of logic lay in the area of developing understanding of the way language works, its modes of signification. Here Oxford's scholars were in the front line with those of Paris. But in Oxford there was also a substantial overlap of logic with mathematics. There Oxford shone.

Why did Oxford produce such a line of leading mathematicians? Probably the stimulus of shared interest was important. The 'Merton Calculators' were a group of mid-fourteenth century scholars, including Thomas Bradwardine, William Heytesbury and Richard Swineshead, who were at some time Fellows of Merton College, though the second two had also been at Balliol while they were students of the Arts. They experimented in the mid-fourteenth century with mathematical concepts applied to questions of exactly the sort which were to excite Newton and his contemporaries in the seventeenth century. What, they asked, *are* light and colour and hear and density? Can they be measured or can we learn about them by any sort of numerical 'calculation'? Or are they to be approached philosophically, by reasoning or speculation? And what is the difference?

Their work was in some respects advanced logic as much as it was mathematical, especially in their choice of topics which challenged the logician as much as the mathematician. They can be glimpsed 'being themselves'. The intellectually ambitious Richard Swineshead composed a 'book of calculations' (in reality a collection of shorter treatises) in 1350. He was no fourteenth-century 'nerd' but a robust and sometimes quarrelsome figure, prominent in a row over who was to be the next Vice-Chancellor which degenerated into a brawl. (He backed the Merton candidate against the candidate from Oriel.) William Heytesbury became quite an asset to Merton as an administrator. He served as its bursar and was energetic in making journeys to oversee its extensive properties in the north of England. He was also to be Oxford's Chancellor more than once. This did not dull his interest in mathematical logic. He wrote *Rules for resolving sophismata* in 1335, in which he set out the law that the same distance is covered in the same time by a uniformly accelerating object as by an object moving steadily at the mean speed of the accelerating object. This law is thought to have been helpful to Galileo when he was considering the problem of the rate of movement of objects in free fall.

Thomas Bradwardine (c.1300–49) eventually became Archbishop of Canterbury, but he spent his earlier career in Oxford, making his name both as mathematician and as theologian. He was a Fellow of Balliol (where at this date, only those who were not yet Masters of Arts might be Fellows) by 1321; but two years later he too appears as a Fellow of Merton, which helps to fix his probable period of inception as a Master. He was almost certainly intending to begin higher studies in theology, for that was the primary purpose of Merton's provision and would have been its expectation in admitting him as a Fellow.

But he was to make a name for himself on the boundary between logic and mathematics too. Bradwardine's *Tractatus de proportionibus* (1328) proved important enough – and sufficiently famous – to be among the early printed books.[35] He examined what Aristotle had to say about motion and asked whether it was enough. He looked at such concepts as force, distance, time, relationship, and considered how to describe acceleration. Was the subject closed? Did Aristotle say everything that needed to be said? Aristotle had suggested that for something to 'move' there must be a moving force strong enough to overcome the resistance of the object. Bradwardine suggested that if the object was to be moved twice as fast, it will not be enough to double the proportion of the force applied to the resistance it encounters; it will have to be squared. If the aim is to move it three times as fast, the proportion will have to be cubed (a matter of dynamics). The same mode of calculation will apply if the object is bigger and if the distance to be moved is greater (a matter of kinematics). These topics were to remain important to the development of modern science. They were to shape the work of Galileo and then of Isaac Newton.

Bradwardine was chosen to be Proctor in 1325 and again in 1327, which provided him with opportunity to learn how the world worked, for in 1328 Oxford University was in dispute with the Archdeacon of Oxford. He was dispatched, perhaps in the mid-1330s, to consult the Pope, who was in exile at Avignon and there he heard or took part in a disputation on the well-trodden subject of future contingents. We shall come to Bradwardine the 'Oxford theologian' in a moment, for like Grosseteste he moved from the study of science to the study of religion.[36]

Roger Bacon's attempted review of the syllabus

The Oxford Franciscan Roger Bacon (c.1214–94) wanted to shake up the university syllabus surprisingly early in its development. It was probably not until the 1250s that he became a Franciscan, though the Oxford Franciscans were later eager to claim him as their own. When they revived the ancient Franciscan study house at the beginning of the twentieth century, they helped to ensure that the ninth centenary was duly celebrated in 1914 and a statue of Bacon placed in the University Museum. He had become something of an Oxford symbol in an era when understanding of the intellectual history of the Middle Ages was largely unformed even in Oxford.

Yet more is known of him as a legend than can be pieced together in any rounded way about the real person, especially his early life. Robert Adamson, in *Roger Bacon: the philosophy of science in the Middle Ages,* which was published in Manchester in 1876, in an era when modern medieval studies were at an early stage in Oxford. It rather naively portrayed the Oxford of Bacon's day as the seat of resistance to the papacy and the place for the study of the natural sciences. In his contemporaries, he claims, are found the 'spirit of scientific inquiry... skill in mathematical investigation of all kinds, and the same proneness to practical invention, that are so markedly characteristic of him' (p.13). 'We can see Bacon deliberately rejecting the whole spirit and method of scholasticism' (p.23). 'To logic, indeed, Bacon is somewhat unjust. He advances against it arguments similar to those afterwards employed by Locke. Logic, he says in effect, is innate. We reason perfectly well without it' (p.28).

So Roger Bacon was seen in Oxford during the period when his 1914 centenary was being celebrated, as a leading light in the philosophy and study of science. Indeed he was regarded as a hero, deemed to have cast aside scholarly obfuscation in favour of pure science. 'His keen sense of the futility of the scholastic quibbling which passed for learning in his day, and of the evils of the use of bad translations of Aristotle and other ancient writers at second or third hand through Arabic and Latin' may explain 'the extreme frankness' with which he speaks of leading contemporaries, 'Roger Bacon', said *The British Medical Journal,* on 20 June 1914 (p.1367).[37]

A *Conversazione* was held on 20 November 1893 in the University Museum in Oxford including a lecture by Falconer Madan on 'Some interesting features in the Past History of Science in Oxford'.[38] Madan's lecture-notes survive, including his summary of key points on a folded sheet of '90, Banbury Rd.' notepaper. In 1265, he proposed to say, 'scholasticism up + all authority against experimental science' 'Yet there came light' (item 8) Meteorology for example, 'sterile till now' was 'founded'. In his actual text (item 13), 'There is no one in the long roll of English scientific men of the past who for real progressive power, real originative force can be set on a level with the Doctor Admirabilis of the 13th century, Roger Bacon.'

The reality is rather different. Bacon began his academic life as a student at Oxford. Robert Grosseteste was lecturing in Oxford from 1229 to 1235, but it is not certain that Bacon could have heard his lectures or known him at the time. Thomas Wallensis lectured to the Oxford Franciscans in the 1240s so Bacon could have known him and he certainly knew Adam Marsh who was lecturing as Regent

Master in theology at Oxford from 1247 to 1250. Bacon, like others among his contemporaries, did not spend his career in one university. He was lecturing in Paris in the mid-1240s, teaching some of the newly introduced and controversial writings of Aristotle on the natural sciences. He can be placed there once more in 1251. Nevertheless, it is the tradition that Bacon died in Oxford, having retired there at the end of a challenging life.

The puzzle is not so much *who* Bacon knew in his intellectually formative years as *how* he came to conceive of so original a way of approaching his work. He was a somewhat rebarbative character, whom the Order kept under strict and repressive control as far as it could, which may be one reason why it insisted that he spend a decade in Paris. He was not the only Franciscan author who had to be discouraged from writing too much too frankly on themes likely to cause offence. This was not only the period of the poverty debates but also an era of Joachimist apocalypticism. It is known that Joachim of Fiore was read in Oxford in the fourteenth century and that at least one copy of his work on the Apocalypse was borrowed.[39]

In the course of his studies and teaching, Bacon had made the acquaintance of the future Pope Clement IV (Pope from 1264), and sent him his work with the claim that the Pope had required to see it.[40] Silenced for so long, he now produced work of great originality and on a huge scale. His *Opus maius* was an attempt to frame an account of all knowledge in a novel way – possibly intending the work to be analogous with the type of *summa* which was now being produced to assist in the comprehensive and systematic study of theology. He began with the causes of human ignorance, discussed the relationship of theology with other branches of knowledge; he continued with grammar in the context of the study of all languages, not merely Latin; mathematics and optics and natural science followed, and finally ethics. In case this great work went astray or the Pope found he did not have time to read it, the *Opus minus* followed, sent off to the Pope by a carrier called John who was apparently a favourite pupil of Bacon's. Then Bacon began on the *Opus tertium,* which he may not have completed and which it is not certain he ever sent to the Pope. Certainly nothing is known of the Pope's reaction to the arrival of any of these texts or whether he read them. The Pope died in 1268 and Bacon was left to go on working, perhaps without his former sense of having a suitable destination for his works, but with a continuing sense that he had not yet quite succeeded in capturing the whole of human knowledge in a satisfactorily orderly manner. The *Compendium studii philosophiae* or *Compendium studii theologiae* survive as fragments. Others had, however, been taking a view of his work and disapproving. The Franciscan order formally condemned it and Bacon was apparently imprisoned. He had made enemies because of his frank criticisms of his contemporaries. This was a nervous age.

An element in the new 'science' was going to be astrology. Bacon's doctrine about this was certainly influenced by Grosseteste, but, it would appear, even more strongly by the *De radiis* of al-Kindi. This work had the ominous alternative title 'Theoretical study of the magical arts' (*Theorica artium magicarum*), and, despite its short length, Bacon's contemporary Giles of Rome felt able to list eighteen serious errors contained in it. Here was a first hint of the problem of identifying proper subjects for serious academic study, for there were many who looked askance at all this, and 'magic' was to crop up more than once in later centuries as a very dubious area of research. Even Newton in the seventeenth century did not regard astrology as unworthy to be taken seriously by a scientist like himself.

Bacon's hypothesis, which enabled him to justify his radical approach to adjusting the framework of learning, was that although God had revealed all necessary knowledge to the patriarchs and the prophets, now corruption had set in, so that it was repeatedly necessary to reform study; here Solomon and Aristotle and Avicenna could be pointed to as having made specially important contributions. Bacon's own time was another period when reform was vital and Bacon seems to have seen himself as the Aristotle of his times. One of his reasons for seeking so assiduously to appeal to the Pope was that being the Aristotle of his times was proving expensive and he needed financial support.

Housing the scholars

Lodgings, town and gown

A few of the buildings which used to house the students in the Middle Ages still survive, for example, 106–7, High Street, once Tackley's Inn, built in the 1320s. The halls had been an integral part of the townscape, not fully distinguishable from student lodgings. As in the case of Tackley's Inn, a Hall could be a hybrid building; halls did not house only students. This one had five shops at the front and chambers above and below them which could be let to ordinary townspeople. Behind, reached through a passage, was an inner area, with rooms for academic use and a hall for the small community of scholars to use as a common area. In the early fourteenth century,

Tackley Hall was sold to Adam de Brome, almoner to King Edward II and Rector of the University Church of St. Mary the Virgin from 1320 to 1326, who wanted it for the scholars of the new foundation which was to become Oriel College. They moved within five years to another house on the site of today's Oriel College, called La Oriole, but they seem to have kept the original house and benefited from the rental income. The internal space was flexible. By the fifteenth century the rooms were divided up in a different way, into two spaces side by side instead of front to back, one used as an academic hall, the other as a tavern.[41] Town and gown relations were subtly affected by the shift from hall to college, for the townspeople no longer lived cheek by jowl with the students and scholars in the same buildings in the same way.

From hall to college: ideas of community and visible displays of benefactor generosity

Halls usually did not have chapels or libraries.[42] Those were the marks of a community. The concept that not only the University but its colleges should be bodies corporate emerged with the development of true colleges, which first appeared as bodies of Fellows, young graduates with first degrees who were going to study for higher degrees. Halls had lodged changing housefuls but the new college communities were to be corporate bodies and their members were going to be bound by the founder's statutes. There was to be continuity and real membership. The 'model' was roughly that of a religious community cross-bred with a great house, of which the houses of the friars already provided examples.

The colleges which now give Oxford its character and much of its beauty were chiefly built surprisingly late in the University's story, for they began to take shape only when the University was a generation or two old. Most of the Colleges are very much younger. But from the beginning, Colleges often bore the stamp of their founders' ambitions. They could be status symbols for their founders. For example, University College is a creation of the thirteenth century (1249), with a claim to be the earliest college in either Oxford or Cambridge. Its founder was William of Durham (d.1249), who intended it to be a home for Fellows engaged in the study of theology, and therefore for graduate students returning to take a higher degree.[43] Balliol College (1263) also claims to be the oldest. Balliol began as a hall provided with places for poor students by the charitable gift of one of Henry III's barons John Balliol, encouraged by the bishop of Durham. From 1280, Balliol had statutes – another mark of the intention to form a community and one which would last and be a memorial to the founder.

Merton College was founded in 1264 by Walter de Merton, who was in the course of his career Chancellor of England and Bishop of Rochester. His foundation at Oxford was intended for twenty Fellows who were to govern themselves as a community. However – and this was an important new trend – undergraduates were also admitted as early as 1380 and provided with scholarships through the generosity of John Wyliot, himself a former fellow and subwarden, who endowed bursaries to be known as 'postmasterships'.

Colleges were conscious that they needed domestic legislation, 'statutes', to govern the activities of the community, together with firm rules about the future modification of those statutes. The founders of New College, Oxford, and Magdalen College, Oxford, declared their statutes immutable in the hope of securing the institutions for the future. Brasenose College had as one of its founders (1511/12) Ralph Sutton, who was also anxious to prevent changes to his statutes because he wanted to be sure that his college would continue to set its collective face against the new learning.[44] Those which lacked one or the other because of the negligence of their would-be founders sometimes did not last long.[45] Founders' wishes have continued to be significant.

There are glimpses of the expanding practicalities which needed to be attended to as the College grew and acquired properties which had to be looked after and administered in their turn. Walter de Merton had an eye for detail in the drafting of the statutes of the college which were revised to meet these new needs. The horse question was as pressing in its time as the modern need to make car parking arrangements. It is not improbable that Peter Abingdon bought the tenements across St. John's Lane especially to provide stabling and then there was hay and harness and farriers' accommodation and the medieval equivalent of vets' bills to be looked to.[46] By 1274 there was provision for the Warden to keep two horses, but he was also allowed a third for a servant to ride to accompany him, and then possibly a fourth for a messenger in case he needed to send one in a hurry when his other three horses were busy.

Exeter College was founded by Walter de Stapeldon in 1314. As Bishop of Exeter he was anxious to ensure a steady supply of properly educated clergy for his diocese, and for some generations it was from the West of England that the college drew most of its students. In the first phase of its existence the college was merely a hall, named after Stapeldon himself. There lived a community of a dozen Fellows studying theology, with a Rector and a Chaplain.

Oriel College, founded in 1326 by King Edward II with the assistance of Adam de Brome, is the fifth oldest of Oxford's Colleges. The Queen's College was founded as a hall in 1341 by Robert Eglesfield, a Chaplain of the then Queen, who paid her the compliment of naming it as an act of respect for her, and with an astute realization that she might be persuaded to endow it. She did, giving it lands in 1343. The intention was that it should confine itself principally to students from the north of England.

The new medieval colleges had to make decisions about the kinds of buildings which would meet their needs. The physical buildings were secondary to the human and legal framework and the sense of 'community', but also shaped by these new preoccupations. The old academic halls had often faced inward round a courtyard. Monastic houses had had cloisters. So Colleges began to be built round quadrangles, sometimes with cloisters in addition as at New College and Magdalen. The purpose of these cloisters is uncertain. Perhaps they were used for teaching in mild weather. Perhaps it was simply felt that something of the sort was required for the look of the thing. Rooms for particular purposes were going to be needed, not only the 'display items', a chapel for worship and a hall for meals, but also administrative rooms, a library, as well as rooms for students to live in. Students' rooms were normally shared among several students, each provided with his own study area.[47] The head of the house would be so much like an abbot or a lord that he would need accommodation of appropriate quality.

The resulting new Oxford buildings were made of local Cotswold stone, which has given a golden visual unity to the whole city ever since. The building of New College was perhaps the most important in establishing the physical norms and parameters of Oxford's colleges, the ways in which these essential elements of the new community life were to be configured in a plan. New College was called 'new' because it had the same patron saint as Oriel and that made it the 'new college of St. Mary', which was abbreviated to New College. It had some new ideas too, particularly the important notion that undergraduates should be accommodated in its rooms as well as graduate Fellows, because that led to the concomitant development of a tutorial responsibility for the younger students, who might need to be taught within the college as well as in the University.

New College's founder was William of Wykeham (c.1320–1404). He was extremely interested in fine building. The immense revenues of his see as Bishop of Winchester (on which he was able to draw from 1367) gave him the necessary wealth. He was responsible for the building of St. George's Chapel, Windsor and parts of Windsor Castle. His good relations with the King helped to protect his New College venture from interruption or interference. The planned site was ripe for rescue and redevelopment because it was run down and known as a place where prostitutes plied their trade. New College, drawing students from Wykeham's other foundation Winchester School, was a success both academically and as a building which had been able to benefit from the services of court architects, so that Henry VI took it as a model when he founded Eton as a feeder school for his own new foundation of King's College, Cambridge. New College seems to have been designed in some detail and built very quickly but Wykeham did not acquire the complete site until after the main quadrangle had been built and occupied so there were some anomalies.

College building went on developing during the medieval centuries and beyond. The elaborate tracery of the early collegiate ambition gave way for a time to a simpler decorative style. This is exemplified at All Souls, which was begun by Archbishop Chichele in 1437–8. Then showing off came back into fashion and mason's workshops began to produce a tempting array of decorative features in the later fifteenth century.[48] A spattering of crenellations was added here and there.

The 'architects' profession', embodied by the masters of various crafts, had some social standing and its members could and did make plans with a patron to ensure that the buildings of a new college spoke well of its founder. Masons were usually slightly subordinate in status but there are examples of the master mason and the master carpenter both being invited to dine with the Master or the Fellows when important work was afoot for a college.[49]

Colleges were not all rich and grand. Little Lincoln was built from 1427 to 1437. Grand Magdalen was the work of 1474–90 with the great tower on the High Street added later and not completed until the beginning of the sixteenth century.[50] And for those with medieval origins there was going to be the question of keeping up with the times and with new rivals when more colleges were founded in the sixteenth and seventeenth centuries and beyond. The colleges were never 'finished', but living and continuing communities endlessly revising their housing.

The first 'University' buildings

The University itself was not to be outdone in the matter of impressive architecture. It had had no buildings of its own until the early fourteenth century. It had not needed them. It too was first a community and only secondarily a 'place' and its possessions, mainly books and documents, could conveniently be kept in the University 'Chest' at first. The University Church of St. Mary the Virgin provided a meeting-place for Congregation when there was University business to be done and a pulpit from which University sermons could be preached.

A Congregation House with a room above it to be used as the first University library was built after 1320 with funding provided by Thomas Cobham, who was planning to bestow his own book collection on the new venture. He died in 1327 before the building was finished, but he had started a trend, and not only in Oxford. Chapels with libraries over them became quite the fashion, as at Canterbury (1420) and Winchester College (1425).[51] The Oxford arrangement was superseded in the 1440s by the plan to put the University's library above the new 'schools', in the space now known as Duke Humfrey's Library. This evolved in the hands of a succession of architects, and not without controversy over the highly elaborate decoration of the stonework. Stone masons and carpenters formed the leading 'architectural-and-building' trades, with certain families prominent in Oxford.[52] The architect who gave the Divinity School its soaring ceiling was William Orchard, and he was also involved in the design and building of parts of Magdalen College.[53] The University was anxious to do itself proud, ensuring that its buildings would stand comparison with the best that was being built elsewhere in England notably at Windsor.[54] St. Mary's Church was in disrepair in the fifteenth century and was rebuilt in 1462, the work paid for by Walter Lyhert, a Bishop of Norwich who had been Provost of Oriel. Fine new carpentry was commissioned, for example, the installation of desks and benches in the Divinity School in 1466.[55] Framing roofs might be done some way away and the timbers ready-prepared would be brought on site to be assembled.

Keeping the record

The construction of a physical University to give location and enduring substance to the community went with the realization that it was going to be necessary to keep a record, and to keep it somewhere safe. At first, archives, legal documents, money and valuables would have been kept in a Chest probably in St. Mary's Church, until the Congregation House was built in 1320 and then they were kept there. Members of the University could borrow money from the University Chest if they left some form of security, such as a book. The Chest had four keys, two kept by the two Proctors and two by a representative from each of the two 'nations'.[56] By the fifteenth century a new Chest was needed, this time with five keys so that the Chancellor could have one. After a robbery in the sixteenth century there began to be concerns about the safety of the record and after an abortive attempt to get All Souls to look after the archives in 1609 the problem was solved by the construction of the Bodleian Library and the Tower of the Schools, to which the archive was moved. The University Chest survives in name and a fifteenth-century example is in the Ashmolean Museum.

Quarrels and confrontations

Visitation and the search for academic respectability

In 1296 Oxford petitioned Pope Boniface VIII for the grant of the *ius ubique docendi,* 'the licence to teach everywhere'. A degree from Oxford would be considerably elevated in status if that was granted, for Oxford graduates could travel the world and teach where they pleased. The request had the support of Winchelsey then Archbishop of Canterbury, and a number of bishops. The University pleaded that if Paris was entitled to this right, Oxford should have it too.

The timing was bad. Oxford had powerful enemies in the mendicant Orders and during the next two decades it was going to be involved in lawsuits against them.[57] The bid prompted a visitation, the nearest thing to an inspection to which medieval universities were likely to be subjected. There was going to be a balance to be struck between inviting popes and princes to grant 'privileges' in the form of exemptions from taxation and protections from interference, and submitting to such interferences where they were pressed for by the granting authorities.

The first such 'inspection' of Oxford had been conducted by Boniface, Archbishop of Savoy in 1252, arriving as 'metropolitan' in the context of a visitation of the Lincoln diocese. The question which had to be answered – and the answer was going to have long-term implications – was what exactly a Visitor of a University was entitled to inspect. The spiritual welfare of the scholars and students was clearly his responsibility. A college's faithfulness to its statutes would later be the business of a Visitor who acted as successor to the founder of an eleemosynary body, but it was too early for that and in any case, the University of Oxford had no founder. It had created itself. The one thing which the University was sure about was that no Visitor ought to be questioning the arrangements it made for the conduct of its academic activities. Those were its 'craft' and strictly the business of the Masters. This was a point which was going to have to be articulated and defended. It was in the context of a

PLATE 1 – Charles Stuart (1600–49) succeeded to the throne in 1625 and reigned as Charles I. However, the King offended his Parliaments, which claimed that he was abusing his royal powers, and civil war broke out in 1642. Charles retreated to Oxford and installed his court in Christ Church. The Parliamentarian General Thomas Fairfax (1612–71) marshalled his troops before the City of Oxford. The siege was successful and the city capitulated in 1646, but the King had already fled.

PLATE 2 – Rupert of the Rhine (1619–82) was Charles I's nephew, a professional soldier from an early age, and a dashing – if sometimes reckless – commander. He was appointed leader of the Royalist cavalry during the English Civil War and became a hate-figure to parliamentarians, who accused him of war crimes in their broadsheets. Prince Rupert's successes were counteracted by misjudgements on the battlefield, in particular his surrender of Bristol in 1645. This lost him the King's favour and he was dismissed from royal service.

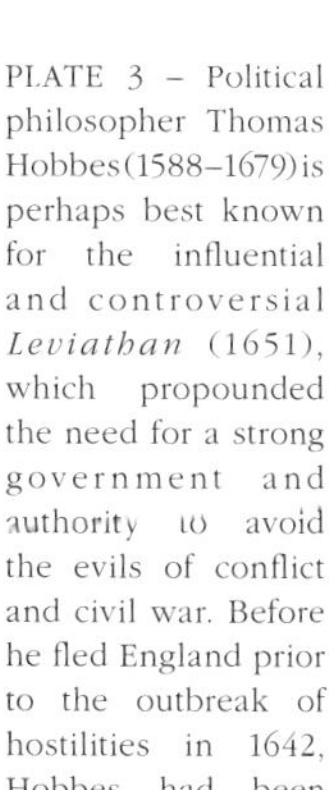

PLATE 3 – Political philosopher Thomas Hobbes (1588–1679) is perhaps best known for the influential and controversial *Leviathan* (1651), which propounded the need for a strong government and authority to avoid the evils of conflict and civil war. Before he fled England prior to the outbreak of hostilities in 1642, Hobbes had been an Oxford student, attending the now-defunct Magdalen Hall at the beginning of the seventeenth century.

PLATE 4 – A staunch proponent of high-church Anglicanism, William Laud (1573–1645) attended St. John's College, Oxford, as a scholar, eventually becoming the College's President in 1611. In 1630, Laud was elected Chancellor of the University of Oxford. One of his most important legacies was the codification of the University's statutes in 1636. Laud served as Archbishop of Canterbury from 1633 to 1645, and was throughout this period a tenacious supporter of the royalist cause. Denounced as a traitor by the Long Parliament of 1640, Laud was imprisoned in the Tower and executed on Tower Hill in 1645.

PLATE 5 – Christ Church (which is also known as 'the House', after its Latin name Ædes Christi, the temple or house of Christ) was founded in 1525 by Thomas Wolsey, on the site of the suppressed Augustinian Abbey of St Frideswide. Wolsey, who rose to greatness as Lord Chancellor, Archbishop of York and the eminent position of cardinal, called this new foundation after himself: Cardinal College. When in 1529 England's most powerful cleric fell from grace, his nemesis Henry VIII refounded it in his own name in 1532 as King Henry VIII's College. The college definitively became Christ Church in 1546, after Henry's break with Rome, when it incorporated the cathedral church of the freshly created diocese of Oxford. The House boasts singularly impressive architecture, notably the Romanesque cathedral, Wolsey's Tom Quad and Christopher Wren's famous bell tower, designed in 1682 and housing the bell itself, Great Tom. Christ Church has since evolved into one of Oxford's most powerful collegiate institution and for many centuries has been a focus of jealousy and resentment from other colleges. It is unique in the world not only for its cathedral, but also in possessing 'Fellows' (called 'Students') who are also the canons of the cathedral, and its Dean, the head of the College, who simultaneously serves as Dean of the cathedral.

PLATES 6 and 7 – In the late 1520s, Thomas Cromwell (c.1485–1540) assisted Thomas Wolsey (c.1471–1530) in dissolving thirty monasteries to raise the money to build Cardinal College, which later became Christ Church. Cromwell later took Wolsey's place as Henry's chief minister, though he forfeited the king's favour after Henry's disastrous marriage to Anne of Cleves. He was executed in 1540.

PLATE 8 – Christ Church boasts the largest dining hall in Oxford, which dates from the Tudor building of the College. It has an impressive hammerbeam (Gothic open timber) roof and a fine collection of portraits. More recently the Great Hall served as the model for the set of Hogwart's dining room in the film *Harry Potter and the Philosopher's Stone* (dir. Chris Columbus, 2001).

PLATES 9 and 10 – Charles Dodgson (1832–98), a mathematician and sometime Student (Fellow) of Christ Church, wrote his charming but sophisticated children's stories under the pen-name of Lewis Carroll. *Alice in Wonderland* and *Alice through the Looking Glass* were written to amuse Alice Liddell, daughter of the Dean of Christ Church and her two sisters. Dodgson used to take the children rowing on the river and tell them stories. He ate his meals in the Great Hall, and based many of his fictional characters on the real people in the college whom he knew.

PLATE 11 – *Prince Caspian* (1951), one of C.S. Lewis's 'Narnia' stories, was released as a film in 2008 (dir. Andrew Adamson). Susan, Peter, Edmund and Lucy return to the Narnia they left a year earlier at the end of *The Lion, the Witch and the Wardrobe*, to help the rightful Prince, young Caspian, to rescue his inheritance from the usurping King Miraz and his army of Telmarines.

PLATES 12 and 13 – Clive Staples ('Jack') Lewis (1898–1963) achieved lasting fame as author of the Narnia stories and a long list of novels and books on Christian themes. A Fellow of Magdalen College between 1925 and 1954, and a senior member of the Oxford English Faculty, Lewis was one of the founder members of the Inklings who met in The Eagle and Child (often colloquially changed to 'The Bird and Baby').

PLATE 14 – John Ronald Reuel Tolkien (1892-1973), celebrated author of *The Hobbit* and *The Lord of the Rings*, held the Chairs of Anglo-Saxon and then English Language and Literature in the University of Oxford. Tolkien was a close friend and colleague of C.S. Lewis in Oxford's English Faculty, and a fellow Inkling. His phenomenally popular fantasy series reached a still wider audience when *The Lord of the Rings* was filmed as a trilogy by Peter Jackson, and released between 2001 and 2003, to considerable critical and commercial success.

PLATES 15–17 – The children's fiction of atheist writer Phillip Pullman has been described as a secular alternative to the Christian allegory of C.S. Lewis's *Chronicles of Narnia*. The first book of Pullman's *His Dark Materials* trilogy, has already been made into a film released in 2007 (dir. Deborah Forte), and features an Oxford both similar and yet very different to our own. In Pullman's books, the characters Lyra and Will move between parallel universes on an esoteric quest. *Lyra's Oxford* elaborates on this alternative Oxford through the further adventures of Lyra Belacqua or Lyra Silvertongue.

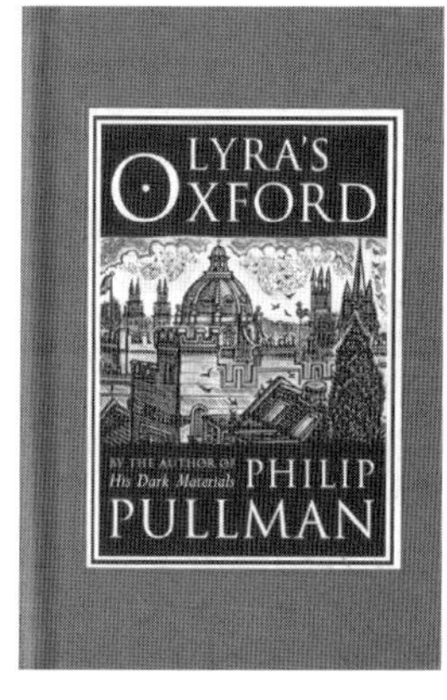

PLATE 18 – Oxford Canal. The picturesque canal which begins in Oxford runs north towards Banbury and links Oxford with Coventry. It is home to many canal-boat dwellers. In Phillip Pullman's *His Dark Materials* trilogy, the Gyptians are modelled on just such boatmen and women who traverse the Oxford Canal in narrow boats. The author himself has been a staunch defender of the Castlemill Boat Yard in Jericho (whose original buildings were demolished in 2008) from property developers.

PLATES 19 and 20 – Evelyn Waugh's 1945 novel *Brideshead Revisited* begins in a pre-war Oxford among undergraduates and dons of exotic kinds. The encounter between the secular and agnostic Charles Ryder (an undergraduate at Hertford College) and the Catholic Marchmains (the aristocratic family of Charles's friend Sebastian Flyte, who is studying at Christ Church) leads to an exploration of serious themes like divine grace, faith and redemption. The story was adapted for TV in 1981, and starred Jeremy Irons and Anthony Andrews as Charles and Sebastian. Julian Jarrold directed a film version of the novel, released in 2008.

PLATE 21 – Evelyn Waugh (1903–66), author of *Brideshead Revisited*, was himself a student (reading history) at Hertford, the college attended by Charles Ryder in the novel, though he never graduated. Waugh famously threw himself into high society, seeking out friendships with Oxford's young aesthetes and aristocrats. His undergraduate experiences served him well in his later writing, which explored – often with dark satirical humour – the failings and foibles of the English upper classes.

PLATES 22 and 23 – Novelist and philosopher Iris Murdoch (1919–99) was an undergraduate at Somerville and then a Fellow of St. Anne's College. She was a natural Platonist and her novels, mainly about the entangled couplings of intellectuals, dons and civil servants, are also full of an idealized beauty. *A Severed Head* (1961) was made into a play. A film about her life, based on the recollections of her husband, the Oxford English professor John Bayley, was released in 2001.

PLATE 24 – 'How cheerful, as if waked from a dream, glides on the famous stream by Christ-Church Cathedral Grove!' The modern Oxford punt is a Victorian design. Punting in Oxford is done differently from Cambridge's equivalent, with the pole wielded not from on top of the raised platform (the 'till' or 'box'), but rather from inside the decking at the opposite end of the boat. To sceptical Cambridge eyes, this means that unorthodox Oxford boaters punt with the stern of the punt first, contrarily propelling their craft with its till end facing forwards.

PLATE 25 – Just as they enjoy contrary forms of punting, Oxford and Cambridge possess rival Bridges of Sighs. Designed by Sir Thomas Jackson (1835–1924), Oxford's 'Bridge of Sighs', which links the Old and New Quadrangles of Hertford College, more closely resembles the Rialto Bridge that straddles the Grand Canal in the centre of Venice than Antoni Contino's original Ponte dei Sospiri near St Mark's Square.

PLATE 26 – The tallest building in the city, at 144 feet (44 metres), Magdalen College Tower was built between 1492 and 1509 and presides dramatically over the road into Oxford from the east. Every May morning at dawn, the College choir sings madrigals from the top of the tower to mark the beginning of summer. Crowds gather in the High Street and on Magdalen Bridge below to listen.

PLATE 27 – Oxford's glamorous summer balls (often called Commemoration Balls') come at the end of the academic year. Their festivities go on all night, at the end of which the streets are full of revellers – still in full evening dress – who make their way home at dawn. Like those who have been to Cambridge's May Balls, those who attend Oxford's balls usually never forget them.

PLATE 28 – William Hogarth's satirical brilliance finds a subject worthy of his skill in this irreverent depiction of an eighteenth century university lecturer and his audience, the latter caught in a variety of attitudes ranging from boredom to astonished incredulity.

PLATE 29 – The Sheldonian Theatre, designed by Christopher Wren as an adventurous imitation of a Roman theatre, was named after Gilbert Sheldon (1598-1677), at different times Warden of All Souls and Archbishop of Canterbury, and Chancellor of the University, who donated the money to enable it to be built. William Laud had suggested that University needed a fine building for the granting of degrees and the holding of ceremonies but only now has the idea become a reality.

Visitation (again ostensibly as part of a visitation of the diocese of Lincoln), in 1277, that Kilwardby, as a Dominican with experience of Oxford and now Archbishop of Canterbury, had made the 'visitation' in connection with which he condemned a list of thirty propositions which he said were improperly being taught in the Arts course.[58] In 1286 Archbishop Pecham pronounced 8 articles to be heretical at the Court of the Arches in London, in the presence of the bishop of Lincoln and the Chancellor of Oxford and others. Winchelsey, who had been Chancellor of Oxford from 1288 seems not to have made a Visitation of Oxford when he became Archbishop from 1293.

However, Archbishops of Canterbury continued to try to interfere during the fourteenth century. Archbishop Langham (1366–8) made a list of theological errors (1368) in connection with a case involving the Dominicans who objected to the views of one of the theologians at Oxford. William Courtney interfered actively because of the threat perceived to be posed by the teaching of John Wyclif, as we shall see in a moment.

Squabblesomeness continues: town and gown

Anthony Wood preserved many tales of the earlier Oxford. He tells the story of an occasion when some scholars in a tavern criticized the wine they were offered and 'several snappish words passed' between them and their host. John de Bereford, Richard Forester and Robert Lardiner did not let the matter lie. There was a lot of longstanding bad feeling between town and gown to be expressed, and there were factions within factions. A good many of these murdered students were believed to be Irish. The townspeople stirred up an armed mob in the town and gathered in people from the surrounding countryside, who broke into Oxford by the West Gate waving a black flag.[59] The argument which followed lasted several days, drew in 'a numberless multitude' of the townsfolk and led to attacks by the Town on 'the Scholars' houses' with 'iron bars and other engines', murders and woundings. Wood favoured the scholars' side in this famous St. Scholastica's Day riot of 1355 and depicts them as innocent victims.[60] The authorities were informed. The Bishop of Lincoln responded at once by excommunicating those who had started the riot and, for good measure, placing the town as a whole under an Interdict, which denied everyone the comfort of the sacraments. The King happened to be at Woodstock, only five miles away. He took action to recall the charters under which the town held its royal privileges. The University broke up and the scholars dispersed and for some time they were reluctant to come back. When they did, it was to an Oxford in which the balance of power had been adjusted in their favour, with the University not the town in control of the market.

Chaucer affords further glimpses of late medieval Oxford life. Chaucer includes three 'clerks' of Oxford in his *Canterbury Tales* and two from Cambridge who both appear in the *Reeve's Tale*. Apart from the Clerk whom Chaucer puts among the story-tellers, he includes an Oxford student called Nicholas in the *Miller's Tale*, who takes part in a riotous farce of a tale involving an attempt to seduce the wife of the keeper of his student lodgings. This student has books, a psaltery and an astrolabe, a quantity of personal equipment for study likely to have been untypical. The third Oxford scholar in Chaucer's tales is the 'joly clerk, Jankyn', whom the Wife of Bath has captured as one of her many husbands.

> 'Sire Clerk of Ocenford,' oure Hooste sayde,
> 'Ye ryde as coy and stille as dooth a mayde...
> I trowe ye studie aboute som sophyme;'[61]

The studious Clerk good-humouredly expresses his willingness to entertain Chaucer's Canterbury pilgrims, and says he will tell a tale he learned at Padua from 'a worthy clerk'. Chaucer paints him as studious and unworldly, though he has, improbably for the times, 'twenty bookes, clad in blak or reed' containing works of Aristotle. Chaucer knew these would have been of enormous value, so he tells his readers that anything the Clerk could come by 'On bookes and on lernynge he it spente', and hints that he came by money by offering his services to pray for the dead.

Higher studies and fiercer disputes among the theologians

All over Europe from the early thirteenth century, leading Masters were having to make a choice. The arrival of Aristotle's writings on natural science was causing as big an upheaval as Charles Darwin caused with the publication of his book on the *Origin of species* in the mid-nineteenth century, and for the same reasons. Here was a secular challenge to Christian beliefs as they seemed to be required by the Bible and as they had been worked out in centuries of Christian writing. The approach was to try to reconcile Augustine and Aristotle but that was not easy. And the youthful Arts students and their young lecturers were studying additional topics in 'philosophy' which overlapped with the questions the theologians were also studying and they loved to throw down challenges. There was, for example, the problem of the incompatibility of Aristotle's theories about the soul with those of Christian orthodoxy.

We have already seen Robert Grosseteste getting to grips with theology, but in a somewhat unstructured way. Very soon, there was a growing European network of scholars and scholarly opinions. By the 1250s Robert Kilwardby was lecturing in Oxford as any theology student was expected to do in the course of completing his theological studies. For once the formality of requirements to be gone through on the way to obtaining a degree was defined, the lengthy process of graduating in theology involved first the study of, and then the giving of 'bachelor's lectures' on, the *Sentences* of Peter Lombard as well as the Bible. Kilwardby's *Quaestiones* on the *Sentences* survive, and they suggest that he knew the contents of the commentary Bonaventure had produced in Paris and also that he had read or heard Richard Fishacre (d.1248) on the subject. It is not easy to be sure, because 'questions' were handled as disputation topics, and the technique was to list alternative and opposing viewpoints. Thus the opinion (*sententia*) of an earlier or contemporary Master might become an entity to be quoted and transmitted independently of familiarity with the whole body of the author's work.

Commentaries on the *Sentences* were already a favourite vehicle of theological publication for ambitious masters and by the fourteenth century it was customary for them to focus on a topic or group of topics particularly fashionable at the time. The effect was not so much to provide a general grounding in systematic theology across the board but to allow advanced and sophisticated publication and review and counter-argument. Secular masters such as Richard Fitzralph (c.1300–60), Richard Kilvington (c.1302–61), Thomas Buckingham (d.1349) were able in that way to challenge the threatened preeminence of the friars.

Thomas Bradwardine's interest in mathematics seems to have given way to a focus on theology. While he was studying for his higher degree or perhaps just before he began, as he says in his *De Causa Dei,* he experienced a personal *metanoia*. He realized that he had, as a young man, not really understood the meaning of the passage in Romans 9.16 which describes the basis on which God shows mercy to individuals. He had, he realizes, been thinking like a Pelagian, assuming that he could live a good life by his own efforts and earn God's good opinion. Now he had discovered the meaning of 'grace'. Salvation, he now thought, 'depends not upon man's will or exertion, but upon God's mercy.'[62]

As Augustine and Anselm had also found, the subject of the relationship of divine foreknowledge, predestination, necessity, contingency, grace and the exercise of human free will spreads out in all directions. One of those directions is the question whether anything a person can do can affect God's decision about his or her eternal future. Bradwardine wrote 'On God's Cause' (*De Causa Dei*), in which the *causa* of the title means something like 'case', as in a lawsuit, not 'cause'. The first two books were written while Bradwardine was still in Oxford but probably not the third. For Bradwardine moved out of Oxford into a series of preferments, holding the Chancellorship of St. Paul's from 1337 to 1349. He could have become a Master in theology in 1336 and completed his obligatory lectures a year later. That could have freed him to continue the lectures from the pulpit of St. Paul's, which were revised for the book which he completed in 1344. In 1339 he was a royal chaplain and it was through this move into court circles perhaps that he became Archbishop. Keeping up with the latest research while out of Oxford did not prove to be a problem.

Bradwardine chose for the arguments in his *De Causa Dei* the closest approximation he could to 'demonstrative method'. This was, essentially, the Euclidean method, and it involved attempting to proceed from self-evident truths, or propositions which had the certainty of Scriptural statements, by tight inference, to what must then be 'necessary' conclusions; these, once demonstrated, then became truths evident to those who understood how they had been arrived at, and could be put forward as building blocks for the next stage. So the *De causa Dei* has its axioms, theorems, proofs, conclusions, and corollaries, beginning with proofs for God's existence as the fundamental axiom to be accepted. The method was highly favoured in medieval scholarly circles and immense effort was put into trying to make it work for theology, although it is probably strictly applicable only to geometry.

The matters being debated here form a key stage in a long history of disputes on this cluster of topics, of which the Pelagian debates of Augustine of Hippo's time to which medieval scholars regularly referred are only a staging-post. It was all to continue into the Reformation and beyond. Chaucer's coupling of Bradwardine's name with the names of Augustine and Boethius on this subject in the 'Nun's Priest's Tale'[63] suggests that Bradwardine was perceived to have made a noticeable dent in the discussion for his times.

Who were the 'modern Pelagians' Bradwardine was attacking? He could have met a fair number in Oxford or Paris among the academics. To the post-Reformation eye, the matters being discussed appear particularly significant, as when Bradwardine raised the question whether human 'free choices' to do the right thing could earn rewards from God. Bradwardine does not seem to have been an out-and-out determinist; he believed that human beings have some freedom of choice. He did not approve of the device of claiming that if one did the right thing God would be somehow compelled in justice to provide the necessary grace to make the act meritorious (the *de congruo* doctrine).

Bradwardine still approached the discussion as a logician, from the point of view of the problems raised by Aristotle at the end of the *De Interpretatione,* about the difficulty of knowing whether any future statement is true or must be regarded as contingent. This textbook of elementary logic which was familiar to every medieval student included a discussion of future contingents. Future contingents for Bradwardine focus on the problem that only in a 'determinist universe' could it be known whether a statement in the future tense was true. But he was not a determinist.

More controversial opinions: Ockham and Fitzralph

The Franciscan William of Ockham (1287–1347) 'read' or lectured on the *Sentences* in Oxford from 1317 to 1319. He left Oxford and never completed his theology degree there, but his work remained the subject of discussion because by 1324 he had been delated to the Pope as a heretic and had to go to Avignon to answer the accusations. He did not return to England after 1324 but his ideas circulated and were debated in Oxford.

Richard Fitzralph (before 1300–60) studied in Oxford from about 1314 and was a Master of Arts by 1325. He had graduated in theology by 1331. His Fellowship at Balliol ended in resignation in 1325 when it was held that the statutes did not allow theological students to be Fellows. He did the usual required lecturing on the way to his theology qualification, and portions of his work on the *Sentences* and on the Bible survive. He became Chancellor of Oxford from 1332 to 1334.

He learned something of the potential fierceness of Oxford dispute while he was in office as Chancellor, for two long-standing tensions erupted almost simultaneously. The town continued to resent the gown; the students claimed in rejoinder that they were exploited by landlords and others who provided commercial services to the students. Among the scholars the Northerners and the Southerners were also at odds. These 'nations' extended beyond studenthood, to divisions among their seniors. Fitzralph himself was a 'Southerner' because he was Irish and the Irish were allocated to that group. The Northerners said the post Fellowship opportunities were going to the

Southerners, so they marched off to Stamford and threatened to set up a rival university there. Fitzralph proved quite unable to handle the matter and became the subject of spiteful taunting verses.

This does not seem to have prevented his advancement in his career, for a series of preferments followed until he became Archbishop of Armagh in 1346. He had useful patrons but he was also able to make an impression in debate on a visit to the Curia where he gave an opinion on the Last Things – contemporary vexed questions about what was to happen at the end of the world – which made his name. From 1337 to 1344 he was at Avignon again and here he discovered the subject on which he was to make his name as a controversialist, amidst the disputes which were the focus of the papal court at the time. One of his ideas concerned the question whether there could be legitimate sovereignty or 'dominion' if whoever exercised it was not in a state of grace.

He proved an active reformer as Archbishop of Armagh, but his view of the mendicants hardened. They were no longer to be regarded as academic colleagues but a nuisance to those responsible for maintaining church order, since they sought to preach outside the normal framework of jurisdiction and licensing. He became interested in the issue of poverty and in 1350 published his groundbreaking *De Pauperie Salvatoris,* 'On the poverty of the Saviour', utilizing and developing his ideas about dominion. The book stimulated strong interest in Oxford and in London, where the Dean of St. Paul's, Richard Kilvington, another Oxford man, invited Fitzralph to preach a series of sermons from his pulpit in the winter of 1356–7. The impact was great enough to prompt the friars to look for royal support, which they obtained, and Fitzralph found himself in trouble and being tried. The case was never concluded because Fitzralph's death in 1360 interrupted the proceedings. But as with the ideas of Wyclif, debate continued in Oxford, in disputation and treatise and sermon.

John Wyclif

The Wyclif affair made Oxford rediscover the importance of its autonomy. Perhaps the most controversial of all the medieval Oxford theologians, John Wyclif (d.1384) prompted strongly independent reaction in the University when it found that Church and state were minded to tell it what to do about its troublesome scholar.

It is not easy to piece together his early life. It is not even possible to do more than guess when he was born and where he came from, though he was probably a northerner. He first appears as a steward at Merton College for a week in the summer of 1356, so he must have been a Master of Arts by that date because it was not yet a college which admitted undergraduates. But he was apparently only a probationary Fellow and he did not complete his period of probation. In 1360 he appears as Master of Balliol College. He then spent a period in parish ministry (and in indignant search of a better preferment which he might hold as an absentee) before returning to Oxford to study theology and to live in lodgings at the Queen's College, though he was never a Fellow there. Meanwhile, the new foundation of Canterbury College by Simon Islip, Archbishop of Canterbury (d.1366), was running into difficulties. The original conception was that this should be a mixed society, including some monks and some 'seculars' such as Wyclif, and when Wyclif was appointed to be warden in 1365, he took the place previously held by a monk. There was trouble. The new Archbishop Simon Langham (d.1376) tried to change the constitution so that the college should henceforth be for religious only. Wyclif and the seculars naturally resisted this. Litigation followed, lasting several years, and the seculars lost. So here we have examples of the miscellaneous and opportunist trajectories careers in Oxford could follow, their dependence on patronage and the constant danger of disputes arising.

Wyclif was undoubtedly ambitious and probably made a bid to break into court circles and the royal service. He got himself appointed as a member of an embassy to Bruges in 1374 to negotiate with envoys from the papacy about papal taxation. This episode was clearly not a diplomatic success for Wyclif, for he was not asked to join the next episode of these protracted negotiations. Yet some three or four years later Wyclif still spoke of himself as *peculiaris regis clericus* ('special clerk of the king'). But it may have been this – his only experience of the real world and its ways – which prompted the insight on which his intellectual work was henceforth to be based.

He began both to teach and to preach doctrines the state considered to be dangerous. In 1376 he was summoned to answer for his ideas before the King's Council. He was summoned again in 1377 to explain himself to the assembled bishops at St. Paul's on a charge of preaching sedition. The occasion turned into a riot, involving ordinary Londoners in the protest. Here was an early example of the capacity of Oxford to hit the headlines. Wyclif is a little unusual in his apparent reluctance to move between universities and teach for a time at Paris or elsewhere. He stayed at Oxford. Although he left England only once, he was demonstrably influenced by both William of Ockham and Richard Fitzralph who was in Ireland as Archbishop of Armagh or in Avignon bearding the Pope in exile, during the years of Wyclif's maturity.

Wyclif's ideas at this stage seem to have been causing offence on three grounds. He was saying that any priest could release someone from excommunication. It did not need to be the Pope himself. He was claiming that lay authorities could legitimately deprive misbehaving clerics of the temporalities of their benefices. He was saying that lay grants to the Church could be withdrawn for good cause and could not be absolute. So he was putting forward ideas with the potential to interfere with powerful vested interests and it seems they came too close to doing so for comfort. For example, in 'On civil dominion' (*De civili dominio*), Book 2, chapter 1,[64] he reports an argument in favour of the right of the secular powers to use church property in time of need which he heard in the Parliament in London; this probably refers to business in the Parliament of February–March 1371.

Papal censure followed. In May 1377 five Bulls were issued condemning nineteen 'conclusions' alleged to be the work of Wyclif and in fact coming mostly from his *De civili dominio*, Book 1. Three were sent to the Archbishop of Canterbury and the Bishop of London; one was sent to the King. The last was sent to the Vice-Chancellor of Oxford. The Pope wanted these various authorities to conduct an enquiry into Wyclif's teaching. The Pope probably had an 'informant' in Adam Easton (d.1397), a Benedictine monk from Norwich who was at the court of the pope in exile at Avignon at the time, and some of whose active letter-writing to gather evidence against Wyclif is still extant. Easton had studied in Oxford at Gloucester College and had been active in the disputes between friars and monks there. This encounter was the one which had earlier involved Oxford and its theologians in the 'poverty' controversy, and the arguments about the authenticity of the Franciscans' claims to be 'holier than thou'. Easton had, it seems, been greatly exercised by the views of Richard Fitzralph on this theme.

Oxford's reaction showed a sophistication of the sort which was to be characteristic of the University in later generations. It was thought politic to seem to cooperate up to a point in case the Pope withdrew some of the University's privileges. Wyclif was subjected to a form of house arrest but in due course the Vice-Chancellor took his place so that he might be released. Wyclif was not let off so lightly by the authorities of Church or state. He was sent for to appear at Lambeth but again there was riot and disruption, with Londoners breaking into the hearing.

Wyclif was not going to be allowed by Oxford to get away altogether with causing so much disruption, for there were fears that his ideas were poisoning opinion in the University. William Barton, Oxford's

Chancellor, arranged for a committee to condemn those who had been spreading heretical teachings in the University.[65] Included were allegedly misleading opinions on the Eucharist. At this stage in the Middle Ages, unsoundness on the Eucharist usually meant seeming to challenge the doctrine of transubstantiation. This had been framed in the late eleventh and twelfth centuries and it stated that when Jesus' words of consecration were said by the priest ('this is my body'; 'this is my blood') the bread and wine literally and physically became the flesh and blood of Christ. Wyclif later wrote, 'I agreed not to use in future outside the university the terms "the substance of material bread or wine"'.[66]

Wyclif was actually lecturing when he was told of this condemnation of unnamed individuals, which obviously included him. In alarm, he appealed to the King (which implicitly raised dangerous questions about the autonomy of the University). William Courtenay, now Archbishop of Canterbury, instigated active attempts to get Wyclif decisively condemned. The Blackfriars Council met in May 1382, accompanied by a minor earthquake in London, which witnesses took to signify divine disapproval. It condemned 24 of Wyclif's conclusions with varying degrees of human disapproval, ranging from calling them 'heresy' to calling them 'error', and in scope, from his views on the Eucharist to his views on unworthy ministers.

The Chancellor of Oxford, by then Robert Rygge (d.1410), resisted the demand that the condemnation should be published in Oxford. He said that was for the University to decide. Philip Repyngdon (d.1424) was one of Wyclif's supporters and a leader of the contemporary movement of popular religious revolt whose association in the popular mind with Wyclif was one of the reasons the authorities so feared him. Repyngdon preached a sermon in Oxford endorsing Wyclif's teaching on the Eucharist. The Blackfriars Council met again on 12 June and repeated the condemnation, and this time there were signatures from a preponderance of Oxford figures; after some debate the condemnation was published in Oxford on 15 June. Wyclif and his followers were forbidden to preach or teach. On 13 July, a purge of Oxford was ordered and the Chancellor and Proctors were instructed to hunt out Wycliffites and their books and hand them over to the Archbishop.

So eventually Oxford spat Wyclif out. He left for his parish at Lutterworth where he spent the last years of his life miserably taking stock and writing salvos. He had an attack which may have been a stroke, to which he referred when he claimed the Pope had sent for him, that 'one who is paralysed and lame has been ordered to that papal court, but royal prohibition stops him going'.[67] In June 1410, a list of eighteen conclusions from Wyclif's works was condemned by Convocation and teaching from his books was banned.[68]

Themes in these debates were going to be of immense importance once the Reformation began. But there was little or no continuity in the threads which were woven in and out of the discussions of these medieval centuries in Oxford. The Reformation did not begin here or quite yet.

3 OXFORD AND THE INTERFERING TUDORS

Renaissance in Oxford

Thomas More

Thomas More (1478–1535) had a career which, except that he was executed in the end, had a distinctly modern profile. He got his scholarly grounding in Oxford, trained for a profession, moved out into public life, kept up his intellectual interests, was active in the public affairs of the day and returned to engage in the University's affairs again. That pattern of conduct of its graduates has kept Oxford in the thick of things. This has worked both ways, giving it influence and exposing it to the desire on the part of the powerful to control its activities and benefit from its influence.

More began his education at a Latin grammar school in London and then went into service in the household of the Archbishop of Canterbury at Lambeth Palace. There was still a need for patronage to help a young man get on. John Morton the Archbishop was also Lord Chancellor of England, so the young More saw something of the high politics of both Church and State. Politics was becoming intellectually sophisticated under the Tudors – while remaining as brutal and violent as ever – and the royal court became a place for advanced forms of wit as well as sycophancy and intimidation. Morton was greatly impressed by this promising boy and sent him to Oxford in about 1492. The objective was not to get him a degree but to give him a period of preparatory study before he concentrated on qualifying as a lawyer. More spent only two years at Oxford before returning to London to study at the Inns of Court with the intention of becoming a lawyer.

It was not usual, certainly not essential, for a future lawyer to go to either Oxford or Cambridge. The Inns of Court would do as well.[1] The Inns resembled the universities in many ways, for the model of governance and of awarding of degrees they adopted was that of the 'guild'. There was interaction and lively rivalry. Brasenose College was founded by a group which included benchers of the

Middle Temple.[2] Indeed, the early sixteenth century proved to be a golden age for the Inns of Court as educational institutions. The 'third universities' of England granted their degrees by mooting, with 'benchers' – those qualified to sit on the benches and examine the students by their mooting skills – assessing the quality of the students' performance.[3] This was in essence the same process as the examination by disputation conducted in the universities. For a time, the Inns were thus almost London's 'alternative university', though after the Civil War of the seventeenth century, students were left to make arrangements themselves. (Moreover, the teaching of canon law was not allowed in the universities after the Reformation.)

Circles: the coming thing in Renaissance studies

At Oxford, More had an opportunity to encounter Renaissance learning. For a decade, before settling to his lawyer's trade under pressure from his father, More met and corresponded with Desiderius Erasmus (1466–1536), whom he met in Greenwich in 1499, Colet, Linacre, Grocyn, Lily, learned Greek and became a 'Renaissance man'. Erasmus made visits to More. *Moriae Encomium,* the Latin title of Erasmus's *In praise of folly* is a sophisticated compliment to More. Thomas More and the circle of friends and acquaintances of which he was a member brought the Renaissance to England and to Oxford. They demonstrate again and again the scope for independent endeavour and the way scholarly standards were able to be set personally not institutionally in this period of intellectual expansion for Oxford.

Some of More's new friends had been to Italy and they were fired with the idea that the study of Greek and Greek literature, including early Christian writers in Greek who had been largely unknown in the West until now, might well lead to new insights in theology. Indeed, from the end of the Roman Empire, for most of a millennium, the very general lack of knowledge of Greek among Western scholars had largely cut them off from this part of the Christian tradition. Mere scraps of Origen may be glimpsed in Bernard of Clairvaux and quotations from John of Damascus in Thomas Aquinas's *Catena Aurea.* William Grocyn was probably one of the first in early modern Oxford to learn Greek.[4] The attempts by Grosseteste and a few others to master the Greek language had not started a trend. Oxford did not regularly include Greek in the syllabus during the Middle Ages.

Grocyn studied at New College, Oxford, and speedily became a Fellow and tutor to Oxford's future Chancellor, William Warham (c.1450–1532). He had become a Master of Arts in 1474 and lingered in the University, studying theology; this was a lengthy course and one which required him to find 'funding', not unlike someone wanting to embark on a graduate course today. In 1481 the College had given him a living. Other preferments followed. Meanwhile he continued in Oxford, becoming Reader in Divinity at Magdalen College. A 'Reader' was a salaried lecturer. The title derives – as does that of 'lecturer' – from the practice of 'lecturing' on set texts by simply 'reading' them (*lectio*) with the students, commenting line by line. The creation of this kind of paid post was soon to undermine the tradition that Oxford's teachers were its Regent Masters.

Grocyn performed as Respondent in a 'display' disputation held before King Richard III in 1483. This was one of several examples of debate-as-theatrical-performance and we shall see them continuing later in the sixteenth century; their popularity for the purpose of demonstrating impressive academic skills to the monarch suggests that an audience could be expected to enjoy the spectacle. Grocyn was paid for his performance on this occasion.

He may have begun to learn Greek before he went to Italy in 1488, where, accompanied by William Latimer and Thomas Linacre, he studied in Florence with Angelo Poliziano and Demetrius Chalcondyles. The circle of acquaintances and intimates who shared this novel interest included Erasmus, a figure in the European Renaissance influential far beyond Oxford; it also included some of those who were studying Hebrew, such as Johann Reuchlin (1455–1522), also the scholar printers Aldus Manutius and Johan Froben. William Lily (1468?–1522/3) was Grocyn's godson. He began to learn Greek not in Italy but in the Greek world, at Rhodes, on his way back from a pilgrimage to Jerusalem soon after he graduated from Oxford. Correspondence survives, showing that the circle, which also included Thomas More and John Colet (1467–1519), drew from all over Europe, Germany, the Netherlands, France and Italy, as well as England. In England it took in London as well as Oxford and Cambridge.

Grocyn's study trip was comparatively brief. In three years he was back in Oxford, and he felt sufficiently well-equipped to give University lectures in Greek in 1498–9. Desiderius Erasmus visited him, making his first visit to Oxford in 1499. Between 1493 and 1496, Colet studied in Paris and in Italy, and learned Greek, before returning to Oxford where he had been a student himself. While he was out of England, he met Erasmus and Guillaume Budé and he kept up a friendship with Erasmus. There were enthusiasts for the work of Marsilio Ficino in Paris at the time. In 1492 Colet was in Rome, apparently with his parents and his brother Richard. Colet came back to England in the mid-1490s and stayed in Oxford until 1504–5. Colet lectured in Oxford on the Pauline Epistles, which was standard fare for theology lectures; throughout the Middle Ages this had been the most usual book of the Bible to be lectured on after the Psalms. Colet and Erasmus both participated in one or two university disputations during Erasmus' visit. Their correspondence continued, reflecting a lively friendship within a world of talk and argument. They show that circles of intellectuals were able to flourish independently of the university.

Colet's approach was something new, and no one could have thought his lectures merely afterthoughts of the Middle Ages. Thomas More wrote him a letter about 1501 which indicates that Grocyn lectured on the *Celestial Hierarchy* at St. Paul's in London and attracted a substantial audience.[5] Like others of the time, Grocyn believed Ps-Dionysus to have been Paul's convert Dionysius the Areopagite and was therefore studying this fifth-century neoplatonist in conjunction with St. Paul. Grocyn was about to be wrong-footed as a scholar here, and there is some uncertainty whether he was aware that this Dionysius was not the Areopagite,[6] but it all made his approach to the Pauline epistles stimulating for his audience.

Thomas More seems to have studied Greek with Grocyn too, probably in London, where Grocyn appears to have been settled by 1501; Erasmus believed More had learned Greek from Grocyn and Thomas Linacre, and he was a close enough friend of Linacre's to stay with him on his London visit in 1506 and possibly again in 1509–11, before he left for his ill-fated period of lecturing in Cambridge.[7] More saw no reason not to speak as a theologian as well as a lawyer. In 1501, he gave lectures on Augustine's *The city of God* at the invitation of his friend William Grocyn (1449?–1519) in the London Church of St. Laurence, Jewry.

John Colet and the school at St. Paul's

Colet became Dean of St. Paul's at the King's wish in 1505 and founded St. Paul's School in 1509. The school was as much a refounding as a founding, for there had been a cathedral school at St. Paul's from early in the twelfth century, but it had lately declined. Meanwhile, St. Paul's was still, as in Wyclif's time, the pulpit for an ambitious theologian to be heard from.[8]

Thomas Linacre, Oxford and the medical profession

Thomas Linacre (c.1460–1524) was another of Oxford's graduates to become a leading 'Renaissance figure' in England. He was studying in Oxford by 1481, where in 1484 he was elected to a Fellowship at All Souls. He went to Italy in 1487, with companions who were travelling to Rome on the King's business. He himself spent a year or two in Florence learning Greek with tutors available there, Politian and Demetrius Chalcondylas. He made the most of his time in Italy, spending time studying medicine at Padua, where he graduated in 1496. It was during this extended trip that he got to know the scholar-printer Aldus and his circle of students of Greek in Venice. It proved useful to be friendly with a publisher, for Linacre's translation into Latin of the *De sphaera* of Proclus was published in a collection by Aldus. Linacre took the opportunity to buy books, including medical texts in Greek, which were to prove important to his future as an authority on Galen. In 1499 Linacre was in London and tutor to the heir apparent, the King's eldest son Arthur. He was successful enough to be chosen to tutor Arthur's niece Mary for a time in the early 1520s. The group in London with whom he could exchange ideas, with links to and from Oxford, included Colet, More and Grocyn. Linacre's medical skills got him an appointment as royal physician in 1509 and he became personal physician to Princess Mary on her visit to Paris in 1514.

Before he died, Grocyn arranged to provide endowments to fund lectureships in medicine in Oxford and Cambridge, to concentrate on teaching Galen's works. The Mercer's Company was entrusted with the duty to ensure that the founder's wishes were respected. They were chosen because they were already supervising the work of St. Paul's School and could be expected to understand their responsibilities from a humanistic point of view. Oxford medicine needed the stimulus. In the Middle Ages, Medicine was the least numerous of Oxford's faculties and it did not produce graduates who made their names outside England, though 'physicians' graduating from Oxford are visible in the fifteenth century. Although medicine leads on nicely from Natural Philosophy, Roger Bacon had previously had perhaps the best claim to be a major Oxford author on the subject. Bacon's *Antidotarium,* a pharmaceutical work, includes a study of how to slow down the ageing process.[9]

Thomas More and the new King

Thomas More, taking the world as his oyster, entered public service as a Member of Parliament (1504) and became a Justice of the Peace and involved with the London guilds. In 1505 he sent a New Year's gift to Joyeuce Leigh or Lee, sister of the Edward Lee who later became Archbishop of York. She had recently entered the convent of the poor Clares. He went to some trouble to explain to her that this was a translation he had made of the *Life* of Mirandula, which he thinks she will find 'profitable', for it would 'delyte and please ony persone that hath ony meane desire and loue to God', as she has.[10]

The 'Renaissance' enthusiasts of England thought the accession of Henry VIII in 1509 promised great things for their new approach to learning.[11] They were full of optimism that they were beginning a new world. In 1515 More was sent on an embassy to Bruges, but with a very different outcome from Wyclif's abortive venture on the unsuccessful diplomatic mission of which he formed a member in 1374. In Bruges, More met the town clerk, Peter Giles. Their conversations led More to write the *Utopia.* This is a book of a genre just evolving from its medieval form, in which the hero makes a 'moral journey' in a dream, often with a 'guide' – as in Dante's *Divina Commedia.*

More pretends at the beginning of his *Utopia* that he had encountered on his travels a surprisingly highly-educated ship's captain, a man who had travelled in newly-discovered lands and found there communities with sophisticated governments.[12] Outstanding among them was Utopia. Utopia is an island on which many of the features of the rich and interesting life the young More was shaping for himself would be tried out in fictional form and the best way of running things discussed. Perhaps it is not too fanciful to suggest that in More's mind Utopia had a certain amount in common with Oxford as it was now emerging, or at least with the new Oxford-and-London world of intellectual, social and political evolution in which he was having such an interesting time.

Academic advisors to Governments

In the Middle Ages, scholars had been used, though somewhat uneasily, as experts at Councils of the Church. There was a new role for them now as advisers to governments. The discovery in the sixteenth century that the world contained peoples and lands hitherto unheard of, and not predicted or accounted for in the Bible, presented a challenge. The Bible had nothing explicit to say about the way Christians should regard such peoples and how they should be treated. French and Spanish universities were made use of by the civil and ecclesiastical authorities to provide expert consultants, and some lecturers took the opportunity to comment in their lectures on matters of current public interest involving ethical dilemmas, such as the rights and wrongs of Christian Princes appropriating new lands from their earlier inhabitants,[13] the slave trade, new financial arrangements for the expanding world of trade (particularly those involving usury, and the manipulation of prices of commodities for profit).[14] Subtle arguments could be adduced to suggest that native American Indians were somehow not quite human, or if human, not entitled to the same consideration or protection of the same rights as Christian peoples. These they could acquire perhaps if they were colonized by such peoples and reeducated. 'Expert opinion' could be quoted in defence of a position. For example, the seizing of lands was justified by a *junta* of theologians, canonists and civil lawyers meeting with representatives of the monastic orders and royal officials.[15]

The universities were being used in a new way here to provide expert advice to governments as well as the Church on matters which were not easily 'placed' in familiar ethical or cosmological frameworks. Possible justifications could be constructed by deliberately opening up possibilities such as the radical notion that the peoples 'discovered' in the new lands were not fully human and therefore did not have the same rights as Europeans, but building a gateway through which they could join the human race by learning European ways and accepting a European religion. These were prompters to a great deal of reshuffling of assumptions about the taxonomy of knowledge and testing of new methods of thinking.

These academic contributions to discussions about urgent practical and political matters might have seemed to put the universities in a strong position to dictate to Governments how they were to be treated. But the effect was rather the opposite. Governments were moved to try to control these useful repositories of expertise. Individuals such as Thomas More who enjoyed walking the corridors of power as intensely as he delighted in the life of the mind, could play on either side, from the point of view of what was to the advantage of the university.

And so it proved, for in the new reign, More was to position himself adroitly in the circles of influence deriving their power from King Henry VIII. He was to become Speaker of the House of Commons and also Oxford's High Steward. When he returned from Bruges it was rumoured that he was hanging almost too obviously around Westminster, and ingratiating himself with Thomas Wolsey (1471–1530), an immensely powerful figure in the Kingdom from about 1514. More was politically astute and not too proud to make friends with the powerful; he knew where it would pay him to form alliances. Yet More was a far more sophisticated and educated figure than Wolsey and they were not in any ordinary sense friends. He wrote to his daughter, family, familiars in a fluent and affectionate Latin, to Wolsey (as to Thomas Cromwell [1485–1540]), in a formal English, in business-letter style. More became a member of the King's

Council in 1518, along with others from his circle of Renaissance enthusiasts. Among his writings was a strategically-angled *History of Richard III,* designed to present the Tudors who wrested the throne from him in a favourable light;[16] and a *Letter to Oxford,* which makes it plain that he was very far from having lost touch with or interest in the University where he had spent two years as a boy.

More's *Letter to Oxford,* written in 1518, was prompted, he says, by a damaging rumour. It is said that some scholars (*scholastici*) of that *Academia* have formed a group which calls itself the 'Trojans', the members taking nicknames such as 'Priam', 'Hector', 'Paris'. The aim of this society is to mount a resistance to the introduction of the study of Greek language and literature. More had heard about this while he was accompanying the King, who had been staying at Abingdon, and he had been prompted to outrage particularly by the story of a sermon preached by one of the Trojans, who had mounted a pulpit wearing an academic gown with its sheepskin hood, *humeros instratum velleribus,* and thus as one who professes to be learned, and *in medio Academiae* he had made a drunken attack on almost the whole world of letters (*omnes ferme literas debacchari*). At issue, as More well understood, was the very old debate as to whether Christians should engage in secular learning. He refers to the topos of the 'spoiling of the Egyptians'.[17] He takes the opportunity to remind Oxford that Cambridge seems to be getting ahead of them in Greek studies, though Oxford usually outshines its younger sister (*cui vos praelucere semper consuevistis*). Does Oxford really wish to be outdone?[18]

In 1523:

> The commons chose for their speaker sir Tho, More, knt who... in his speech brought in a story of Phormio, the philosopher, who desired Hannibal to come to his lectures, which when he consented to and came, Phormio began to read De Re militari, of chivalry; that as soon as Hannibal heard this, he called the philosopher an arrogant fool, to presume to teach him, who was already master of chivalry and all the arts of war So, says sir Tho. If I should presume to speak before his maj. of learning and the well ordering of govt. or such like matters, the king, who is so deeply learned, such a master of prudence and experience, might say to me as Hannibal to Phormio.[19]

In his elegant and coded way he insisted on freedom of speech for Parliament and defended it as Speaker.

Oxford wrote to its increasingly influential ally More in June 1523 pleading poverty and asking for exemption from taxes, in a series which also includes letters to Wolsey and the King. Benefactors are not as generous as they were and students are hard up, the University complains. The colleges are protected by their statutes from divulging the exact state of their wealth.[20] In 1524 More was invited to become the High Steward of Oxford, almost simultaneously with his acceptance of the same office at Cambridge.

More, never far behind the trend of events, was also interesting himself in the new reforming ideas which were abroad in England by the 1520s. He himself never became a protestant, but it was going to be some years before the taking of sides decisively affected his career prospects, and he began to write on this subject as a defender of the faith as he had always known it. His *Diatribe against Luther*, the *Responsio ad Lutherum*, appeared in 1523.[21] It was written in Latin, in dialogue form between two characters, Baravellus and Lucellus. That marks it as intended for a continental and an educated audience. His theme is that Luther is a pygmy, not a serious threat to religion.[22] More's *A dialogue concerning heresies*, of 1531, however, was written in English and takes the Lutheran threat more seriously. More was quick to identify the key issues of the Reformation debates, as in his *A dialogue concerning heresies*, 1531, and his *Confutation of Tyndale's Answer* written in English (1532?).[23]

His usefulness to Oxford came to an end with his fall from grace at court. He found himself imprisoned and executed in 1535 for failing to support the King in his endeavours to achieve a divorce from Catherine of Aragon. A different More is visible as the author of the *Dialogue of comfort*, a fictional conversation which he set in the context of the invasion of Hungary by the Turks. This device allowed him to explore the implications of political house arrest without too obviously writing about his own situation. He advises those facing such troubles not to hope but to prepare for death:

> And in any sick man it doth more harm than good, by drawing him in time of sickness, with looking and longing for life, from the meditation of death, judgment, heaven, and hell, with which he should beset much of his time – even all his whole life in his best health.

But this is more easily said than done. 'And yet there is (as Tully[24] saith) no man so old but that, for all that, he hopeth yet that he may live one year more, and of a frail folly delighteth to think thereon and comfort himself therewith.' The device of setting the discussion in the context of a Moslem invasion of a Christian country allows him to tiptoe close to his concern that a Christian King is now treating his Christian subjects as infidels:

> Because of the great Turk's enterprise into these parts here, we can scantly talk nor think of anything else than his might and our danger. There falleth so continually before the eyes of our heart a fearful imagination of this terrible thing: his mighty strength and power, his high malice and hatred, and his incomparable cruelty, with robbing, spoiling, burning, and laying waste all the way that his army cometh.[25]

Reformation in Oxford

The ascendancy of Thomas Wolsey

Thomas Wolsey, Archbishop of York from 1514 until his fall in 1530, was baulked of the See of Canterbury by Warham, who held the senior Archbishopric from 1503 to 1532.[26] The consequent rivalry and resentment may have driven some of Wolsey's energetic attempts to stamp his memory on Oxford, where Warham was Chancellor of the University from 1506 until after Wolsey's fall from power. Certainly Warham was very annoyed when his own preferred candidate for the post of the ceremonial officer of deputy Bedell was not chosen by Convocation.[27]

Wolsey's plan for the vast new college which eventually became Christ Church was communicated to the University in 1523, although it took the Cardinal another year to obtain papal permission to destroy or close down the monastic houses and St. Frideswide's, which would have to be got out of its way. He linked his six new lectureships with his new college. The University, somewhat awed, but keen to make the munificence quite secure, wrote him an unwise letter or two imputing to him the credit for acts which veritably make Oxford his own ('your Oxford, and truly yours').[28] To him the University attributes its having risen in status so high that really no one need study anywhere else.[29]

At Wolsey's request the University foolishly (although Warham warned them that it would be dangerous to their future academic independence) invited him to reform the statutes for the Arts faculty.[30] But Wolsey did not find the task easy and by 1524 he had to invite assistance from the University and the task remained uncompleted when he fell in 1529.[31] He wrote his testy letter asking for two suitably qualified men from the University to assist him in drafting the statutes for 'his' lectures and he undertakes to rely on their help and consider the good of the University in the drafting, as long as he finds that their view accord with his own longstanding opinion (*sic nobiscum decrevimus ut quod diu nostro inhesit animo*).[32]

The 'little congregation' and the youthfulness of its members

These exchanges threw up some of the implications of the significant mutations in the governance of the University that had taken place at the end of the Middle Ages. Late fifteenth-century Chancellors often preferred to be non-resident and Vice-Chancellors began to be appointed to deal with the daily business of the University. The structure was roughly like that which obtains in the running of a modern company between the Chairman of the Board and the Chief Executive. Their absence from the scene did not prevent Chancellors taking an active and sometimes interfering interest in its affairs from a distance. The Archbishop of Canterbury, Warham, a graduate of New College and a doctor of canon law, was made Chancellor in 1506 and he remained in office until 1532.

He was an active Chancellor even when he was not in Oxford. The University wrote to him anxiously in January 1509 to ask him to ensure that its privileges were protected.[33] They were writing again about this in November 1509,[34] and he was not the only senior churchman approached for such protections.[35] Between May and July 1509, there was an exchange of letters about the need to look into the behaviour of the keepers of the University Chest, where its assets including important documents about property were kept, since they are said to be nearly empty and this is alleged to be the fault of negligent custodians; there is also a request to overhaul the statutes, though the University explains that this will not be easy and will take some time.[36]

In the Congregation house were held meetings of the Masters in a tradition already some centuries old. But here too there was significant change. The old pattern, which required Bachelors to give lectures under close supervision before they could become Masters, and recently-qualified Masters to lecture for a prescribed period as Regent Masters before they were considered to have completed the requirements for their degrees, had given the University a relatively young direct democracy to conduct its business and to take decisions by debate and voting. It should never be forgotten how young these Regents were (just as the majority of college Fellows were to be young men, recent graduates, until the end of the nineteenth century when Fellows were allowed to marry and did not have to resign their Fellowships and go off to be parish clergy if they wished to do so).

In Oxford as in Cambridge the salaried Professor and Reader arrived with the sixteenth century to do the work of the Master. Posts were created in colleges as well as in the University, as the responsibility for teaching began to be undertaken by the colleges. This began to create a dangerous separation between the work of teaching and the exercise of power. The medieval convention of distinguishing the full assembly of the senior members of the corporation which was the University into 'Regents' and 'Non-Regents' continued. An assembly of the whole body was known as Convocation, though a meeting of that body might also generally be described as a 'congregation'.[37] The Regent Masters, those actually teaching at the time, met formally as the 'Congregation', sometimes known as *congregatio minor* or *congregatio parva*.[38]

Congregation was 'in session' for each term, although it might actually meet several times during the term, rather like the national Parliament. It was summoned by the Chancellor and Proctors when a 'meeting' was needed. Convocation by contrast remained nominally in being from term to term. The meeting place was the University Church of St. Mary's. At meetings of Convocation, each faculty had its allotted place in case it became necessary for Regents with a common interest to confer. When Convocation was summoned the members of Congregation were automatically 'summoned' too, because its members were also members of Convocation, so it was convenient for them to hold their own meeting afterwards. There was a certain amount of dispute and proposed change in the agreed manner of voting, as to whether it was to be by faculties or by individuals.[39] The same applied to debate. The Regents in Arts constituted the largest faculty 'body', and they tended to debate matters as a group. Those who taught the higher degree subjects were older and fewer and even seemed to have been consulted as individuals, a less efficient system when it came to forming a common mind.[40]

The division of powers between the larger and the smaller body gave the making of statutes to Convocation and also major decisions about money (for example large building projects such as the one which permitted the building of the Divinity School) and the use of the property of the University. The Convocation also had the right to take a collective view on behalf of the University on matters of importance, for instance the theology of the King's divorce. To Congregation fell the academic administration, curriculum, timetables, student fees, election of administrative officers. This distribution of tasks was not to be substantially adjusted until the passing of the Oxford and Cambridge Act of 1923 and the statutes of 1926.

When the University wished to express an opinion and Convocation had settled what it thought, the Registrar wrote the agreed letter and it was submitted to Congregation for approval, being sealed – so as to ensure that nothing was rushed or slipped through – only the next day on a separate occasion.[41] The outgoing letters, once approved, were formally sent as from the University only after they had been approved by the Commissary, the Proctors and representatives of the Masters. They also had to be sealed, which had to take place in a separate session, where at least in theory Congregation had to approve their sealing in its name.[42]

Oxford's letter-book, *Epistolae Academicae*[43], was given to the Bodleian Library between 1603 and 1605 and borrowed by the Parliamentary Visitors of 1647, though they returned it to the University. One of the most interesting features is the variation in the description of the corporate body sending or receiving them (*universus Oxoniensium cetus, totus eiusdem gymnasii grex*), making it apparent that both the Congregation of Regent Masters and the Convocation of all graduates were actively involved in the conduct of the business of the University. They seem to amount, taken together, to the Registrar's record.[44]

Town and gown still at loggerheads

The aftermath of the St. Scholastica's Day riot of the fourteenth century lingered in continuing ill-will for generations. Town and gown were active in petitioning Wolsey with complaints against one another. The town said the University had no right to run the market. It complained that the University was exceeding its jurisdiction by arresting townspeople or releasing townspeople arrested by the Mayor and Alderman, or the Justices of the Peace:[45]

> Item the officers of the Vniversitie take felons' goodes.
> Item the free men of the towne be arrested, attached, cited, supended, cursed, banished, wrongfully imprisoned by the commandement of Mr Commissary of the Vniversitie.[46]

The University insisted in its reply that it had not only the right but also the duty to protect its scholars 'where the one partie is the scholler or a scholler's servante' and could choose whether to try the matter in the University's courts or allow the common law to take its course.[47] The problems are real. There are 'conspirases continually and pykinge of quarells day be day in divers sondrie places of the Vuniversitie'.[48] The University wishes to remind Wolsey and the town of the agreements reached after the riot of St. Scholastica's day. The town, indignant, replied that this is all an example of the 'craftie and suttle meanes' by which the University 'have from tyme to tyme devised ways and meanes' to get for themselves privileges long held by the town.[49]

Some Reformation moles

Just as in the Civil War of the seventeenth century, Oxford was going to be Royalist and Cambridge Roundhead (broadly speaking), so in the Reformation of the sixteenth, Oxford remained mainly of the old religion while Cambridge was quickly caught up in the shift to reforming ideas. Ironically, it was partly as a result of Wolsey's own head-hunting activities for scholars from Cambridge to come to Cardinal College, that orthodox Oxford, which Wolsey had chosen as the theologically safer of the two universities in which to establish his College, became infected with some of the ideas which were attracting such interest in Cambridge. John Clarke was one of these. He was found to have been reading the Pauline Epistles to young men in his rooms in 1527. In the same year Thomas Garrett arrived from London bringing copies of Tyndale's New Testament in English and various 'Lutheran' publications. Wolsey gave orders that the commissary, John Cottisford, should have him arrested and he was found to be associating with twenty-two suspects,[50] most of them young (*homunciones, tyrones*),[51] the bulk of them from Cardinal College. The Cardinal College miscreants were imprisoned and the host of books (*libros complures*) found hidden[52] were seized.

Wolsey wrote back to say how concerned he was, for he had always regarded Oxford as a bastion of orthodoxy. He wanted the suspects imprisoned, including any who have been let out, and he ordered that they be questioned to extract everything which could be got out of them, on pain of excommunication.[53] The University inquired of the Bishop of Lincoln whether it was to send all the heretics to the Cardinal or just the older ones, keeping the younger ones, who are full of remorse, in Oxford. It stressed that John Clarke is a Cambridge man who has only recently come to Oxford.[54] The Bishop told the University to concentrate on maintaining the orthodoxy of the University.[55]

Oxford mishandles its part in the King's divorce

Wolsey left his mark on the appearance of Oxford. James Ingram, in his 1841 *Memorials of Pembroke College, Oxford*,[56] says that the area round St. Aldate's Church used to be full of 'decayed tenements', which were demolished by Wolsey before 'his sudden fall suspended all his great designs'. In the 1530s, things changed radically for Oxford with the fall of Wolsey, in ways which went far beyond an interrupted building project, however grandiose. It learned the hard way how unwise it was to have trusted so much to such a patron. The building of Cardinal College was not yet complete and the funding for the lectureships now looked uncertain. Moreover, future relations with the court seemed likely to be strained.

Seeking a divorce from Catherine of Aragon, in the hope that a new wife might bear him a son, Henry VIII asked Cambridge for a view on the validity of his marriage. Cambridge obliged with the opinion he wanted. Archbishop Warham almost simultaneously asked Oxford to do the same. Oxford found that it could not agree with itself. Attempts were made to arrange that the more senior, the theologians with their higher degrees, should do the job, excluding the Regent Masters, the young, and comparatively recent Arts graduates. The struggle raised with a new sharpness the question who had authority to make representations on behalf of the University. Warham the Chancellor advised the University to present a united front and appear unanimous,[57] with the more junior giving way if necessary to the more senior. The King, irritated, wrote to express his displeasure that Regent Masters in the Arts should have been intruding their own opinions rather than leaving it to the experts, the theologians.[58] He said that he expected the seniors to control the juniors, to 'conduce and frame the saide yonge personnes into good ordre and conformitie, as it becommythe you to doo'. He does not think the 'youthe' of the University should 'playe maistres, as they begynne to do'. Moreover, he reminds them that Cambridge has prepared and delivered its answer in a 'farre shorter tyme'.[59] A worried Warham followed with a letter urging them to haste, writing in English, 'for I must make you understand what I have to say', 'as ye intende the contynuall preservation of the commyn weale of that universitie in tyme to cume' (Letter 197a, p.274). He too urged that the Masters of Arts should be taught obedience and required to accept a report made on their behalf.

Royal interference grows

The King decided that Oxford must be brought under better control. Wolsey's charter already purported to confirm the University's existing medieval privileges in the form of a royal grant.[60] The way was open for the King to assert himself. Warham died in 1532 and was replaced by the Bishop of Lincoln, at the King's insistence.[61] He told the Regents how he wished them to vote and they duly voted. In a town-gown dispute in 1532, the University as well as the town was persuaded to surrender their privileges as well as their charters to the Crown, for their better 'protection'. This was politically naïve, for it put

Thomas Cromwell, Henry's chief officer of state from 1532 to 1540, in a position to play town off against gown, and the control of the University was what the Government was after:

> After these troubles ... between the University and Town, concerning divers Libertie and Privileges, the report of which coming to the King's hearing, Instructions were sent down from him to make a surrender of their Liberties.[62]

Liberties not only needed to be renewed to keep them fresh, but could be withdrawn.

Thomas Cromwell sends in the Visitors (1535)

By 1532, Thomas Cromwell was taking charge at court, and Thomas More was no longer able to protect the University by offering Oxford his diplomatic support. Cromwell sent Visitors to Oxford in 1535, in the persons of Richard Layton and John Tregonwell. They were intrusive. They saw no reason to refrain from imposing requirements about academic activities. The Visitors removed the requirement for theology students to study Peter Lombard's *Sentences* in favour of a new 'protestant' study of the Scriptures based on the Greek and Hebrew text.[63] They also abolished the study of canon law. College libraries were invaded and books destroyed if they were deemed 'scholastic'.[64] (However, this had a positive side, for it seems to have encouraged colleges to buy in the books of the new humanist learning, particularly the Greek one.)

The Visitors set up new public 'college lecture' series at the richer colleges, which could afford to finance them.[65] Wolsey had launched this idea of sponsored public lectures as Cardinal, providing funding for a salary and establishing terms which allowed the 'college' lecture to be open to the wider University audience. In his own new Cardinal College he had ambitious schemes for public professors to be carried on the foundation, with costs of residence and food and clothing as well as a salary paid out of endowments. The professors were to undertake not to intervene in college affairs and provision was made for depriving them of office if they neglected their duties or behaved inappropriately. A theology professor was to give his lectures between 9.00 and 10.00 and to lecture either on Scripture or on the theology of Scotus, because Scotus was currently fashionable as a reliable source for those anxious to scotch heresies. There was here the germ of what was to become the tutorial system, with its balance of lectures and regular 'required work' by students. The idea was that the lecturers should set their students 'themes' each week and test them regularly.

Other benefactors creating such new posts were no less interventionist in the arrangements proposed for making appointments and for determining the content of the teaching to be undertaken by the appointees. There was none of the sort of talk which was heard in Oxford over the arrangements for the Said Business School.

Wolsey's fall put an end to his particular plans, but not to the recognition by the State that it had (in its own view) a proper interest in ensuring that there was adequate provision of public lectures in the University. The series of Regius Professorships established by Henry VIII sought to provide Oxford and Cambridge with salaried senior teachers in the higher subjects.[66] All this may have helped further to erode the 'Regent Masters' system of obligatory lecturing by recent graduates which had obtained from early in the history of the University. It meant that instead of each new graduate Master spending a required period lecturing to the next generation of students and presiding over the disputations at which they practised their skills of argument, responsibility for organizing teaching would move to the emerging colleges. The centre of gravity of the University would shift with this change. The corporation of Masters would continue to exist and to take decisions as a *universitas*, but wealth and power and state approval was now beginning to lie with the colleges.

Graduation, inception, incorporation

This separation of degree and post did not undermine the framework of the award of degrees. The conventional distinction of graduation and inception continued despite the progressive shift away from the old 'Regent Masters' system to the creation of salaried posts for lecturers and readers and professors.[67] Those proceeding to a Bachelor's degree in Arts were still said in the sixteenth-century record to 'graduate' (*graduare*), that is, climb a rung of the ladder, while Masters 'incept' (*incipere*) or begin as full members of the corporation and of its governance arrangements, and potential teachers.[68] The higher degrees entitled the holder to call himself *doctor* or *professor* in the case of theology. The academic title became the leading title in the way a graduate described himself, even when the graduate was a monk or a friar. As well as provisions for incorporation, there were arrangements for undergraduates to 'transfer credit' from work in other universities and have it counted towards their Oxford degrees.[69]

The queen of the sciences: the theology syllabus old and new

Medieval theology had always been a 'higher degree' subject, not to be entered upon by boys, at least not the still-youthful students of Arts;

and of the three traditionally available, it had been uncontested chief. Corpus Christi College, founded in 1517, had its theological *lector* 'on the foundation'. By the sixteenth century, most colleges required their resident MAs to join a higher Faculty, normally Theology, and continue to study, as a condition of continuing to hold their Fellowships once they had completed the required period of lecturing on obtaining their MAs. This requirement seems to have led to a certain amount of chopping and changing in the choice of specialist study. Thomas Mosgroff of Merton lectured in Astronomy (1517) and was then Public Reader in Medicine (1523–4). John Throwley of Canterbury College was a Bachelor of Theology in 1524 and, perhaps seeking a career change in the context of the Reformation upheavals, was also lecturing in Medicine. This kind of thing had precedent in the Middle Ages, when it was not uncommon for students to move among the higher degree subjects in a similar way. The need to concentrate specialist provision was glanced at by the Visitors of 1549, who seem to have made an effort to persuade All Souls and New College to exchange some of their Fellows so that All Souls might specialize in civil law in future, but this seems not to have been pursued once the Visitors had left. Oxford had practised skills in biding its time and waiting out external requirements for change.

Despite the modernizing insistences of the 1535 Visitors, the theology course formally remained much as it had been in the Middle Ages until 1549. It lasted seven years. Its syllabus, as everywhere in Europe since the early thirteenth century, concentrated on the Bible and Peter Lombard's *Sentences*, which provided a textbook of systematic theology, geared to reliance on extracts from the Latin Fathers. As their courses progressed, these extremely 'mature students' were allowed to practise some of the skills they would need as academic theologians, to participate in disputations (formal degree exercises); to preach Latin sermons; to lecture on the *Sentences* and finally to lecture on Scripture itself. They were also subject to what would now be thought of as 'fitness to practise' regulations, in that they had to show themselves to be of good character by the testimony of three doctors of theology before they could incept as doctors themselves.

Consequences for the colleges

Possibly spurred to it by 'philanthropic' rivalry with Thomas Pope, who founded Trinity College in the same year, Sir Thomas White (1492–1567) founded St. John's College in 1555. His heart is buried in the chapel. White's plan was to educate a new generation of Roman

Catholic clergy to serve the Church which was being restored by Queen Mary. This scheme was quickly frustrated by her death in 1558, but the College continued and adapted and proved an acceptable Tudor foundation even when Mary's sister Elizabeth came to the throne and reversed her sister's policies.

The early statutes of St. John's had a repressive air. There was to be no football in the quadrangles. The Fellows were not to keep singing birds (*aves cantatrices*) and students were not to sing in their rooms. Serious conversation was permitted in the appropriate place and at the right time, but students were to talk quietly. No one was to play cards (and certainly there was to be no gambling).[70] The porter acted as barber and no one was to wear long hair or an elaborate beard.[71]

The pattern of life for students was to be plain and rigorous. They are to be: 'content with a penny piece of beef between four, having a pottage made of the same beef with salt and oatmeal and nothing else'.[72] Echoes of the monastic life sound in the custom of having improving readings at meal-times:[73]

> After their dinner they are reading or learning until five in the evening, when they have supper not better than their dinner, immediately after which they go to reasoning in problems or to some other study till nine or ten; then, being without fire, are fain to walk or run up and down for half an hour to get a heat in their feet, when they go to bed.[74]

Sleeping arrangements at St. John's in the late sixteenth century might now raise an eyebrow but they reflected the custom of the time in not assuming that sleepers would necessarily have beds to themselves. Separate beds were permitted only to those over 16. Each Fellow was to sleep with a chorister or scholar, if he so wished, in order to ensure that the young had someone to care for them and also to provide the Fellows with convenient servants. On the other hand, women were not to be admitted within the College, with the possible exception of a member's mother or sister (but even she was not to stay long).[75]

To contemporaries, the questions probably of greatest overarching importance do not concern these domestic arrangements (though they would have thought the discipline essential) but the arrangements for the governance of the colleges. Today Oxford and Cambridge colleges remain autonomous charitable corporations but the universities allow them to admit students (which they undertake to matriculate as members of the University), as well as to house them and to teach them; for their part, the universities set the curriculum, offer 'courses' and grant the degrees.[76] The distribution of functions between colleges and University was at a crucial stage of evolution in Oxford in the early sixteenth century. The modern style of collegiate life in which the colleges take partial responsibility for the teaching of undergraduates had begun to evolve in Oxford at the end of the Middle Ages, for example, with the foundation of New College in 1379. New College added an undergraduate population to the graduate Fellows of which other, older colleges had been formed. The idea of having undergraduates 'on the foundation' had a precedent at Winchester, which was the grammar school of New College's founder, William of Wykeham.[77] When Magdalen College was founded in 1458 by William of Waynflete, Bishop of Winchester, and successor of William of Wykeham, it too made provision from the first to admit first-degree students. Magdalen 'Demys' were scholars who counted as 'half' Fellows. They were to study poetry, grammar, logic and sophistry. There was to be a feeder school on the spot in the form of Magdalen College School.

With the admission to the colleges of these sometimes very young students came fresh responsibilities. A new system began to involve providing for student teaching, with 'college' lectures supplementing the University ones. College 'repetitions' began to be held. These took place in the afternoons and required the students to rehearse what they had heard in the morning. So college tuition became important and some of the 'senior' members of the colleges became, perforce, teachers and tutors to boys who might be only in their early or mid-teens. This was happening at the same time as the old Regent Master teaching framework was being undermined by the arrival of salaried lecturers and Readers and Professors, paid by a college or the University and when the long-standing requirements to give a period of lecturing in partial fulfilment of the requirements for a degree were not always being enforced.

The new-style colleges, if they were to survive better than the medieval halls, would need endowments. Until 1520s Oxford college endowments tended to be like those which would be provided at the foundation of a religious house, such as manors, lands, rectories, houses and sometimes capital for buildings for the new college.[78] This proved to be a danger when the King of England turned against the monasteries and their like. Henry VIII threatened to seize the colleges' endowments.[79] An Act for the Dissolution of Colleges[80] empowered the King to enter into all Colleges and have all their possessions vested in him.[81]

The Vice-Chancellor (1547–52) and Dean of Christ Church, Richard Cox, was anxious to know more about what this would mean and wrote urgent letters. The King promised the 'heads of house' that they should keep their houses and lands, but soon after, he died. The first Parliament of Edward VII November 1547 passed a new Chantries Act, with a preamble saying that the intention was to give the King, 'the power of converting the foundations' which came under the Act, 'to good and godly uses as in erecting of Grammar Schools, the further augmenting of the Universities,' and better provision for the poor and needy, leaving some over for the Exchequer.[82]

The sixteenth century was a period of considerable enlargement of the stock of colleges. Both Oxford and Cambridge brought forth new colleges with a strong sense of their collegiate identity and this decisively shaped the future of both 'collegiate universities'. That this route of development was not inevitable is clear from the history of the early Inns of Court in England. A shadowy *studium* preceded the inns where law students practised their trade by mooting. The degree was taken by the act of mooting as in the academic disputation.[83] Yet these were not and did not become universities:

> Nor were the inns founded in the way that colleges were founded, with royal charters and licences to be preserved, and benefactors to remember in prayer. They have never been incorporated, and they did not until the sixteenth and seventeenth centuries own freehold property.[84]

Brasenose and Corpus Christi

In 1500 there were ten Oxford colleges and by the beginning of the Henrician reformation there were thirteen. Brasenose College was the first of the new sixteenth-century creations. It was founded in 1509 by William Smith and Richard Sutton, absorbing up to ten of the existing small halls for students which stood on its site. Brasenose was regarded as a rather conservative foundation, whereas its rival Corpus Christi College was seen as forward-looking. There was even rivalry between the builders of the two colleges, who came to blows in 1512 and 1514.[85]

Corpus Christi College was founded with more ambitious intellectual pretensions by Richard Fox. Richard Fox was by no means exclusively an Oxford man. In 1500 he was elected Chancellor of Cambridge and in 1507 he became Master of Pembroke Hall, forerunner of Pembroke College, Cambridge. Lady Margaret Beaufort regarded him sufficiently highly to make him one of her executors and he was actively involved with John Fisher in establishing St. John's College, Cambridge. In such circumstances the evolution of the college life of the two universities was bound to run in tandem. Fox acquired land from Merton College in 1511 and in 1516 he got a licence from the King to establish his college. He evidently took a continuing interest in it, for the statutes were revised and he signed the new version with a shaky hand a few months before his death in 1528.[86]

This was a founder with a strong personal interest in learning. The copy of Lorenzo Valla's *Elegantiae* he gave to the library had been his own and seems to have been in his possession since his student days in Paris. He had made neat notes in it.[87] His great innovation in the Corpus Statutes was to set up a *lector publicus* or 'reader' in Greek, whose lectures were to be open to the whole University. The founder called his college a 'beehive' and he certainly expected this lecturer to be busy. He was to lecture on Mondays, Wednesdays and Fridays through the year on the Greek Grammarians (a subject on which Erasmus had found it singularly difficult to hold an audience in Cambridge). On Tuesdays, Thursdays and Saturdays, throughout the year, he was to lecture on Greek poets and playwrights (Aristophanes, Theocritus, Euripides, Sophocles, Pindar, Hesiod) and on orators, historians and philosophers (Demosthenes, Thucidydes, Aristotle, Theophrastus, Plutarch). In the vacations, this heavily-loaded lecturer was to give teaching in Greek to every member of the college who was not yet an MA. Another lector or *Professor artium humanitatis* was to attend to the quality of the Latin and ensure that none of the Corpus students is guilty of barbarisms. For the students too there were many requirements, to attend disputations and other exercises. Vacations, it seems, were no such thing.

Fox's principal stated reason for the foundation was to provide support for the study of theology. There was also a theological *lector* whose duties were to give daily lectures on Old and New Testaments, these lectures to be based on the Greek and Latin Fathers and not on the *glossa ordinaria* and its later developments in Hugh of St. Cher (c.1200–63) and Nicholas of Lyre (c.1270–1349).

Power and wealth and Christ Church envy

Thomas Wolsey had had immensely ambitious plans for his proposed Cardinal College in Oxford, which he began to implement in 1525. The funding was easily arranged. He used the opportunity to transfer money released by the dissolution of Wallingford Priory, and suppressed the ancient abbey of St. Frideswide in Oxford so as to take over its lands. He started to look about him for leading scholars to 'head-hunt' and made some overtures. Wolsey's fall in 1529 meant that his college was never completed, but the King did not waste the opportunity to take over his work. He suppressed Wolsey's foundation and refounded it as his own College in 1532, calling it King Henry VIII's College. It kept that name for a time, until in 1546 the King, now, as he saw it, liberated from the Church of Rome, refounded it once more as Christ Church and made its chapel the cathedral of the new diocese of Oxford. He treated Cambridge similarly, founding Trinity College there in the same year. Christ Church became the object of some envy and resentment in sixteenth-century Oxford because of its wealth and influence. In the seventeenth and eighteenth centuries High Anglicanism at Christ Church was strongly marked by fears that anything less would hand the country over to the dogs, in the form of social reformers, levellers, dissenters and other left-wing undesirables.

Another inspection: Edward VI goes 'visiting'

Richard Cox (1500–81) became Oxford's Chancellor at the beginning of the reign of Edward VI. In 1545 a series of appointments had culminated in his being made Dean of the new cathedral which was to become part of Christ Church. He had been one of the Cambridge crowd whom Wolsey had succeeded in attracting to Cardinal College, and after getting into trouble for his reforming opinions, and spending some time teaching at Eton, he had returned to Cambridge in 1535. Anthony Wood, who was hostile to Cox, says that Cox was 'so busy in placing his friends in Colleges, that though they were uncapable and altogether unfit for Scholarships and Fellowships, yet if he did but utter his mind, none dared to deny him'.[88] But he was not so busy in Oxford as to prevent him becoming a valued contributor to the changing views of royal circles. He was Edward's tutor from about 1543, an appropriate choice since in his years at Eton he had shown himself an imaginative and successful teacher. So all looked fair for Oxford.

The task Richard Cox now faced in Oxford was to make the University, hitherto of mixed opinions, into a 'Protestant Academy'. It was convenient that, disturbed by the Interim 'settlement' recently put out by the German Emperor, several leading protestant scholars from continental Europe were keen to come to England. The Diet of Ratisbon of 1541 had concluded what proved to be only an interim Interim, seeking to bring about a pause in the protestantizing of Europe while everyone took stock. In 1548 a further Diet at Augsburg resulted in another Imperial decree, instructing protestants to return to Roman Catholic beliefs and practices. The protestants objected and drew up a counter document, in whose drafting Melanchthon had a leading part, and which was adopted by the electorate of Saxony and came to be known as the Leipzig Interim. This made use of the notion of *adiaphora,* or inessentials, to provide a list of points conscientious protestants might regard as things indifferent. That device did not mollify everyone, however.

'Melancton's coming was expected, but he not appearing' in Oxford,[89] substitutes were sought. Peter Martyr arrived in 1548 to take over the professorial lecturing when Richard Smith was put out of the Regius Chair of Theology; and at Cox's instigation eleven other protestant scholars from Switzerland came too. Peter Martyr, having spent a period on arrival in England 'with the Archbishop in his house at Lambeth'[90] proved to be a considerable influence in Oxford,[91] where it was fully understood that as Regius Professor he lectured on the King's authority. He presided over weekly disputations in Christ Church and fortnightly ones in the University, held after 1549.[92] He was energetic in giving private talks (sermons or lectures) in his own rooms at which John Jewel (1522–71), the future bishop of Salisbury, was sometimes present. This protestantizing of the universities was not seen as an exclusively Oxford project. 'You ... ought to come over ... you are very much wanted in these universities,' Martyr wrote to Bucer in January 1549,[93] and Bucer came, but to Cambridge not Oxford.[94]

Cambridge proved more compliant than Oxford. The attempt to force Oxford's hand ran into difficulties from the outset. 'It being now thought high time to make a Reformation of the University', letters were sent to the colleges instructing them to 'make no Election of Head, Fellow, Scholar or of other place within their Coll. Or attempt any other Act'. They regarded this as unreasonable 'least the decay of Learning should follow' if posts were left vacant.[95]

John Ab Ulmis wrote to Heinrich Bullinger from Oxford on Ascension Day 1548 to described the changes he already observed in England:

> 'The mass ... is shaken ... the images too are extirpated root and branch in every part of England', clergy are allowed to marry and 'it has been proved by Peter Martyr to the great satisfaction [of his hearers] ... that there is no other purgatory than the cross to which we wretched beings are exposed in this life ... he speaks with caution and prudence ... with respect to the real presence, so as not to seem to incline either to your opinion or to that of Luther'.[96]

Edward VI and the Visitation of 1548–9

> The K. or Lord Protector and his Council having the year before made an enquiry into the state of the University and finding it altogether, or at least for the most part out of order, as they pretended ... resolved to have it visited.[97]

In 1548 the King appointed the royal Visitors who were to inspect both universities. Cox was one of those appointed for Oxford, together with John Dudley, Earl of Warwick Viscount Lisle, Chamberlain of England; Henry Holbech, Bishop of Lincoln; Nicholas Heath, Bishop of Worcester and others.[98] Edward VI, however precocious, was still a little boy when he became King. His 'agenda' was that of his advisors.

The Visitors arrived in Oxford and met the University in its University Church of St. Mary's on 24 May 1549, where everyone heard a sermon preached by Peter Martyr. Then the Visitors' Commission was read, 'most of the University being then present', but no more could be done until the proposed set-piece disputation on the Eucharist had been held.[99]

The importance of the wider debate on the Eucharist

The Eucharist was the sacrament about which fiercest controversy raged during the Reformation. This was because continental reformers had maintained that the Church had gone seriously astray in regarding to the celebration of the Last Supper as a 'sacrifice', for that, they said, was to diminish the completeness of the sacrifice Christ had made when he was crucified. It was also the strong contention of the reformers that the doctrine of transubstantiation was false. In Peter Martyr's *The common places* (1583), something of the reach of the topics it was found to raise and the passion with which they were debated may be glimpsed.[100] Peter Martyr was writing to Martin Bucer from Oxford in December 1548 concerning his worries about the pervasive disputatiousness on the Eucharist he found in Oxford ('every corner is full of it') and the 'most obstinate pertinacity of the friends of popery'.[101]

Martyr was in discussion with Cranmer on the subject, while Cranmer was crafting his liturgical reforms:

> And this is the onelie way that the scripture alloweth and knoweth of eating the bodie, and drinking the bloud of the Lord, namlie, when we apprehend by a constant and firme faith, that Iesus the sonne of God our Lord and sauiour gaue his body vpon the Crosse, and shed his bloud for vs. Herein standeth the whole power and reason of this meate and of this

> drinke; whereunto our faith is stirred up and kindled... Christ gaue in the supper, bread and wine for signes, the which by his institution and his wordes are made sacraments, that is to wit instruments, whereby the holy Ghost stirreth up faith in our mindes, that by the same faith we may be spiritually, but yet truely nourished and sustained with his bodie and blood.

The debates about transubstantiation gave way in part to debates about justification in 1550 and Martyr wrote to Bucer in September 1550 remarking that he had taken part in a discussion recently about different degrees of reward for the blessed.[102]

Some Heads of House in Oxford forbade their scholars to go to Peter Martyr's lectures on the Eucharist. Others, especially Richard Smith, a great attender of the lectures, could not rest until they had had the chance to refute what he said in a public disputation. John Jewel (1522–71) went to Oxford at the age of 13, studying first at Merton and then along the street at Corpus Christi College. John Parkhurst was his tutor at Merton and encouraged him to take an interest in the new humanist learning. By 1548 Jewel was Reader in rhetoric and a popular lecturer. Jewel formed a friendship with Peter Martyr after he had been invited by Thomas Cranmer to come to England to be Regius Professor of Divinity at Oxford and took notes of the debate on the Eucharist.[103]

Some of Peter Martyr's friends went to warn him not to attempt to lecture for 'his adversaries were prepared to encounter him rather with arms than arguments'. Bravely, he went forth, to tell his audience that he was perfectly willing to 'frame himself for a disputation', and then to lecture calmly as usual, despite the noisy protests, and 'though the noise of the Juniors and Lay-people of the adverse party was much, yet he finished his lecture in that sort, that there was little change of countenance, stammering of speech, or faltering of tongue'.[104]

The lynch-mob atmosphere seriously threatened a disturbance of the peace. Peter Martyr insisted that a formal disputation would need to be properly set up and arranged. Richard Smith mockingly said that after lecturing on the subject so much he should be able to dispute on the spot and 'proposed one or two arguments' which he 'urged to the quick'. 'Martyr drew back, and told them that he could not nor would not undertake such a weighty matter without the King's Leave'; the younger students and the 'vulgar sort' of ordinary townspeople 'began to make a tumult' and the Vice-Chancellor had to step in, declare that a proper disputation would be arranged and get the Bedells to 'remove the multitude', leading Peter Martyr off to his own house to ensure his safety. There too went Smith, and the other leading combatants went too and there was a lengthy discussion about the content of the proposed disputation.[105] It was decided in the end that 'the whole manage of it was, by the consent of both parties, to be referred to the King's Council',[106] and the King's Council referred it to the forthcoming Visitation of Oxford, to be held when the Visitors came. The thing was a challenge to a duel, as the notice of 'provocation' made plain when it was eventually put up on the doors of St. Mary's Church.[107] The duel was to be about transubstantiation.

Between 28 May and 1 June, the debate took place. Its official purpose was to try to eradicate the doctrine of transubstantiation in Oxford, with Peter Martyr and Cox supporting that objective. It is not clear that anyone changed his belief as a consequence but the Visitors were able to see that Oxford was taking seriously its duty to establish a protestant position. Cox perhaps had it in mind that the whole set-piece disputation would be more decorous and less contentious if it had to be conducted in the presence of the Visitors.

John Ab Ulmis wrote again in August 1549 (and many times between) to tell Bullinger that

> there has been a sharp disputation in Oxford respecting the eucharist, where the subject was made so clear and easy of comprehension, in the very presence of the king's commissioners, that any person of ordinary capacity might easily understand on which side the truth lay, and detect the absurdities of our opponents.[108]

And he told Bullinger in August 1549 that 'the Oxfordshire papists are at last reduced to order, many of them having been apprehended, and some gibbeted, and their heads fastened to the walls.[109]

New statutes for Oxford

On 4 June the Visitors met again in St. Mary's Church and 'put' new statutes in the place of the University's old ones:

> and therein allowed more liberty to all. Especially the Juniors, and commanded that they be religiously observed of all, whereby not only the whole frame of the Government was altered, but most of the customs relating to religion changed.[110]

This set the tone before the Visitors began the rounds of the colleges. Wood deplores the ejecting of old members and their replacement with 'strict Calvinists'. At Christ Church, Richard Cox and Peter Martyr, being married, set an example other canons followed, and 'women and idle huswifes' were allowed with their 'bawling children', which so annoyed the Catholics that they called them 'whoores'. The 'weekly corrections of the youth in every House of Learning' came to an end, to the great detriment of Education.[111]

Colleges seem to have been put under pressure to use some of their resources to purchase suitably protestant books for their collections. These inspectors were also keen to supervise closely the content of the books Oxford's students and scholars were exposed to. This led to book-burnings. It should not be taken for granted that books were always seen as sacrosanct; valuable, yes, but not objects of a respect based on any belief that unpopular opinion must be respected. Wood records with horror how:

> The antient Libraries, a glory to the University, as containing among them many rarities ... were by them or their appointment rifled. Many MSS, guilty of no ither superstition than red letters in their fronts or titles, were either condemned to the fire or jakes. Others also that treated of controversial or scholastical divinity were let loose from their chaines, and given away or sold to Mechanicks for sevile uses ... sure I am that such books wherein appeared Angles, or Mathematical diagrams, were thought sufficient to be destroyed, because accounted Popish, or diabolical, or both.[112]

This applied to the 'public library', that is the University's own, and also to those of the colleges, from which were thrown out the works of scholastic authors:

> From Merton Col. Library a cart load of MSS and above were taken away ... at the disposal of certain ignorant and zealous coxcombs.[113]
>
> What this generation did with scorn throw aside, the following did gather up with care.[114]

Academic freedom is a comparatively modern idea. Matthew Parker (1504–75) describes with regret the loss of the great ancient libraries at Alexandria and Constantinople and Rome and more recently those lost with the dissolution of the monasteries:

> What other great Libraries have there been consumed, but of late Dayes? And what Libraries have of old throughout this realme, almost in every Abby of the same, been destroyed at sundry Ages, besides the loss of other Mens private Studies, it were too long to reherse.[115]

Parker, who was one of the Cambridge scholars Wolsey had unsuccessfully tried to 'head-hunt' for his new college, did not necessarily think that books should be preserved at any cost. He approved of the destruction of books if that would encourage the reading of Scripture instead. Medieval books were deliberately destroyed, those of Duns Scotus, for example,[116] and Edward VI's Act of 1550 against Superstitious Books and Images destroyed more, especially liturgical books, by burning or defacing. Duke Humfrey gave Oxford two hundred books. Only two survived the Reformation.[117] These destructions were not the only ones to which Oxford was party. Wyclif's books were burned in 1410, so thoroughly that most of the texts have come down in copies preserved in manuscripts carried off to Hussite Bohemia.[118] Some of Milton's writings were to be burned in the late seventeenth century.[119]

At the end of the Visitation the University was presented with its new statutes by the Bishop of Lincoln, Richard Cox (who seems to have drafted them), Morrison and Nevison. They were intended to effect an interim change in the curriculum requirements, laying stress on Greek and Hebrew studies and removing from the University the requirement to be bound by older statutes made in 'popish' times.

So the Statutes of Edward VI (1549) were academically intrusive. They stipulate times for lectures in each subject and list set books. The lecturer (*lector*) in Philosophy is to lecture publicly on Aristotle's *Problemata, Moralia, Politica* and on Pliny or Plato; the lecturer in Medicine is to lecture on Hippocrates or Galen; the Mathematics professor 'if he teaches cosmography' must use such authors as Pliny, Strabo or Ptolemy; the Greek lecturer should choose Homer, Demosthenes, Isocrates, Euripides, 'or another ancient author' and also teach the Greek language; while the Hebrew lecturer is to teach the grammar of the language and the Old Testament. The students who have just arrived from their elementary grammatical studies (*a ludo literario*) should first study mathematics, maintaining a modified version of the medieval *quadrivium*.[120]

The Visitors were further engaged in close supervision of the spiritual life of the University. They were eager to ensure that worship in the University and its Colleges would henceforth be decidedly protestant, and that the theological education of students should be encouraged, even if they were not studying theology for a higher degree. Peter Martyr wrote to Bullinger in June 1550:

> a new burden has been imposed on this university by laws lately enacted by the king's majesty. For it is decreed that

> public disputations upon theological subjects should be held frequently, that is, every alternate week, at which I am required to be present and to preside, then, in the king's college, where I reside, theological disputations are held every week, which, inasmuch as all persons are freely admitted to hear them, may in like manner be called public; and over these I am appointed moderator, as over the others. I have therefore a continual struggle with my adversaries, who are indeed most obstinate.[121]

Martyr complained to Bullinger in January 1551, of 'minds hardened against the truth'[122] He wrote about getting something printed at Zurich and the need for careful proof-correction by someone who could correct Greek and Hebrew and was 'godly' (Oxford, April 1551).[123]

Clever evasions of requirements were to be expected, for example, the New College Fellows claimed that they could not afford to replace their coloured glass with plain.[124] Yet the effect on the morale of the University is colourfully described by Wood:

> 'The scholars were reduced to an inconsiderable number ... they choosing rather to undergo misery elsewhere, than lay at the mercy of such whom they accounted no better than mad men', and parents no longer wanted to send their sons to the universities.[125]

Mary Tudor's Visitors: the volte-face

Despite considerable Government pressure and intimidation, including the imprisonment of some academics and interference in colleges in the form of requirements to remove Fellows of unacceptable opinions,[126] Oxford's theological conservatives were resistant to change as prescribed by Edward's Visitors. But Edward died, and Mary's accession in 1553 appeared to vindicate their resistance. She favoured Oxford and provided it with additional funding so that it might be valiant in the defence of the 'old religion'. Christ Church's endowment was made up so that it became richer still, the 'schools' in which the University did its teaching were repaired at royal expense, and two new colleges (St. John's College and Trinity College), were founded, with royal support.

There ensued a 'musical' chairs of leading figures, as exiles returned and others went into exile. Thomas Bodley's family went to Geneva where the future founder of the Bodleian Library was able to hear Calvin lecture. Peter Martyr left the country and wrote to Bullinger from Strasbourg in November 1553,[127] where he had fled from the dangers of the new reign. Richard Cox returned from Louvain and was reinstated as Dean of Christ Church and Regius Professor of Theology (Richard Smith also got his Chair back). Jewel's position of respect as a theologian in Oxford was to be modified during the reign of Mary Tudor, although he astutely wrote her a formal letter as public orator expressing Oxford's congratulations on her accession. He was expelled from Corpus for his now dangerous opinions. Jewel gave in, admitting that it was because he was afraid of martyrdom.

Others left Oxford altogether, including Vermigli, who went back to Strasbourg. Jewel stayed and moved to Broadgates Hall (which was later to become Pembroke College), where his friend Thomas Randolph was in charge. About this time – perhaps prompted by fear of the consequences of the Visitation of Oxford which took place in October 1554 – Jewel subscribed himself a Catholic. But it became clear that it was too late for him and he fled Oxford at last, moved from one hiding place to another, and eventually joined his protestant friends in Europe, probably going first to Strasbourg; in March 1555 he was seen in Frankfurt with Richard Cox, Dean-of-Christ-Church-in-exile. There John Knox and his allies were calling for the use of the Calvinist form of worship as followed in Geneva. Jewel seems to have felt it politic to confess that in Oxford he had recanted his Protestant faith altogether.[128] Jewel prevailed in the Frankfurt controversy, though he wrote later to try to mend fences.[129]

He then returned to Strasbourg and worked with Vermigli in a capacity of 'research assistant' and secretary, learning much himself as a scholar in the process. Vermigli was lecturing on Aristotle's *Ethics* and the book of Judges. But he was far from alone with his old colleague. In Strasbourg he came into contact with Edwin Sandys, Edmund Grindal, John Cheke, Anthony Cook, all fellow-exiles. Heinrich Bullinger invited Vermigli to move to Zürich, where Jewel accompanied him in 1556 and made new contacts. He also found his old tutor Parkhurst there. A consequence presumably unforeseen by the counter-reformers was that Mary's reign thus became a period of significant 'networking', both among the English exiles and with the key continental figures in the Reformation.

The new Government instigated the show-trials of the 'Cambridge men' Cranmer, Latimer and Ridley at Oxford, bringing together the theological expertise of Oxford and Cambridge and drawing out the condemnations while public attempts were made to bring the miscreants to recant.[130] It was perhaps felt that they were more likely to get their just deserts in conservative Oxford than in protestant Cambridge.

The process of bringing Oxford minds back in frame began with disputations in 1554, focusing once more on the Eucharist. The issues for debate still included the disputed points about the doctrine of transubstantiation which had been thoroughly thrashed out in the Middle Ages but were still generating conflict. It remained, for example, still a spatial problem to explain how Christ could simultaneously be on the right hand of God and in the consecrated bread. Once the visitors from Cambridge had been 'incorporated' by consent of the Regent Masters so as to make them members of the University of Oxford, a solemn Convocation was held in St. Mary's to determine what was to be done, and then 'all the Doctors and Masters went in a solemn procession to Quatervois (Carfax) and thence to Christ Church, where they heard divine service, and so they went to dinner'. After dinner they returned to the University Church and 'soon after was brought in Cranmer, then Ridley, and last of all Latimer, to subscribe to certain Articles then proposed, but they all denied them'.[131] These were not mere popular dissidents. They were senior figures in the Church, or had been. Cranmer had been Archbishop of Canterbury from 1532, Ridley Bishop of London from 1449, Latimer Bishop of Worcester from 1535.

On 16 April, the Oxford and Cambridge Doctors conducted the Disputation at which the three were to be given an opportunity to defend their position. Jewel was still in Oxford and he was deputed to take the notes for the record. Everyone walked from Exeter College, where they had all assembled, and was seated in the Divinity School. Cranmer was brought in first and set in the Respondent's place and a formal debate was conducted just as if they had been sitting a conventional University examination. The next day Ridley had his chance and the third day, Wednesday 18th, Latimer. Three days later the Doctors assembled again in the University Church and once more the three were asked whether they would subscribe to the Articles, 'but they refusing, were solemnly pronounced no members of the Church, and were forthwith remitted to their respective prisons', where they were kept until the autumn of 1555.[132]

In November 1554, the Revival of the Heresy Acts brought back into use three former Acts of Parliament against heresy, of 1382, 1401, 1414, all of which had been repealed under Mary's father and brother.[133] The Revival Act regretted the resulting lack of 'authority' to proceed against 'errors and heresies, which of late have risen, grown, and much increased within this realm': it therefore reinstated 'every article, branch, and sentence contained in the same three several Acts... in full force, strength, and effect to all intents, constructions, and purposes for ever', although the earlier Acts had been concerned not with recent protestant ideas but with the suppression of Lollardy.

Anthony Wood relates how:

> Ridley and Latimer being kept prisoners until 16 Oct. 1555, were then brought to that place where they were to be burnt, that is to say over against Balliol Coll. where now stand a row of poor cottages; a little behind which, before this time, ran [a] clear…stream under the Town wall.…There I say being brought suffered death with courage for the Religion they professed, in the presence of the chief Magistrates of the University and City, with multitudes of Scholars and Laicks.[134]

Armed peace-keeping forces were brought in by the authorities to ensure that there was not going to be a riot. A sermon was preached from a roughly-constructed pulpit, by Richard Smith, again perhaps in the hope of ensuring that the crowd did not get out of hand. Cranmer was able to watch from his nearby prison in the Bocardo, near the North Gate of the city where St. Michael's Church still stands, for he 'ascended to the top thereof to see the spectacle, and kneeling down prayed to God to strengthen them'.[135] They encouraged one another. Latimer's words have become legendary:

> Be of good comfort, Master Ridley, and play the man. We shall this day light such a candle, by God's grace, in England, as I trust shall never be put out.

The smell of burning human flesh must have been obvious very quickly. Latimer died rapidly, but Ridley was glad of the bag of gunpowder his brother-in-law George Shipside was permitted to hand him to hasten his end, though his desperate efforts to speed up the process by piling on the faggots seems to have slowed down the fire and left Ridley screaming in agony for his torment to end. The spot is marked in the roadway of Broad Street today.

Cranmer's turn came a few months later, in March 1556, when again a crowd assembled. He tried to say his farewells to 'some of his Friends standing by', for example William Ely of Brasenose, who was later to be President of St. John's, but he drew back and would not touch his hand, says Anthony Wood. Cranmer's own feelings were equivocal. His mind was complex, balanced, and he found himself writing two versions of a farewell speech for the occasion. He seems to have been trying to say that the truth was not and could not be so simple as his condemnation would seem to suggest, that he did not know what he was to die for since he freely admitted that he had not always been right. But since it was his hand which had written those things he now fears were not right he would put it first into the flames.

Mary Tudor's reign now brought a further Visitation, in 1556, instigated by Cardinal Pole, and more book-burning.[136] Reginald Pole (1500–88) was a graduate of Magdalen and a former Fellow of Corpus Christi. He had enjoyed the patronage of Henry VIII but had gone into exile in 1532 when relations broke down over the King's proposed divorce. He returned in Mary's reign to become her Archbishop of Canterbury.

Pole had Legatine authority from the Pope, and he used it to appoint fresh Visitors for Oxford. He chose the Bishop of Gloucester, James Brokes, 'a man for Literature not vulgar, for Eloquence not to be contemned, for his manners and curtsey to be beloved and respected, though much changed, and perhaps to be weakened as to his Religion, by the variety of these times,' as Anthony Wood describes him. This mingling of cultivation of mind and time-serving was, Wood suggests, also to be found in Walter Wright the Archdeacon of Oxford, another of the Visitors, while the other three were unblinkingly arrogant and ruthless. They ejected 'those persons that were active and forward in the late times' and burnt in the market-place all the English Bibles they could find 'and all Commentators on it in the same language', with all books that 'made for the Protestant Religion', found in libraries, 'Scholars studies' and 'in the houses of lay persons', which suggests that the search was both thorough and intrusive. 'Such a close and strict enquiry made they after Hereticks ... that they were forced either to dissemble or to fly into corners.' This was an activity fired by hatred. Peter Martyr's deceased wife was dug up on the instructions of the Dean of Christ Church and her body thrown into a dung-hill on the grounds that she and Peter Martyr had both taken vows of religion before they had been married and had therefore lived 'in cursed fornication'.[137]

Pole issued Injunctions for Oxford in 1556[138] in which he noted that the existing Statutes of Edward VI 'stood in need of considerable amendment' (*non modica indigere emendatione*). His Injunctions covered the governance not only of the University but also of the colleges, and the importance of lecturers fulfilling their duties. He set out a list of matters for further discussion, proposing that when the professors have finished their lectures they should make themselves available for a while so that students who want to disagree with what they may have said in the lectures, or who have some other point of difficulty to raise, may do so and the lecturers will listen to them 'kindly' and respond so as to help them with their difficulties and doubts.[139]

An almost deserted Oxford

These repeated frightening arrivals of punishment brigades in the form of Visitors had so purged Oxford that it had become seriously short of academics and students.[140] Wood suggests that more attention was now being paid to the 'establishment of the Catholick Religion, than for the retrieving of learning'. 'What shall we say of Divinity, when the School thereof was seldom opened for Lectures?' Sermons were rare events and lectures in general were scarce. 'The Greek tongue also was so rare, that it was scarce professed in public or private by any body.'[141] John Jewel wrote to Bullinger on 22 May 1559 to bewail the fact that, in his view, the universities are ruined (*afflictae et perditae*) and scarcely two people can be found in Oxford who agree with 'us', the reformers.[142]

Elizabeth places Oxford under the statutes of the realm

Wood describes how both sides hoped to benefit when Elizabeth succeeded her sister in 1558.[143] Jewel returned to England a few weeks after the news of the death of Queen Mary reached him in Zürich. He wrote to Peter Martyr in some despair at what he had found on his return at the beginning of Elizabeth's reign:

> The bishops are a great hindrance to us; for being, as you know, among the nobility and leading men in the upper house, and having none there on our side to expose their artifices and confute their falsehoods, they reign as sole monarchs in the midst of ignorant and weak men, and easily overreach our little party, either by their numbers or their reputation for learning. The queen, meanwhile, though she openly favours our cause, yet is wonderfully afraid of allowing any innovations: this is owning partly to her own friends, by whose advice everything is carried on, and partly to the influence of Count Feria, a Spaniard, and Philip's ambassador.

He had been invited to assist at a disputation in Westminster set up to enable the 'Marian' bishops to be outpointed. He explains in this letter that a disputation is to be held before the Council between nine of the reformers ('Scory,[144] Cox, Whitehead,[145] Sandys, Grindal, Horn,

Aylmer, a Cambridge man of the name of Gheast,[146] and myself') and five bishops, so as to air three key issues, liturgy in the vernacular, variation of rites locally, and the non-sacrificial character of the Eucharist. It was not a success.[147] The conference turned out to be 'useless,' he says.[148]

He takes the opportunity to comment gloomily once more on the state of Oxford, how 'religion, and all hope of good learning and talent is altogether abandoned' there.[149]

He was still writing in the same vein to Peter Martyr on 22 May 1560,

> Our universities and more especially our Oxford, are now most sadly deserted; without learning, without lectures, without any regard to religion (*sine bonis literis, sine lectionibus, sine studio ullo pietatis*).[150]

Nevertheless, Jewel was now back among the darlings of Government; he was sent on a royal visitation of the West and made Bishop of Salisbury in short order. He took his episcopal duties seriously, pressed for a better-educated clergy, and was himself an energetic preacher.[151] He left his mark most deeply in the *Apologia pro Ecclesia Anglicana* (1562) which he sent to Vermigli. The immediate prompter of this may have been the Council of Trent which was being reconvened (from 1560 to 1563). Jewel's idea was to lay out the faith of the English Church as a defence against the misrepresentations which were current. The *Apologia* made a stir all over Europe and prompted a particularly strong reaction from the English recusants who were now taking their turn in exile in Europe, mainly at Louvain.[152]

Work after work appeared contesting Jewel's claims. Of these the most important was that of Thomas Harding (1516–72). He had been Jewel's near-contemporary as a student at Oxford though he had been at New College, and he had been made Regius Professor of Hebrew in 1542. (The Regius Chair in Hebrew in Oxford was founded in 1540.[153] A number of Oxford Hebrew scholars are known from the sixteenth century,[154] although they did not publish on the subject until the seventeenth-century Regius Professor of Hebrew Edward Pococke, appointed in 1648, began to do so.)

Though Harding had been with the protestants in Oxford, he became a Roman Catholic on Mary's accession. When Elizabeth became Queen, the rewards and preferments of her sister's reign were stripped from him and he went to join the exiles in Louvain and became involved in the founding of the English College at Douai. For ten years, 'answer', 'defence', 'reply', 'confutation' flew between him and Jewel in a pamphlet warfare. Battles were waged in detail over point after point.

Calvinism and the puritans

> [In Geneva before Calvin arrived] neither king, nor duke, nor nobleman [had] any authority or power over them, but officers chosen by the people yearly out of themselves, to order all things with public consent. For spiritual government, they had no laws at all agreed upon, but did what the pastors of their souls by persuasion could win them to. Calvin, being admitted one of their preachers, and a divinity reader amongst them, considered how dangerous it was that the whole estate of that Church should hang still on so slender a thread as the liking of an ignorant multitude is, if it have power to change whatsoever it itself listeth.[155]

Richard Hooker (1554–1600) describing this in his *Ecclesiastical polity*, explains that Calvin took matters in hand and got the people to agree to obey their duly appointed ministers. It was evident to this late-Elizabethan divine, who had become a student at Corpus Christi College in 1577 and published his hugely influential book in 1593, that religion and government could not easily be separated in sixteenth-century England. If Henry VIII's Reformation had been stamped with Lutheranism and its ideas about the Christian Magistrate, the strong influence in Elizabeth's reign came from the Calvinists and the focus of debate throughout the Kingdom shifted to the rights and wrongs of Puritanism and whether governance and oversight of the Church should remain in the hands of bishops.

The Calvinists had had their impact on higher education in France and in Switzerland too, and latterly in Scotland, whence Presbyterianism remained a perceived 'threat' for some generations. Reforming ideas also entered parts of Switzerland in the sixteenth century, where John Calvin founded an 'Academy' at Geneva in 1559. This eventually became the 'University' of Geneva, though it did not so describe itself at its beginning. At the outset it taught theology and law, though its curriculum expanded during the eighteenth century.

Laurence Humphrey and the Calvinists in Oxford

An example of the way this Calvinist influence spread is to be seen in the career of Laurence Humphrey. He was one of the Demys of Magdalen[156] from 1547, and was quickly made a probationary Fellow, even before he had graduated as a BA. Almost as soon as he was an MA, in 1553, he had been given a lectureship in philosophy.

The power of the University sermon to move and persuade its hearers should never be underestimated. Popular preachers were feared by the authorities with good reason and inside the Universities they had a specially dangerous reach. In July 1550 Humphrey heard Martin Bucer preach from the pulpit at Christ Church. He and several others joined forces to try to bring a new zeal for the Reformation to Oxford. They wrote to the Privy Council accusing the President of Magdalen, Owen Oglethorpe, of resisting reform. In one of the numerous interventionist coups which removed Fellows and Heads of House from colleges in Oxford and Cambridge in the sixteenth and seventeenth centuries and replaced them with those of temporarily more acceptable opinions, Oglethorpe was ejected and replaced by Walter Haddon. But when Mary became Queen and Stephen Gardiner the Bishop of Winchester, Magdalen found itself with a Visitor of a very different colour. Stephen Gardiner had met Erasmus in Paris in 1511 when he was probably already a student at Trinity Hall. In Cambridge he turned into a lawyer and came to prominence sufficiently to be chosen by Thomas Wolsey as his secretary, and he entered the King's service within three years.[157] He paid Oxford a Visit in October 1553 and the Master and a dozen of the Fellows were removed. Humphrey survived, probably because he was not there, having got permission a month earlier to travel abroad without giving up his Fellowship.

With others anxious to get out of dangerous Oxford, he had gone to Zurich, where he arrived in the Spring of 1554. Magdalen continued to pay his salary and he was therefore obliged to request the College to continue to support him if he wished to stay away. It agreed, but it imposed the condition that he ought not to associate with heretics. In the end, he was removed from the list of Fellows of Magdalen in 1556, but by then he had worked his way into circles where printers and publishers could provide him both with a means of earning his living and with a means of having his say in print.

The exiles in Zurich during Mary's reign had included a group of Oxford men of his stamp, who remembered it with affection and enthusiasm for the quality of the discussions they had enjoyed.[158] Magdalen took Humphrey back when he returned from exile at the beginning of Elizabeth's reign (in 1560). He was needed, and the shortage of experienced academics speeded his progress. Even though Humphrey was not a theologian and did not have the doctorate which was a formal qualification for the Professorship, Mathew Parker, now Archbishop of Canterbury, tried to get him appointed to the Lady Margaret Chair of Divinity. Peter Martyr decided not to come back to Oxford, so a still richer prize came his way instead and Humphrey was made Regius Professor of Divinity. In 1561 (though it took some active campaigning on his behalf), he was chosen to be President of Magdalen and took a rapid doctorate in theology in order to comply with requirements.

Vestments and vestiarians

The returned Humphrey made himself unpopular in Oxford by his public and increasingly obsessive opposition to the clergy wearing surplices. Extreme protestant views regarded these as popish vestments and 'Romish rags'. He wrote to ask Bullinger whether vestments could possibly be considered 'things indifferent'. The Queen wrote firmly to the Archbishop of Canterbury in 1565 that the requirement of order and uniformity in the Church of England applied everywhere and the universities were to be no exception. Parker sent to Magdalen to inquire what the practice was in its chapel. The President and 25 Fellows wrote indignantly back saying that the Bishop of Winchester was their Visitor and only he had jurisdiction to inquire about this.

The question of vestments became a trial of strength, and a matter in which Humphrey and others claimed liberty of conscience when attempts were made to force their personal submission. Humphrey was not the only one to preach at Paul's Cross in early 1565 and alarm the authorities. He and Sampson, the Dean of Christ Church, were censured and Sampson ejected from office, though Humphrey clung on until he became something of a left-over from an earlier generation of reformers and younger men became impatient with his preoccupation with the battle over vestments.[159] On the other hand, he won a degree of acceptance which encouraged Matthew Parker and the Bishop of London to ask him to write the *Life* of John Jewel. The biography, almost an early modern hagiography, became one of the instruments for persuading readers towards Calvinism. Humphrey presented Jewel's recantation cosmetically and suggested he went bravely into exile in defence of the faith rather than capitulating ignominiously to save his skin.[160]

Elizabeth comes to Oxford

On 3 September 1566, on her first visit to Oxford,[161] Elizabeth heard a disputation conducted before her. The Queen arrived at the University Church of St. Mary's on Tuesday with a great crowd of the nobility. It is likely that she was able to take a strong intelligent interest in what followed. She was quite capable of holding a conversation in Latin with the academics,[162] for although she had never been to school or university herself, she had enjoyed the best possible private tuition.

Disputations were still regarded as good theatre and an appropriate kind of performance for the University to put on to honour a notable visitor.

Two questions within the compass of the Arts Faculty were first proposed for debate. These were prudently selected from the field of 'natural philosophy'. The first attracted several disputants on the question whether things 'lower' are governed by 'higher' things. The second question, whether the moon is the cause of the tides, attracted no challengers at all. Then questions of moral philosophy were propounded, likely to pique a monarch's interest – whether a Prince ought to be elected or to succeed by inheritance; and whether it is better to be governed by good law or a good monarch.[163] These are themes of the sort which are to be found in her *Sententiae* of 1563, so perhaps her courtiers advised the University what would please her.[164]

On Wednesday there were more disputations, this time in the field of Law, and on Thursday the disputations were on Medicine and Divinity. The Queen was interested by the theological disputation, for the question proposed was whether it is permissible for an individual to take up arms against a bad prince. It was carefully explained to her Majesty that the doctors of theology had no seditious intentions and abhorred disturbance of every kind. Then the proposer of the questions explained the practice of the gentiles and of the Jews and other theologians added their opinions, before everybody cried *Vivat Regina,* just to make sure she could not possibly be left with the wrong impression about their loyalty. She vouchsafed them a speech of thanks.

The Latin record of these events has a counterpart in an English narrative by Neale, the Reader in Hebrew, abbreviated by Richard Stephens, which yields a full picture of the visit as a whole.[165] Elizabeth had visited Cambridge in 1564, so Oxford was eager to impress. It had even sent its Proctors to observe on the earlier occasion, and it had seen that the Queen was in a mood for dignified ceremonial and expected to be received with dignity and obedience. It was deemed fitting for her to be met by the University's senior officers at Wolvercote and to received the staves of the three bedells in token of the University's submission. She processed into the city pausing to hear a series of speeches of respectful welcome in English (from the town), Latin and Greek. She stayed at Christ Church, which had been done up lavishly in her honour with gold and other fitting decoration; she did not sit patiently through all the festive events in her honour by any means, though she did attend a play.[166]

The colleges were persuaded into an appropriate acceptance of the Elizabethan Settlement, even if some had leftward leanings. Jesus (1571) was the only college founded in Elizabeth's reign. It was not a completely new foundation. It replaced White Hall, one of the medieval halls. Jesus was the enterprise of a group of clergy and lawyers with a preponderance of Welsh influence,[167] who saw a need to ensure a high quality of training for clergy in the new Elizabethan Church. A census of 1577 carried out by the Privy Council found only All Souls, Balliol, Exeter and Queen's Colleges infested with Roman Catholic sympathizers. In 1578, Convocation agreed to amend the University's counter-heresy Statute *De inquisitione et cautione faciendis contra haereticam pravitatem,* so as to ensure that junior members would not be endangered by any conservatives who put pressure on them in favour of the 'old religion' and that the health of their souls would be looked after. Texts, including some from Calvinist continental theology, were prescribed for catechetical purposes: Nowell's *Catechism,*[168] Calvin's Catechism, and the Heidelberg Catechism. Laurence Humphrey served on the committee which selected and promoted these.

The first Act of Parliament to address the status of the universities in law

The Oxford and Cambridge Act of 1571[169] ('An Acte for Thincorporation of bothe Thunyversities') was short, but potent in its implications. On its face, it was merely 'confirming the Priviledges of the Two Universities':

> For the greate Love and Favor that the Queenes most excellent Majestie beareth towardes her Highnes Universities of Oxford and Cambridge, and for the greate Zeale and Care that the Lords and Commons of this present Parliament have for the Mayntenaunce of good and Godly Literature and the vertuouse Education of Youth within either of the same Universities.

However, its effect was to incorporate the two universities in law, almost as though they had never been corporations all along. Oxford was to go by the 'Name of Chauncellor Maisters and Schollers of the Universitie of Oxford, and by none other Name or Names, ... for evermore'; there was to be a perpetual succession of the corporate body, which was to have the power to sue or be sued. Everything was confirmed as it had been before and everything was to be continued, but now the authority for this lay with the state and not with the University itself. It had the potential now to be moved from being a private to something close to a public body. There was also a stipulation attempting to fix for the future the legal basis of the relations between town and gown, for:

> this Acte or anye Thinge therin contayned shall not extend to the Prejudice or Hurt of the Liberties & Privileges of Right belonging to the Maior Bayliffes & Burgeses of the Towne of Cambridge and Cittie of Oxford

The creation of this piece of legislation appears to have taken some of the intensity out of royal concerns about the universities, though the Elizabethan Statutes were in some respects a backward step.

Elizabeth's second visit to Oxford, in 1592, seems to have been a solemn occasion in a different and more repressive spirit. There were also visits to colleges this time.[170] But the standard of the entertainments was felt to have dropped and the Queen expressed herself bored. It was apparently her pleasure and distraction to translate one of Cicero's speeches, the *Pro M Marcello,* on this later visit to Oxford.[171]

Teaching the Arts from the late sixteenth century

Humphrey Gilbert (1537–83) in *Queene Elizabethe's Achademy,* proposed in the 1570s the establishment of an academy for the instruction of the Queen's wards and other young gentlemen, whose syllabus was to cover the conventional liberal arts, together with the skills which would be needed at court and by future civil servants, such as heraldry. He includes a requirement that the lecturers shall regularly publish research:

> All the fforesaid publique Readers of arte and the common lawes shall once within every six yeares set forth some new bookes in printe, according to their severall professions. Also every one of those which shall publiquely teache any of the languages as afforesaid, shall once every 3 yeares publish in printe some Translation into the English tounge of some good worke, as neare as may be for the advawncing of those thinges which shalbe practized in the said Achademy. All which bookes shall for ever be entituled as set forth by the gentlemen of Queene Elizabethes Academy, wherby all the nations of the worlde shall, once every 6 yeares at the furthest, receave greate benefit, to your highness immortall fame.[172]

There is a hint here that despite the continuing monopoly of Oxford and Cambridge, higher education could in principle be provided elsewhere on a freelance basis. There was competition.

Sound pedagogy was certainly considered important in Oxford itself. Izaak Walton (1593–1683) describes how Richard Hooker (1554–1600) pieced together some modest funding to go to Oxford and distinguished himself and was awarded a scholarship and was getting pupils almost at once and proved to be an exceptionally good teacher with a rare capacity to make things clear. Walton's Hooker is a hero of scholarship, 'enriching his quiet and capacious Soul with the precious Learning of the Philosophers, Casuists and Schoolmen'.[173] He was also a martyr for his opinions, for scarcely had he been invited to read 'the public Hebrew lecture' but, within three months, he was expelled from his college with John Reynolds.

What really happened to the syllabus in the Arts?

The Oxford Statutes of 1564–5 preserved the framework of the old curriculum with its seven liberal arts.[174] They say that the undergraduate must spend two terms on arithmetic, two on music, four on rhetoric, two on grammar and four on dialectic. (The roughly equivalent Cambridge statutes of 1570 say the first year is to concentrate on rhetoric, the second and third on logic, the fourth year on philosophy.) Their more old-fashioned provisions were often observed only in the imaginative ways in which they were breached.

When it came to the study of grammar, 'modernization' took place with the introduction of the study of Greek and Hebrew. With logic the story is rather different. Debate and disputation still formed the backbone of the work of the University, both as a teaching method and for the purposes of examining the candidates. Richard Hooker commends it as a useful way of conducting public discussions on important issues, something the universities are peculiarly well-fitted to do:

> earnest challengers ye are of trial by some public disputation. Wherein if the thing ye crave be no more than only leave to dispute openly about those matters which are in question, the schools in universities (for any thing I know) are open to you. They have their yearly Acts and Commencements, besides other disputations both ordinary and upon occasion, wherein the several parts of our own ecclesiastical discipline are oftentimes offered unto that kind of examination.

He points out that those who are clamouring for the opportunity to debate know this perfectly well and

> have been of late years noted seldom or never absent from thence at the time of those greater assemblies, and the

> favour of proposing there in convenient sort whatsoever ye can object (which thing myself have known tem to grant of scholastical courtesy unto strangers) neither hath (as I think) now ever will (I presume) be denied to you.[175]

So the medieval disputation did not die with the decay of the highly demanding teaching of logic in the late medieval syllabus. It was as well adapted for pamphlet warfare and for the conduct of trials for heresy as for routine teaching and for examinations.

Syllogistic logic remained useful for testing the steps in an argument to make sure they were valid. Euclidean demonstrative method was still much admired because it proceeded from self-evident truths to necessary conclusions. The sixteenth century was thick with 'commonplaces' and 'articles', in Oxford and outside it. These are the *loci communes* or 'topics' of ancient logic and rhetoric.[176] They are also the equivalent of the *conclusiones* of medieval disputations.

There was a distinct move, though, to simplify the enormous complexities of the late medieval logic course. Concerns had been expressed about the need for reform of the logic syllabus in the fifteenth century, for example, by Rudolph Agricola (1444–85), in his *De inventione dialectica* (1479). The fashionable but often muddled simplified logic of Peter Ramus (1515–72) was introduced in many of Europe's universities. Peter Ramus's system concentrated first in an area which loosely equates with 'topics', and belongs equally to the *Art of Rhetoric*, emphasizing the importance of applied skills of argumentation, the disposition of arguments and their presentation for purposes of persuasion as well as conviction.[177]

Robert Sanderson (1587–1663) published a logic textbook which was widely recommended in Oxford during the seventeenth century and which reflects the mixed character of the late sixteenth-century changes in the logic course there.[178] Sanderson evidently considered some elements of the traditional medieval logic course still relevant to the needs of his pupils. He has a chapter in his *Logicae Artis Compendium* (published anonymously, but based on his teaching as a tutor) on 'supposition of terms' (*suppositio terminorum*)[179] and other aspects of 'terminist' logic; this book was quite widely used until the nineteenth century in English universities, so some coverage of these topics evidently persisted in the syllabus. He refers those who are interested in knowing more to the *summularii* ('little summaries') or digests, that is textbook summaries. His teaching was evidently a success, and he is said to have given great satisfaction to his hearers as a lecturer. A letter from the Bishop of Lincoln contributing a recollection to the writing of Isaac Walton's *Life of Robert Sanderson* (first printed in 1678), remembers him as Regius Professor of Divinity in Oxford, giving his public lectures. 'A Person of Quality (yet alive) privately ask'd him What course a young Divine should take in his Studies to inable him to be a good Casuist,' for he had been much impressed by Sanderson's ability to split hairs.[180] Abraham Fraunce in his *Lawiers Logik* (1588, II.iv.92b), was impatient with the whole business, for he saw the teaching of skills of argument for lawyers in vocational and practical terms. 'Suppositions are built rather upon idle supposals of schoolemen, then grounded upon any sure foundation of naturall experience.' Logic in the English universities was now going to be done from somewhat motley collections of textbook materials.

Improving the teaching of formal reasoning occupied some generations. It was the task to which Descartes' *Discours de la Methode* (1637) is addressed, just as much as Fraunce's *The Lawiers Logick.*

4 OXFORD KEEPS UP WITH THE TIMES

Oxford and the state

The Hampton Court Conference and the King James Version of the Bible

On his way to London in 1603 to become King on the death of Elizabeth, James VI of Scotland, soon to be James I of England, was presented with a Petition. This Millenary Petition was the work of puritans who had grievances against the Church of England. Its tone was moderate and James was sympathetic to the benefits of being seen to listen. But not all puritans were moderates. From one extremist strand was to come Civil War and disturbing times for Oxford.

It was a time of repositioning for scholars with sensitivities. When Queen Elizabeth made her first official visit to Oxford in the 1560s, John Reynolds (1549–1607) took part in the festivities, performing as Hippolyta in a production of *Palaemon and Arcyte* put on in her honour at Christ Church and presenting her with verses. Reynolds (or Rainolds) came from a family of brothers who were all sent to Oxford, and, like others during Tudor times, he had suffered interruptions to his studies. He experienced a gradual conversion during the changes of the century, from his original Roman Catholicism to a moderate but decided Puritanism. By now he was strongly critical of theatrical performances, but when James I succeeded to the throne he still thought it worthwhile to present such compliments in verse to the monarch in a collection put together from within the University and proffered on its behalf.

The Hampton Court Conference of 1604 was convened by the new King, James I, in an attempt to find a resolution to the problem of apparently irreconcilable differences between those who favoured Presbyterian Church government and the supporters of the Elizabethan Church Settlement with its built-in bishops. Oxford's scholars had had an equal involvement with those of Cambridge. John Reynolds led the moderate puritans who came from Oxford. The Hampton Court Conference was set down for January of 1604, but Reynolds as leader of the puritans seems to have misjudged the temper of the King. The suggestion that it might be sensible to create a synod composed of bishops and Presbyterian leaders to decide disputes prompted the famous cry, 'No bishop, no King', and an indignant royal departure.

The Church of England Canons finalized in 1604 caused Reynolds and others considerable problems of conscience. Reynolds wrote letters on points of principle and tried to hold off the moment when he would be required to 'subscribe' to beliefs he did not wholly share. The King was due to come to Oxford in August 1605 and perhaps Reynolds hoped to use the opportunity to win him over, for he was due to give a lecture to honour the King. The King, however, was not to be outmanoeuvred. He gave orders that the Vice-Chancellor was to force Reynolds into compliance or he must be expelled from the University. Reynolds kept his nerve, and continued to write letters, and seems to have survived without being expelled. Oxford was also fully represented in the team of translators which produced the King James Version of the Bible, published in 1611, and here again Reynolds was heavily involved. The Oxford committee entrusted with the translation of the major and minor Prophets met three times a week under the chairmanship of the Regius Professor of Hebrew in Reynolds' President's lodging at Corpus, even as he became seriously ill.

Regents revolt

In 1613 there was a stirring of 'revolution' when the Regent Masters decided to rise up against the Vice-Chancellor and Doctors on the subject of the wearing of caps in the Convocation House. It had become the custom to sit bareheaded but one of the dissidents had observed in the stained glass of the large west window of St. Mary's Church that the Regents and Non-Regents were wearing their caps, and took that to be an indication that it was historically the right thing to do. So he put on his own cap and got others to do the same. The Vice-Chancellor had him charged with trying to subvert the honour and government of the University.[1]

These latter-day Regent Masters had good reason to feel insecure. Not only were they being replaced by salaried postholders, but they were losing their old monopoly of the route to clerical life. Students who were not training to be notaries or preparing for ordination, graduated, now left Oxford and got on with lives which might include free-ranging intellectual activity, or lives as country clergy, or merely comfortable existences running their estates and otherwise largely pleasing themselves as country gentlemen. These educated lifestyles were accessible by other routes than studying for a degree at Oxford or Cambridge.

William Laud and Oxford's new Statutes

Internal tensions continued to be flavoured with religious differences. This was the century in which Oxford's reputation established itself for a conservatism both religious and political. At St. John's College, founded in the reign of Mary Tudor, some of the membership continued to have strong Roman Catholic sympathies. In any case there was reason to suspect that Roman Catholicism and high church views had not been wholly purged from the University. When one of the chaplains of Christ Church, Humphrey Leech, left Oxford to become a Roman Catholic in 1608, he took the opportunity to claim that he was not the only person in Oxford to hold his particular views, and that there were numerous anti-Calvinists there.

William Laud entered St. John's College in 1589 and lingered there for the best part of thirty years. Laud himself became a controversial figure as a young man, energetically advancing views which his critics said he had taken from the Roman Catholic apologist Robert Bellarmine (1562–1621). When he preached in the University Church of St. Mary's in 1606, the Vice-Chancellor sent for him to explain himself. His arguments offended chiefly those of Presbyterian preferences with a dislike of an episcopal ecclesiology, for he maintained that a priest and a bishop are in different 'orders' and that only a bishop can make priests. This was also offensive to those who were eager to ensure that the reforming communities of continental Europe did not feel separated from the Church of England, a matter which in due course turned out to be close to Oliver Cromwell's heart.

In 1610–11 Laud became President of St. John's, though the election was contested by his enemies. Laud did not cease to be controversial and a controversialist. A 'Conference' between William Laud and 'Mr. Fisher the Jesuit' was held on 24 May 1622, in London, quite in the spirit of the public disputations of the medieval and sixteenth-century universities.[2] Meanwhile he had become a made man at court as a close friend of the King's favourite, Buckingham. He was worried that James I's son Charles might prove to be no friend to the Church of England and sought reports from those who had come back from Spain and spent time with him recently in 1623.[3]

At the time when Charles I came to the throne in 1625 there were rumblings of criticism – against Cambridge as well as Oxford – for in both universities, it was alleged, Heads of House (specifically those of Corpus Christi College in Oxford and Trinity College in Cambridge) had been behaving improperly; there were even claims that simony was interfering with elections to Fellowships. Charles's resentment was sharpened when students killed game on his estate at Woodstock, and when the University made difficulties about agreeing to appoint his favourite, Buckingham, as Chancellor. Laud wrote a letter about the game in July 1630, requesting 'that you would all be careful, that the university may stand right in his majesty's good opinion for not spoiling his game'.[4]

Laud could be as soothing and diplomatic as he could be troublesome. About 1630, he wrote to the Master of Trinity College Cambridge, Samuel Brooke, who had apparently circulated a treatise on predestination expressing Arminian opinions, respectfully conceding that 'fifteen years study cannot but beat out something'. He even promises to read the work 'if God give me leisure'. But he doubts whether such matters can finally be resolved and he wonders whether the King will want 'these controversies any further stirred, which now, God be thanked, begin to be more at peace, etc'.[5]

William Laud was made Chancellor of Oxford in 1630, expressing his delighted 'surprise', and he held the post until 1641. High offices followed during the period while he was riding the crest of a wave. Laud was Archbishop of Canterbury from 1633. But this success was not to last. He later wrote his account of how he felt about being Chancellor while he awaited his fate at the hands of an angry state, itself being tossed about in the throes of incipient civil war. For Laud was to end his life in disgrace, imprisonment and in execution, bayed at by a popular mob. The finger was pointed at him for events and developments in which he may indeed have had a hand but these were political matters, and great efforts were made to construct a case against him.

In prison he kept up with the reports of debates in Parliament and wrote his history of his time as Oxford's Vice-Chancellor:

> As soon as I was admitted to the chancellorship, which God knows I little expected, I thought it my duty to reform the university, which was extremely sunk from all discipline, and fallen into licentiousness; ... Hereupon I resolved within myself to set close to a reformation. And though I understood most of the defects of the university, as having lived there many years ... yet the first thing I thought fit to do, was to lay a command upon the vice-chancellor for the time being, that he should give me an account by letters every week of all necessary occurrences which happened at the university ... with a promise that he should weekly, without fail, receive a letter from me expressing what I disliked or

> approved, and with directions what should further be done for the good of that place.[6]

He continued to take the job of Chancellor very seriously and write his weekly letter to the Vice-Chancellor. He considered himself entitled to say 'I think I have not so carried business in the University, as that you should suspect my justice' on 11 February 1630, to Dr. Christopher Potter, Provost of Queen's.[7] Among the things Laud disapproved of were sermons preached in the University with unacceptable content, for example, a sermon 'by one of Exeter college, who preached directly against all reverence in churches'. Then there were the unfortunate opinions of John Tooker of Oriel.[8]

In a letter to Frewen the Vice-Chancellor, on 28 May 1630, Laud wrote:

> I am given to understand that formalities, which are in a sort the outward and visible face of the university, are ... utterly decayed ... insomuch that strangers which come thither, have scarce any external mark by which they may know they are in a university. If this go on, the university will lose ground every day both at home and abroad.

Laud tried to curb the more decadent habits into which the University had fallen. He wanted care taken 'that there be no gowns made out of the ancient fashion of the university'. He wanted to see everyone properly dressed, so that 'the university may have credit by looking like itself: and then I doubt not but it will be itself too'.[9] And he wanted a curb of dispensations, which allowed men to take their degrees when they had not completed the requirements. There was 'muttering in the university'.[10] The Proctors wrote in November 1630 to thank Laud for his reforming efforts, and 'to congratulate your lordship's honourable reformation of the university so well begun. ... The corruption was gotte up high. ... Some medicinal hand was of necessity, and that speedily, to undertake the cure.'[11]

He was also willing to put up a public fight on the University's behalf when necessary. Laud was alerted by the University to the King's plans to inspect both universities, and he and Cambridge's Chancellor, Henry Rich, 'resolved to go both together to him, and humbly to move him in the universities' behalf, that no foreign power might be sent to the prejudice of their privileges'. It took some persuasion, but at last he consented. One of the issues was fees.[12]

Laud may have been a disciplinarian in his visions of an improved Oxford, but he did not disapprove of patronage. The proprieties of public life were not the same then as now. John Birkenhead (1615–79), servitor at Oriel, impressed Laud as a good transcriber, so 'the Archbishop recommended him to All Soules College to be a fellow and he was accordingly elected. He was scholar enough, and a poet'. 'After Edgehill fight, when King Charles I first had his court at Oxford, he was pitched upon as one fitt to write the Newes, which Oxford Newes was called *Mercurius Aulicus,* which he writt wittily enough, till the surrender of the towne (which was June 24, 1646).' A sample will give the flavour:

> The Rebells intending a Reformation by the sword, will square their Church according to their Arm; and therefore they thrust all Trades into the pulpit.
>
> *Mercurius Aulicus, 24 February 1643.*[13]

In 1629 Convocation had entrusted a committee with the reframing of the Statutes of the University, which had been added to and changed until they were in a higgledy-piggledy muddle. This committee '*de redingendis Statutis Universitatis in certum ordinem et certam formam*'[14] handed over the work to a small sub-committee of itself, which delegated it further to two of its members, who were to produce drafts for the committee to look at, the Regius Professor of Civil Law and the Antiquary, Bryan Twynne. The most important task Laud undertook for Oxford was the completion of this new attempt at a proposed reform of the Statutes of the University,[15] which 'had lain in a confused heap for some ages, and extremely imperfect in all kinds'.[16] Laud knew that Thomas Wolsey had attempted to do something about the statutes and that others had since done the same, but 'it came to nothing'. He did not see how reform could achieve what it needed to unless the statutes were first put into order. He 'resolved to go on against all difficulties which were likely to oppose me in the body of that university... such bodies never want factions'.[17] These achievements were capped by a royal visit to Oxford in August that year, at which Laud presided.

Laud was impeached for treason in the House of Lords in March 1644, but it proved impossible to make the charge stick. In November he was attainted – that is, declared guilty by Parliament without trial – and the House of Commons bullied the House of Lords into agreeing that he was a traitor. Laud offered the King's pardon, which he had been given in 1643, but they refused to accept it. He was executed on Tower Hill in

January 1645, still protesting his innocence. The only concession he was able to obtain was that he should be executed briskly with an axe.

In 1663, long after his execution and the failure of the puritan experiment, when the monarchy had been restored, Laud's body was brought back to St. John's and lies in the chapel of the College still. He proved a generous benefactor to his own college of St John's by building it an impressive new quadrangle; to the Bodleian Library, to which he donated over 1000 manuscripts as well as coins and books; and to the university by founding a lectureship in Arabic and enlarging the stipend of the Professor of Hebrew.

Civil War

As the conflict between King and Parliament began to drift into civil war in the early months of 1642, the King began to look for a safe place to go. On 9 August 1642, Charles declared that the country was at war. He tried to raise an army in the Welsh Marches near Shrewsbury. At first he had fair success in battles at Edgehill and in Yorkshire, but he needed a suitable long-term 'base'. Nowhere in the country outside London was so well-provided with fine and suitable buildings in which to billet a court and its supporters than the two Universities, and Cambridge was showing signs of favouring the Parliament side. Besides, Charles expressed it as his opinion that Oxford was 'the only city of England that he could say was entirely at his devotion'.[18] In this he may have been mistaken because Oxford contained resentful puritans and supporters of the Parliament as well as loyal subjects of his own.

So Charles took up residence in Oxford, where Christ Church gave him hospitality. Christ Church had been 'given' to Henry VIII by its Dean in 1545 and a royal connection persisted. The Deanery provided a location for the court to convene and the 'Parliament' of the royalist side met in the Hall. The King worshipped in the cathedral every day and sat in the stall normally reserved for the Vice-Chancellor. Queen Henrietta Maria stayed at Merton, and other colleges were commandeered to help with accommodation or storage.

This honour did not come cheap for the University. Thomas Baskerville (c.1630–1700) was Lord of the Manor of Sunningwell, a few miles outside Oxford. His father had studied at Oxford, though he never went there himself, so his account of the gossip of the place in the period when it was settling down after the Restoration is an indicator of the way Oxford looked at this time to those who were not its members. He had friends who were insiders though:[19]

> I am informed by my worthy friend Mr Richard Rod [he writes,] yt when King Charles ye first had his residence in Oxford, in ye time of our Civil wars, the King wanting cash to pay his soldiers, he was necefsitated to send for the Colledge Plate to Coyne money and accordingly had it delivered to him.

St. John's hastily struck a bargain to pay him a sum of money instead and got their plate back. But Charles 'sent to demand it a second time, and had it' ('urgent occasions for money still prefsing him forward'). Coins were produced 'Coyn'd with ye Plate'.[20] The College has a letter from the King in which he explains that he has 'removed' his Mint to Oxford in order to coin money from the 'seuverall quantityes of Plate' which he has received 'from divers' of his 'loving Subts [subjects]'. The King promises to restore the value of the plate as soon as he can:

> Wee shall neuer let Persons of whom Wee have so great a Care to suffer for their Affection unto Vs but shall take special order for repayment... well knowing [the plate] to bee the Goods of your Colledge, that you ought not to alien, tho noe man will doubt but in such a case you may lawfully lend to assist your King in such visible necessity.

The Fellows agreed to allow their plate to be turned into coins but insisted that they should have some of the coins to help pay for the running of the college and to 'provide Commons for ye Students'.[21]

Prince Rupert's advice was to build fortresses round Oxford and ensure that there was adequate cavalry to add extra protection. Rupert was young, dashing, a professional soldier and Charles's nephew. At the early age of 23 he was given charge of the Royalist cavalry, though as it turned out he had been over-optimistic about the size of the force which would be needed to be effective. In any case, he was intent on going north to try to secure that part of the country for the King. Fortifications were duly built in the late autumn after the King had come into residence in Oxford, north of St. Giles's Church and close to the walks of St. John's College, near Merton College and to defend Magdalen Bridge, thus attempting to seal off all points of entry to the city. Guards were posted at strategic places.[22] There was also a notion that Abingdon and Reading could act as part of an outer ring of fortifications. Oxford thus invited attack and consequently found itself besieged by the Parliamentarian armies in 1644. Charles prudently withdrew in June, in the direction of Worcester because he had no wish to be trapped in the city of Oxford. He was to return to the area and there were to be further skirmishes around Oxford.[23]

Academic life could not go on unaffected in such circumstances. The town was desperately overcrowded and tempers frayed, with fights reported between soldiery and townspeople in the taverns. These were prompted in part by popular resentment that the military men were getting the best food and commons were short for the natives. Infections such as typhus and smallpox broke out.[24] Waggons and carts were provided for the army, by the simple expedient of seizing them as necessary, though a voluntary handing over was preferred and encouraged. This transport was needed for arms and ammunition, for provisions and for carrying the wounded.[25] The King had a hospital set up at Yarnton near Oxford in the house of Sir William Spencer.[26] The provision of artillery and other weaponry required considerable organization and the taking over of college ground. Oxford had gunsmiths but blacksmiths were needed too and skilled workmen were brought in from the local villages and even greater distances. A list kept at New College records a blacksmith of Dorchester, an armourer from Bicester, a wheelwright from Burford. There were Frenchmen, Germans and craftsmen from the Low Countries too. An 'artillery' park was set up at Magdalen College Grove and a foundry for the casting of cannons at Christ Church. Metal was requested and requisitioned. Mills for making gunpowder were constructed on the banks of the Isis and Cherwell and the army's chief engineer supervised the improvement of the channels from the rivers so that the better water-power could drive the mill-wheels more forcefully. Earthworks for defensive purposes were also being constructed to the south of the city.[27]

This kind of thing cannot have made for a relaxed atmosphere for scholarly endeavour. Moreover, scholars could not travel freely in these difficult times. The young Isaac Barrow (1630–77) was accepted as a foundation scholar at Peterhouse, Cambridge, in December 1643, thanks to the patronage of his uncle, another Isaac Barrow, who was a Fellow of the College. His arrival was deferred because almost immediately his uncle was forced to leave as a result of the Parliamentary Visitation of the University of Cambridge. One of his friends, Edward Walpole, promised to accompany him there and help him financially. He too was about to go to Cambridge, but to Trinity College; so Barrow was admitted there instead, in 1646. James Duport was to be his tutor. When, several months later, Walpole went down, Barrow was once again faced with uncertainty:

> During this time old Mr. Thomas Barrow was shutt up at Oxford and could not heare of his sonne .... [Isaac] was unsure what to do and was assisted by Mr. Walpole of Norfolk when he told him he 'knew not what to doe; he could not goe to

> his father at Oxford'. Walpole was going to Cambridge so he took him there and 'maintained him' and so he did for half a yeare till the surrender of Oxford; and then his father enquired after him and found him at Cambridge.[28]

Barrow's father, Thomas, was eventually able to make contact with him when he was able to leave Oxford where he had been trapped by the siege. He promised him money for maintenance and Duport arranged for him to have free tuition and free lodgings in the college. Barrow did well and won a college scholarship and soon after his graduation in 1649, a Fellowship.[29]

John Aubrey (1626–97) wrote of his own life as well as the 'Lives' of others.[30] He went to Trinity College Oxford in May 1642, but his father made him return home when the peace of Oxford was threatened by the impending Civil War. So students as well as dons were affected by the danger of the fighting, as we saw in the case of Isaac Barrow and his father. In the following February, Aubrey 'gott my father to lett me to beloved Oxon againe, then a garrison pro rege'.[31] He was soon taken home again after he caught the smallpox in April, but complained of feeling bored there:

> where I conversed with none but the servants and rustiques and soldiers quartred, to my great grief...for in those days fathers were not acquainted with their children. It was a most sad life to me, then in the prime of my youth, not to have the benefit of an ingeniose conversation and scarce any good bookes – almost a consumption.

He was made to linger at home until 1646 when his father permitted him to go to study at the Middle Temple. On 24 June following, 'Oxon was surrendered'. He was allowed to return to Oxford in November and there and in his time at the Middle Temple he 'enjoyd the greatest felicity of my life' until he had to go home once more on Christmas Eve 1648 because his father was ill, and after that he had to 'look after his country business'.

Another kind of reporting altogether was going on among the historians. *Behemoth: the History of the Causes of the Civil Wars of England* by Thomas Hobbes (1588–1679),[32] set out to cover the events of 1640–60, identifying three groups of 'seducers' of the people, those who rejected episcopacy, namely ministers 'pretending to have a right from God to govern every one his parish, and their assembly the whole nation'; those who remained loyal to the Pope; those who 'declared themselves for a liberty in religion'; sects such as Quakers and Adamites 'whose names and peculiar doctrines I do not well remember'. This was going to be a new kind of history-writing flavoured with religious party-politics.

Oxford in a bunker: the Protectorate

Charles I was executed in 1649, and soon after several of the leaders of his armies. The Earl of Cambridge, the Scottish nobleman James Hamilton, mounted the scaffold and behaved impeccably:

> Some part of the time was spent in a speech to the people, other part of the time was spent in speaking to those on the scaffold.... And prayed very humbly (and with a deal of Reverence) to God... putting on a white Satten Cap, he fitted himself to lye down, imbraced his Servants... and then he prayed at the Block. A piece of red silk was spread upon the block... to receive his head when it was cut off. He having put off his Doublet was in his shirt and prepared himself to dye.

It took a single stroke.[33]

There followed a decade of rule under the Protectorate by the victorious puritan leaders, Oliver Cromwell and for a short time his son Richard. Oxford faced the consequences of its support for the dead King. Its colleges were cleansed of persons disapproved of by the new Government. Thomas Hobbes describes the subsequent purging of Oxford 'by virtue whereof they turned to all who were not of their faction' and 'divers scandalous ministers and scholars'.[34] It became necessary to toe a party line if one wanted to be secure. Academic activity inevitably suffered, or was at least displaced, heightening the awareness that a higher education could be got outside the Universities. As Hobbes put it, 'As for natural philosophy, is it not removed from Oxford and Cambridge to Gresham College in London, and to be learned out of their gazettes?'[35]

The University feared damage to its reputation. Henry Stubbe wrote to Hobbes in late November 1656:

> Another request I haue to put up to you is yt you woulde speake favourably of this vniversity, wherein you haue many favourers, a wch hath undicated you so much by slighting both the lectures & bookes of yor Antagonists.... In particular Mr. Barlowe Keeper of ye publique library told mee yt thee had such an esteeme for you; yt if you would send him one of yor physiques, hee would not only give it entertainement in ye library, but honourably register ye worthy donor.[36]

Oxford was short of apologists capable of hitting the note required. The poets of the Protectorate, able to celebrate what had happened not regret it, were mainly Cambridge men. Oxford had produced William Davenant (1606–68), who had been born in the city, and had briefly been a student at Lincoln College in 1620, though he never completed his degree. He had been Poet Laureate from 1638, but his career had veered between approval and condemnation, and he had spent the year 1651–2 in the Tower of London.

The heavy hand of Parliament was everywhere, lending its approvals and permissions:

> 28 October, 1651, 'That the thanks of this House, be given to Mr. Owen Dean of Christ Church in Oxford, for his great paines taken in his sermon preached before Parliament ... on Friday the 24 day of this instant October.'

The same wording is used to thank Mr. Thomas Goodwyn, President of Magdalene Colledge in Oxford.[37] These gentlemen were licensed to have their sermons printed.

Stephen Penton (1675–83), the future Principal of St. Edmund Hall, described the way Oxford taught itself to hope for recovery 'when *Oliver* was dead and *Richard* dismounted'.

> They saw through a maze of changes that in a little time the nation would be fond of that government which twenty years before they hated. The hopes of this made the scholars talk aloud, drink healths, and curse *Meroz* in the streets ... they were mad, stark, staring mad. To study was *fanaticism*, to be moderate was downright *rebellion* ... and thus it would have continued ... if it had not pleased God to raise up some Vice-Chancellors who ... reduced the University to that temperament that a man might study and not be thought a *dullard*.[38]

The Restoration of the Monarchy and Oxford's continuing troubles

Royalist Oxford embraced the Restoration of the Monarchy in 1660. There were more removals and insertions of leading figures in Oxford designed to align the University with the new politics:

> The Publick Intelligencer 12–19 March 1660, includes the resolution of 13 March 'That Dr. Owen be and is hereby discharged from being Dean of Christ Church, Oxon, [and that] Dr. Reynolds be and is hereby restored to the Deanry of Christ Church, Oxon',

along with various other removals and replacements.[39]

Oxford wisely came into its own as the seat of a middle-of-the-road Anglicanism. Presbyterians found themselves able to be less extreme. High Anglicans discovered that they could be more moderate.

The story goes that a student called Thomas Brown (1662–1704), later to make his name as a satirist, was set the task of translating Martial's *Epigram* (I.32)

> *Non amo te, Sabidi, nec possum dicere quare;*
> *Hoc possum tantum dicere, non amo te.*[40]

as a punishment by Dr. Fell (1625–86), famed as a draconian disciplinarian. He was reprieved when he neatly and accurately turned the Latin into the quatrain:

> I do not love thee, Dr. Fell
> The reason why I cannot tell;
> But this I know and know full well;
> I do not love thee Dr. Fell

John Fell became a Canon of Christ Church in 1660, then Dean later in the same year. This was a double reward for some active canvassing for the Restoration. In 1666–9 he was Vice-Chancellor, behaving rather in the spirit of Laud in his determination to maintain good order and good manners in the University (also the wearing of appropriate academic dress). His career was crowned in 1676 by his election to the Bishopric of Oxford. The taste for harsh measures did not diminish with the bishopric. In 1684 Fell famously and summarily deprived John Locke (1632–1704) of his Studentship[41] at Christ Church where he had seemed to be beginning a promising career, because he had enjoyed the patronage of the first Earl of Shaftsbury and was under suspicion of having been involved in the creation and dissemination of seditious pamphlets.

The problem of the 1670s and 1680s was how to secure the succession, for Charles II had no children. Could his Roman Catholic brother James lawfully be 'excluded' from the succession? His religion could be no secret after he had refused to take the oath under the Test Act of 1673. The record of the last two Roman Catholic monarchs of England had not been encouraging.

The Popish Plot of 1678–81 was the 'war on terror' scare of its times. Titus Oates, a complex character who had been a student at Cambridge, created a story that there was a Roman Catholic conspiracy to assassinate Charles II, with a lengthy (forged) document giving the particulars. Oates was exposed as a liar and convicted of perjury for swearing that he had overheard the plotters at work and giving testimony that a number of named individuals were involved, particularly Jesuits, but not before there were arrests and executions and a general panic, precipitating the 'Exclusion Crisis'.

The panic made its way from London to Oxford, where Anthony Wood reports that in October 1678, accusations were being made that various persons in Oxford were papists. Walker, the Master of University College, was alleged to be one, and 'many of the divines in Oxford ... pricks up their eares and crests upon the discovery of the plot' and 'talk very boldly and undaunted'.[42] By November, when 'popish recusants' were banned from coming within ten miles of London, the heat grew in Oxford. Wood reports John Hall of Pembroke College preaching 'sharply and bitterly against the papists' in St. Mary's and an effigy of the Pope was burned at St. Edmund's Hall:

> He was brought out in a chaire, set before the fire, shot at, and then (his belly beng full of crackers) was burnt. A great white cross made of papers and sticks burnt in St. Clement's.[43]

There were proposals to search the rooms and papers of scholars[44] and alleged 'papists' were ostracized.

In May 1679 Anthony Ashley Cooper, the Earl of Shaftsbury, introduced an Exclusion Bill in the House of Commons, whose objective was to ensure that no Roman Catholic could succeed to the throne. The Queen, Catherine of Braganza, was herself a Roman Catholic, so this was sensitive territory. The King dissolved Parliament to prevent the Bill becoming law. A party which was to become the Whigs petitioned the King to call Parliament again so that the Bill could complete its passage and did their best to maintain public concern about the now debunked 'Popish Plot'. Those who 'Abhorred' the Bill were to emerge as the 'Tories'. Oxford was reckoned to be Tory.

Anthony Wood had particular reason for concern on Oxford's behalf over the turn events were taking. His *Historia et antiquitates universitatis oxoniensis* was criticized, as he himself records, on the grounds that it said 'many unseemly things of the reformation'.[45] Old scores were settled in Oxford by the simple expedient of denouncing one's enemies as crypto-papists. An official request from the King was engineered, 'requiring' the Vice-Chancellor, then Nicholas, Warden of New College and anxious to steer the University through these choppy waters by making what accommodations he could, to make an inquiry and root out scholars with papist sympathies.

John Evelyn (1620–1706) may have been a material help in encouraging the King in his patronage of Oxford.[46] Charles II visited Oxford in the spring and is said to have watched the men at work building the new 'scientific' Museum next door, when he went to inspect the Sheldonian Theatre, so as to see whether it could be adapted to use as a House of Commons. It was planned that Parliament should meet in Oxford from 21 March. Parliament duly met in Oxford for a week in 1681,[47] with colleges rather conservatively providing rooms. Exeter College, for example, offered three rooms in the Rector's house 'but the whole college could by no means be had' as John Locke reported during his negotiations on behalf of Shaftsbury.

Holding Parliament in Oxford in 1681 may have represented a move by the King to balance the country's allegiances by countenancing a 'Tory' venue. He could not get the members to agree and he never called a Parliament again. Wood refers to 'some hot discourses' in Oxford and threatenings of some in power against the 'Universitie' as the Parliament assembled and the way 'parliament men lately endeavour to intrap scholars in discourse' and 'provoke them to talke of parliaments and state affaires'.[48] On Palm Sunday, Dr. Fell, now Bishop of Oxford, preached in the cathedral before the King. But the King was already uneasy. On the Monday he 'did about ten of the clock in the morning send for his robes and crown privately', sent for the Speaker and dissolved the Parliament without attending in person for the purpose. Then he left for London. Wood notes the contrast between the civility of the courtiers towards the scholars and how 'uncivill' were the 'parliament men'.[49] The dissolution of the Oxford Parliament in March 1681 was a significant moment for the University and for the country.

The new royalist thinking had to be articulated and defended, and an academic context was not proving a comfortable or safe place to do it. On 21 July 1683, Congregation made a Decree and books were burned in the Bodleian Library quadrangle. Condemned by the decree as dangerous to the state or the souls of men were 'certain Pernicious books and Damnable Doctrines Destructive to the Sacred Persons of Princes, their State and Government of all Humane Society', and also twenty-seven opinions or 'Propositions', judged to be 'false, seditious and impious; and most of them to be also Heretical and Blasphemous, infamous to Christian Religion and destructive of all Government in Church and State'. Among the condemned authors and works were Hobbes (his *Leviathan*), political works of John Milton, works of John Owen and Richard Baxter and others.

Uncomfortable consequences continued to flow when Charles II's brother James II became King. The Cambridge figure Robert Brady (1627–1700) was appointed physician-in-ordinary to Charles II in 1682, a year after publishing the first version of his *True and Exact History of the Succession.* In 1687 Brady accompanied James II on a visit to Oxford during which, with Brady's encouragement, the King attempted to impose a Roman Catholic president on Magdalen College.

Letters of 1688 described the outbreaks of violence in the indignant city:

> how the Rabble were offended, & fell upon breaking windows of the few Papists we have with us; wch riot continued that whole day.[50]

'The middle part of our University doe stick well enough to Old Principles.'[51] Nevertheless, to some observers the intrusion seemed beneficial. At Wadham, for example, there has been a 'turning women bedmakers out of Colledge' and changes to ensure that 'the publick revenue be better managed thereafter than it hath been Don for many yeares'.[52]

Oxford and the Glorious Revolution: honest brokers and propriety in public life

The events of 1688–9 precipitated another crisis for Oxford. In April 1688 seven bishops led by the Archbishop of Canterbury submitted a petition requesting the King to rethink his religious policies. In June, the Queen gave birth to a son and the nation feared that this would be the beginning of a dynasty of Roman Catholic monarchs. Before the end of the month William of Orange, a protestant married to Mary, one of James's two moderate Anglican daughters, had received an invitation to come to England and take over the reins of Government. He was happy to oblige. James II fled from England at the end of 1688.

Would Oxford support William and Mary as joint monarchs? The Oxford decree of 1683 had condemned the deposition of an anointed king.[53] Could that now be disavowed? The constitutional position was unclear, indeed unprecedented. Pamphlets and counter-pamphlets flew about in Oxford, arguing the case for and against the succession of William of Orange. The Vice-Chancellor was wisely not at home when the city celebrated the proclamation that William and Mary were to share the monarchy.[54]

The Prince of Orange summoned an assembly of Lords and Commons at the end of December 1688 at the request of both Houses, and the resulting Convention Parliament met in January 1689. It was this body which resolved that in effect James had abdicated and the throne was vacant and, on 6 February, that the Prince and Princess of Orange should be made King William and Queen Mary, preserving the succession as well as might be done, through Mary, James II's eldest daughter. A Declaration of Rights was framed to legitimate what was being done, including a list of the misdoings of James II. The Convention enacted the Parliament Act of 1689 to make itself into a Parliament and the new sovereigns gave the Royal Assent on 23 February. When they themselves summoned a Parliament the declaration that it was indeed a Parliament 'notwithstanding any fault of writ or writs of summons' was repeated. Everything was done, in short, to ensure that this unprecedented mode of succession would be safe from challenge.

Oxford sent Heneage Finch and Thomas Clarges to represent it at the Convention Parliament of 1689. Heneage Finch (1621–82) had been at Christ Church before he entered the Inner Temple to pursue a career in the law. He was a consistent Royalist and sufficiently courageous to detach himself from public affairs during the period of roundhead supremacy and the Protectorate. At the Restoration he came into high favour marked by rewards and offices. At the election of 1661 he became member of Parliament for the University of Oxford, was active on committees and a frequent maker of speeches.

But these were dangerous times to be so visible. Finch had enjoyed the patronage of Edward Hyde, Earl of Clarendon (1609–74), and Chancellor of the University of Oxford from 1660 to 1667, and he found himself in a difficult position when Edward Hyde was impeached in 1667. Finch spoke out, but equivocally, and perhaps fortunately for him Clarendon fled and was formally banished. He himself became a baronet and was removed to the House of Lords.

Sir Thomas Clarges (1617?–1695) began his Oxford connection not through the University, but as apprentice to an Oxford apothecary. This trade took him into the Royalist armies during the Civil War. He earned sufficient respect in the entourage of General Monck to be entrusted with tasks as his agent in London while Monck was commanding armies in Scotland. That led to Clarges becoming a member of the Protectorate Parliament in a Scottish seat. He was said to have been influential in persuading Monck to urge the restoration of the monarchy; he voted in the Convention Parliament of 1660 and when on 1 May it voted to restore the monarchy, Monck sent him to take the news to the future King Charles II. However, he became critical of the Court, lost favour and his offices, as he spread anxiety about the rise of 'popery' and misconduct in public life. Yet he was back in Parliament again in 1685, for Christchurch in Hampshire, and an active opponent of James II's policies affecting religion. His selection to represent Oxford in the Convention Parliament of 1689 was therefore not the choice of a 'safe pair of hands'. He worked actively to help shape the legislation which underpinned the Revolution Settlement, though he seems to have had some hope that James II might be brought back. He kept his seat for Oxford in the election of 1690. Bishop Burnet described Clarges as an:

> honest but haughty man, who valued himself upon opposing the court, and on his frugality in managing the public money, for he had Cromwell's economy ever in his mouth.... Many thought he carried this too far, but it made him very popular. After he was become very rich himself by the public money, he seemed to take care that nobody else should grow as rich as he was in the same way.[55]

Into the eighteenth century with a grin

The high seriousness of these events did not reduce the inveterate Oxford taste for gossip. Thomas Tanner received a letter from a friend in 1699 describing how

> The Oxford Ladies are in bodily fear least the French should come and ravish 'em. And some of them say what a strange thing it is to be ravish't. They were ne're ravish't in their lives. If I could send thee a Ream of paper full of news I would: but there is none here, but that Randal of Oriel has powderd his hair.... Dr. Rogers has a new pair of breeches in order to stand for President... Ives the poticary is ready to break, having no vent for his chocolat.[56]

Thomas Hearne's *Collections* are in part a diary of his encounters and of the local gossip of Oxford in the first decades of the eighteenth century:

> Mr. Robt Wood told me yesterday that his Uncle Ant Wood was a wonderfull Pryer, that he used to go out by himself in by-Places, wore his hat over his eyes, seemed to take notice of nothing and to know nothing, and yet he took notice of everything and knew everything.[57]

There is a jumble of trivialities and serious comment. On May 26 (1713), he was telling the story of a young gentleman of good prospects and recently a Gentleman-Commoner of Merton College, accidentally drowned in a well in Yorkshire in an episode involving several of his friends in the middle of the night, Thomas Hearne breaks off to remark that 'The present Vice-Chanc: Dr. Gardiner hath the Character of a Man of no credit'.[58] For 19 March 1715 we read:

> Yesterday about 3 Clock in the Afternoon died of a Feaver my great and good friend Mr. John Urry, Student of Christ-Church. This gentleman was Bachelor of Arts, & bore Arms against Monmouth in the Rebellion called Monmouth's Rebellion, as several other Oxford Scholars did. He was a stour, lusty Man, & of admirable Principles. His Integrity & Honesty & Loyalty gain'd him great Honour & Respect. He refused the Oaths, & died a Non-Juror.... He had published Proposals for a new Edition of Chaucer, which he had almost prepared for the Press before he died, & he was like to meet with very great Encouragement.[59]

The 'Non-juror' question began to present itself as a matter of 'integrity in public life' in Oxford minds. It was one of the factors which was to lead to the 'ejectment' of Thomas Hearne himself from the Bodleian Library.[60] The Non-Jurors were so-called because they refused to take the oath of allegiance to William and Mary. Their leaders on the episcopal bench numbered more than half a dozen and saw it as a matter of conscience, since they considered that they would be traitors to James II if they did. They were deprived of their sees in 1691 solely by Act of Parliament, and not by any canonical action of the Church. The issue was important to Oxford because Oxford (and of course Cambridge) was always busy with the education of future Anglican clergy. This was regarded as an activity carried out in trust for the nation, for these were to be the clergy of the established Church. Colleges commonly required ordination as a condition of the holding of Fellowships.

New styles of Oxford Toryism

'Conservative' Oxford now became 'Tory' Oxford, after the foundation of the 'Tory' party in 1678. It was also to be in a small way a hotbed of Jacobitism, the movement to restore the succession through the son of James II. This was the infant James whose birth had precipitated the flight of his father and was to become the Old Pretender. Rightly or wrongly, Oxford was widely perceived to be dangerously eager to unseat the current Hanoverian monarchy and restore the Stuart line. Oxford was regarded by Whig politicians as very positively Jacobite. The Jacobite leader known as 'Colonel Owen' was entertained by Heads of House and he and his gang strutted about the streets in broad daylight attended by an avid mob of townspeople:

> huzzaing King James...in defiance of the government and the friends of the government; and that the few friends it had

> there went every day in danger of their lives from them and their abettors; that they actually besieged Oriel college and demanded out of it two gentlemen, remarkable for their zeal for the protestant succession, to sacrifice to the mob... I need not mention that the pretender's health was drunk openly and unreservedly in all places... and... at last, a regiment of dragoons march'd into Oxford, sword in hand, to prevent their rising in open rebellion.[61]

'Tory' Oxford in the eighteenth century was to suffer attack from the 'Whigs', led by Shaftsbury, who loosely represented the heirs of the various left-wing challengers to conservatism of the seventeenth century (though the Whig party came formally into being at the time of the Exclusion Bill, when its focus was on preventing the succession of James II).[62] Exeter, Wadham and Merton were 'Whig' colleges, but they were in a minority and were suspected of acting as Government spies, relaying disadvantageous stories of what went on at Oxford.

For a time Oxford had no Chancellor. The second Duke of Ormonde had followed his grandfather as Chancellor in 1688 and he had won general goodwill by his hospitality, but the memory of the way his own election had been fixed had not been lost in Oxford. Charles Butler, Earl of Arran, was appointed in 1715. Thomas Hearne's *Remains* comment on the political coloration of university sermons as Oxford positioned itself for the Hanoverians and took a stance on the Pretender.[63] So this became a period, unusual in the history of the University, where Convocation had parties or 'factions' bigger than the coteries which have always engaged in horse-trading.

Francis Atterbury (1663–1732) entered Christ Church in 1680 with a coterie of fellow-students from Westminster School, a social and intellectual élite. Atterbury was a particular favourite of the then Dean, Henry Aldrich, author of the standard student logic textbook. Atterbury began to find the intense but closed-in life of Christ Church suffocating. 'I am losing time every minute I stay here,' he wrote to his father.[64] He began to seek, and obtain, preferments in a wider world, and to make his name as a society preacher.[65] His first publications evinced a lively anti-Catholicism and were positive about Lutheranism. His ideas changed and he began to be known as a High-Churchman anxious to re-establish the Established Church in society in more than name. After a period of political negotiation he got his wish and was made Dean of Christ Church (1710–13), where he set about politicking again, with the objective of adjusting the balance of power among the colleges to the advantage of a prospective alliance between Christ Church and Magdalen (with its current head Sachaverell as his ally).

Oxford and the Jacobites

The first Jacobite Rising occurred in 1715, and in the same year there was a notorious riot in Oxford. On 29 May a Presbyterian meeting house was half pulled-down in a disturbance, which Heads of House were quick to blame on Whigs who were members of the Constitution Club, not on Tories or Oxford 'Jacobites'. A second riot took place the following year, again allegedly instigated by the discontented young Whigs – and perhaps exacerbated by the fact that a regiment of foot-soldiers had been quartered in Oxford since 1715. There was a riot in a coffee-house between some students and an officer of the army. There began to be talk of setting up an Inquiry into Oxford by the House of Lords.[66]

John Toland (1670–1722) published a *State Anatomy of Great Britain* (1717) in which concerns were expressed about the propensities of the universities to be politically dangerous. (His own time spent in Oxford in 1693 to work in the Bodleian Library on the compilation of an Irish dictionary had consolidated a friendship with John Locke and brought him a reputation as a coffee-house orator.) Public concern grew. It went as far as the drafting of a University Reform Bill regretting that 'many in those Nurseryes dedicated to Religion Learning Loyalty and peace have been infected with principles of sedition' leading to 'Riots and tumults'.[67]

The plan was to vest in the Crown the right to make all appointments in the University and to set up a body of commissioners to administer the process. Oxford was saved partly by the realization that the vested interests in the existing framework of property and endowments were huge and complex and reached far beyond the University. The University put its collective mind to holding off the danger of further state interference though, unusually, it does not seem to have made much of a fist of the sort of political networking which has stood it in good stead in most centuries.

In 1745 came the Second Jacobite Rising, and with it heightened concern in London about the involvement of Oxford. In Oxford, drunken parties were reported, at which, it was said, there were toasts to 'the King over the water'. William King (1685–1763) a known Jacobite, gave a speech at the opening of the Radcliffe Library in the newly-built Camera in April 1749. The architect, Gibbs, was a personal friend of his. He spoke enthusiastically about the trustees, who included several Jacobites and various High Tories. He proffered familiar topoi linking the decline of national standards with the decline of virtue in the nation and cried 'redeat' six times, a choice of term which could easily be, and was, construed as a call for the return of the Stuart monarchy.[68] Thomas Warton (1728–90), Oxford's in-house poet laureate in 1747 and 1748, captured the scene in verse:

> See, on yon Sage how all attentive stand,
> To catch his darting eye, and waving hand.
> Hark! he begins, with all a Tully's art,
> To pour the dictates of a Cato's heart:
> Skill'd to pronounce what noblest thoughts inspire,
> He blends the speaker's with the patriot's fire;
> Bold to conceive, nor timorous to conceal,
> What Britons dare to think, he dares to tell.[69]

In Government there were more calls for Oxford to be brought to heel. But it was realized that it would be difficult to create regulations for Oxford which would not also have to apply to Cambridge and Cambridge was not thought to have been behaving badly. The trouble was that those in power in the country were almost inevitably *parti pris* on the subject of the universities, from personal experience. The Whig rival of William Pitt, Charles James Fox had been a student at Oxford at Hart Hall from 1764, but he never took his degree and left murmuring about the 'nonsenses' of the University. His sympathies were with the dissenters and their educational experiments in the dissenting academies. William Pitt the Younger (1759–1806), his Tory adversary, was a Cambridge man. The threat of state interference lingered.

A society of scholars: student life in the seventeenth and eighteenth centuries

What was life like for the students during these centuries of political drama? A lively appetite for the details of the life of a small but vivid society seems to have been as characteristic of Oxford as it is today. Senior and junior members of the University met in the streets and enjoyed mutual hospitality. It was said of Thomas Allen of Trinity (1542–1632) that 'every body loved his company, and every howse on their *Gaudie-dayes*[70] were wont to invite him'.[71]

John Aubrey was an antiquarian in an age when the curious was the legitimate object of curiosity. A notable human character was a collectable item as much as an object of interest brought back by a traveller to be put in a 'cabinet of curiosities'. He collected his 'specimens' in his *Lives*. One of Aubrey's most memorable 'Oxford' portraits is of Ralph Kettell who was President of Trinity College, Oxford, for nearly half a century, from 1599 until he died in 1643.[72] Kettell was generous to his college. In 1616 or not long after, he leased the site of the house which is now 54 Broad St. from Oriel College and built 'Kettell Hall' for the use of the College. Aubrey says he was

> a very tall well growne man. His gowne and surplice and hood being on, he had a terrible gigantique aspect, with his sharp grey eies.... One of his maximes of governing was to keepe-downe the juvenilis impetus.

Aubrey would have been able to observe him keeping the students 'down' when he was a student and Kettell near the end of his time. This manner of looking after the welfare of the young in his charge involved assiduous effort on the President's part:

> The Doctor's fashion was to goe up and down the college, and peepe in at the key-holes to see whether the boyes did follow their bookes or no. He observed that the howses that had the smallest beer had most drunkards, for it forced them to goe into the town to comfort their stomachs; wherfore Dr Kettle alwayes had in his College excellent beer, not better to be had in Oxon.

Kettell apparently particularly disliked 'long-haired students':

> He was irreconcileable to long haire; called them hairy scalpes, and as for periwigges (which were then very rarely worne) he beleeved them to be the scalpes of men cutt off after they were hanged, and so tanned and dressed for use. When he observed the scolars' haire longer than ordinary (especially if they were scholars of the howse), he would bring a pair of cizers in his muffe.... I remember he cutt Mr. Radford's haire with the knife that chipps the bread on the buttery-hatch. He dragg'd with one (i.e. right) foot a little, by which he gave warning (like the rattlesnake) of his comeing.

His vocabulary of criticism when he found fault was ripe and robust:

> When he scolded at the idle young boies of his colledge, he used these names, viz. Turds, Tarrarags (these were the worst sort, rude raskells), Rascal-Jacks, Blindcinques, Scobberlotchers (these did no hurt, were sober, but went idleing about the grove with their hands in their pocketts, and telling the number of trees there).

Yet he was quietly generous to poor students:

> In his college, where he observed diligent boyes that he guessed had but a slender exhibition from their friends, he

> would many times putt money in at their windowes; that his right hand did not know what his left did.

He also seems to have had a delicious sense of fun:

> Dr. Kettle was wont to say that 'Seneca writes, as a boare does pisse', scilicet, by jirkes. He sang a shrill high treble; but there was one (J. Hoskyns) who had a higher, and would play the wag with the Dr. to make him straine his voice up to his.

Of Kettell's own intellectual pretensions Aubrey has a mixed report:

> Mr. –, one of the fellowes, was wont to say, that Dr. Kettel's braine was like a hasty-pudding, where there was memorie, judgement, and phancy all stirred together.

But he was shrewd as a 'governor' (Head of House). One of Kettell's most lucrative innovations was a College rule (*Decretum de Gratiis Collegio Rependendis*), which bound members of the College to pay it a proportion of any financial bonuses or outside sources of income they might acquire. The Fellows agreed in 1602 to give 20 per cent of the annual income if they inherited a property and if they accepted a benefice, to give 12.5 per cent; in their wills they would leave Trinity 5 per cent of the capital of which they died possessed.[73]

Self-education and intellectual self-reliance for students

In the seventeenth and eighteenth centuries a student's allocated tutor largely shaped the student experience and also the course of his studies, for from the seventeenth century, these principally took the form of 'directed reading'. The Oxford student, if he was fortunate, was advised by a good tutor how to conduct his inner intellectual life and manage his energies and interests, but ultimately the responsibility was his own.

This tended to encourage an ambitious and independent 'lifelong learning'. Aubrey comments on the early reading habits of William Brereton (1604–61), who was a student at Brasenose. 'I have heard him say that when he was young, he read over Cowper's dictionary' which is why he has such a mastery of Latin.[74] Brereton was upright in every way. 'He is very tall (about six foot high) and straight, very temperate, and vertuouse, and frugall,' says Aubrey. He was to be prominent in the Civil War and was going to spend much of his life as a soldier in the Parliamentary Army and a student of military affairs, but he never ceased in the active pursuit of his intellectual interests, reaching out to others with similar enthusiasms. He was generous to fellow chemists from abroad:

> his greatest delight is chymistrey. He has at his sister's a noble laboratory, and severall servants (prentices to him) to looke to it.[75]

An example from 1701 gives a picture of the way a tutor might guide a student seeking to equip himself intellectually in the traditional way within the University:

> If you find yourselves indisposed for such studies which require intenseness of mind, divert yourself by reading [something light which may] yet withal profit you. Or, if of that standing [i.e. a graduate] that you may be admitted to publick Libraries, go thither... withal you may happen on some book, that may be of more advantage to you, than what you was reading in your own Study, and find that time most beneficially spent.[76]

(In these centuries, undergraduates were still not admitted to the Bodleian, which remained the 'public Library' in contrast with the College libraries.)

So it was the expectation of these times that students should make themselves responsible for their own learning. This was not peculiar to students educated at Oxford. Daniel Waterland provided 'Advice to a young student' (not published until 1730 but originally devised three decades earlier to meet the needs of the students to whom he was tutor at Magdalene College, Cambridge).[77] He too takes it that the task of the tutor is to guide and encourage what is essentially the independent effort of the young man to educate himself by reading. 'Design your own Accomplishment, and therewith the truest Pleasure'[78] urged a commentator in the 1770s. (These were the sentiments of Joseph Priestley, too, in his prefatory remarks to his students at the beginning of a set of science lectures given in the world of the dissenting academies at the end of the eighteenth century.[79])

Lectures in Arts for undergraduates in the University of Oxford stopped in the seventeenth century, though colleges sometimes still provided them, and the 'lecture' as a mode of instruction survived in the lectures on novel extra-curricular subjects given by the new breed of salaried professors. Tutors not only directed students' private reading, but instead might provide further teaching materials written by themselves.[80] The consequences of this shift from the medieval practice of familiarizing oneself with a text by hearing it lectured upon (with concomitant problems in getting hold of one's own copy), to the seventeenth-century emphasis on private study, is exemplified in the surviving notebooks of some leading intellectual figures.

Teaching, by whatever method, involved a transaction for which the student was expected to pay. In some places and at some periods a generous academic could provide lectures free, but this was highly unusual. The rarity of such 'offers' cannot be overemphasized. It happened in Oxford at the beginning of the Michaelmas Term in 1764, when Edward Bentham (1707–76), Regius Professor of Divinity, offered some free lectures. He confined his offer, however, to those intending to prepare for ordination, who were already graduates, the kind of young man who held a college teaching Fellowship for a time after graduating and then wished to marry and consequently had to qualify himself to accept a living and become a parish priest. 'For the benefit of the younger Members of the University, from three to seven years standing, who are designed for Holy Orders,' he 'proposes to give gratis a Course of Instructions relative to Theological Knowledge'.[81] The course was to include the following:

> 'The chief Doctrines and duties of Natural and Revealed Religion will be stated, and the proofs of them produced'; ... 'The rise and Progress of erroneous Opinions among Christians'; 'A general View of Sacred and Ecclesiastical History'; 'The most useful Books in these Branches of learning will be recommended.'

Forming the mind, forming the man: Oxford and the Christian gentleman

'My intention was to outline a way of life for you, not a course of study,' says Erasmus in his *Enchiridion* (1503). One of the most important new dimensions of the post-medieval universities was the expectation that they would form not only the mind but the man. Medieval education for the younger child had coupled study and discipline – particularly in monastic schools where it was considered a sort of martyrdom to die of a beating in the school. But medieval universities did not beat their students to encourage them to learn; instead they concerned themselves with maintaining good order in the town.[82]

The notion that a university should fit the ordinary student to be not only a good man but also a good citizen can be seen to be influencing discussion from the sixteenth century.[83] When he made the remark just quoted, Erasmus had something rather different in mind from the medieval model, perhaps closer to the way classical philosophers had understood the intimate relationship of 'progress in understanding' with 'progress in right conduct'. His thinking was more in tune with Cicero's *De officiis,* with its practical notions of the way to ensure the fulfilment of duties in public life. A serious-minded sixteenth-century approach to forming the student to fit him for life's duties, extended to princes too.[84]

'The change from young men of position studying law and the muses before entering upon life to a more plebeian and puritanical class of undergraduate coincides more or less with the conversion of the Hall into a College,' writes the nineteenth-century historian of Pembroke College, noting that this change was widespread throughout the University. He gives the example of George Hughes (b.1603), who became a Fellow of Pembroke and was ordained, then 'preached in and around Oxford' until 'silenced by Laud', when he 'had thoughts of transferring himself to New England' until dissuaded and given a living at Tavistock where by his efforts 'a mighty Reformation was wrought'.[85]

It was a paradox of this shift that it carried with it expectations about both these early 'middle class' students and the students who were 'gentlemen'. For a further evolution of the sense of moral responsibility for students can be observed in the seventeenth and eighteenth centuries with the development of the somewhat equivocal notion of an English gentleman. Robert Boyle (1627–91) got his schooling at Eton but he continued it independently. In 1639, when he was 12, he was sent with his brother to tour the continent with a French tutor, Isaac Marcombes, a French-speaking protestant. He had successfully conducted the boys' older brothers on a similar tour. They passed through France to Geneva, where they stayed for nearly two years and where Robert studied history, ethics and natural philosophy. Writing on the qualities of *The Christian Virtuoso,* he lists:

> greatness of mind, noble aims, courage or valour, constancy and patience in afflictions, bounty or liberality, forwardness to oblige, readiness to forgive, a just and impartial estimate of riches, humility, contempt of all that is base.[86]

He wrote moral essays and religious meditations in the 1640s in which such themes appear.[87] In 'Of Publicke-Spiritedness' he explored the relation between virtue in the abstract, personal virtue and 'the role of the individual in society'.[88]

> the great and deplorable Growth of Irreligion, especially among those that aspired to pass for Wits, and several of them too for Philosophers, / And on the other side, it was Obvious, that divers learned men, as well as Others, ... had

> brought many Good Men to think, that Religion and Philosophy were incompatible ... the Libertines thought a Virtuoso ought not to be a Christian; and the others, That he could not be a true One.[89]

One should not be led into thinking that this necessarily meant that young men at Oxford or their tutors behaved well. But it set a standard of expectation:

> Among the many methods by which a Revealed Religion has advanced Morality, this is one, That it has given us a more just and perfect Idea of that being whom every reasonable Creature ought to imitate. The Young Man, in a Heathen Comedy, might justify his Lewdness by the Example of Jupiter; as, indeed, there was scarce any Crime that might not be countenanced by those Notions of the Deity which prevailed among the common People in the Heathen worlds. Revealed Religion sets forth a proper Object for Imitation, in that Being who is the Pattern, as well as the Source, of all Spiritual Perfection,[90]

said the *Spectator* in 1714.

'Honour' could be accommodating. Nicholas Amhurst of St John's wrote in January 1720/1 about the dilemma which faced many young men arriving at Oxford. When they were admitted to their colleges they were required to take an oath to obey its statutes and often to give undertakings which had been created because of problems which had arisen in the past. For example, it might be a requirement to swear that one did not have an estate of more than a certain value though one had much more wealth than that in reality. One boy made his estates over 'to a bed-maker ... who locked her up in his closet, till he had taken the oath, and then disposses'd the poor old woman of her imaginary estate, and cancell'd the writings'.[91]

Moral education as 'vocational'

This was still the age of the 'pious' founder and the 'pious benefactor' and the tutor with a sense of pastoral responsibility. This meant that students would expect their tutors to behave as 'moral' tutors, as well as guiding them intellectually in their reading. William Laud, when he was Chancellor of Oxford, wrote to Oxford's Vice-Chancellor in June 1637 to express his dislike of the idea of allowing students access to a riding school. He says it will be a thoroughly bad thing 'to suffer scholars to fall into the old humour of going up or down in boots and spurs'. And if one student goes riding 'you shall have twenty or forty to look on, and there lost their time'. And 'though the exercise in itself be exceedingly commendable' the students 'are most part too young and not strong enough'.[92]

Seventeenth-century histories of morality heralded new fashions in good behaviour, and 'formation' of the boy as future citizen as well as good Christian was thought important.[93] Thomas Barlow wrote to Thomas Hobbes from Oxford in 1656:

> Tis true, (as you well observe) that Vniversities ... are (good or bad) as they are vsed; ... It is my hope, and prayer, yt our Vniversityes may be such, as they should, Seminaries of all good Letters; in wch the youth of this Nation may (upon just principles) be taught religion and Piety towards God, and obedience and duty to their Gouvernors [= fathers].[94]

Pedagogical objectives: polished manners or enlargement of mind?

There was a perceived danger in the eighteenth century that the temptation of any family with wealth enough to afford it was to educate at least the eldest son to be good for nothing. 'Why should my son be a Scholar, when it is not intended that he should live by his learning?' And the Father has grown rich by 'Avarice, Injustice, Oppression; he is a Tyrant in the neighbourhood over Slaves and Beggars, whom he calleth his Tenants'. That has served him well enough, the hypothetical father thinks and he sees no reason to expose his son to higher standards.[95]

> Another Hindrance to good Education ... is that pernicious Custom in rich and noble families, of entertaining French Tutors in their Houses. These wretched Pedagogues are enjoyned by the Father, to take special care that the Boy shall be perfect in his French; by the Mother, that Master must not walk till he is hot, nor be suffered to play with other Boys, nor be wet in his Feet, nor daub his Cloaths: And to see that the Dancing-Master attends constantly, and does his Duty: She further insists, that the Child be not kept too long poring on his Book, because he is subject to sore Eyes, and of a weakly Constitution. ... By these Methods, the young Gentleman is in every Article as fully accomplished at eight Years old as at eight and twenty ... the same Airs, the same Strut, the same Cock of his Hat ... the same Understanding, the same Compass of Knowledge, with the very same Absurdity, Impudence, and Impertinence of Tongue.[96]

The Irish satirist Jonathan Swift (1667–1745), having evoked this sprig of juvenile arrogance, contrasts the effect of being sent to a good school which takes learning seriously, and then to university, where a young man would read books 'full of incitements to Virtue and discouragements from Vice', and be exposed to larger ideas, 'the Points of Honour, Truth, Justice and other noble Gifts of the Mind'. Edward Gibbon too thought this a sensible way to ensure that a boy was imbued with desirable characteristics:

> At [public] school, 'a boy of spirit may acquire a praevious and practical experience of the World'... 'In a free intercourse with his equals the habits of truth, fortitude and prudence will insensibly be matured.'[97]

Swift had studied at Trinity College, Dublin, but he was admitted to Hart Hall (later Hertford College) and in 1692 he became an example of the practice of 'incorporation', admission to an Oxford degree which was the equivalent of a degree already held.

The 'formation' of the student of modest means

Daniel Fleming (1633–1701), entered Queen's College in 1650 and remained in Oxford for two years. It was always the norm for students to pay fees for their tuition. Even in the Middle Ages, completion rates were aversely affected by poverty and even sometimes by the need to earn while studying.[98] In Oxford as in Cambridge arrangements could be made to enable an impecunious student to earn his way by acting as a gentleman servant to other students or to tutors. These 'sizarships' were distinct from exhibitions or scholarships, which were granted on merit but also assisted with the costs of study. But there remained many students for whose parents it was a struggle to afford to send a son to Oxford. Daniel's mother wrote him an anxious letter – of only modest literacy – in January 1650; the family was in straitened times because it was involved in a lawsuit, but she will try to send him the shirts he has asked for as soon as they can be afforded, which will probably be 'abut Whutsonday abut then they are the whitest and chipest'.[99] His tutor wrote a report of him to his father, on which his father comments shrewdly in a letter to his son in May 1651: 'Yor Tutor is pleasd by his letter to give you a very ffaire Character: I hope it is yor merritte in some measure; as well as his Good will.'[100] He was a generous father and sent the Tutor the necessary money. 'I shall bee loath to see you want anythinge ffitt ffor you.' He wants to help his son, 'to make you a Man; & indeed a Gentleman...yu must bee a good husband, and frugall; as Civilitye & your Reputacõn will pmitt.'[101] Daniel was apparently not a good correspondent and his family's letters grumble about his silence.

Student life in the eighteenth century

In the eighteenth century the age of admission typically rose from 15–16 to 18–19. Students were now young men rather than children, with consequences for the way they were to be 'formed'. Dr. Johnson (1709–84) 'went to Oxford, and was entered a commoner of Pembroke College' in 1728 at 19. He arrived with his father, 'who had anxiously accompanied him'.[102] His father ensured that he was introduced to his tutor that very evening, though Boswell suggests that like Robert Burton, 'he wanted not a tutor':

> His father seemed very full of the merits of his son, and told the company he was a good scholar, and a poet, and wrote Latin verses.....He [Samuel] sat silent, till upon something which occurred in the course of conversation, he suddenly struck in and quoted Macrobius; and thus he gave the first impression of that more extensive reading in which he had indulged himself.

Boswell is disparaging about the tutor. Johnson had described him as 'a very worthy man, but a heavy man, and I did not...attend him much'. He 'waited upon him' the first day and then spent four days sliding on the ice on Christ Church meadow instead of returning for more tuition. He retrieved tutorial good opinion through a 'masterly' translation of Pope's Messiah into Latin verse, a vacation task which he tossed off 'with uncommon rapidity' but which greatly impressed the college. Johnson's Oxford career was brief because of shortage of family funds.

At Magdalen, gentleman-commoners became comparatively numerous; they had superior gowns, ate with the Fellows and were distinct both from the scholars or demys on the foundation and the ordinary commoners.[103] Arriving in Oxford on 3 April 1752, Edward Gibbon says:

> I felt myself suddenly raised from a boy to a man: the persons whom I respected as my superiors in age and Academical rank entertained me with every mark of attention and civility; and my vanity was flattered by the velvet Cap and silk gown which discriminate a Gentleman-Commoner from a plebeian student....A key was delivered into my hands which gave me the free use of a numerous and elegant library; my apartment consisted of three elegant and well furnished rooms in the

> new building, a stately pile, of Magdalen College: and the adjacent walks, had they been frequented by Plato's disciples, might have been compared to the Attic shade on the banks of the Illissus.

Eating with the Fellows may not have been quite the social privilege it sounds. As a gentleman-commoner, Edward Gibbon 'was admitted to the society of the Fellows, and fondly expected that some questions of literature would be the amusing and instructive topics of their discourse'. But no. 'Their conversation stagnated in a round of College business, Tory politics, personal stories and private scandal.'[104]

The gentle teasing of Thomas Baskerville echoes more hollowly against such criticism. Scholars must be allowed to have some fun, thought Thomas Baskerville:

> Before I leave this Colledge and the good people in it I must remember their mallard night. For the grave Judges have sometimes their festivall days, and dance together at Sergeants Inn; The Country people will haue their Lott-meads, Parish feasts; And Schollers must haue some times of mirth to meliorate their great sobriety.

He does not know when the Magdalen Mallard Ceremony began but he describes how 'when they have a mind to keep it' a Lord of the Mallard is chosen, who bears the costs of the ceremonial and there is a procession with songs in which a mallard is carried fixed to a pole, and a game of forfeits, followed by a night's drinking in the common room. The ceremony ends with the beheading of the unfortunate duck and the distribution of drops of its blood into everyone's 'tumbler' 'which being drunk off', the College disperses.[105]

Edward Gibbon quotes the enthusiastic description of what Oxford had to offer intellectually speaking by Robert Lowth (1710–97), who entered New College in 1729 and became Professor of Poetry in 1741:

> where a liberal pursuit of knowledge, and a genuine freedom of thought was raised encouraged and pushed forward by example, by commendation, and by authority. I breathed the same atmosphere, that the HOOKERS, the CHILLINGWORTHS, and the LOCKES, had breathed before: whose benevolence and humanity were as extensive as their vast Genius and comprehensive knowledges, who always treated their adversaries with civility, and respect,

only to reject this view and regret his own experience of fourteen idle and unprofitable months at Magdalen.[106] Gibbon's main impression is of the orderliness of Oxford life compared with what he has since seen 'in the most celebrated Universities of Holland, Germany and Italy'. He notes a little later that he fears the universities will be hard to reform, since they have 'the spirit of monopolists'.[107]

John Wesley at Lincoln College

John Wesley, founder of Methodism, was a student at Christ Church before he obtained the 'Lincolnshire' Fellowship at Lincoln College which became vacant in 1725, for which he was eligible by reason of his birthplace.[108] He got it by examination and interview, not mere patronage, though some effort had been put in on his behalf in that quarter. In 1730 he became a tutor, with eleven students to supervise. This was the period when the Holy Club was formed and Methodism emerged.

These earnest seekers after truth and holiness were only one of several types of student to be met with in Oxford's streets. Among the freshmen,

> we see the public schoolman, just freed from the rod of Busby's successors, strutting about town for a week or so before entrance, courting his schoolfellows' envy ... swaggering at coffee-houses, and giving himself a scholar's airs at the bookshops. We see the country greenhorn ... trotting with father and mother along the Oxford road; or meet in the High the rough country farmer with his equally unkempt hopeful, staring moodily about

each clad according to his class and pretensions. 'A month or two sees them metamorphosed into complete smarts.' What used to be a pattern of early rising in Oxford has changed. Now 'the smart's breakfast is scarcely over by ten'.[109]

There is the student who is there for the social life, an 'assignation to tea with some fair one' and who comes to wear a gown and be able to say in later life that he has been at university.[110] For such social purposes the coffee-house was added to the ale-house. Coffee was first sold in Oxford in 1650, and in 1759, in the *Oxford Journal* of April 13, 'The Masters of Coffee-Houses in Oxford' regretfully have to announce a price-rise ... chocolate to go up from four pence to five pence a dish and coffee from four pence to five pence a pot.[111]

For students as for their seniors time at Oxford was likely to create lasting ties of robust and not uncritical friendship. Richard Radcliffe, who graduated from Queen's College, Oxford, in 1748, became a clergyman and served in various parishes until in 1777 Queen's gave him one of the preferments in its gift, the Rectory at Holwell. In the meantime he had been a Fellow of Queen's from 1762, and a somewhat absentee Bursar from 1776. His friend John James was a year or two younger and embarked on a clerical career which took him into schoolmastering, including seventeen years as a successful headmaster of the previously declining St. Bees' School. Joshing with his friend, Radcliffe wrote to James in November 1755 to describe a visit he has paid to Queen's in August:

> but what a dull and desolate place is it become ... not a soul to be found of all our acquaintance except Tom Hodgson [now chaplain]. ... The bottom of number six [staircase], formerly the scene of mirth and joy, is in a manner quite forsaken: all unity, friendship and society have been banished in it long ago. ... The latter part of my stay in Oxford was made agreeable enough by the arrival of Barnett, Jefferson, and Denton, senior: the two first came I suppose, a fellowship-hunting; the last, with a couple of his country acquaintance, purely upon a party of pleasure. Denton is excessively sleek and jolly, and is encreased in corpulency most surprisingly.[112]

The essayist William Hazlitt (1778–1830) respected a boy with a 'wayward disposition' much more than those who 'submit their imaginations so servilely to the trammels of strict scholastic discipline':

> Any one who has passed through the regular gradations of a classical education, and is not made a fool by it, may consider himself as having had a very narrow escape.[113]

Hazlitt observed that it is the boy who complies with requirements, has a good memory and lacks the independence to develop other interests and challenge what he is taught, who generally comes top of the class. The distinction he was trying to draw is between the student whose knowledge comes entirely from the books he is told to read and the possessor of a mind which grapples with what it is told and challenges it.

Jane Austen could be sure of an appreciative readership when she wrote in *Sense and sensibility*:

> [A]s there was no necessity for my having any profession at all, as I might be as dashing and expensive without a red coat on my back as with one, idleness was pronounced on the whole to be the most advantageous and honourable. ... I was therefore entered at Oxford and have been properly idle ever since.[114]

Independent intellectuals and new styles of academic life

Oxford's Colleges provided a base, and could sometimes provide funding, from which to go out into Europe, on paper or in person, and discuss ideas. Writing on 'the present state of polite learning in Europe', Oliver Goldsmith (1730–4) emphasizes the benefits of the 'social' and interactive character of higher intellectual activities. 'Among strangers, we consider ourselves as in a solitude, and 'tis but natural to desire society.'[115] Could it all have happened without the universities? The outflow of people and activity from Oxford (and Cambridge) into an active intercourse with the scientific, philosophical and literary world outside raises again the important question how central the universities were to the developments of the key period when science found its feet. The freedom scholars felt to 'desire society' and discuss their ideas with one another was to transform the intellectual life of Europe in the seventeenth and eighteenth centuries.

Wadham and the circle of 'scientists'

Wadham College was founded in 1610, under the will of Nicholas Wadham 'gentleman', whose widow had an active interest in taking his wishes forward. She found a site and pressed in court circles for support for the venture, giving generously herself; she was able to achieve the remarkable feat of getting the College open for business within four years. She chose the Warden and the first Fellows. Until she died in 1618 the College remained her hobby and she tended to interfere. There was more interference after the Civil War. Wadham, like other colleges, was the subject of draconian action by the Parliamentary Visitors in 1648. They ejected the Warden and thirteen Fellows and brought in a new Warden.

John Wilkins (1624–72) was only 34 when he became Warden, but he seems to have had excellent 'survival' skills, remaining on good terms with all sides in the period of mending of fences which took place in the succeeding decade. For example, he was friendly with the diarist John Evelyn, who had no love of the revolution or its instigators and came into his own in public life with the Restoration of 1660. He gave him a transparent beehive in which the bees could be seen at their construction and storage work. It was ornamented with little statues.

But Wilkins found himself in a somewhat conflicted position. He became Cromwell's brother-in-law when he married Cromwell's sister in 1656. He was to be made Master of Trinity College, Cambridge, on Cromwell's recommendation in 1659, though it was a post he did not hold for long, for Cromwell's appointee was removed at the Restoration.

During his time at Wadham he rescued the young College from an early decline and its undergraduate numbers rose. Christopher Wren went there as a student in 1650. Wilkins exercised considerable influence in encouraging independent intellectual journeying. The Warden's lodgings in Wilkins' time became the regular meeting place of a circle of 'scientists' who were to form the nucleus of the Royal Society on its foundation in the 1660s. Not all of these were insiders in the University, or connected with Wadham. Robert Boyle was one, living as he did in Oxford, without formally studying there. Wilkins, ever a diplomatist, welcomed Cambridge exiles to Wadham, one of them Seth Ward, after the Parliamentary Visitors had put him into the Savilian Chair of Astronomy. Another of Wilkins's friends, John Wallis, took the Savilian Professorship of Geometry at Merton.

Boyle in his turn brought in Robert Hooke, who was his assistant and a former sizar of Christ Church. It is unclear how far John Locke of Christ Church was regarded as a 'member' of the group surrounding John Wilkins at Wadham College. Yet by 1660 he knew Robert Boyle and was reading him, together with Descartes and Gassendi. Locke worked on some chemical experiments at his own expense. Christopher Wren went to All Souls as a Fellow in 1653, but he went on attending the meetings of the Wadham circle and kept a room at Wadham. He became Professor of Astronomy before he moved into architectural design, which lent a pleasing fitness to his appointment as architect of the Royal Observatory at Greenwich. Robert Payne (1596–1651) was at Christ Church from 1611 and seems to have remained in Oxford, exploring the ideas on natural philosophy which were attracting interest, reading Roger Bacon and learning Hebrew. In 1624 he became one of the first Fellows of Pembroke College. He offered himself as a candidate for the Gresham Professorship of Astronomy in 1624, but failed to get it. A few years later he had joined the circle of those who enjoyed the favour of the Cavendishes, Charles and William, Earl Cavendish. In 1638 Payne was back in Oxford, as Canon of Christ Church, where he remained until the parliamentary visitors ejected him in 1648 for being a royalist. They went further, imprisoning him for a short time while they searched his house.

So this was far from being a cosy inward-looking 'Wadham' circle. Individuals such as Boyle and Locke exemplified an important feature of this early scientific Oxford. It allowed scope for original work among its scholars, for the following of one's specialist interests, but it also welcomed 'outsiders'.

Some of this scientific inquiry was driven by mere curiosity and the love of a show and a wonder. John Evelyn noted in his *Diary* for 13 July 1654 a visit to 'Waddum' in which Wilkins had shown him his transparent apiaries and a great many curiosities: 'a variety of Shadows, Dyals, Perspectives ... and many other artificial, mathematical, Magical curiosities'.[116] Evelyn remarked in his *Kalendarium* for July 1675,[117] how he went to hear:

> *Dr. Morison Botanic Professor,* reade on divers plants in the Physic Garden; & saw that rare collection of natural Curiosities, of Dr. *Plots* of *Magdalen* Hall: author of the Natural hist: of *Oxford-shire;* all of them collected in that shire, & indeede extraordinary, that in one County, there should be found such varietie of Plants, Shells, Stones, Minerals, Marcasites, foule, Insects, Models of works &c: Chrystales; Achates, Marbles ...

So it is possible to see the phenomenon of collaborative Oxford scientific work as having its locus at Wadham, but it remained apparent that an individual could do a very great deal with only glancing contact with the University and its colleges.

The Royal Society: societies for holding experiments and discussing scientific questions

The most important potential challenge to the universities as the natural leaders in the advancement of knowledge was the formation of learned societies. The strong curiosity of a number of individuals such as these brought like-minded people together to discuss, hear papers and watch experiments in a free-ranging attempt to work out how to answer the legions of different kinds of questions now arising. Societies sprang up, locally and nationally, independently of the universities but including in their membership a good many interested academics.

Sir Robert Moray (b.1608/9, so about 50 at the time), had a key role in the founding and the early development of the Royal Society. A decisive meeting of twelve at Gresham College in London on 28 November 1660 launched what became the Royal Society. It was the culmination of earlier meetings over a decade or more, held in Oxford as well as London. Moray stands out as the driving force. Yet it is unclear how much formal higher education he had. He may have studied in France but he was a soldier by profession. He was one of the early Freemasons. He had been a Royalist during the Civil War. He was attracted to a Christian stoicism and practised the control of feeling and its expression. His own special scientific interests were in magnetism, tides, horology and chemistry.[118]

In a letter to the Earl of Kincardine of 31 December/10 January 1658, he comments on his own strong consciousness of the ill-focused character of the new experimental and practical scientific work:

> All my physicall skill, I mean in the medicall sphere, is nothing else but the effect of loose ratiocinations built upon no great stock of knowledge of natural things, and managed with a pretty baugh [= weak] logick.[119]

John Evelyn's *Diary* for 25 April 1661 also describes the amusement to be had by watching the experiments conducted at meetings of the Royal Society but now with an undertow of more serious intent:

> I went to the Society, where were divers experiments with Mr. Boyle's pneumatic engine. We put in a snake, but could make it only extremely sick by exhausting the air, and could not kill it; but a chick died of convulsions in a short space.

He went again:

> July 17, 1661, I went to London. At our assembly, we put a viper and a slow worm, or aspic, to bite a mouse, but could not irritate them to fasten at all. Mr. Boyle brought two polished marbles of three inch diameter which, when first well rubbed and then treated with a drop of olive oil which was afterwards clean wiped off, and when clapped together, stuck close – even so close that the nether stone, having a hook inserted, and the upper a ring, took up forty-two pound weight by the power of contiguity before they separated. The oil was added to fill up any possible porosity in the polished marble. The 19th, we tried our diving bell, or engine, in the Water Dock at Deptford, in which our curator continued half an hour under water.

These are descriptions of enquiries more ambitious than just trying things to see what would happen. The experimenters were searching for natural laws (such as might govern the effects of 'contiguity'), and for the properties of living things (a snake seems to need less air than a chicken). Underlying the relatively simple question whether it was better to try things out or to arrive at conclusions by thought was the need to revisit profound epistemological and metaphysical presumptions.

The Royal Society and other bodies and institutions like it were attempting something which was not being done by universities as 'institutions', although many of the leaders were dons and Oxford men were indisputably among the leaders. Part of the problem was that they did not have the equipment. This lack was not confined to England. J.T. Needham (1713–81), an English priest who hoped to obtain a post for himself, complained in 1759 that the scientific instruments at the University of Louvain were kept in unsatisfactory conditions, exposed to the risk of damage and rusting. A contemporary suggested that the teachers were not equipped to use these instruments in any case and scarcely stayed long enough to learn.[120] Most Catholic universities did not have a collection of scientific instruments before 1750.[121] Nény ordered library books at Louvain to be sold if they were not on philosophy so that the money could be spent on instruments.[122] The Louvain science course tended to deal with problems in separate disputations and not to try to create a grand unified theory or to allow one set of conclusions to illuminate a problem in another area (tides and eclipses of the moon, for example).[123]

Professorships and university science

One of the weapons the universities had in the face of this challenge from gentleman amateurs was the pull of the prestigious institutional appointment. But it was by no means a regular expectation either that an appointee would be especially outstanding in the relevant 'field' or that he would take the job seriously. On 19 February 1732, we read that 'D. Newland of Magdalen College, Oxon. is elected Geometry Gresham Professor... 'Tis a gentle Sinecure'.[124]

Oxford had a Sedleian Professor of Natural Philosophy from 1611 and a Reader in Experimental Philosophy from 1810. The Regius Chairs founded in the sixteenth century continued to be of particular importance in both Oxford and Cambridge. Physic (Cambridge, 1540) was medical and fitted into the medieval syllabus which had always included medicine among the three higher degree subjects. Oxford's counterpart was the Regius Professorship of Medicine (1535). But Chairs were now being founded in studies which lay outside the traditional curriculum and in the spheres of modern science. The Cambridge Professorship of Anatomy (1707) could also be deemed medical, as could the Oxford's Tomlin's Praelector of Anatomy (1626) and the Professorship of Clinical Medicine (1772). In Cambridge there were Chairs in eight subjects which would now be regarded as scientific, established before the end of the eighteenth century. A Cambridge Professorship of Chemistry was established in 1702 and an Oxford counterpart in 1803. Cambridge had a Plumian Professorship of Astronomy and Experimental Philosophy in 1704. Oxford had a Professor of Astronomy from 1619. Botany was provided with a professorship in

Cambridge in 1724 and in Oxford in 1728; Oxford also had a Professor of Rural Economy from 1796, whose proceeds were used to publish its founder John Sibthorp's *Flora graeca* until the first holder of the Chair was appointed in 1840. Cambridge's Professorship of Geology was established in 1728, and Oxford's Readership in Mineralogy in 1813 and that in Geology in 1818, both first held by William Buckland. Cambridge had a Professorship of Astronomy and Geometry in 1749, and the Jacksonian Professorship of Natural Experimental Philosophy was established in Cambridge in 1783.

Natural philosophy and the experimental method

Thomas Hobbes (1588–1679) and the Irishman Robert Boyle (1627–91) became embroiled in controversy over the advantages of experimental method. Hobbes grouped 'light, sound, and all phantasms and ideas' as involving human responses, which were subjective, learned from experience, and not inherent in the external world as objective qualities of things. This was in itself a substantial departure from the Aristotelian foundations on which science still rested. It made light and heat into mental 'fancies', as Hobbes is reported to have put it. He became very excited by all this in the 1630s and wrote in a letter that he aspired to be the person who first satisfactorily explained the faculties and passions of the soul. This took him into a cluster of related subjects, stretching from logic and metaphysics and epistemology and what would now be described as psychology, to experimental science subjects such as optics. Boyle wrote *An Examen of Mr. T. Hobbes's 'Dialogus'* (1662).[125] Boyle identified 'mechanical' laws as superior to the Aristotelian explanations. He approved this approach partly because it allowed for God's acting or operating in the world according to laws of nature he had himself built into it.

Teaching: the changing intellectual life of Oxford

Francis Bacon's programme of academic reform

While these individual 'researchers' enjoyed their freedom to experiment, Oxford had students to educate, courses of lectures to deliver and degrees to award. The question was how far these were going to be changed by the new experimental approach to learning.

> His lordship would many times have musique in the next roome where he meditated. The aviary at Yorke-house was built by his lordship ... at every meal, according to the season of the yeare, he had his table strewed with sweet

> herbes and flowers, which he sayd did refresh his spirits and memorie.... None of his servants durst appeare before him without Spanish leather bootes: for he would smell the neates-leather, which offended him.... His dowager married her gentleman-usher... whom she made deafe and blind with too much of Venus.[126]

In 1605, Francis Bacon (1561–1626) presented his plans for the 'advancement of learning' to King James I. He was anxious to ingratiate himself with the new monarch, but he also had warmly-held views to put in defence of the idea that scholarship is both morally defensible and of advantage to the nation. These themes were not original. It had long been argued that the pursuit of knowledge is merely an aspect of the curiosity which led to the Fall, that it leads to intellectual pride, makes men hard to govern and given to holding politically dangerous opinions; or conversely that it unfits men for active life and participation in practical affairs by encouraging them to retreat to their studies and spend all their time with books. Bacon tried to give force to his refutation of these ideas by reminding James that his predecessor Elizabeth was a 'learned Prince' and flattering him that he is too, so that they are 'Castor and Pollux... Starres of excellent light'.[127]

> Those who have taken upon them to lay down the law of nature as a thing already searched out and understood, whether they have spoken in simple assurance or professional affectation, have therein done philosophy and the sciences great injury.... They have been effective in quenching and stopping inquiry.[128]

Francis Bacon noted the difficulty that a familiar syllabus of accepted materials may tend to fix knowledge and prevent it advancing.

Bacon was particularly keen to see theoretical and practical education put together in useful and appropriate ways. He was not of course a 'provider of education' himself. He did not have to try to bring about syllabus change in a university. So he was free to suggest ideas. Among the notions he conjured with were suggestions which others were making and some of which proved to be immensely important in shaping future academic priorities. One of his notions was that the King might put in hand the composition of a fitting new *History of England,* concentrating, if the whole story seemed too much, on the 'storie... from the Vniting of the Roses, to the Vniting of the Kingdomes, Portion of time wherin, to my vnderstanding, there hath bin the rarest varieties' in styles of monarchy which have ever been known.[129] This was before history became quite so sensitive a subject in the aftermath of the Civil War.

It seems that those who had universities to run were not over-enthusiastic about Bacon's programme and plans. He sent a copy of a draft towards this work to the Warden of Merton, Sir Henry Savile, but Savile is not know to have replied. Thomas Bodley did respond and was positively hostile, evidently considering that Bacon had failed to grasp the 'holdfaste of Certainetie' in the sciences the universities enjoyed.[130]

The mutations of Oxford and Cambridge with the religious allegiances of England's sixteenth-century monarchs had a counterpart in Ireland when Trinity College, Dublin, began in 1594. James Ussher was one of its first students. Although Trinity College was enthusiastically protestant, the syllabus adopted there was essentially based on the conventional one of the medieval university, grammar, logic, rhetoric, some of Aristotle's philosophical works. Some quarter was given to the students in the form of the adoption of Peter Ramus' simplified logic course, to which Ussher was unaccountably loyal, given its flaws.[131] Dudley Fenner had translated Ramus into English and substituted biblical examples for the ones taken from classical texts and thus made it attractive to protestant students and their teachers.[132] Ussher was ordained to the protestant ministry and taught as Professor of Sacred Theology at Trinity from 1607 until 1621 when he became a bishop. He understood the importance of creating a good library for the new university and he did more than anyone else to build up what would now be regarded as a 'research' library, an innovative notion at a time when universities saw themselves primarily as teaching institutions. He also made regular journeys to England (Oxford, Cambridge and London) every few years in order to buy books. This led him into research of his own. He was one of the leading seventeenth-century divines in establishing the academic study of Greek patristics.

The emergence of modern scholarship

The expression 'deepe witted schollership' appears in 1589.[133] In 1784 Cowper couples 'scholarship' with 'genuine worth'.[134] 'Scholarship' is a word which retained its dignity in the early modern world, for this was the age when the modern concept of 'scholarship' emerged. But by contrast, 'scholasticism' began to be regarded as a thoroughly bad thing, from which universities urgently needed to move on. The pejorative use of the term 'scholastic' seems to begin with the sixteenth century.

Before that date, *scholasticus* describes the master of a school in what seems a perfectly neutral way. Afterwards, unflattering associations cling to 'scholastic' and to its partner 'schoolman' for centuries.

A 'scholastic' syllabus, as characterized by Milton in 1644, expects students to struggle with too many abstractions and does not prepare them to apply their knowledge in real life. It is:

> an old errour of universities not yet well recover'd from the Scholastick grosnesse of barbarous ages, that…they present their…novices at first comming with the most intellective abstractions of Logick and metaphysicks.[135]

Scholasticism's failure to be practical is said to make it dry and pedantic, obscure and preoccupied with trivialities. Scholastic learning is described as shallow and absurd. Milton again:

> Doubt not, worthy Senators, to vindicate the sacred honour and judgment of Moses your predecessor, from the shallow commenting of Scholasticks and Canonists.[136]

In 1651 Hobbes writes in his *Leviathan* of the 'frivolous Distinctions, barbarous Terms, and obscure Language of the Schoolmen'.[137] Scholastic learning is over-subtle. John Donne (1572–1631), who was in his teens a student at Hart Hall, now Hertford College, before he went to study at Cambridge, links the 'Schools' and the 'Casuists'.[138]

It would not be true to say that the condemnation was unequivocal. There is grudging respect too. It is sometimes difficult to be sure in a reference in a sermon whether John Donne intends his remark ironically, for example, in 'And it is usefully moved, and safely resolved in the School, that the devil himself cannot deliberately wish himselfe nothing'.[139] There is often an air of ambivalence, a grudging respect for a particular argument, to balance a consciousness that it is precious or casuistical. 'We have in the Schooles, a short and a round way, to prove that the world was made of *nothing*.' One must ask the enquirer 'of *what* it was made' and when he postulates some substance used for the purpose, one asks him what *that* was made of, until he is driven into infinite regresse.[140]

Donne displays a certain ambivalence about particular scholastic opinions, for he can see that sometimes they are very sound:

> This Doctrine of a sin against the Holy Ghost, is not a dream of the Schoole-men, though they have spoken many things frivolously of it, but grounded in evident places of Scriptures.[141]

There is sometimes a hint of Donnish recognition that even a Schoolman may jest, and that in fact there was a good deal of fun to be had by medieval disputants. 'They are all (as we say in the Schoole) *Co-omnipotentes*, they have all a joynt-Almightinesse',[142] or respect for the sheer cleverness of the device proposed. 'It is said sometimes in School, that *no man* can keep the commandements, yet man, collectively, may keep them.'[143]

John Dryden (1631–1700), though of puritan stock and a prominent figure in the Cromwellian revolution, was converted to Roman Catholicism between 1685 and 1688. In a biography of 1688, he describes how Francis Xavier (1506–52) was sent to the University of Paris at the age of 18 and had a hard struggle at first with logic, though he battled manfully to master it. The system of study and knowledge Dryden describes as 'crabbed' and 'subtle' was frequently caricatured in a similar way by others in the early modern period. John Donne (1572–1631), was brought up a Roman Catholic and spent time at Oxford, though he did not take his degree, displays a great deal of knowledge of academic theology and of the source-texts, both patristic and 'scholastic' in his sermons, also speaks of 'the intricacies, and subtilties of the Schoole'.[144]

Some still found scholasticism attractive, however. The books Richard Baxter (1615–91) was able to get hold of as an autodidact took him into the regions of what he still found it natural to call 'scholasticism' as well as the realms of practical Christian living. He liked the 'scholastics' precisely because they were subtle. 'I thought they narrowly searched after Truth, and brought Things out of the darkness of Confusion.' He records how in time he learned to place 'smaller stress ... upon these Controversies and Curiosities' and put first 'the fundamental Doctrines of the Catechism'.[145]

Ancients and moderns and the battle of the books

Looked at from the distance of some centuries, the process by which the mediaeval syllabus became the modern one appears a modulated mutation rather than an abrupt shift. Nevertheless, it was seen to raise fundamental questions, pitching progress against conservatism. But the period at the end of the seventeenth and the beginning of the eighteenth century saw Oxford participation in a debate in which 'ancients' were pitched against 'moderns' and their respective claims seen as alternatives. An issue of particular interest at Christ Church was whether Cambridge's Isaac Newton and his system had made everything earlier dated or obsolete. Against that hypothesis it was argued that Newton had himself relied upon earlier literature and did not appear to have considered the classics of no account.[146] This was not merely an Oxford debate; in fact the Oxford challenge was a small part of a European one, in which Fontenelle was prominent. And it was not restricted to secular literature. There were fears that going 'modern' might lead to the reading of the Bible as though it were just another old book. This was a concern raised by Sir William Temple (1628–99) in his 'On ancient and modern learning',[147] in which he borrows Bernard of Chartres' twelfth-century image of recent scholars as mere dwarfs sitting on the shoulders of the giants of old. Critics, he jibed, 'are a race of scholars I am very little acquainted with; having always esteemed them to be like brokers, who, having no stock of their own, set up and trade with that of other men'.[148] He was scathing about the lack of discrimination shown by modern scholars who dabbled in alchemy, which has 'enchanted, not to say turned, so many brains in later ages', and which he regards as a waste of money.[149] Richard Bentley was one of Temple's opponents, and Jonathan Swift took the whole affair as a motif for his *A tale of a tub* (1704, but written in the mid-1690s).

Continuing eighteenth-century anti-scholasticism

'Scholasticism anxiety' persisted beyond the period of the 'battle of the books' and continued to colour the mental lives of intellectuals. Because scholastic learning was held to be out of touch with real life, it was alleged that academics are, at best, innocents abroad. *The Tatler* in 1710 remarks that 'the Town Orators ... despise all Men as unexperienced Scholasticks who wait for an occasion before they speak'.[150] In 1770 Edmund Burke remembers 'an old scholastick aphorism, which says, "that the man who lives wholly detached from others, must be either an angel or a devil"'.[151] Hume (1751) has the schoolman, or rather his ass, so torn both ways by the habit of adversarial disputation that he cannot make a decision at all. 'He would stand, like the Schoolman's Ass, irresolute and undetermin'd, betwixt equal Motives.'[152]

Not everyone would grant that the 'schoolmen's' absurdities rendered them harmless to the modern world. The 'schoolmen' appear in Swift's satire as active conspirators against a more open, secular and sophisticated learning:

> When the Works of Scotus first came out, they were carried to a certain great Library, and had Lodgings appointed them; but this Author was no sooner settled, then he went to visit his master Aristotle, and there both concerted together to seize Plato by main force, and turn him out from his antient

> Station among the Divines, where he had peaceably dwelt near Eight Hundred Years. The Attempt succeeded, and the two Usurpers have reigned ever since in his stead.[153]

Swift goes on to suggest that the best way to prevent any more such episodes is to chain up controversial books in their own separate section of libraries, so as to prevent them disturbing the peace of the others.

Above all, 'scholastic' learning was regarded as out of date. It belongs to a less civilized age. It is 'barbarous'. A century later in 1759, Oliver Goldsmith uses the same terminology as we saw Milton employ above, when he wanted to argue for shorter university courses. 'This slowness of conferring degrees is a remnant of scholastic barbarity.'[154]

David Hume in 1748 feared that he was 'in Danger ... of passing for a Pedant and Scholastic'.[155] Goldsmith was still speaking in 1759 of 'the absurdities of scholastic philosophy'.[156] Another eighteenth-century commentator speaks of 'the thorny paths of scholasticism'.[157] For it was recognized that scholastic study was demanding. It was difficult for students. 'Whatsoever his Inclinations were towards a knowledge so crabbed and so subtle, he tugg'd at it with incessant pains.'[158]

Similar complaints were still to be heard from James Yates two centuries later in 1826. 'Leotichidas, the Spartan, having been asked what free boys ought most to learn, answered, "what will be most useful to them, when they have become men."' Yates deplores the fact that, on the contrary, the educators of young men of rank have been exclusively 'professed philosophers', 'schoolmen' and 'ecclesiastics'. 'The situation of such persons causes their knowledge to be speculative rather than practical.'[159]

The 'schoolmen' were seen by Coleridge as little more than commentators on antiquity, not as taking forward any branch of learning themselves.[160] In the mid-nineteenth century, Matthew Arnold notes the condemnation of 'the Averroist doctrines' by the Lateran Council of 1512 but remarks that

> still the theologians were, at bottom, not ill-disposed to the routine, the respect for authority, the clinging to established texts, which the Averroist teaching shared with their own, and which both of them had learned in the same uncritical school of the Middle Ages.[161]

Moving on from scholasticism involved not merely the abandonment of a scholastic methodology but also of a set of assumptions and starting-points about the very content and nature of knowledge. It remained the case even though the textbooks began to change a little. In Cambridge the *Advice* of Daniel Waterland's (1683–1740) *To a Young Student. With a Method of Study for the first four Years* (1730 republished 1740) gives a list of advice about reading which suggests that the 'scholastic' authors were being replaced – often, rather, added to, by important recent work, such as Hobbes, Descartes, Leibnitz, Butler, Berkeley, Locke and Newton.[162] But behind the 'modern' recommendations for reading stood the old set books; they remained in use for communicating some of the fundamental intellectual skills they had been employed to teach in universities since the Middle Ages.

The *Spectator* (1711) could see that the obscurest of scholastic questions could provide a challenging modern metaphor:

> The following question is started by one of the Schoolmen. Supposing the whole body of the Earth were a great Ball or Mass of the finest Sand, and that a single grain or particle of this Sand should be annihilated every thousand years?

Would you prefer to be happy while this was happening and miserable ever afterwards or miserable all this time and happy ever afterwards? But this is how people behave in giving all their energies to this life and not thinking as much as they should about preparing for the next.[163]

And Samuel Taylor Coleridge (1772–1834) was still engaging with scholastic opinions as fellow students of common questions:

> I know that several of the School-men, who would not be thought ignorant of any thing, have pretended to explain the Manner of God's Existence, by telling us, That he comprehends infinite Duration in every Moment; that Eternity is with him a punctum stans, a fixed Point; or which is as good Sense, an Infinite Instant; that nothing with reference to his Existence is either past or to come; To which the ingenious Mr. Cowley alludes in his Description of Heaven.[164]

The enduring basic syllabus: the liberal arts

> The liberal Arts, though they may possibly have less Effect on our External Mein and Behaviour [than 'the Carriage of a Seaman or the Gaite of a Taylor'], make so deep an Impression on the Mind, as is very apt to bend it wholly one way.[165]

This claim in the *Spectator* in 1711 acknowledges a truth. The content and assumptions of an education tend permanently to form the mind.

The resulting patterns of intellectual behaviour manifest themselves in the way former students approach their careers:

> The Mathematician will take little less than Demonstration in the most common Discourse, and the Schoolman is as great a Friend to Definitions and Syllogisms. The Physician and Divine are often heard to dictate in private Companies with the same Authority which they exercise over their Patients and Disciples; while the Lawyer is putting cases, and raising Matter for Disputation out of everything that occurs.[166]

This makes the continuation of the old 'liberal arts' course, with a number of shifts of emphasis and innovations, of central importance to the ways in which the university syllabus formed the mind.

The liberal arts: grammar

The study of grammar still meant learning Latin. Latin was still alive in England in the early eighteenth century for scholarly use and among gentlemen who wished their publications to have a wide-ranging readership throughout Europe, though not for much longer.[167] It was mastered to a level where it could be used for reading and writing and (haltingly) for the conduct of examinations, even though it no longer seems to have been used routinely for actual conversation. But even though it was dwindling as a vehicle for academic discourse, the underlying assumptions about the nature and structure of language were still governed by the way Latin had traditionally been studied; these continued to shape the student's intellectual formation at the most basic level.

That medieval theories were not trivial questions of an age long past is evidenced by the fact that they were tackled by John Locke. John Locke's *Essay concerning human understanding*[168] reinvents this account of language and signs which had been the subject of an immense amount of discussion in the course of the Middle Ages. Locke, like Augustine in the *De magistro* recognizes that 'negative or privative words', words which 'mean nothing', 'such as are nihil in Latin, and in English, ignorance and barrenness' present a paradox, They 'cannot be said properly to belong to, or signify no ideas: For then they would be perfectly insignificant sounds; but they relate to positive ideas; and signify their absence'.[169]

But seventeenth-century Oxford glimpsed wholly new grammatical horizons, stretching beyond the new dimensions which had been afforded by the arrival of Greek and Hebrew at the end of the Middle Ages. It discovered the Orient. Two professorships at Oxford were established, with the requirement that lectures be given on Arabic. The Chair established by Archbishop Laud in 1640 required the professor to lecture for an hour a week on Wednesdays in the University vacations, so as to explain the similarities of Arabic, Syriac and Hebrew. The emphasis on assistance with the study of Hebrew for the purposes of Bible study began to be complemented during the later seventeenth century by the recognition that the study of Arabic could give access to an enormous body of literature and learning in the field of philosophy. It was recognized that the Arabs had been invaluable custodians of the learning of ancient Greece, in centuries when the Greek language had fallen out of use in the West. Laud and others started to collect manuscripts, something lost sight of from the thirteenth century in the West.

Edward Pococke (1604–91) was chaplain at the Levant Company from 1630. He seized his chance to study Hebrew, Syriac, and Ethiopic as he travelled in connection with his pastoral duties, and to collect manuscripts, forming lasting friendships in the Middle East. In October 1631 the Chancellor of Oxford, William Laud, arranged that all ships of the Levant Company entering English ports must bring at least one manuscript with them. Laud's plan was to build up the collection in the Bodleian Library and to establish a professorship of Arabic in Oxford, with Pococke his choice for its first holder.

To Augustine of Hippo at the end of the ancient world, Greek was not an oriental or even an 'Eastern' language, but merely the other main language of educated people in the Roman Empire, and he perhaps barely thought of Hebrew as remote from his own 'world' of Romano-Christian thought. Quite different was the perception of William of Auvergne in the thirteenth century to whom Islam was a challenge without antique precedent, and distinctively 'eastern'.[170] The coupling of Hebrew and Arabic as 'oriental' languages, together with a related interest in other 'Eastern' languages, was something new in early modern Europe.[171] Seventeenth-century critics display still more new dimensions of 'cultural awareness' because of the emerging early modern consciousness that 'Eastern' or 'oriental' languages came from a cultural context different in many ways from that of the West. The study of Hebrew ultimately led to an interest in Arabic. New 'oriental language' professorships in the universities reflected a trend, a developing interest in a wider world and the dawning realization through trading contacts that there were quite other cultures, especially in Asia.

Not everyone among the early moderns who perceived that such differences existed had made a profound or extensive study of the necessary languages. Robert Boyle wrote letters to his friend John Mallet in which he speaks (November 1651) of his spending time with a 'very learned Amsterdam Jew', who had recently arrived in London so as to perfect his Hebrew (the 'Holy Tongue') and ensure that he accurately understood the 'Tenents and Rites' of the modern Jews.[172] Oriental languages are discussed in Robert Boyle's 'Essay of the Holy Scriptures' (c.1652–4), part of which has survived in manuscript and was adapted to form part of his *Some Considerations Touching the Style of the Holy Scriptures*, published in 1661.

Boyle remarked that however 'charming its Eloquence may be in its Original, I confesse my self too unskilfull in the Arabick Tongue, to be a competent Judge' (he has had many distractions and has forgotten much of what he once knew). 'The Alkoran have stolen too much from the Bible, not to contain/divers Excellent Things.' Yet 'the Antient Latin Version of it, made by orders of the Abbot Petrus Cluniacensis' and published by Bibliander (1543), the Swiss orientalist and protestant theologian. This 'would scarce by our European Orators be thought so much as of kinn to Eloquent'; he has, however, seen recent translations in French and of parts in Latin 'making it very Conformable to its Eastern Original'.[173]

Boyle was confident enough to make pronouncements admittedly going beyond his personal knowledge:

> The Eastern Eloquence differs widely from the Western. In those purer Climates, where Learning, that is here but a Denizon, was a Native. Boyle suggests that what seems a lack of eloquence, 'their Dark and Involv'd Sentences, their Figurative and Parabolical Discouses; their Abrupt and Maimed way of expressing themselves' ... often leaves us at a losse for the Method/and Coherency of what they write.[174]

Hebrew and Arabic shared in contemporary eyes, and in contrast with Greek, the feature of lacking a 'literature'. There was, at any rate, a wish to find this so, for protestant scholars were nervous of discovering that they had admitted materials which might be the Jewish equivalent of the 'traditions' of the Church, and might compromise the purity of 'Scripture alone'.[175] In the case of Hebrew this excluded Rabbinic, Talmudic and other literature. In the case of Arabic, the enormous debt of the medieval West to the Arabic transmission of Aristotle and to the work of Arab scholars in exploring and developing ancient Greek philosophical thought, had been partly lost sight of. The translation of the Koran into Latin was achieved in the twelfth century, at the instigation of Peter the Venerable, Abbot of Cluny. William of Auvergne was still thinking about the implications as we have seen, but it was not until the early modern period that it was actively revisited by Western scholars. Johann Heinrich Hottinger (1620–67) was the author of a *Historia orientalis quae ex variis orientalium monumentis collecta* (1651) which was cited second-hand by Boyle when he wanted to draw stylistic and other comparisons between Bible and Koran.[176]

Robert Boyle's *On the diversity of religions* reviews the world's alternative religions disapprovingly, but in a way which indicates some of the preoccupations of contemporary debates on the subject. The 'Ethnick,' he says, 'comprizes a Multitude of Sects' which maintain 'absurd' and 'contradictory' opinions. He knows this from 'Credible Persons, some of them Navigators, and some Divines, who speak upon their own knowledg [*sic*]'. These other religions have common belief in many gods and often also idolatry. As to Islam, which Boyle calls 'Mahometanism', he dismisses the 'Alcoran' as full of 'Falsities & Absurdity's' and he makes it a point against it that the 'Author' was 'averse from having it disputed of'. Yet he points out that 'it bears Testimony to the Old Testament and the New; and acknowledges Christ to be not only a great Prophet, but the Son of a Virgin, thô Christ's Religion did altogether condemn the Mahometan'.[177]

The recognition that there might be a gulf between a 'Western' and an 'Eastern' way of seeing questions of language began to affect the academic study of the languages themselves. The study of Hebrew had begun to be conducted in the context of the study of Arabic and even of other languages. In Oxford there was a contention that Hebrew studies required a knowledge of Arabic,[178] and many competent in one also studied the other. So by the seventeenth century the netful of ancient languages considered requisite for the study of the Bible included Chaldaic, Syriac and Arabic.

This meant that provision needed to be made in universities to study 'oriental languages' as a group. Yet at no stage did Greek or Hebrew threaten to replace Latin for academic purposes. The normative academic use of Latin throughout Europe had not changed since Valla had remarked in the fifteenth century that it was a 'great mystery' how Latin had been religiously preserved as a holy language for so many centuries among strangers and barbarians and enemies of the Romans:

> *Magnum igitur Latini sermonis sacramentum est ... quod apud peregrinos, apud barbaros, apud hostes, sancte ac religiose per tot saecula custoditur.*[179]

Nevertheless, the enlargement of academic language study to include Greek and Hebrew had shaken up presuppositions radically and in various ways and encouraged new combinations of traditional academic approaches with something quite new.

New theories of language and the beginning of linguistics

The advent of a scholarly interest in Greek and Hebrew had reawakened and heightened a much earlier awareness that there are differences between languages; this too had had to find its way into academe and into the syllabus and from the seventeenth century it began to do so by way of hard thinking about linguistics. Augustine of Hippo (354–430), in an earlier era when the three 'Biblical languages' were in active use, already understood the need to take careful note of linguistic differences in studying the text of the Bible:

> Users of the Latin language ... need two others, Hebrew and Greek, for an understanding of the divine scriptures, so that recourse may be had to the original versions if any uncertainty arises from the infinite variety of Latin translators.[180]

The liberal arts: logic

Francis Bacon's *Novum Organum* in 1620 was a frank challenge to Aristotle. The term *organon* seems to have been first used in the sixteenth century to describe Aristotle's six books on logic and the choice of title calling Bacon's work a 'new' *organon* was presumably intended to strike the contemporary reader with appropriate force.

The syllogistic method is no way to make discoveries he says:

> As the sciences which we now have do not help us in finding out new works, so neither does the logic which we now have help us in finding out new sciences. (Axiom XI)

The syllogism forms a closed system and does not necessarily say anything about the truth of a conclusion; it merely establishes its validity:

> The syllogism ... commands assent therefore to the proposition, but does not take hold of the thing. (Axiom XIII)

Within each proposition lies a mass of traps for the unwary, and students trying to use this method of reasoning may get a false sense of the certainty of their conclusions:

> The syllogism consists of propositions, propositions consist of words, words are symbols of notions. Therefore if the notions

> themselves (which is the root of the matter) are confused and overhastily abstracted from the facts, there can be no firmness in the superstructure. (Axiom XIII)

So, he insists:

> The logic now in use serves rather to fix and give stability to the errors which have their foundation in commonly received notions than to help the search after truth. So it does more harm than good. (Axiom XII)

Disputation lives on: William Chillingworth

Grenfeild was writing in March 1658:

> I question not, how you have shifted at Oxford ... 'tis impossible to be cold in a schoole; and indeed; I think it an excellent refuge from the frost, when well heated with a disputation.[181]

William Chillingworth (1602–44) was educated at an Oxford grammar school and at Trinity College, Oxford, where he was elected to a Fellowship in 1628. He 'studied not much, but when he did, he did much in a little time,' says Aubrey. He was noted for his outstanding skills in disputation. Aubrey says he was persuaded to go to Douai, 'where he was not so well entertained as he thought he merited for his great disputative witt' so he returned 'and came to Trinity College againe, where he was fellowe'. 'William Laud ... was his godfather and great friend. He sent his grace weekly intelligence of what passed in the university.' He was ambitious. Aubrey has him as a competitor for the Presidency of Trinity against Kettel.

Anthony Wood, assiduously collecting information about Oxonians, and Aubrey in his *Brief Lives*, both say that 'he would often walk in the college grove and there contemplate, and meet with some *cod's-head* or other, and dispute with him and baffle him. He would always be disputing.'[182] Aubrey's *Lives* confirms his reputation as 'the readiest and nimblest Disputant of his time in the university, perhaps none haz equalled him since'.[183] This was a natural bent, enhanced but not created by the mode of his education, though it manifested one of the important characteristics of the formal disputation of the Middle Ages, an ability to get so caught up in the thrust and parry that the pursuit of a particular line might be lost sight of. Thomas Hobbes, who was a friend of his during the 1630s, said 'he was like a lusty fighting fellow that did drive his enemies before him, but would often give his owne party smart back-blows'.[184]

The satirist Nicholas Amhurst (1697–1742) describes less impressive aspects of 'late-period' disputation:

> The persons of this argumentative drama are three, viz. the Opponent, the Respondent, and the Moderator. The Opponent is the person who always begins the attack, and is sure of losing the day, being always (as they call it) on the wrong side of the question; tho' oftentimes that side is palpably the right side, according to our modern philosophy and discoveries. The Respondent sits over against the opponent, and is prepared to deny whatever he affirms, and always comes off with flying colours; which must needs make him enter the lists with great fortitude and intrepidity. The moderator is the hero, or principal character of the drama, and is not much unlike the goddess Victoria, as described by the poets, hovering between two armies in an engagement, and with an arbitrary nod, deciding the fate of the field.[185]

So the study of logic at Oxford still involved live disputing long after the content and approach of the medieval syllabus had changed. This was a required element in undergraduate study and performance was expected before graduation, but the expected level of expertise became superficial to the point of absurdity, and the whole business was often mocked and sneered at, both inside and outside the University.[186] Locke was made censor of moral philosophy at Christ Church (1664). This required him to preside over scholastic disputations. Locke's *Essays on the Law of Nature* are derived from a series of eight of his own disputations on the standard theme of natural law.

Textbooks: Henry Aldrich

In 1691 Henry Aldrich (1648–1710) published the *Artis logicae compendium*, a small treatise on logic which became a standard textbook at Oxford, and remained so into the late nineteenth century. Into a notebook six inches by three and half an inch thick, he tried to compress the efforts of more than a thousand years of Latin scholarship. Most of his preface is concerned with an account of the classical background and then the medieval.[187] He knows the important names (for example, 'Albertus Magnus, Thomas, Scotus, Burlaeus, Occam'). He provides a list of 23 names with their dates of death. He knows of various schools of thought, the Scotists and Thomists and the Nominales and Reales. It is his view that the earlier scholastics were the best and the later *degeneres*. It is hard to judge how far Sanderson's *Logicae artis compendium* (1615) proved a rival to that of Aldrich, or to the independent efforts of individual tutors who provided their own teaching materials for their students.[188] But seems that Robert Sanderson's was often found too difficult and Aldrich an easier option for the tutors who were obliged to try to ground young gentlemen in the elements of logic. Aldrich includes, in an extracted form, the appendix of Sanderson's *De usu logicae*.

Logic, as Aldrich understands it, has two objectives. One involves the use of argumentation to establish a point. The other is concerned with putting the subject-matter in order (*ordinando*), in such a way that the parts of a subject are arranged so as to make the whole more readily comprehensible (*talis dispositio partium alicuius disciplinae ut integra facilius discatur*). But he includes the main conventional elements in a simplified form, even a brief treatment of the logic of terms and supposition and categorematic terms.

Aldrich's work held its popularity as a standard textbook. Daniel Wilson wrote in 1807, 'Next term I have to lecture on Aristotle and the tragedies of Aeschylus...and the New Testament has to be critically and copiously dealt with, and Aldrich's *Ars Logica* to be entered on. I will do what I can'.[189]

Textbooks: John Milton and the case for Peter Ramus

John Milton remained persuaded of the value of Peter Ramus' work. His own *Artis Logicae Plenior Institutio ad Petri Rami Methodum concinnata* was published in 1672, though it was probably prepared (in the main) thirty years earlier.[190] Milton's method is to interweave his own explanations into Ramus' text. Ramist logic had had its day, and interest in the controversies surrounding it was fading by the end of Milton's life, but his own training in logic had apparently been Ramist and the method remained his natural first choice.[191] It was apparent to many by the early seventeenth century that Ramus had not proposed a profound new insight, a true simplification of old complexities, but an untidy and superficial substitute for the Aristotelian real thing.

Isaac Watts

Isaac Watts (1674–1748), dissenting minister and educationalist,[192] published a *Logic*[193] which exemplifies very well the way the process of reworking the syllabus had begun to yield dividends in enhancing the ability of those who taught and used logic to adapt its technicalities to practical general use. Watts's *Logic* ends with a summary of practical considerations and general rules for the user to bear in mind. Among them is the advice to make thorough studies of the evidence:

> Enlarge your general acquaintance with things daily, in order to attain a rich furniture of things ... But especially meditate and inquire with great diligence and exactness into the nature, properties, circumstances and relations, of the particular subject.[194]
>
> By ... a large survey of the whole subject in all its properties and relations, you will be better secured from inconsistencies, that is, from asserting or denying any thing in one place, which contradicts what you have asserted or denied in another.[195]

He himself was sure that talking to other intellectuals and observing the ground-rules of logic should be treated as complementary activities:

> 'Accustom yourselves to clear and distinct ideas.'[196] ... Converse much with those friends, and those books, and those parts of learning, where you meet with the greatest clearness of thought and force of reasoning. The mathematical sciences, and particularly arithmetic, geometry, and mechanics, abound with these advantages. ... Something of these sciences should be studied by every man who pretends to learning ... [and here he cites Locke] not so much to make us mathematicians, as to make us reasonable creatures.[197]

Watts's ideal is the thinker who has so thoroughly internalized good habits that he is unlikely to be misled by sloppy thinking in himself or others, however persuasive the others may be:

> We should gain such a familiarity with evidence of perception and force of reasoning, and get such a habit of discerning clear truth, that the mind may be soon offended with obscurity and confusion. We must apply ourselves to it till we perform all this readily, and without reflecting on rules. For want of this care, some persons of rank and education dwell all their days among obscure ideas; they conceive and judge always in confusion; they take weak arguments for demonstration; they are led away with the disguises and shadows of truth. Now, if such persons happen to have a bright imagination, a volubility of speech, and a copiousness of language, they not only impose many errors upon their own understandings, but they stamp the image of their own mistakes upon their neighbours also, and spread their errors abroad.[198]

Watts laments the easy susceptibility of the common people in this respect.[199]

Watts is also highly conscious of the relevance of all this to the discussion of 'association' which was to be of such interest to Coleridge. 'The casual association of many of our ideas' can give rise to prejudice or rash judgement, he warns. Here, too, he fears the practical consequences of confused thinking in making the populace easily misled:

> So a child who has been let blood joins the ideas of pain and the surgeon together. It is for the same reason that the bulk of the common people are so superstitiously fond of the Psalms translated by Hopkins and Sternhold, and think them sacred and divine, because they have been now for more than a hundred years bound up in the same covers with out Bibles.

Mistakes can arise from the ways 'ideas and words' are 'linked together'. He uses familiar notions of the logical tradition. This can be because the words are 'insignificant and have no ideas' (are meaningless); when they are 'equivocal and signify two or more ideas'; and when 'two or three words are synonymous and signify one idea':[200]

> The best relief against this prejudice of association, is to consider whether there be any natural and necessary connexion between those ideas which fancy, system, or chance, hath thus joined together.[201]

Edward Bentham (1707–76) published *Reflections upon the Nature and usefulness of Logick* (1740), examining both old and new kinds of logic, also an *Introduction to Logick (Scholastick and Rational)* (1733). He was not ready to dismiss scholastic logic as roundly as Locke wanted.

Another attempt to remove Aristotle

It still took daring to suggest removing Aristotle two centuries on, but the question was robustly raised. Edward Copleston (1776–1849), Bishop of Llandaff and moral philosopher, mooted the idea that keeping to an outdated set book might actually mislead students:

> The only parts of Aristotle's writings, which can interfere with the Student's progress in natural philosophy, are his Physics; the doctrines of which, it is well known, were formerly made the basis of instruction in that department of science through all the Universities of Europe.

He describes how Francis Bacon 'succeeded in dislodging the Aristotelian philosophy from its strong holds'; Oxford 'although the place where this new fledged philosophy tried her earliest flights' was also one of the last fortresses, of which she took a formal possession:

> For the Aristotelian Physics were interwoven with the whole course of our studies and exercises; and it was not easy to reconcile the abandonments of them with the language of the Statutes, which public officers were bound to inforce.[202]

The demonstrative method

In his prose autobiography Hobbes stated that it was during his European travels that he acquired his special interest in geometry, when he happened to look at a copy of Euclid's *Elements*. (Aubrey, telling this story, gives the place where this happened as '..... a', with the number of dots corresponding to the missing letters of Geneva; Bodl. Oxf., MS Aubrey 9, fol. 36*r*.) What Hobbes emphasized in his account, however, was that Euclid impressed him 'not so much because of the theorems, as because of the method of reasoning': in other words, he may well have known some geometry before this, but he had not previously thought about the power of a deductive method based on definitions and axioms (*Opera philosophica*, 1.xiv). This suggests that he was already thinking about some philosophical problems to which Euclidean method seemed to supply a solution.

The survival of the disputation

Well into the eighteenth century, John Wesley (1703–91) was appointed to teach Greek at Lincoln College, Oxford, soon after being appointed to a Fellowship there. Robert Southey comments in his *Life of Wesley* that 'at that time disputations were held six times a week at Lincoln College; and however the students may have profited from them, they were of singular use to the moderator'. He quotes Wesley who, he remarks, 'during a most restless life of incessant occupation...found time to register not only his proceedings, but his thoughts, his studies', and much else. Wesley noted that the result of all this hard practice was that he acquired 'some degree of expertness in arguing; and especially in discerning and pointing out well-covered and plausible fallacies'.[203]

So just as disputation had early become the second method of instruction in medieval universities after lectures, like the lecture it evolved; but it remained a pedagogical staple, much as described in Balliol's foundation deeds:

> We desire also that every other week a sophism shall be disputed and determined among our Scholars in their own house [practice for determining in the Schools].[204]

The liberal arts: rhetoric and Boyle on the style of Scripture

In July–August 1655, John Locke had exchanges with Thomas Grenfeild, who had studied at Oxford himself and was now was a local clergyman at home and more than a dozen years Locke's senior. Locke wrote to him in a stylistically self-conscious way. Grenfeild writes, 'If your rememberances had come to me in a plainer dresse, they had bin more welcome to him, that now studyes playnesse, more than ever quayntnesse heretofore'. He teases that it shows that 'a good spirit mixes itself with that high Genius of your university, that you stoope to the notice of him, who has almost forgotten, he was ever there; and can hardly give any other Testimony of it, then the names of Colledges, and formes of streetes'.[205]

> Eloquence, the Dresse of our Thoughts, like the Dresse of our Bodies, differs not only in several Regions, but in several Ages. And oftentimes in That, as in Attire, what was lately Fashionable, is Now Ridiculous, and what New makes a Man look like Courtier, may within these Few Lustres make him look like an Antick.[206]

Robert Boyle understood very well not only these matters of changing taste in the choice of literary style, but also the difference between proving and persuading, between logical and rhetorical argumentation.[207] He speaks in his preface to the Reader about using texts 'by way of Allusion' or 'rather ... to Expresse than Prove my Thoughts'. In reading 'Popular Discourses,' he remarks, 'Men use not so much to look whether Every thing be a Strict Truth; as whether it be Proper to perswade or impresse the Truths they would inculcate'.[208]

The classical rhetorical distinction between figures of thought and figures of diction – well set out in the *Rhetorica ad Herennium*[209] – was a favourite theme of the Middle Ages because the form of the Latin language makes it easy to match parallelism or antithesis in the ideas being expressed with a parallelism or antithesis in the word-endings. This held for Scripture too in the Latin Vulgate. There may be more than decorative purpose in the use of figurative language. Bede clarified and emphasized this point in his *De Schematibus et Tropis,*[210] distinguishing the 'decorative' from the 'necessary' use of extraordinary language. The same point struck Robert Boyle, who remarked that 'Few books of similar length in the world' have 'greater Plenty of Figurative Expressions' than the Bible, and here it is important to distinguish 'the Embellishment of our Conceptions' and 'the Congruity of them to our Designe and Method'.[211] It is hard to know whether he was (directly or indirectly) indebted to Bede for this realization.

> Some Ratiocinations of Scripture remain undiscern'd or misunderstood, because of our unacquaintednesse with the Figurative, and (oftentimes) Abrupt way of Arguing usual amongst the Eastern People, who in their Arguments us'd to leave much to the Discretion and Collection of those they dealt with; and discours'd at a wide distance from the Logical Forms of our European Schools.

Sometimes in Paul 'a tacit kind of Dialogue' is to be noted.[212] The perceptive ought to be able to identify technicalities of logic in the Bible too:

> The Prophets and Apostles do make frequent Deductions and inferences, and that their Arguments, though not cast into Mood and Figure, are oftentimes as cogent as theirs, that use to make Syllogisms.[213]

Sometimes 'use Arguments, not to Convince Opposers, but to Confirm Believers'.[214]

Another shift of stylistic fashion

We can see an altogether different set of approaches in the eighteenth century. Dr. Johnson appeared to contemporaries the practised professional. 'Sir Joshua Reynolds once asked [Johnson] by what means he had attained his extraordinary accuracy and flow of language.' The answer was that 'he had early laid it down as a fixed rule to do his best on every occasion and in every company; to impart whatever he knew in the most forcible language he could put it in, and that by constant practice and never suffering any careless expression to escape him or attempting to deliver his thoughts without arranging them in the clearest manner it was become habitual to him'.[215] He did not ask himself whether he was in the mood for writing. His stated view was that 'A man may write at any time if he will set himself doggedly to it'. Johnson 'answered the stated calls of the press twice a week... from the... stores of his mind', despite being busy with his Dictionary and in 'frequent depression of spirits'.[216] The admiring Boswell claimed that 'his various learning and knowledge were arranged in his head as if in different drawers, any of which he could pull out at his pleasure', and thanks to long practice he could give the hastily-written the appearance that he had 'laboured with all the slow attention of literary leisure'.[217]

What became of the old higher degree subjects?

The old 'higher degree' subjects of law, medicine and theology had always been 'taught', not research degrees, and that did not change in these centuries.

Among the fraternity of those with medical interests was William Harvey (1578–1657), one of the subjects of Aubrey's merciless *Lives*. He became Warden of Merton from 1645 to 1648, after studying at Cambridge and Padua where he became interested in the question how the blood moved in the body and conducted experiments. His theory of the circulation of the blood, put forward in 1616 and published in 1628, met with a hostile response because he was contradicting the orthodoxy of the day and it never had much effect on the practice of blood-letting in his lifetime, although it began to gain acceptance as he grew older. He rode out the political storms of the early Stuart period by enjoying royal favour as personal physician to the monarchs in turn. Aubrey was more interested in his eccentricities. 'He did delight to be in the darke, and told me he could then best contemplate.... His chamber was that roome that is now the office of Elias Ashmole Esq:'[218]

> He was wont to say that man was but a great mischievous baboon...that we Europeans knew not how to order or governe our women, and that the Turks were the only people used them wisely. He was far from bigotry.... I remember he kept a pretty young wench to wayte on him, which I guesse he made use of for warmeth-sake as King David did, and took care of her in his will, as also of his man servant.[219]

He was generous to Merton College, giving it money for buildings and a library which had its dedication in 1654. He paid for a Librarian's salary and an annual oration.

Medicine had become rather a do-it-yourself affair. Isaac Barrow (1630–77) did not have to pursue a higher degree in medicine when he considered entering the medical profession. He merely had to read. And the reading included contemporary fashions in natural science, specifically in chemistry and botany, astronomy and mathematics, as well as anatomy. John Locke's notebooks show that he began to teach himself medicine in his twenties, and perhaps it was in that way that he got interested in natural science and the new philosophy. In Shaftsbury's employ, Locke found he could study medicine at a clinical and not merely a theoretical level. He made the acquaintance of Thomas Sydenham, who had recently published a book on infectious diseases, the *Methodus curandi febres* (1666). He started to go on his ward rounds with him and make notes, and they began to collaborate. Locke kept records of Sydenham's methods of treatment with a view to furthering their collaboration.

Oxford can claim a number of the great names among its lawyers. John Selden (1584–1654)[220] entered Hart Hall in 1600, though he moved on to the Inner Temple in a few years (1604). Selden became a friend of Ben Jonson, Robert Coron, Camden. Either in Oxford or in London he learned a vast array of languages,[221] or at least acquired the confidence to use words and expressions from them in his writings. He had among his friends John Donne, Edward Herbert and Lord Herbert of Cherbury, Lancelot Andrewes. Selden became MP for the University of Oxford in the Long Parliament, managing to retain the goodwill of both Parliament and King. As a working barrister, Selden seems to have perceived the importance of 'constitutional' history, which he understood in the terms of the 'Norman Yoke' theory. It is not clear that he would have gone as far as some of the seventeenth-century holders of this viewpoint, but he seems to have believed that a true picture of the English constitution would include the Anglo-Saxon heritage.[222]

Oxford now became a rival to the Inns of Court as a training ground for lawyers.[223] Until the mid-eighteenth century Oxford taught only Roman Law and Canon Law until that was banned at the Reformation. The launch of the Vinerian lectures in Common Law under the will of Charles Viner (1755) meant that Oxford could offer the teaching of common law practising lawyers needed. Danby Pickering was retained by Gray's Inn in 1758 to give lectures for an annual fee, so as to compete with Oxford's provision and in 1795 Lincoln's Inn made it known that it had a syllabus.

This new law lecturing at Oxford was not launched without its hiccoughs, however. Sir William Blackstone (1723–80) was the first holder of the Vinerian Chair. Blackstone had entered Pembroke College in 1738. In 1741 he was admitted to the Middle Temple, and it was decided that he would study for the BCL at Oxford. He had diverse interests at Oxford; one of the pieces of work he completed there was a treatise on architecture, illustrated by himself. In 1746 he was elected Dean of Laws and Bursar at All Souls, where he was rightly judged to be efficient and hard working and well-suited to such responsibilities. The architectural interests came in useful too, and he made sure the Codrington Library was finished at last.

In the case of the new Vinerian Professorship of English Law in Oxford, the difficulty was to get the Professor to reside in the University at all. The (absentee) Professor was to read a solemn lecture at the beginning of each term but a resident tutor was to cover the teaching for the subject. Blackstone:

> apprehends he has a Right to read his four solemn Lectures by Deputy, provided he appoints a proper one ... He is not conscious of having given just Cause (or any Cause that dares be avowed) for the Series of peevish Opposition and personal Insult, which he has met with in the Execution of his present Employment (1761).[224]

Theology remained the dominant discipline because Oxford as well as Cambridge was supplying the Church of England with its ordinands. A Doctorate in Divinity no longer required the immensely long course for a select and usually middle-aged few that it had been in the Middle Ages, but it was expected of senior figures in the University.

Theology made its impact everywhere in seventeenth- and eighteenth-century Oxford, as we have amply seen. Something of the complexity of the situation at the beginning of the seventeenth century can be seen in Wood's *Annals*. Protestantism triumphant had become Protestantism divided. James I tried to impose 'Instructions' on Oxford, including directions that 'young students in Divinity be directed to study such books as be most agreeable in Doctrine and Discipline to the Church of England, and excited to bestow their time in the Fathers and Councels, Schoolmen, Histories and Controversies'. Wood makes it clear that some saw this as an opportunity to take 'the first step ... towards the suppressing of that reputation which Calvin and his writings had attained to in this University'. But the Dean of Christ Church so handled matters that the proposals 'gave general alarum to the Puritan Faction' so that 'the terror of it could not be forgotten in twenty years after'.[225]

Against this conflicted background, and the theological warfare that succeeded it, would-be Fellows of College continued to be ordained and in due course went out to parish life, often to college livings, when they were ready to marry. Undergraduates were required to worship regularly in their college chapels and their conduct was measured against Christian principles. Their studies encouraged frequent intellectual encounter with Christian theological assumptions, for example, in grammar and the study of the Biblical languages.

The immense pressure to conform and the dangerous chopping and changing of approved attitudes did not prevent radical ideas emerging. The Deist Herbert of Cherbury (1583–1648) was an Oxford graduate. He had been struck by the contradictions in religious views and applied a reductionist approach. These could not all be correct, he maintained. Perhaps the truth was something far simpler, that there was indeed a God, but one who did not interfere with his creation once he had made it, constantly adjusting and demanding and punishing and rewarding.

By contrast, Joseph Butler (1692–1752) moved from an 'extreme left' position. He began as a student at a dissenting academy and entered Oriel College in 1715 when he realized that he wished to be ordained in the Church of England. He found the teaching at Oxford consisted of 'unintelligible' disputations and disappointing ('frivolous') lectures, as he wrote to his friend Samuel Clarke.[226] He even thought of going to Cambridge instead. Once ordained, he became a famous preacher. His Sermons in the Rolls Chapel made a considerable impact on fashionable London, but he preferred to retire to parish life and write the *Analogy of religion*. His intention was to rebut the kind of thing the Deists were saying in the context of the concerns of a later generation now preoccupied with new issues. Butler took a higher degree (in law) at Oxford in 1733.

Experiments in collegiate life and new ideas about universities

Colleges have always been the beneficiaries of gifts, but they have not always been able to receive them with unmixed pleasure. Richard Busby (1606–95) graduated from Christ Church in 1628. He became Headmaster of Westminster School and gained a reputation there for delivering beating and also for molesting at least one of the boys. Pupils at the school during his time included Christopher Wren and John Dryden and John Locke. He stayed doggedly in his post until his eighties. Meanwhile, he made active efforts to become a benefactor to his 'ever honor'd Mother, the University of Oxford', the benefaction to take the form of 'a Catechetic Lecture to be endowed by me with a Salary'. He had to repeat the offer several times, while the University argued about accepting it. 'When ever I understood that an objection was made against the terms proposed by me, I accordingly altered them', he complained in 1682. A strong reason for not accepting the money seems to have been a familiar one – jealousy of Christ Church getting an advantage. He became very fed up with the repeated refusals and began to threaten to take his money elsewhere.[227]

The flurry of college founding at Oxford and Cambridge in the fifteenth and sixteenth centuries subsided after Wadham's foundation in 1610. Pembroke got its royal 'foundation charter' in 1624, but it had a long medieval history. Worcester College (1714) was founded on the site of the medieval Gloucester College, a Benedictine foundation from 1283, which had come to an end with the Dissolution of the Monasteries in 1539.

Cromwell's would-be college

There is some evidence of an attempt to found an Oxford college in the period of the Protectorate,[228] during which Oliver Cromwell was Chancellor of Oxford. Cromwell's[229] Letters Patent survive in draft from 1657 to 1658:

> We being satisfied that the erecting and endowing of a colledge…for the purposes hereafter mentioned, will be a good meanes, tending to the glorious end specified [of 'propagating the true, reformed, Protestant, Christian religion and the Gospell or Jesus Christ'].[230]

The governance model was not to be that of a body of Fellows running their own affairs but of obedience to the 'Christian Magistrate' rather in the Lutheran spirit. The propagation of 'the true reformed, Protestant, Christian religion, and the Gospell of Jesus Christ' was said to be 'the chiefe care and endeavour of all Christian Magistrates and people'.[231]

Cromwell's college was to be an international school and a research institution (to begin with).[232] Its first task was to appoint 'tenne godly, able men' chosen from the universities and from the City of London, who were to make 'a generall synopsis of the true, reformed, Protestant, Christian religion professed in this Commonwealth', to be written in both English and Latin and completed within three or four years. So that it might be: 'communicated and sent abroad unto forraigne Churches' together with additional material 'to prevent misconstructions theruppon', together with a note of 'cases of conscience'. Once that is accomplished the new college is to turn its attention to its teaching responsibilities:

> into this Colledge shall be received and there maintained, poore Protestant ministers and schollers, being forreaigners and strangers born, who shall reside in the said Colledge, and apple themselves principally to the study of divinity, and be made use of according as they shall be capable, for the promoting of the ends above mentioned.

It should not be assumed that the idea originated with Cromwell. The handwriting of the lawyer Bulstrode Whitelocke (1605–75) appears on the draft Letters Patent. He had been a student at St. John's College, leaving before taking his degree to study at the Inns of Court, and he sent three sons to Oxford as well as taking an active part in lobbying for the University's benefit. He was opposed to the Presbyterians in the Westminster Assembly in 1643 and his own personal mission is strongly reflected in the proposal to use the new college for ecumenical purposes and bring together the right-minded protestants of Europe an enterprise in which Samuel Hartlib seems to have shared his interest. The venture to create a 'college' failed with Cromwell's death and the end of the Protectorate.

The Greek College plan

The Greek College[233] was a project of 1699–1705, involving the notion of creating a college where Greeks could study in Oxford. Some were already doing so. Metrophanes Critopoulos was sent to Balliol in 161 by the Archbishop of Canterbury as a gesture of friendship to the then Patriarch of Alexandria. Others asked to enjoy the same privilege. John Evelyn writes about Greeks beginning the drinking of coffee in Oxford. Wood, in his *Life and Times*, suggests that in the 1670s there were schemes to turn Gloucester Hall (now Worcester College) into a Greek College for about twelve Greek students. The idea revived in the 1690s, for Gloucester Hall had fallen into decay and badly needed rescuing:

> I look at Loggan's print of 1683. The remains of a Chapel and a Hall and a Library, crumbling walls and half-decayed buildings; the end is in sight. A few undergraduates still come from time to time to shelter themselves in those rooms which remain habitable; a few families have settled or squatted among the ruins; the Principal is still housed on the north side of the old quadrangle. Life goes on, but surely the end is in sight – soon Gloucester Hall will be a memory, just as its former neighbours, Oseney Abbey and Beaumont Palace, are already memories! Fortunately the event was otherwise. Benjamin Woodroffe, who became Principal in 1692, was a disgruntled crank, but he was at least man of ideas, and he set himself to revive the failing fortunes of his hall. His first experiment was hardly a success. In an attempt to reunite the Church of England and the Orthodox Church, he turned Gloucester Hall into a Greek College, and summoned his undergraduates from Constantinople. Alas! The orthodoxy of the newcomers was not proof against vacation visits to the continent of Europe; Woodroffe was soon engaged in

litigation with his peccant undergraduates, and his academic life was interrupted by visits to the Fleet prison.[234]

The dissenting academies as rivals to Oxford?

There were moves which might have threatened the monopoly of Oxford and Cambridge as the only universities allowed in England. From the Restoration of Charles II in 1660, those who would not join the Church of England and subscribe to its Articles were denied admission to Oxford and Cambridge. 'Academies' began to be set up for these 'dissenters'. Richard Frankland (1630–98) was born in Rathmell, the village where he eventually established his academy. He was educated at Oxford but then became a Presbyterian minister. Frankland founded the Rathmell School as an academy where the sons of dissenters could be taught to a 'university' standard. Such academies were regarded with suspicion as potential breeders not only of more nonconformists but also of more potential sedition. This first dissenting academy had to move several times and it did not long survive Frankland's death.

A new higher education college for dissenters was begun in 1699 in Manchester by John Chorlton, and fourteen of the students at Rathmell transferred to it. This academy lasted for a decade and a half. Again, it was comparatively shortlived, though, ironically, among its distant descendants was the originally Unitarian Manchester College, eventually licensed by Oxford as a Permanent Private Hall intended for mature students and now Harris Manchester College. Nettlebed Academy lasted from 1666 to 1697 and its tutor, Thomas Cole of Christ Church, Oxford, had had John Locke as one of his students. Newington Green Academy (c.1665–c.1706) had another former Fellow of an Oxford College as tutor (Theophilus Gale) and Isaac Watts among its students. One of the longer-lasting examples of these earlier academies was that at Taunton which seems to have lasted from 1672 to 1759. Among the longest enduring of all was the academy at Carmarthen, which began in 1700 and still survives.[235]

All this experimentation reflected a growing awareness that the Oxford (or Cambridge) way was not the only way of running a university and that in times of dissatisfaction it was necessary to look at alternatives. 'The greatest number of universities have ever been founded in times of the greatest ignorance,'[236] claimed the Irishman Oliver Goldsmith (1728/30–1774). He himself studied at Trinity College, Dublin, and later at Leiden and Padua. His analysis, ranging across Europe, identified three classes of contemporary universities, 'those upon the old scholastic establishment, where the pupils are immured, talk nothing but Latin, and support every day syllogistical disputations in school philosophy'. Prague, Louvain, Padua are his examples. In a second type 'under few restrictions', the students 'take a degree when they think proper' and 'live in the city' not a college. Instances are Edinburgh, Leyden and Gottingen. The third type offers a mixture of the two, as happens, he suggests, at Oxford, Cambridge, Dublin.[237]

Francis Bacon, the ideal college environment and thoughts of reform

Francis Bacon's *New Atlantis* (1626) had proposed setting up a new kind of college:

> (4) The works which concern the seats and places of learning are four – foundations and buildings, endowments with revenues, endowments with franchises and privileges, institutions and ordinances for government – all tending to quietness and privateness of life, and discharge of cares and troubles; much like the stations which Virgil prescribeth for the hiving of bees.[238]

Bacon saw the importance of the provision of an appropriate environment for university study, and his list of requirements includes adequate funding and good governance, as well as the physical 'infrastructure' needed to ensure that standards were maintained.

Meanwhile, an acrimonious debate about the future purposes of universities rumbled on beneath. John Webster (1611–82) called for radical changes to the syllabus and approach of Oxford and Cambridge, though there is no evidence he ever attended either University.[239] His *Academiarum examen* (1654), attacking the way the universities trained the clergy as well as their scholasticism, made John Wilkins (1614–72) and Seth Ward very angry and Ward responded with *Vindiciae academiarum* (1654). Wilkins wrote it an introduction. Wilkins was one of the committee of five to whom Cromwell had largely entrusted the work involved in his role as Oxford's Chancellor in 1652, so he was not one of the Oxford old guard. Seth Ward (1617–89), it may be remembered,[240] had moved from Cambridge to Oxford and had become one of the Wadham circle, and a leading astronomer. Their book mounted a defence against other attacks, too, including critical comment made by Hobbes in his *Leviathan.*[241]

> A contracted Brow, a lumpish down-cast Look, a sober sedate Pace, with both Hands dangling quiet and steddy in Lines exactly parallel to each Lateral Pocket of the Galligaskins, is Logic, Metaphysics and Mathematics in Perfection. So Likewise the Belles letters are typified by a Saunter in the Gate, a Fall of

> one wing of the Peruke backward, an Insertion of one hand in the Fobb, and a negligent swing of the other.... Again, a grave solemn stalking Pace is Heroic Poetry.[242]

This waspish sketch of the poses struck by students affecting various disciplines in the early eighteenth-century English universities appeared in the *Spectator* in 1711.

Public unease and calls for reform

Alongside the historic experiments with a new style of higher education going on in the dissenting academies, various proposals for change and reform in traditional universities were in the air in England. Some took the form of plain calls for reform of what was perceived to be a decayed system of higher education where standards had slipped. Books and articles began to appear and there is evidence that these were not the work of isolated individuals but the indirect products of active discussion.

On 12 May 1735, Thomas Hearne noted that 'Yesterday morning died of the small Pox Mr. Sayman MA.... This is the Gentleman it seems that occasioned Dr. Newton, Principal of Hart Hall to write his 8vo book called University Education'.[243]

> A series of papers on subjects the most interesting to the nation in general and Oxford in particular, containing well-wishers to the University of Oxford and the answers, collected together and subjected to the judgment of the public (London, 1750), Being a series of extracts from the *General Evening Post*, January–May, 1750 [claims that universities have fallen into bad habits in the pursuit of 'Luxury' and students are being led astray].[244]

Far-reaching structural proposals were being made. Perhaps degrees could be got more quickly in this new world? This was not a new idea. Milton writes of

> that voluntary Idea, which hath long in silence presented it selfe to me, of a better education, in extent and comprehension farre more large, and yet of time farre shorter, and of attainment farre more certain, then hath been yet in practice.[245]

Some English parents were choosing to send their sons abroad, not independently accompanied by tutors, but to foreign universities. Gilbert Burnet (1643–1715), a graduate of Aberdeen and subsequently a professor at Glasgow, disapproved of that. 'Trust me, they who send their Children for Learning or Manners to any foreign Universities, are not worthy of the Benefits they may enjoy in their own Country.'[246] If universities at home were unsatisfactory, perhaps new ones could be created on sound principles? Gilbert Burnet put forward proposals for the founding of a new university, to which young men were to come with 'a good Degree of understanding the Latin tongue' and where they were to be put at once to the study of logic and practical disputation. He proposed to allow no exemptions from serious study for boys of better breeding.[247] Everyone was to take equally seriously the opportunity to study for a degree and work hard.

Among the possibilities being canvassed was the shortening of courses and the reduction of the number of years required before obtaining a degree. One of the enticements to go to Europe in the eighteenth century was that in some places a degree might be achieved much more quickly than in England. It will be remembered that Goldsmith thought that a sound plan. To his thoughts on the 'slowness of conferring degrees', he added: 'Those universities must certainly be most frequented, who promise to give in two years the advantage which others will not under twelve.'[248]

In an extract from the *General Evening Post* of 15 February 1750 (given on p.21 of the above pamphlet) is a call for Government intrusion[249] into the self-governing universities of England, especially Oxford:

> Our rules and statutes, it seems, intended by founders to be the best provision for good government, are, by alteration of times and circumstances, become a hurt to the societies by them founded.... And therefore the assistance of the legislature is called in, to provide a remedy for this evil, and to alter, and even to annul, all such statutes as this gentleman shall not approve of. But I humbly presume, that all wise governments will be very cautious how they break in upon ancient establishments.

The Bodleian Library and the University Press

> All those thousands of meanings... Gone.
>
> 'They're not gone, though, Lyra,' said Dame Hannah. 'The books are still in Bodley's Library. The scholarship to study them is alive and well.'[250]

Academic libraries were not a feature of university provision until late in the Middle Ages. They did not need to be. The fortunate medieval student might have the use of books made available to their students by the religious orders. Many depended on lecturers carefully reading out in full the passages on which they were commenting so that they could note them down with the lecturer's explanations. Chaucer's Poor Clerk of Oxenford in *The Canterbury Tales,* had his twenty books 'at his bed's head', but he was a graduate. It was not until comparatively recent generations that undergraduates were allowed to use the Bodleian Library in Oxford.

In the Middle Ages, a collection of books was as likely to be kept in a chest as on shelves in a room, and the University's comparatively modest collections seem to have been accommodated in that way until Duke Humfrey of Gloucester (1390–1447), an unusually well-educated aristocrat and a patron of literary figures, gave some hundreds of books to Oxford and helped to found its first modern library. These were of course manuscripts; the enlargement of library provision was not going to be possible on a grand scale until after the invention of printing.

Thomas Bodley (1545–1613), a student of Lawrence Humphrey at Magdalen, and a Fellow of Merton until he married in 1587, wearied of the risky diplomatic life he subsequently led as a royal emissary for Elizabeth I, and took stock of his life:

> Examining exactly for the rest of my life, what course I might take...I concluded at the last to set up my staffe at the library doore in Oxford; being thoroughly perswaded that...I could not busy myself to better purpose than by reducing that place (which then in every part lay ruined and wast) to the publique use of students.[251]

Thomas Bodley's idea was to provide a great library in Oxford (launched 1602), as a gift jointly to the University 'and the Republic of Letters' or the Commonwealth of Learning, as the legend over the door still says.[252] He imposed strict terms and conditions. He expected his librarian to be a scholar, or at least able to hold an intelligent and helpful conversation with scholarly readers. He wrote 'about the appointment of an Vnderkeeper' competent to 'enterteine comers in, aswel of other nations as our owne, with meete discourses for the place', emphasizing that he 'must needes be a scholler of some good abilitie in Learning, and not a drudge altogether to deliver out bookes'.[253] Bodley was energetic about providing buildings, about the form of which he had decided opinions. He was also insistent that there should be appropriate rules for the running of the Library.

> As now for the present, my opinion is this, that before they goe about to establish statutes for continuance, it would availe

> very muche, to make proofe beforehand, for one whole yere, howe all things will be guided by the practise of some fewe, or their ancient order: and then after to goe forward, vpon a deeper inspection into all inconveniences, with a perfecter plotte of gouernment.[254]

Should such a library really be available to everyone with scholarly needs, or principally a private resource of the institution to which it belonged? Bodley insisted that any external readers were to be people of whom the University approved (*omnibus et singulis (ne peregrines exceptis) de quibus bene sentit Academia*). Oxford addressed the question of admitting outside readers early in its history. The Frenchman Jean Basire was admitted by permission of the University, in 1603. He was a lawyer, attracted to Oxford by the high reputation of its civil law teaching. The problem was that he was unmatriculated, and therefore not a member of the University, so this was the first real test of the meaning of Bodley's conception of a library which should serve the republic of letters. Basire was soon followed by a stream of others, mainly from 'protestant' continental Europe.[255] The arrangement which evolved under Cromwell and the Protectorate was that candidates from abroad were to be admitted on proof of academic suitability and personal impecuniousness, with testimonials required from Protestant Churches at home and they were to be examined by a board of ministers and laymen appointed by Cromwell, the 'Triers' under an ordinance of 20 March 1654.[256]

Since the very idea was still in process of definition, there were many questions to be addressed about what a university library should contain and the responsibilities it had to maintain a balanced collection and treat it in a 'scholarly' way. Between 1690 and 1720 there was a 'battle of the books' between those who maintained that everything worth knowing was contained in the classics and those who favoured the addition of new works on new subjects.[257]

The first Librarian of the Bodleian Library at Oxford, and its founder Thomas Bodley's own preferred choice for the post, had been Thomas James. Politically, he was a controversial figure because of his strong anti-Papist views. But he was a librarian of considerable practical imagination when it came to anticipating readers' needs. He published Bodleian catalogues in 1605 and 1620. Like an early seventeenth-century Google, he wrote out finding-aids and topical concordances to help readers locate material on particular themes. He had the idea of negotiating with the Stationers' Company to win the first 'copyright deposit' privileges on behalf of the Bodleian.[258] He

PLATE 30 – 'There's been a murder, Lewis.' Colin Dexter's fictional detective Chief Inspector Morse became the hero of a thirty-three-episode television series filmed in Oxford, with John Thaw in the title role. The series has been so popular worldwide that many tourists now travel to England almost exclusively to visit 'Morse's Oxford'. The crossword- and opera-loving Morse never completed his Oxford degree, but his cerebral and intuitive approach to crime-solving presents a sometimes baffling intellectual challenge to his colleagues of the Thames Valley Police, particularly Morse's sidekick, the earnest Sergeant Lewis (Kevin Whately).

PLATE 31 – The Ashmolean Museum was first housed in Broad Street, where the original seventeenth century building still stands, though it is now the Museum of the History of Science. The Ashmolean was intended to hold Elias Ashmole's collection of 'curiosities', which he bequeathed to the University in 1677. The building was designed by Charles Cockerell and was built in 1845 to hold the original collections, pictures, statues and a prominent collection of Greek, Minoan and Egyptian materials. The rear of the museum has been completely rebuilt to add gallery space, opening in 2009. The museum was used as a set for the Inspector Morse episode 'The Wolvercote Tongue'.

PLATE 32 – Brasenose College, which was used in the TV adaptation of Inspector Morse to represent the fictional Lonsdale College, was built on the site of the old residential halls ('Brasenose Hall'). It became a proper College at the beginning of the sixteenth century, when building work began and a royal charter was granted to create a body of Fellows and a Principal who would govern their own community. The founders were the lawyer Richard Sutton and the Bishop of Lincoln, William Smyth. The College celebrated its quincentenary in 2009.

PLATE 33 – The Franciscan philosopher Roger Bacon (c.1214–94), who lectured on Aristotle at Oxford, made a name for himself as a scholar willing to challenge contemporary certainties. He won a largely undeserved reputation for having founded the very idea of modern scientific method. He was awarded a statue in the Oxford University Museum to honour this uncertain achievement. Nevertheless, his intellectual legacy, as well as his experiments and investigations within the medieval fields of alchemy, astrology, optics and mathematics, have an enduring importance. This image offers a modern imagining of Bacon's *scientia experimentalis*.

PLATE 34 – Author of a groundbreaking early modern work on chemistry, *The Sceptical Chymist*, Robert Boyle (1627–91) was a leading member of that fraternity of gentleman-scientists (including Robert Hooke, John Wilkins and Christopher Wren, whom Boyle described as fellow members of an 'invisible college') involved in the foundation of the Royal Society. Boyle lived in Oxford from 1654 and joined in the meetings there. He was equally interested in theology, and wrote on the study of the Bible, and like other contemporaries he was fascinated by alchemy, the proto-chemistry of its time.

PLATE 35 – Boyle's fellow 'new scientist', the brilliant English architect Sir Christopher Wren (1632–1723), completed his undergraduate studies at Wadham College, where he studied Latin and Aristotle, and joined a group of natural philosophers whose discussions led to the formation of the Royal Society. In 1661 Wren was made the Oxford's Savilian Professor of Astronomy. He eventually became Surveyor of the King's Works, and a major influence in the reconstruction of London after the great Fire of 1666. He built the Sheldonian Theatre, commissioned by John Fell, the Dean of Christ Church, in 1663 to be used for degree ceremonies. Wren modelled it on a Roman theatre. He also designed Tom Tower above the gate of Christ Church (1681–2). The Sheldonian Theatre became the University's formal ceremonial hall, where today degrees are granted and debates of Congregation take place.

PLATES 36–38 – Pioneering naturalist Charles Darwin (1809–82) created a storm with the publication in 1859 of his revolutionary book *On the Origin of Species*. The British Association for the Advancement of Science called for a formal debate in 1860, and staged it at Oxford University's Museum of Natural History (above). Often regarded as one of the most significant debates in scientific history, its moment of high drama came when the Bishop of Oxford, Samuel Wilberforce, enquired as to whether it was through his grandmother or his grandfather that his opponent, Thomas Huxley, considered himself descended from a monkey. Huxley, an associate of Darwin and a fellow-champion of evolution, is said to have rejoined that he was by no means ashamed to have a monkey for an ancestor, but would be ashamed to be connected with a man who used great gifts to obscure the truth.

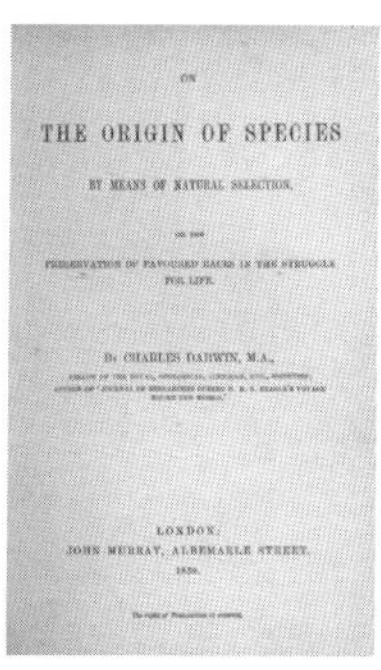

ON

THE ORIGIN OF SPECIES

BY MEANS OF NATURAL SELECTION,

PRESERVATION OF FAVOURED RACES IN THE STRUGGLE FOR LIFE.

By CHARLES DARWIN, M.A.,

LONDON:
JOHN MURRAY, ALBEMARLE STREET.

PLATE 39 – Albert Einstein (1879–1955), to whom the University awarded an Honorary Doctorate of Science, visited Oxford in 1931 to deliver the Rhodes lectures and stayed at Christ Church. He visited the College in three short periods between 1931 and 1933 and was elected to a Research Studentship, becoming the first German-Jewish scholar to hold an academic post at the House. The blackboard from one of Einstein's lectures on relativity was preserved and is now the most famous exhibit in Oxford's Museum of the History of Science (formerly the Old Ashmolean Building).

PLATE 40 – Nicholas Hawksmoor, who began his career as a clerk to Sir Christopher Wren, was the architect of the Clarendon Building, built in 1711–13 to provide a home for the University Press. The Press began in the space at the top of the Sheldonian Theatre, but the sheer weight of the books was thought to be endangering the ceiling. In 1832, 'The Printing House', as it was called, moved to its present site in Walton Street.

PLATE 41 – Charles Williams (1886–1945) began his literary career as a proof-reader for Oxford University Press, and was then promoted to the position of editor. He became a member of C.S. Lewis's informal literary society the Inklings when the Press moved him from London to Oxford before the beginning of the Second World War. Though chiefly remembered for his novels, the multi-talented Williams also wrote volumes of history, theology and literary criticism. Williams himself thought his Arthurian-style poetry was his best work and his gravestone in Holywell Cemetery appropriately bears the epitaph 'poet'.

PLATE 42 – An officer in the Royal Welch Fusiliers, Robert Graves (1895–1985) was one of the popular First World War poets who survived, despite receiving serious wounds at the Battle of the Somme. He studied at St. John's College after the end of the Great War, and subsequently made a living as a writer, publishing numerous novels, volumes of poetry and works of criticism. From 1961 to 1966 he served as Professor of Poetry at Oxford. His best known book is perhaps *I, Claudius* (1934), which was adapted in 1976 into a successful television series by the BBC.

PLATE 43 – Ill-fated Romantic poet Percy Bysshe Shelley (1792–1822) studied at University College, from 1810 to 1911, though it was later said that he had only ever attended one lecture. He read hard, as students were then expected to, but was sent down for publishing a pamphlet under the title 'The Necessity of Atheism'.

PLATES 44 and 45 – Balliol College was founded in the 1260s by Professor John Balliol, husband of a Scottish princess and father of a King of the Scots. John Wyclif (1320s–1384), was in his day one of the University's most prominent and troublesome academics. Master of Balliol in the early 1360s, he is said later to have taken rooms in the Queen's College. Though he was protected by John of Gaunt, Wyclif antagonized many of England's leading clergy with his reformist preaching and writings – an inspiration to the Lollard movement – and his criticism of temporal papal power. Eventually the University spat him out and he died in exile while crossly revising his writings for re-publication. The College remained all-male until 1979, when the first female undergraduates were admitted.

PLATE 46 – Wadham College was founded in 1610 by Nicholas and Dorothy Wadham during the reign of James I. Its famous former members include Sir Christopher Wren and Rowan Williams, the current Archbishop of Canterbury, and it celebrates its 400th anniversary in 2010. Famous raconteur and wit Sir Maurice Bowra served as Warden between 1938 and 1970. The College's impressive and strikingly symmetrical main building (traditional Oxford Gothic with classical modifications) was erected in a single operation from 1610 to 1913. William Arnold was its architect or 'master mason', who was also responsible for Montacute House and Dunster Castle in Somerset.

PLATE 47 – The College of All Souls of the Faithful Departed was founded by Henry VI and Henry Chichele in 1438. Chichele was at the time Archbishop of Canterbury and a Fellow of New College. All Souls is unique among Oxford Colleges today in maintaining the early medieval tradition of having no undergraduate students. Shown here is Nicholas Hawksmoor's North Quadrangle, which along with his creation of Radcliffe Square and its library was part of the great architect's refashioning of the centre of Oxford in the early eighteenth century.

PLATE 48 – The medieval University Church of St. Mary the Virgin, site of the 1555 trial of the Oxford Martyrs. The earliest part of the church, its tower, dates from 1280, and the elaborately decorated spire from between 1315 and 1325. Meetings of Congregation were held there from the thirteenth century onwards, and it was also used for the granting of degrees and for lectures and University sermons. John Wyclif preached in St Mary's, as later did John Wesley and John Henry Newman.

PLATE 49 – The Martyrs' Memorial at the bottom of St. Giles was erected in 1843 to commemorate the Protestant martyrdoms of Mary Tudor's reign. (The Memorial is not built on the actual execution site, which lies in nearby Broad Street, just outside the walls of the medieval city.) The Memorial was designed by Gilbert Scott, and incorporates statues of Thomas Cranmer, Hugh Latimer and Nicholas Ridley, by sculptor Henry Weekes.

PLATE 50 – Hugh Latimer (c.1485–1555) and Nicholas Ridley (c.1500–55) died at the stake in Oxford under the reign of the Catholic queen, Mary Tudor, when the reformist policies of the previous (Protestant) monarch, Edward VI, were reversed. The same ghastly fate befell Thomas Cranmer in March of the following year, 1556, and all three are known as the 'Oxford Martyrs'.

PLATE 51 – New College (so-called because it is the 'new college of St Mary') is actually one of Oxford's oldest true colleges, and the first to admit undergraduate students as members. Part of the work of reconstruction after the Black Death, it was founded by William of Wykeham (c.1320–1404), Bishop of Winchester and Chancellor of England, to provide a place of study in which the depleted clergymen of England could rapidly be replaced by new ordinands. It still retains strong links with Winchester College (another St Mary's College), and many Old Wykehamists – such as Hugh Gaitskell (1906–63), sometime leader of the Labour party – have gone on to attend New College.

PLATE 52 – Merton College was founded in 1264 by Walter de Merton, Chancellor of England and later Bishop of Rochester, as one of the first true 'colleges' in Oxford, where a community of Fellows ran its own affairs. Merton's Mob Quadrangle is the oldest 'quad', or courtyard, in the University, while its Mob Library is the oldest continuously functioning library for scholars and students in the world.

PLATE 53 – Worcester College originated in the thirteenth century, as a medieval cluster of halls of residence for students from various monasteries, with Gloucester College – which was founded in 1283 for the Benedictines – being the main such cluster. The present College was founded as Worcester College in 1714, after a benefaction by a leading Worcestershire baronet Sir Thomas Cookes (1648–1701). Although located in central Oxford today, in the eighteenth century the College was on the semi-rural periphery of the city, and its large and rustic gardens date from this period.

PLATE 54 – Shotover was once a royal forest and game reserve, and for centuries the road from London to Oxford took the traveller over it to see the 'dreaming spires' of Oxford stretching out below. According to Anthony Wood (1632–95), the Oxford antiquarian, Shotover could itself be seen from the top of the tower of St Mary the Virgin. He remarks how on 7 September 1661 senior members of the University assembled in St. Mary's to wait for a visit from the Earl of Clarendon (Lord Chancellor of England and Chancellor of the University) and 'caused a man to goe up to the battlements of the steple and there to watch his coming over Shotover Hill'. John Baptist Malchair's watercolour shows that Oxford, in past times as now, has been vulnerable to flooding.

PLATE 55 – A watercolour of Exeter College in 1835 by Joseph Murray Ince (1806–59). Exeter was founded in 1314 by Walter de Stapeldon, Bishop of Exeter, with a view to educating clergy from his own diocese. It was originally known as Stapeldon Hall. The original college comprised a Rector, a Chaplain and twelve or fourteen Fellows, all clergymen. It seems that from the late fifteenth century the College offered rooms to a few students. Its present Hall dates from 1618.

did not confine his sense of duty to meet the needs of the community of scholarship to the resources of Oxford. As early as 1600 he had published – again a first – a catalogue of the manuscripts which might be consulted in the colleges of Oxford and Cambridge. This was the first manuscript catalogue to be printed in Britain and the first 'union' catalogue in Europe.[259] James seems to have used it to assist him in identifying authors and their writings and to guide him in acquiring a great many manuscripts for the Bodleian during his tenure as Librarian.[260] This early modern librarian exemplifies an attitude. He provided for readers in the library for which he was responsible. But he thought on a grand scale and in the long term.

From burning to banning

The fundamental principles that books were in a sense sacred and must be guarded fiercely were somewhat shaken during the period of the seventeenth-century revolution in England. John Milton's books, like those of Locke, proved controversial, particularly the political ones. *The judgement and decree of the University of Oxford against certain pernicious books and damnable doctrines,* of 1683, forbade the reading of such stuff in the University. 'We also order the before recited books to be publicly burned by the hand of our Marshal in the court of our Scholes.' The book burning took place on 21 July 1683.[261]

The 'official' burning of political writings of John Milton in the Bodleian Library quadrangle may be read as an indicator that (in the seventeenth century) it was still much too early in its history to talk of a taste for 'academic freedom' at Oxford.[262] But scientific ideas could seem dangerously challenging too.[263] Students read what they chose, particularly, it is suggested, once they had graduated. When Locke published his controversial *Essay concerning human understanding* in 1689, it was bought at once by many in Oxford who were anxious to read it, senior as well as relatively junior. Locke was asked to present a copy to the library of his college, Christ Church and a Christ Church tutor is known to have recommended it to his students.[264] Heads of House were nervous of the effects however, and an unsuccessful bid was made to have the book banned in Oxford.[265] One of the conscious concerns was that the syllabus would become unbalanced, with the traditional elements taking second place to novelties; another that the new ideas would actually mislead students. A second sustained attempt to have Locke's ideas condemned was led by William Lancaster between 1706 and 1709, during which time he was Vice-Chancellor.[266]

The endless need for procuring of books

A later librarian who made a real effort to improve the collections was John Hudson. He wrote to John Locke on 6 February 1703 to say that the University was 'intending shortly to give the world an Appendix to their Catalogue of printed books, in which I doe not find one of those excellent pieces writt by you'. He takes the opportunity to mention this to Locke so that he may do himself and the University 'justice in this matter'. He mentioned that the 'Booksellers, as being of the company of Stationers' had a duty to 'send us a copy of every book they print', but this has fallen into disuse for many years. Locke replied early in March that he had written to remind his booksellers of their duties, and promising that if they do not send the books he will do so himself. The Bookseller obliged and sent a few and Hudson wrote again in April, disingenuously, not 'to enquire, whether these be all you intended us', but just to thank Locke. In the summer of the following year he wrote again to say that they had been placed in the library and on the register and 'not to discourage you from adding now and then a Book to our slender stock in comparison of what has been printed'.[267]

The collection was to become a consciously 'learned collection', and research and publishing ventures might be linked to the Library as a repository for the results. There was a proposal by Robert Holmes that he should collate the manuscripts of the Septuagint subscribers sought and the Oxford University Press Delegates in 1788 undertook to give him £40 a year for three years on condition that 'he shall deposit his Collations in the Bodleian Library ... to be there preserved'; the Oxford University press was to publish the result at Mr. Holmes's expense. He points out that collation of the Hebrew manuscripts has already shown the existence of 'interpolations in the Prophetical Text ... mutilations of it ... and lost readings supplied, so frequently, that beneficial consequences of the same kind may be justly expected from a similar application of other Septuagint-MSS to other parts of Scripture'. He raises scholarly concerns. 'Editors of the Septuagint have sometimes ventured to adjust the Greek version to the Hebrew test and to the New-Testament Citations, as they severally stood at the time.' He ventures a scholarly view: 'for as this Version was made long before the coming of Christ, the Copies, which the Seventy had in their hands, were necessarily more pure and perfect than any later Transcripts' (1788). The work was completed in 1827 by James Parsons, though the Oxford University Press was never able to raise subscriptions sufficient to publish it.[268]

'Ejectment': an eighteenth-century Bodleian moment

> So far I compard this very faulty edition with the original MS before I was ejected (upon account of ye oaths) the publick Library. After which I could not have liberty (as I desired) to compare the rest. The Corrections which come after are only some that I did now and then before my Ejectment. But I designed to have examin'd the whole most nicely, as it ought to be done.[269]

Thomas Hearne (c.1678–1735) was a non-juror and pedant who rose to become second librarian at the Bodleian. John Hudson, newly elevated to the position of Bodley's Librarian himself, was instrumental in making his original appointment as library assistant or janitor in 1701. Their working relationship deteriorated until Hearne was locked out of the Library when he would not take the Oath of Allegiance in January 1716. He refused to resign and kept his keys, although they no longer opened any Bodleian doors. Hudson had had the locks changed. In a copy of *Commentarii de Scriptoribus Britannicis auctore Joanne Lelando* (ed. Anthony Hall, Oxford, 1709), is a note on the flyleaf 'Thomas Hearne. *Suum cuique.* 1722'. Corrections in the same tetchy hand appear throughout and on p.135 in the right-hand margin the remarks just quoted. Here is the very man, still vividly present three centuries later in this marginal note.

Hearne had his reasons for being so keen to check Hall's edition against Leland's manuscript. While Hall was busy transcribing this work, which he published in 1709, Hearne himself had been making a parallel edition of the Itinerary, published in 1710–12. There are hints that their rivalry in these heated times in the Bodleian may have had many dimensions and it certainly outlasted Hearne's 'ejectment'. Hearne wrote in a manuscript (now Rawlinson MS D.984) that 'this manuscript came out of the study of Dr. Anthony Hall, of Queen's College, Oxford, who married the widow of Dr. John Hudson, to whom this book once belong'd'. So Hudson's widow was snapped up by his friend Hall (her third marriage). And Hall was in for Hudson's job after he died of dropsy in 1719. Hearne's comments in his diary on the short-list are printable, but only just, though his chiefest ire is reserved for the successful candidate, his old enemy Hudson's assistant 'that pert conceited coxcomb Mr Bowles', who had at the time, he growls in his 145-volume diary, not even taken his MA.

After he was thrown out of his paradise, he began a self-financing publishing enterprise. He was a collector and hoarder who could be shrewd about what was important. Richard Rawlinson later acquired many of his items and gave them to the Bodleian on his own death, so Hearne's books came home.

The Radcliffe Camera

The Radcliffe Camera was built between 1737 and 1747 with the aid of a benefaction in the will of John Radcliffe (1652–1714), formerly royal physician. His intention was that it was to hold a scientific and general library. The scheme prompted much activity even before Radcliffe's death. James Gibbs and Nicholas Hawksmoor competed with other architects invited to submit designs and Gibbs won with a Palladian design. There were plans for there to be a Radcliffe Library Librarian and Thomas Hearne was spoken of before he became *persona non grata.* Thomas Allen (University College) wrote to him in June 1713 with a report of a conversation he had had with Dr. Radcliffe:

> He told me he designd to make you his Library-keeper & to send you abroad to buy bookes for his library. I assured him he could not send a more faithfull, skillfull and industrious person on that errand.[270]

Francis Wise (1695–1767) was under-keeper of the Bodleian Library from 1719. He was ambitious, but it seems more for position than for the opportunity to make a difference. He fought hard for election as keeper of the University Archives, a position he gained in 1726, though he seems to have done little work on the archives while he had charge of them. He tried to become president of Trinity in 1731, but failed. In 1748 he was successful in his candidacy for the post of first librarian at the Radcliffe Library.

His pridefulness does not seem to have grown less. There was a memorable episode in 1759 when Wise put a padlock on the door to signify that the Radcliffe Library did not belong to the University. He wrote that Smith had:

> brought me word that the Vicechancellor had ordered him to take it off again. Upon which I got another Smith to put it on again, and told the Vice-Ch.s man I would bring an action against any one who should break it open. Soon afte the Vice Ch.came himself broke it open and sent me my padlock, with a letter. The letter summoned him to explain himself because he has 'clapt a padlock on our Radcliffe Library' ... 'if you don't come, and ask my pardon for this strange, and unprovok's insult on me, and the whole University, I shall cite you into my Court next term'.[271]

The University Press

Meanwhile, the University was acquiring a printing-house. The first book was printed in Oxford in 1478, two years after William Caxton had set up his English printing press. This was not yet an Oxford University Press; that first began to come into existence in the late sixteenth century, when Joseph Barnes was granted the privilege of printing books outside London in 1586, apparently on the basis of his own claim to enjoy the University's approval. Both Oxford and Cambridge were granted licences to print books by royal charter in 1632. This was an arrangement in which William Laud had a hand. In both universities the business of the press was to be supervised by the academics. In Oxford, Delegates of the Press were appointed straightaway, in 1633, but the regular way of going on which Laud had envisaged took some time to settle down so that books could actually be produced.

The notorious John Fell, Dean of Christ Church, took a lease on the University's licence in 1672 and began energetically to pursue objectives of his own. He wanted to see Oxford printing in the enlarged range of newly-fashionable 'oriental languages' so he began to acquire fonts to enable books to be printed in Greek and Hebrew and other alphabets. He set up his own practical realization of the University's Press in the basement of the Christopher Wren's Sheldonian Theatre. This had the advantage of providing the University with some equipment when he died, so that it was able to begin production in earnest.

The first great financial success was the publication in 1702 of Clarendon's *History of the Great Rebellion*.[272] On the proceeds the Clarendon Building was built between 1711 and 1713, to the design of Wren's pupil Nicholas Hawksmoor. This enabled the Press to set up a 'Clarendon' arm, so that it could publish the learned monographs of its own scholars and others. Printing Bibles was also to be a considerable money-spinner. A Bible Press was set up from about 1690 to exploit the potential of the licence the University held which allowed it to print the King James Version, then the standard translation. The Press was to become one of the Oxford's most important sources of income, especially from the later nineteenth century.[273]

5 THE NINETEENTH-CENTURY TRANSFORMATION

Varieties of student life at Oxford

School to university

The poet Arthur Hugh Clough (1819–61), who went to Oxford in 1837 from Rugby School, writes of the difficulty of motivating himself to work for an Oxford examination, and remembers fondly the supportive routine of his school days:

> I wish with all my heart that my ordeal was over, even though it were a failure. I have but little appetite for Work mathematical or Classical, and there is as little compulsion to it and as much enticement from it as is possible in our ways of life in Oxford. I would give much for the pleasant treadmill routine of school.[1]

Oxford, he found, was not like school:

> That I have been a good deal unsettled in mind at times at Oxford, and that I have done a number of foolish things is true enough, and I dare say the change from Rugby life to its luxury and apparent responsibility has had a good deal of ill effect upon me.... I have had things come across my way at Oxford which could not but be very absorbing.[2]

The worlds of school and University were not, however, so far apart. Until late in the nineteenth century, Fellows of Colleges still had to give up their Fellowships on marriage, and those who did not become parish priests often became schoolmasters. Charles Dodgson (Lewis Carroll) quotes a testimonial provided for a would-be headmaster in 1880, by Thomas Podmore, MA, Head Master and 'late Fellow of St. John's College, Oxford'. Podmore describes how the candidate has performed as a teacher in his school and remarks:

> I have, in fact, been glad to avail myself, to the utmost, of the accurate scholarship, wide range of reading, refined taste, firm yet gentle discipline which he uniformly brings to bear on all his work.[3]

So we begin with a paradox. The schoolboy might not notice much change in what he studied or even the level at which he was expected to study it when he went from school to Oxford, but he would find himself in a very different mode of life, and no longer much restricted in the way he chose to live. Oxford was liberty, but too much liberty can be hard to cope with.

Improving the tutorial system

John Henry Newman (1801–90) went to Trinity College very young, at 16, for it was now common to begin at Oxford about the age of 18. He says that advice on study-methods (how the student was to read, how 'learn' from his reading), was patchy or non-existent in Oxford when he himself had been an undergraduate. And not all students were as well-prepared as Rugby boys. Newman had already progressed some way through Euclid and was surprised to find his tutor asking him whether he knew what a point, a line and a plane angle were. Once Mr. Short had the measure of him he gave him more advanced books and apologized for the elementary level of the lectures he was obliged to give.[4]

Newman drove himself hard, was a perfectionist and yet lacked the maturity which would have enabled him to study to the best effect. In his 'autobiographical memoir' he describes how, without adequate guidance, he 'read books, made ample analyses and abstracts, and entered upon collateral questions and original essays which did him no service in the schools [Oxford University examinations]'. In the Long Vacation of 1818 he was taken up with Gibbon and Locke. At another time, he wrote a critique of the plays of Aeschylus, on the principles of Aristotle's *Poetics*:

> though original composition at that time had no place in school examinations.... Moreover, though the examiners were conscientiously fair and considerate in their decisions, they would understand a candidate better, and follow his lead and line of thought more sympathetically, if they understood his position of mind and intellectual habits.[5]

Newman read much too long each day and overworked himself into near failure in the examination. In the end, he was not even listed in mathematics in his final examinations and was placed low down in the class list[6] in classics, where he obtained only a 'fourth', the lowest class.

Nevertheless, Newman won one of the coveted Fellowships at Oriel in 1822. Richard William Church was elected a Fellow of Oriel in 1838 and describes the mode of obtaining an Oriel Fellowship.[7] The Fellowships were not advertised. The aspirant wrote to ask if there was a vacancy, was given a preliminary weeding-out interview by the Provost, then wrote a Latin letter to each of the Fellows pleading his cause. He then sat an examination, bringing along a certain volume of the *Spectator*, from which a passage was set for translation into Latin. Then there was 'an English essay to write on a passage of Bacon'. That was on a Monday. On the Tuesday the candidates wrote a Latin essay and translated from English into Greek:

> The Oriel common-room was rather proud of its seeming easy and commonplace and unpretending tests of a man's skill in languages and habits and powers of thinking for himself. They did not care if he had read much.[8]

Then the Fellows considered the papers together 'each of us having one man's essay or translation'. They read bits aloud and compared their impressions. There was criticism of this method of selection in the July 1821 issue of the *Edinburgh Review* ('who can be surprised if, under a system like this, genius and knowledge should so seldom strike a lasting root?').[9] But eccentric though the system was, it got the industrious but maverick Newman his Fellowship.

One of the changes which needed to be brought about in nineteenth-century Oxford – a change of which Newman soon became a leader – was the revival of a 'tutorial' system which had grown up since the colleges had begun to take responsibility for undergraduate teaching but could be patchy, leaving students to flounder. To work well, a tutorial system depended on the conscientiousness of tutors and the assiduousness of the young men. A student's task was to 'read'. His tutor's role was to direct his reading.[10] (Hence perhaps the relatively modern Cambridge terminology of 'Directors of Studies'.)

The pious young Newman thought there was a danger that students would neglect their spiritual lives. He wrote a *Letter to the Editor of the Christian Observer* on the subject on 22 September 1822. The student, he regrets:

> must labour diligently for honours which he affects not to desire.... His literary duties, which require intense devotion of mind, necessarily call off his thoughts in a great measure from dwelling on heavenly objects.

He fears that students leave themselves too tired by academic effort to pray before bed.

In 1826, much to his pride, Newman became a tutor at Oriel himself:[11]

> I have a great undertaking before me in the Tutorship here.... There is always the danger of the love of literary pursuits assuming too prominent a place in the thoughts of a College Tutor, or his viewing his situation merely as a secular office, a means of a future provision when he leaves College.[12]

In his new office, Newman wrote himself notes on things both practical and spiritual he must not forget to say to new arrivals:

> As to Freshmen – on matriculation explain to them the nature of subscription to the Articles, and of taking oath to obey the University statutes. Tell them the day they must come into residence – and what books they must read in the meanwhile. Take caution money[13] and fees, and explain about it to them.
>
> Explain to them the reason of paying tuition in absent terms – talk to them about the Sacrament.[14]

Among his letters are several which show how carefully he attended to his tutorial duties. He wrote to Henry Wilberforce in July 1827. He thinks he has been right to take his name off the list because it would not have been a good idea to be 'examined in a part of Horace you had never read' (though it would have been sensible 'to have been ready'). Self-reproach is healthy. 'Take up for your responsions [examinations] in October, *all* Sophocles, *all* Horace, and *all* Euclid.' This will 'improve you greatly'. My letter is 'too like a sermon' but 'it is written from real regard for you'.[15] In another, to Arthur Tarbutt, 4 December 1827, Newman is pressing him to read hard, but not to get over tired of particular books.[16] This eager young John Henry Newman was not far from his own student years. He was a latter-day version of the young Regent Masters of medieval Oxford.

The Oxford Movement

Six students were expelled from St. Edmund Hall in 1768 on the accusation that they were Methodists.[17] Conformity with Anglican belief was taken seriously as a requirement in Oxford and Methodism was perceived to present an ecclesiological challenge. The broader Evangelical revival of the ensuing decades was more diffuse and a boy could be an Evangelical member of the Church of England as he could not be a Methodist member of the Church of England. So Evangelicalism could be compatible with the required subscription to the Thirty-Nine Articles.

A number of notable students arrived in Oxford who had been brought up to hold Evangelical views. Newman came from an evangelical background too. The future Prime Minister, William Ewart Gladstone (1809–98), is an example. He arrived as a student at Christ Church from Eton in 1828. He came from an Evangelical family and took life so seriously that indignant fellow-students beat him up in his rooms in March 1830 for being too assiduous when it was his duty to keep a record of compulsory student attendance at services in the Cathedral. He tried to found a rival fraternity to the Cambridge Apostles. But despite serious attempts to make common cause with the Calvinists and other evangelical groups in Oxford he found himself dissatisfied.[18]

These ripples on the surface of religiously conservative and traditionally High Church Oxford were important. They helped to prompt the 'Oxford Movement'. The 'Tractarians', as its leaders were known at first, were would-be reformers of the University, the Church and the religious orientation of the nation. They were (loosely speaking) heirs of the religious hotheads who had sought to control the University in earlier centuries. Among the leaders of the Oxford Movement were Newman, who left it in 1845 when he became a Roman Catholic; John Keble (1792–1866), after whom Keble College was later named; E.B. Pusey, whose legacy was Pusey House (1884), with its Chapel and Library (but with no pretensions to a part in the academic activity of the University); and the passionate and challenging Hurrell Froude (1803–36) who died young from tuberculosis. As Newman said of him:

> Froude had that strong hold of first principles, and that keen perception of their value, that he was comparatively indifferent to the revolutionary action which would attend on their application to a given state of things.[19]

This was in large measure initially an 'Oriel' movement. Edward Hawkins (1789–1882) was Provost of Oriel for the best part of sixty years from 1828 to 1882. It was Hawkins who took Newman under his wing as a young Fellow and coaxed him away from his family's Evangelical opinions. When Newman succeeded in his bid for an Oriel Fellowship in 1822 he went to live with Richard Whately at Alban Hall for a year. Whately was interested in overhauling the teaching of logic, 'which, in spite of the Aldrich read for his BA examination, was quite a novelty to Mr. Newman'. He lent Newman his unpublished 'Analytical dialogues':

> At length he went so far as to propose to him to cast these dialogues into the shape of a synthetical treatise. It was a peculiarity of Whately's to compose his books by the medium of other brains. ...Others did but stimulate his intellect into the activity necessary for carrying him through the drudgery of composition.

He gave Newman generous acknowledgement in the book which appeared four years later, though Newman was surprised that so much was credited to him.[20] Whately was to become an active adherent of the Movement.

The Oxford Movement was launched by an Assize Sermon preached by John Keble in Oxford in 1833, on the theme of 'national apostasy'. The semi-political theme was appropriate enough for an official sermon to inaugurate one of the regular appearances in Oxford of the itinerant justices. Keble was referring to the consequences of the 1832 Reform Act, which included the reduction of the number of bishops in the Church of Ireland, a province of the Anglican Church. The campaign he launched was a mixture of patriotism, ecclesiology and university reform and it was to change the style of Oxford.

For Keble and his friends had large ambitions. They wanted the Church of England to awaken to what they now saw as its profound continuity with the ancient Church; they wanted the restoration of medieval liturgical elements; they wanted it accepted that there had been no fundamental division of theological opinion in the sixteenth century, for in their view the Thirty-Nine Articles were perfectly compatible with the Counter-Reformation decrees of the Council of Trent if one thought about it.

Charles Lloyd (1784–1829) was a particularly assiduous tutor at Christ Church, who included Robert Peel among his pupils; he was Regius Professor of Divinity at Oxford from 1822, then Bishop of Oxford. He gave his required public lectures but also private classes which were attended by several of the leading names in the new Movement. Perhaps it was partly under the influence of his lectures, which had emphasized a historical continuity and a legacy of pre-Reformation ideas in the Church of England, that the Tractarians began actively to seek to establish that continuity. The fifth-century Vincent of Lérins' dictum in his *Commonitorium* that the Church is to be known because it has the faith held by 'everyone, always and everywhere' was to burst upon Newman and become the defining moment in his conversion to Roman Catholicism.[21] The Tractarians also had a concomitant interest in the writings of the Fathers of the early Church, whose works, they thought, needed new editions and translations. They began publication of a new *Library of the Fathers*. Newman was already at work on the Fathers, writing a series of papers for the *British Magazine* which were to be gathered together and published in 1840 as *The Church of the Fathers*. Newman also began to write *The Arians of the fourth century,* which he published in 1833, and which began to open his eyes to the way the doctrine of the Church had evolved.[22] This strong scholarly dimension was particularly important to the success of the Tractarians in Oxford.

From September 1833, members of the group began to publish a series of *Tracts for the Times*. Newman wrote Tract I 'To the clergy' (*Ad clerum*), expounding the doctrine of the apostolic succession. For what else could they rely upon for the authority of their calling should the Church of England be disestablished?

> Should the Government and Country so far forget their GOD as to cast off the Church, to deprive it of its temporal honours and substance, on what will you rest the claim of respect and attention which you make upon your flocks?

Newman did not allow any formal structure to determine the activities of those involved in the new movement. He wanted it to remain a 'living movement'.[23] Its sympathizers were to act and write as they felt themselves moved. He himself was very much in the public eye of the University, giving a series of sermons in the University Church of St. Mary's throughout the period from 1834 to 1842, which were eventually published as *Parochial and Plain Sermons*. There was controversy and debate and other activists such as Edward Bouverie Pusey were rapidly drawn in. The strongest objections came from those who alleged that the Tractarians were stripping the Church of England of her protestant character. Newman sought to counter this in his series of *Lectures on the prophetical office of the church, viewed relatively to Romanism and popular Protestantism* (1837), again delivered in St. Mary's, and nicely making the point that the ancient tradition of maintaining the fine line between sermon and lecture was still alive.

The movement – or its adherents – had a powerful influence on susceptible students. They were able to have their effect in part because the spiritual guidance of the student was still seen as central to a tutor's duties. The aims of the Oxford Movement within the University were – as Pusey put it – to restore it to a sense of itself as a primarily ecclesiastical institution, teaching young men who were to be ordained and were expected then to spend their lives in the service of the Church. There were other, rival, 'shows', especially those of a Methodist bent, but it was the Tractarians who managed to unite demagoguery with a sure sense of new institutional possibilities. Ripostes appeared, for example, the Martyrs Memorial to the protestant martyrs Cranmer, Latimer and Ridley, whose foundation-stone was laid in 1841 as a gesture of protest organized by C.P. Golightly, a local cleric. The monument became a point of controversy between the extreme religious left and the extreme religious right in Oxford.

Convocation rather favoured the Tractarians until 1837. Then it began to reject them, with the decision of 1845 coming as the climax of that process. R.D. Hampden (1793–1868) had become an Oriel Tutor in 1832 when Newman (with others) had been forced to resign. In 1834 he became Professor of Moral Theology, though this was a post Newman also aspired to, mainly for strategic reasons. In 1836, Hampden was made Regius Professor of Divinity. He was an advocate of admitting dissenters to the University and of ceasing to require subscription to the Thirty-Nine Articles. On his appointment to the Regius Chair, a disappointed Newman wrote an attack on his liberal ideas. Oxford became increasingly polarized, with the formation of cliques of loyalists to individual leaders of opinion.

Arthur Hugh Clough went to Balliol as a scholar in 1837 at a time when Balliol was beginning to rival Oriel as top College. Balliol was consciously continuing the attempt to reinvent the tutorial system which had begun at Oriel earlier in the century. Benjamin Jowett (1817–93) was a fellow-student and W.G. Ward (1812–82) was one of his tutors. Jowett, who was to become a towering figure in the University later in the century, had gone from St. Paul's School in London to a scholarship at Balliol in 1835, where, although his family was inclined to the evangelical, he was influenced for a time by the ideas of the Oxford Movement. He was quickly offered a Fellowship, even before he had graduated, and then a tutorship. He began to make his name as something of a radical and even planned a history of the University which he was going to write with Arthur Stanley. All that has survived is a pamphlet, published in 1848, containing *Suggestions for an improvement of the examination statute.* Eventually he was to become Master of Balliol and Vice-Chancellor.

Ward became a somewhat insistent friend to Clough and drew him temporarily into the Oxford Movement, against the tendency of his evangelical upbringing and his 'liberal' grounding at Rugby.[24] He wrote of his confusions:

> I don't know how we shall get on in Oxford against those very opposite sort of enemies – the Newmanists – they are very savage and determined, and such good and pious men to boot. I do not know what would become of the various shades of Whigs now existing in the University, if Hawkins were to be made a Bishop. These people however have done a vast deal of good at Oxford, where anything so 'ungentlemanly' and 'coarse' and 'in such bad taste' as 'Evangelicalism' would never be able to make very much way.[25]

After a somewhat chequered performance as a student, which was perhaps the result of the pressures he had been put under, Clough eventually won a Fellowship at Oriel in 1842, but he was progressively to be driven by discomfort towards a political as well as a religious radicalism in reaction against Ward and others.

Meanwhile, in 1841, Newman publish Tract 90, in which he argued that a believer could subscribe to the Thirty-Nine Articles and simultaneously hold Catholic beliefs, offering a '*prima facie* view of the Thirty-nine Articles as not excluding a moderate Catholicism (that is, Roman doctrine, as far as it was Catholic)'. This was widely felt to go too far. William Palmer of Worcester College wrote a *Narrative of events connected with the publication of the tracts for the Times* (1843), with the intention of rebutting any such claim. Ward responded with *The ideal of a Christian Church considered in comparison with existing practice* (1844), which caused huge offence in the University.

By December 1844 Convocation was getting ready to put an end to the Tractarian Movement as an 'Oxford Movement'. It had before it a series of resolutions, to take away the degrees of W.G. Ward, to condemn his book, and to require everyone on subscribing to the Thirty-Nine Articles also to declare that he held them in the sense in which they were 'both first published and were now imposed by the University'. The problem was that this would affect those of liberal views as much as the Tractarians themselves. When Convocation met on February 13 (it was snowing), Ward was called upon to explain himself. The voting took place. The book was condemned by 777 votes to 386. The decision to strip him of his degrees was narrower (569 to 511), perhaps in token of the seriousness of the loss of rights which would follow. The last vote was the most important for it was essentially a judgement on Newman's claim in Tract 90. When the matter was put to the vote, the Proctors stood up and the Senior Proctor cried loudly *Non Placet.*

After this the Movement fractured, careers were ended, some followed Newman himself into the Roman Catholic Church. If 13 February 1845 ended Tractarian hopes, it also saw the final discomfiture of the Evangelicals. Clough wrote on the effect of the news about Newman that 'a great many will be rendered uneasy by his departure; and one may look out for changes in one way or another. ...Pusey, of course will stay, and Marriott, and Church, and Keble'.[26] They did.

State interference and the threat of external 'reform' brings about major change

> The fact cannot be concealed from Oxford residents that they are the objects of dislike to a considerable portion of the community, and of assault in certain august assemblies; and, in consequence, there has been, more or less, a revival in the members of the University of that energetic spirit, that resolve to take part and have a voice in the world's matters, which is one of its distinguishing marks in history.

Newman had written in *The British Critic* in July 1938.[27] This was not the first time in the nineteenth century that there had been public criticism of Oxford and demands for change. Maria Edgeworth's father had published a book in 1809[28] which had given rise to lengthy correspondence in the public prints and caused Oxford to make significant changes.

The excitements of the rise and rejection of the Oxford Movement were followed breathlessly in the national press, and there began to be renewed calls for the reform of the University. Readers of newspapers and periodicals, among which the *Edinburgh Review* continued to be immensely influential, included families in which there were likely to be several graduates of Oxford or Cambridge, with that sense of continuing membership and lasting voting rights which made what happened there seem very much still their business.

The Times was often especially fierce with Oxford in the mid-nineteenth century:

> The Conservatives fancy that they can govern England because they have the support of the nonage and dotage of Oxford. That University is the seat of isolated barbarism amongst an ocean of wholesome knowledge and of useful action. It is generations behind the rest of the kingdom, and

> fitter to sympathize with the monks of the Escurial than with a free and reflecting people. Yet the oligarch faction will take Oxford for their guide.[29]

But who was to pay for these expensive new studies? The first category of available funding which would not call on the taxpayer was the existing endowments of Oxford and Cambridge and their colleges (which enjoyed the income from the bulk of them). In the House of Commons debates of 23 April 1850 on the English and Irish Universities, Mr. Heywood was eloquent about the discrepancy which had grown up between the sums of money available to colleges and the small numbers of students some of them were actually educating (col.692).[30] The motion was put:

> That all systems of academical education require from time to time some modification, from the change of external circumstances, the progress of opinion, and the intellectual improvement of the people (col.697).

Sir R.H. Inglis objected that Mr. Heywood had given no sufficient notice of his intention to put this motion and had left the Universities unprepared to respond. He questioned the jurisdiction of Parliament to enquire into the affairs of the universities at all (cols. 697 ff.).

Popular ignorance drove a resentment of a perceived combination of 'privilege' and the 'uselessness' of what was taught at Oxford and Cambridge. Mark Pattison was well aware of this when he wrote, 'We have no longer the difficult task of justifying science in the eyes of the nation'. However, the nation wants to see what it is getting:

> The public recognizes results. In the last fifty years the physical sciences have filled the world with their marvels. Gas, steam, locomotion. ...It might not be impossible to bring home to the public conviction the real connection which exists between these striking conquests over the material world and the abstract study of the laws of that world.[31]

The University Commissioners

Oddly, the call for the setting up of a Royal Commission to reform the Universities came partly from the academics themselves. In 1849 Fellows of the Royal Society from both Oxford and Cambridge signed a petition. The then Prime Minister, Lord John Russell (1792–1878), proposed that Commissioners should be set up. Russell was neither an Oxford nor a Cambridge man but a graduate of the University of Edinburgh. The Royal Commission of 1850 was envisaged by its instigators as an attack upon an area of vested interest, namely the two ancient English Universities. Oxford's Chancellor, the Duke of Wellington, wrote him a letter in alarm. Oxford wished to point out, through the Hebdomadal Board, that it had thoroughly overhauled its statutes in 1636 and there could be no need for further changes now. 'The nature and faculties of the human mind were exactly what they are still.'[32] Cambridge was more receptive to the idea. These initial attitudes were curiously reflected in the outcomes, with Cambridge receiving an encouraging pat on the head and Oxford a harshly critical report.

The internal politics of the hearings at Oxford were complex. The Oxford Commissioners included insiders such as H.G. Liddell of the Greek Dictionary and A.C. Tait who had been a Fellow of Balliol. Hinds, the Chairman, was an ally of Richard Whateley. Only one member of the Commission, Jeune, was the head of a College, and this may have meant that the Commission focused more strongly on the University's needs than those of the colleges. This became a consistent theme through the series of Commissions, running through the 1870s and the period after the First World War, for each time the colleges suffered and their position was weakened.

It was proposed (for Oxford though oddly not for Cambridge) that non-collegiate students should be encouraged, so that students who could not afford college life might get an Oxford degree. The result was the Oxford University Act of 1854 (Cambridge's Act was dated 1856) and some substantial changes to governance, with the state taking powers to make changes to trusts if they had been in existence for more than half a century, so as to diminish the number which were essentially closed except to a narrow category of students favoured by the original benefactor.

The Oxford Commission Report reads rather irritably, beginning with a protest about Oxford's uncooperativeness:

> The Governing Body has withheld from us the information which we sought through the Vice-Chancellor as its chief resident officer; and this, as has been since intimated to us, with the purpose of disputing the legality of your Majesty's Commission.

The Commissioners seem to have felt that they had had to make do with mere conversations with the Heads of Houses 'as a body'. The colleges succeeded in giving the Commissioners the impression that they were now doing all the educating, while the University was twiddling its thumbs. They were irritated not to have been able to get the figures they sought which would have enabled them to assess the university's financial position. They grumbled that if a student at Durham could get a degree for £60 a year it ought not to be necessary for an Oxford student to be able to find £300.

They reported that there had been improvements and certain reforms appeared to be in hand. Vices 'such as drunkenness and riot' among the undergraduates showed a downward trend and students seemed to be seeing more of their tutors. The Commissioners were not entirely happy about the vice, particularly the 'sensual vice' for 'in the villages round Oxford', 'the opportunities to vice are too abundant'. Then there was gambling and extravagance (excessive spending on 'driving, riding and hunting').[33]

The Commissioners remarked on the desirability of 'wider courses of study':

> It has been held to be the sole business of the University to train the powers of the mind, not to give much positive or any professional knowledge.

Standards had declined ('suffered to decay'), and it was time for a review of the syllabus. They were also anxious 'to place the best education within the reach of all qualified to receive it'.[34]

Russell was coming to the end of his period in power; he resigned in 1852. But the process which was to lead to the enactment of legislation for the two ancient universities was already in train.

Gladstone entered Christ Church in 1828 and by the time he graduated he had already distinguished himself as a promising young politician, prominent among the would-be politicians of the college. He founded an Essay Club which was intended to rival the Cambridge Apostles and became President of the still-novel Oxford Union. As Member of Parliament for Oxford he took a considerable interest in the drafting of the 1854 Act, with the young Benjamin Jowett helping him. But by 1865 he had lost his seat (rather badly; he came third in the poll); Oxford was showing its reluctance to return a Liberal MP.[35] An Act to make further Provision for the good Government and Extension of the University of Oxford, of the Colleges therein, and of the College of St. Mary, Winchester (c.81) came onto the Statute Book in 1854. The Preamble pleads the public good as a justification for the State's interference ('Whereas it is expedient, for the Advancement of Religion and learning') and the Act uses a device which was to become familiar in the Acts which followed, of setting up Commissioners and naming the individuals who were to act in that capacity, to ensure the University did what it was told.

The contrast of style in this mode of state interference compared with the methods of the Tudor Visitors and the Puritan purgings of the next century reflects the expectations of a new age.

Commissioners again

Some freeing up of the outdated restrictions attached to old gifts to Oxford and its colleges began. The Oxford University Act 1863, s. 3 allows Oxford to suppress old professorships 'of political economy, chemistry, geology or mineralogy' and use the professor's salary:

> in promoting or assisting, by the purchase of materials or apparatus, by the support of assistant teachers, or by such other means as the University may by statute determine, the study and cultivation in the University of the science which forms the subject-matter of the suppressed professorship.

Some flexibility is allowed in transferring the mineralogy income 'to the study of geology or any branch thereof and vice versa'.

Royal Commissioners were appointed again in 1872–4, this time chaired by Lord Cleveland, and chiefly intent on scrutinizing the finances of the two universities. The objective was to rebalance their funding and reconsider the uses to which the endowments of Oxford and Cambridge and their colleges should be put, transferring wealth from the colleges to the universities and ensuring that the Universities could afford to pay salaries for professors.

This time Oxford made some attempt to get ahead of the game. In 1873, the Hebdomadal Council set up a committee to consider how better to organize the endowment of professorships. Oxford's cooperation was forthcoming with much less protest than at the time of the Commission of the 1850s, but in the case of Oxford that may have been partly because the Vice-Chancellor, Liddell, had himself been a member of the earlier Commission.[36]

The legislation of 1877, which was a combined Oxford and Cambridge Act, once more created Commissioners to ensure that its provisions were put into effect, in rather the same way as had been done in 1854 and was to be done again in 1923. The Chairman was to be Lord Selborne, an Anglo-Catholic and a Liberal, who seems to have been persuaded that if he did not agree to take on the job there would be a risk that someone else would do so who had an agenda potentially harmful to Oxford. The Act was to intrude still further than the earlier one upon the autonomy of the Colleges and the terms of old trusts. It did however provide the only definition of the purposes of a university in English law, in terms of the fostering of 'education, religion, learning and research'.

John Ruskin records how he lectured on the last day of this post-Act University Commission's visit to the University and had to take Lord Selborne in:

> I had to take him into the lecture and couldn't get him in! nor myself neither at first, for the room was crammed, and the crowd in actual corridor as at door of a theatre,

he wrote in a letter to Mrs. Severn on 7 November:[37]

> But I began clearly, and got them interested ... & the audience all as quiet as mice to hear.

John Ruskin had become Oxford's first Slade Professor of Fine Art in 1869, and although he was appointed for three years in the first instance, his appointment was renewed twice before he resigned in 1878. He was an active lecturer, giving eleven series of lectures during this decade. He was also popular. The University could be confident that the Commissioners would receive a favourable impression of its activities if they watched one of his performances.

One result of the work of the Commissioners was some tightening up of expectations. The Commissioners of the 1850s had been particularly scathing about the convention which resulted in most dons being young Fellows of Colleges, who had to leave as soon as they wished to marry. It meant that a Fellowship did not count as a recognized 'profession': 'where was the necessary income for a marriage to come from? Roger had his Fellowship ... but the income for that would be lost if he married; he had no profession,' as Elizabeth Gaskell asks in *Wives and Daughters* (1866).[38] This was the decade in which the problem of getting and keeping the best tutors if they were required to be celibate was reaching crisis point. Young men soon abandoned academic life for homes and families. There was a consequent lack of mature academics. 'The fact that so few books of profound research emanate from the University of Oxford materially impairs its character as a seat of learning.'[39]

In future, Professors were to be required to show that they were carrying out their duties. The *Gazette* of 21 November 1882 (p.130) records the attempt to regulate the duties of professors in the wake of the 1877 Act. The Corpus Christi Professor of Jurisprudence, for example, was (1) required to 'reside within the University for twenty-eight days at least in each academical year during full University Term; and in order to complete such residence the Professor must have passed twenty-eight nights in Oxford' and (2) 'One clear week-day at least shall intervene between the delivery by the Professor of any two of his Statutable Lectures', so the Professor could not come to Oxford and rattle them all off in a hurry and go away again.

The University Press becomes a moneyspinner

One of the consequences of the work of the 1850s Commissioners was a radical rethinking of the mode of operation of the University Press. Some of the best long-term investments of the Press began now in the late nineteenth century, for example the publication of the *Oxford English Dictionary*. The modern Oxford University Press emerged as a serious commercial venture, and it remains a major source of the University's funding. This did not take place without some initial division of opinion. Factions began to appear among the Delegates. Mark Pattison visualized a future for the Press as principally scholarly and Benjamin Jowett was all for making the Press a commercial success.

Jowett became Vice-Chancellor in 1882 and was instrumental in securing the appointment of Lyttleton Gell, a protégé and a commercial publisher; Pattison conveniently died and he was able to push the matter through in the Long Vacation of 1883. He survived in the post until 1898 and made himself thoroughly unpopular, but he brought about a change of approach and set the conditions in which the Press could become a commercial success.

Family connection to employment relations: the modern development of the University Press

The resilience of what was achieved has been demonstrated again and again in the course of the Press's progress through the changing methods of book production. At the end of the fifteenth century, the making of books moved from the creation of the individual volume by scribal skill using oak-gall, goose-quill and vellum, into print and mass-production. A change of equal moment has taken place in the last decade and in the twenty-first century, 'processes once controlled by a craftsman with a seven-year apprenticeship behind him, are now governed by a single silicon chip'.[40]

The evolution of the Press exemplifies what was to be a significant change in town-gown relations too. The 'craftsmen' of the Oxford University Press were, a part of an arm of the University and an exemplification of the way town and gown could be united in a common cause, from the mid-nineteenth century until the Printing Division was closed down in 1989 and much of the production sent out to be carried through in remote parts of the world where labour was cheaper. In 1883 E.L. Gass joined the Press as an errand boy or 'printer's devil', and worked his way up the ladder of the production process, to compositor, then reader. He had 'known' the Press as a child because one of his parents' neighbours was a compositor. On Tuesdays this neighbour had the task of setting up for printing the weekly official record of the University's business, the *Oxford University Gazette,* which had begun publication in 1870. As a small boy Gass had the task of taking him his tea, since he was always working too late on Tuesdays to go home for it. 'I well remember the climb up to the top of the dark staircase on the learned Side, lit by two feeble gas-jets of the old flare pattern, one on each landing,'[41] he recalled. His perception was that this had been the end of an era in which families of employees had a strong sense of connection with the Press, and the Printer to the University would 'accompany the brass band on its annual excursion by boats to Godstow' and march 'his company of volunteers' from the Press quadrangle to the University Parks 'for their weekly drill'.[42]

Horace Hart (1840–1916), author of *Hart's rules for compositors and readers*[43] became Printer to the University and Controller to the University Press from 1883 to 1915. 'The intimate association of master and man along with his family became a thing of the past.'[44] Hart was a hands-on master of the Press, opening or inspecting all the incoming post personally before sending it on to be dealt with as he deemed appropriate. Young Gass, however, began his career by arriving at work in the company of his father, in time for the six o'clock start of the day, and going up the back stairs, because the composing-room staff (male) were not allowed to 'walk through the stitchery, on account of the girls employed there'.[45] The culture of the Press was still 'old-fashioned', with compositors and many other employees 'who still retained the dress of their youthful days and came to work regularly in tall hats and frock coats'.[46] Despite the new régime introduced by Hart, a cheerful culture persisted among the staff out of his sight. Beer could be smuggled in by the boys. 'One particularly artful card had a coat made specially for the job with a pocket running all round the skirt from one side to the other; here he could conceal as many as 6 or 8 half pint bottles which he retailed at a profit of a halfpenny on each bottle.'[47]

Gass did not work out his full term of apprenticeship as a compositor, being transferred after a couple of years to the ranks of the readers. For him, being a reader meant moving away in due course from the Bible Side and the noisy presence of the machinery to the Learned Side, where the atmosphere was quieter. The Readers were few. Gass recollects the names of only seven and four 'clerks'.

Of the next generation but of the same tradition who began work as late as 1943 was Gilbert Williams, who was proof-reader for the Jobbing Ship at the time when it was the chief remaining old-style production room. Automation was creeping in elsewhere in the Press, but the Jobbing Ship dealt with its work in the old way; 'everything was handset and put through the compositors' stick before being imposed into a chase and then proofed ready for the proofreader':

> Gilbert was the epitome of what a proofreader should look like. He was small, sat on a high stool and was crouched over a Spartan desk with just a single metal lamp casting a bright light over it. The rest of the 'box' was in shadow. He had thick pebble glasses and his pristine shirtsleeves were held up by bright gold-coloured expanding armbands, he wrote on the proofs with his old pen that he dipped meticulously into the inkwell on his desk, and on his head he wore a visor to keep the glare away from his eyes.... Gilbert was fanatical about keeping up OUP's reputation and would ensure that every proof that left him had the hallmark of quality scribbled all over it.[48]

If he could find nothing wrong he would add a one-point space somewhere, to the annoyance of the compositors, just for the sake of achieving perfection.

The story which can be told about the interior life of the employees of the Press has its parallels in the working lives of college servants and porters, the descendants or heirs of the early lodging-keepers, who had moved gradually over the centuries from embattled resentment of the University to becoming part of its inner world. But the division between insider and outsider had more subtle dimensions. The 'Inkling' Charles Williams was a graduate. The Readers and those who were engaged in the physical production of the books were of mixed educational level. Among the Press's Readers, as Mike Belson recollects them, were former errand boys like himself and some were prodigiously learned men, including 'a refugee German lawyer, a maths professor, a Quaker missionary who was proficient in at least ninety languages, teachers from several public schools' and 'a claustrophobic ex-vicar, who spent his day kicking the wooden partitions of his "box".'[49]

What became of the liberal arts?

The scaffolding of the 'classical' education which was now in danger of losing its central position had originally been the study of the liberal arts, with grammar and logic prominent among the seven. Classical literature treated as a study for edification and cultural enrichment was an arrival of the sixteenth century. It was from the old Arts course with its thirteenth-century addition of some 'philosophy of science' that the modern syllabus emerged. But the essence and some of the particulars of the old syllabus persisted. Daniel Wilson, just appointed Vice-Principal of St. Edmund Hall, was dryly sceptical in 1807 about his capacity to do justice to the syllabus that he was expected to teach:

> Next term I have to lecture on Aristotle and the tragedies of Aeschylus ... and the New Testament has to be critically and copiously dealt with, and Aldrich's *Ars Logica* to be entered on. I will do what I can.[50]

Games with words: moving on from the Middle Ages in the study of linguistic theory

Late in the nineteenth century 'Lewis Carroll' (Charles Dodgson, 1832–98) was still teaching in the University of Oxford a syllabus which owed a great deal to medieval grammar and logic. In Alice *Through the looking-glass* in 1872, he teased his fictional Alice in the person of Humpty Dumpty on exactly the long-standing question of the nature of the link between a word and its signification:

> 'Don't stand there chattering to yourself like that,' Humpty Dumpty said, looking at her for the first time,' but tell me your name and your business.'
>
> 'My name is Alice, but –
>
> 'It's a stupid name enough!' Humpty Dumpty interrupted impatiently. 'What does it mean?'
>
> 'Must a name mean something?' Alice asked doubtfully.
>
> 'Of course it must,' Humpty Dumpty said with a short laugh: 'my name means the shape I am – and a good handsome shape it is, too. With a name like yours, you might be any shape, almost'.
>
> 'There's glory for you!'
>
> 'I don't know what you mean by "glory,"' Alice said.
>
> Humpty Dumpty smiled contemptuously. 'Of course you don't – till I tell you. I meant "there's a nice knock-down argument for you!"'
>
> 'But "glory" doesn't mean "a nice knock-down argument,"' Alice objected.
>
> 'When I use a word,' Humpty Dumpty said in rather a scornful

> tone, 'it means just what I choose it to mean – neither more nor less.'
>
> 'The question is,' said Alice, 'whether you can make words mean so many different things.'
>
> 'The question is,' said Humpty Dumpty, 'which is to be master – that's all.'[51]

If Alice wants to convince Humpty Dumpty that '"glory" doesn't mean "a nice knock-down argument"', she needs to find a way to identify the concept that 'glory' signifies so that Humpty can be persuaded that he is wrong.

There ran throughout the syllabus which developed from the eleventh century a heritage which goes back to Augustine (354–430). There is not only *verbum* but also *res*, not only the word but the thing, and the 'thing' may be an idea or a particular exemplification of an idea. For example, the word 'lion' may signify a particular lion met in the course of an afternoon stroll. Or it may signify the idea of a lion, so that when I meet a lion in my path I can compare it with the idea, identify it at once, and make my escape. Carroll-Dodgson was still conjuring with the sophisticated legacy of medieval logic in *Alice through the looking glass.*

> 'You seem very clever at explaining words, Sir,' said Alice. 'Would you kindly tell me the meaning of the poem called "Jabberwocky"?'
>
> 'Let's hear it,' said Humpty Dumpty. 'I can explain all the poems that were ever invented – and a good many that haven't been invented just yet.'
>
> This sounded very hopeful, so Alice repeated the first verse:
>
> 'Twas brillig, and the slithy toves
> Did gyre and gimble in the wabe;
> All mimsy were the borogoves,
> And the mome raths outgrabe.'
>
> 'That's enough to begin with,' Humpty Dumpty interrupted: 'there are plenty of hard words there. "Brillig" means four o'clock in the afternoon – the time when you begin broiling things for dinner.'
>
> 'That'll do very well,' said Alice: 'and "slithy"?'
>
> 'Well, "slithy" means "lithe and slimy." "Lithe" is the same as "active." You see it's like a portmanteau – there are two meanings packed up into one word.'
>
> 'I see it now,' Alice remarked thoughtfully

Humpty Dumpty goes on:

> 'Impenetrability! That's what I say!'
> 'Would you tell me, please,' said Alice 'what that means?'
> 'Now you talk like a reasonable child,' said Humpty Dumpty, looking very much pleased. 'I meant by "impenetrability" that we've had enough of that subject, and it would be just as well if you'd mention what you mean to do next, as I suppose you don't mean to stop here all the rest of your life.'
> 'That's a great deal to make one word mean,' Alice said in a thoughtful tone.
> 'When I make a word do a lot of work like that,' said Humpty Dumpty, 'I always pay it extra.'

Aristotle treated nouns and verbs, the parts of speech most likely to be included in a glossary, as the principal elements in connected discourse. Verbs he saw as 'nouns with a time-reference' (*Perihermeneias* III 16b). Later generations, especially the 'terminist' logicians,[52] heirs of Porphyry and anxious to be clear about the way words were being used in propositions, identified these as 'categorematic' words, which can signify without assistance from others.[53] Boastful Humpty Dumpty instructed by Charles Dodgson knew something of this and expressed a particular respect for the way verbs could stand their ground. 'They've a temper, some of them – particularly verbs, they're the proudest – adjectives you can do anything with, but not verbs – however, I can manage the whole of them!'

The 'others', what the medievals called the 'syncategorematic' parts of speech such as prepositions and conjunctions,[54] were deemed to need to be conjoined with nouns and verbs in order to make up one of the 'terms' (the subject or the predicate) in a proposition. Aristotle recognized that although nouns and verbs can 'stand alone' they cannot individually form sentences (assemblages of words with an overall meaning) or propositions (sentences which may be true or false) (*Perihermeneias* III 16b; *Perihermeneias* IV 17a). If we take an example of one of these needy and incomplete syncategorematic words, this distinction is easy to understand. 'Before,' I say. 'Before what?' you ask. 'Beforc tomorrow?' 'Before going?'

Charles Dodgson was never afraid to tease. A comparable lively revamp called 'Euclid and his modern Rivals' he made fun of Euclid. As one critic put it:

> Mr. Dodgson's discussion of the various systems of geometry which have been put forth as rivals to Euclid, is enlivened

> by occasional flashes of humour which make the work as amusing as it is profound.[55]

Charles Dodgson may have been tossing these ideas about as a mathematician and logician, but he was also doing so as an heir of hundreds of years of teaching on all this in Oxford. The lingering of old grammatical themes was, however, a minor aspect of a modernized study of ancient literatures and languages which had more or less incorporated rhetoric, and was no longer the focus of calls for reform.

From Aristotle to Bacon? The battle to modernize logic

It was the legacy of medieval logic teaching that caused the trouble and got Oxford attacked for being old fashioned. There had been energetic debate from early in the century over the change to the Examination Statute which was going to be needed in Oxford. One of the matters on which the Rector of Lincoln had been most heated was the proposed change to the study of Logic, particularly Aristotle.[56] Strong feelings were expressed for and against and the first proposed version had to be revised. The 'old Scholastic Discipline [of logic is] in its dotage and now exploded', it was asserted, but it was not certain that Bacon's substitution of the new scientific 'inductive' for the 'deductive' method would really do instead. It was a fair question whether:

> Bacon's Dialectics are much superior and of more utility to the Scholar than Aristotle's Organon; but it is still mere matter of opinion ... though you may judge the method by Induction to be far more serviceable than the Syllogistic form, still it by no means follows that the latter is false in its conclusions.[57]

The change was made and the syllabus revised. Some of the elements of medieval linguistic theory which had persisted for centuries moved quietly into the sphere of mathematicians. Upon the recognition of the value of the inductive method alongside the old syllogistic rested the possibility of the introduction of the systematic study of the sciences.

In 1809, the *Edinburgh Review* was sharply critical of the old-fashioned character of the logic syllabus at Oxford:

> The examinations at Oxford, until within these very few years, so far as they were scientific at all, and not confined to the learned languages, turned entirely on the Aristotelian and Scholastic logic; and that the new logic, such as is explained in the *Novum Organum* of Bacon, was never mentioned. ... Some few individuals might pursue natural philosophy to a certain

> length, but it entered not at all into the general plan of education. Examinations have now been reformed.[58]

Edward Copleston (1776–1849), formerly an Oriel Tutor, later bishop of Llandaff, Professor of Poetry at Oxford from 1802 to 1810, mounted a stout defence of Oxford's syllabus in his 'Three replies' of 1810–11 to what had been said in the *Edinburgh Review*.[59] Aristotle, he said:

> is most generally known as the author of the Syllogistic form of reasoning, in which his aim has been commonly misunderstood, and misrepresented even by those who should have pointed out and corrected the vulgar error.

As a logician Aristotle has merits:

> His chief characteristic is a resolute endeavour to get to the bottom of his subject, whatever it may be. ...And however thorny and desert the tracts through which he pursues his prey, however far he may be led from the cultivated and elegant walks of life, the fear of losing admiration, or of disheartening his companions, never bends him from his purpose.[60]

Much of the *Organon*, Copleston coaxes, 'has been judiciously compressed and re-cast', and 'modern compendiums' such as that of Aldrich 'contain the substance of the original, relieved of its tedious explanations and subtleties, and totally free from the barbarous jargon with which the later Schoolmen had overloaded and corrupted it'. 'It is in this reformed shape that his system is now studied in the University.' So modern study of Aristotelian logic has already been 'reformed'.

He then turns to the undeserved reputation of Aristotle for turning logic into an excuse for endless petty argument. No, he says, Aristotelian logic teaches the student to think. Aristotle:

> has been absurdly supposed to have forged this weapon for the purpose of endless wrangling.... Its principal use and advantage is to cut short wrangling, by marking out precisely the real object of dispute, and by confining the disputant to correct reasoning.[61]

In this call for modernization there was a danger of conflation of two strands of Aristotle's legacy. By the nineteenth century, works such as Aristotle's *Physics* were quite plainly out of date as serious textbooks of their subject, although they arguably still had value as classical reading. The *Edinburgh Review* contained an accusation that 'the dictates of Aristotle are still listened to as infallible decrees, and the infancy of science is mistaken for its maturity'.[62]

Whether the *Organon* was out of date is another matter. Here it was not always clear whether Aristotle or the whole subject of deductive logic was being attacked, with all its modern textbooks. The essayist Thomas De Quincey (1785–1859), who had been a student at Worcester College, was very disparaging about Isaac Watts's 'Improvement of the mind', still being reprinted (for example in 1818 and 1821); he calls it 'the most imbecile of books', and its success he attributes partly to Dr. Johnson's having praised it.[63] And he says he ventures 'to denounce, as unprofitable, the whole class of books written on the model of Locke's *Conduct of the understanding*'.[64]

This dangerous tendency to confuse the quality of the methodology he used in formal reasoning with the merits of Aristotle's treatment of natural science, politics and ethics, was still being noted in the 1830s. Frederick Oakeley made a shrewd guess that:

> many ... persons confound the Moral Philosophy of Aristotle ... with his Logical System, which is only studied here as a means to other ends; or with his Physics, a subject plainly depending altogether for its perfection upon progressive discovery.

Such confusion could lead to the rejection of Aristotle's legacy, particularly when coupled with other assumptions:

> and that, having heard of the Scholastic philosophy in connexion with the Dark Ages, they naturally enough, suppose, that Bigotry, as it is called, and the Aristotelian Philosophy, are, in some way or another, connected.[65]

Oakeley robustly defends the retention of the traditional material in the syllabus:

> Heathen philosophy is not wrong, but imperfect; and Revelation has not reversed, but corrected and completed it.[66]

John Henry Newman did not want to see it disappear altogether either, certainly not out of a sense that the morality of some of the content might be inappropriate to the forming of a Christian gentleman:

> You have refused him the masters of human thought, who would in some sense have educated him, because of their incidental corruption.[67]

John Ruskin expressed some highly independent thoughts about Aristotle, calling him a 'muddlehead' in a letter to a college friend in 1840. He would like to see students encouraged to make their own decisions about what to accept and what to reject in what they read and not to be obliged to accept the thoughts they read in set books with uncritical respect as authoritative:

> I have come to the conclusion that Aristotle was a muddlehead. ...If they read him as they ought at the University – that is, telling the student to find out what was nonsense and what was falsehood... they would do good, for what is good of the 'Ethics' is very good; but as they do at present – reading as if it were all gospel – I am certain it does as much harm as good.[68]

This was a view he returned to later, in *The stones of Venice*:

> reading Aristotle, whose system is so false, so forced, and so confused, that the study of it at our universities is quite enough to occasion the utter want of accurate habits of thought, which so often disgraces men otherwise well-educated.[69]

In a letter to his father of September 1853, he describes how he once tried to write a better ethics but gave up as he came to realize (partly through reading Plato and Bacon) that Aristotle's Ethics were 'a mere bog of glittering mud'.[70]

Meanwhile a series of tutors and others began work to try to design the new course materials which would bring the inductive method into its proper place alongside the syllogism. Among them was Coleridge,[71] always game to attempt a subject whether he was specially qualified or not. Coleridge's long-delayed and much-revised attempt to write a simple introduction to logic makes it plain how difficult a task others accomplished with such comparative elegance.

> If, then... pure and simple logic be neither an organ for the discovery... nor a test for the distinguishing of truth... what may it be affirmed to be? The answer is that it is a canon or form to which all legitimate constructions of the understanding must correspond.[72]

But if books were to be added, something would eventually have to be removed, or the syllabus would become impossibly crowded. It took daring to suggest removing Aristotle, but the question was robustly raised. Edward Copleston (1776–1849) mooted the idea that keeping to an outdated set book might actually mislead students:

> The only parts of Aristotle's writings, which can interfere with the Student's progress in natural philosophy, are his *Physics*; the doctrines of which, it is well known, were formerly made the basis of instruction in that department of science through all the Universities of Europe.

He describes how Francis Bacon 'succeeded in dislodging the Aristotelian philosophy from its strong holds'; Oxford 'although the place where this new fledged philosophy tried her earliest flights' was also one of the last fortresses, of which she took a formal 'possession':

> For the Aristotelian Physics were interwoven with the whole course of our studies and exercises; and it was not easy to reconcile the abandonments of them with the language of the Statutes, which public officers were bound to inforce.[73]

The uncertainty about the way to strike a balance between the syllogistic and the inductive method may be seen in examination questions late into the nineteenth century:

> Second Public Examination, Trinity Term 1879, Logic Paper
> Translate and explain briefly [one of three gobbets]
> *(a) Syllogismus ad principia scientiarum non adhibetur, ad media axiomata frustra adhibetur.*
> 2. 'State and explain Bacon's judgements upon Plato and the Atomists'.[74]

Bringing the syllabus up to date: the Oxford reform of classical education

The public good: classics and citizenship

The home-educated John Stuart Mill (1806–73) thought there was a public interest in the creation of:

> an enlightened public: a body of cultivated intellects, each taught by its attainments in its own province what real knowledge is, and knowing enough of other subjects to be able to discern who are those that know them better. The amount of knowledge is not to be lightly estimated, which qualifies us for judging to whom we may have recourse for more.[75]

This educated power of discrimination in a population would work, he thought, both ways. It would be hard to fool such an enlightened public. And the same public will be capable of giving work of high quality the appreciation it deserves:

> The elements of the more important studies being widely diffused, those who have reached the higher summits find a public capable of appreciating their superiority, and prepared to follow their lead.[76]

Early nineteenth-century Oxford assumed that the ideal formation of a person included making him a good citizen, able and willing to take an active part in public life. As long as it remained the case that Oxford and Cambridge required that all their students and Fellows of colleges should be practising Anglicans, it was a strong presumption that that also meant making him a good Anglican Christian. The 'secularising' of this presumption in the universities was one of the more complex processes of the nineteenth century and it went far beyond and behind the University Tests Act of 1871 which at last allowed non-members of the Church of England to take degrees.

Among the defenders of the study of the classics in the nineteenth century were those for whom the classics had become inseparable from the transmission of this Christian culture. John Henry Newman's *Lectures and essays on University subjects* (Longman, 1859) was a collection of papers written in pursuit of his scheme to set up a new Catholic University in Ireland. The first is an address on 'Christianity and letters' which he delivered in November 1854.[77] He suggests that it is worthy of note that a 'University ... should be formally based ... and should emphatically live in, the Faculty of Arts'. He recognizes the historical importance of the medieval 'higher' studies of Theology, Medicine and Law, though he now sees these as 'the three learned professions'. He invites his audience to go back with him and 'review the course of Civilization since the beginning of history'. He does not 'deny a civilization to the Hindoos, nor to the ancient Mexicans, nor to the Saracens, nor (in a certain sense) to the Turks; but each of these races has its own civilization, as separate from one another as from ours'. But he intends to concentrate on a civilization which he identifies as Christian. 'Christianity waited until the *orbis terrarum* attained its most perfect form, before it appeared'.

He goes on to trace a series of points of analogy between Christianity and civilization, in support of the argument that the future of civilization depends on higher education being conducted in a Christian environment of a particular kind. In itself this was no different from the assumption of most of his Oxford and Cambridge contemporaries that a Church of England Christianity provided the essential climate for the forming of the mind of a cultured gentleman. But he needed to adapt the case so as to make it argue the need for a Roman Catholic university in Ireland, and that meant considering the larger question of 'civilisation'.

His case is argued largely from his own somewhat imperfect understanding of the way the classics had been studied down the centuries. In the centuries after the fall of Rome the classics continued to be studied with approval, he suggests. Then he comes to 'the notorious fact, that, Universities introduced certain new sciences into the course of education, which threw the Seven Liberal Arts into the shade'. These, 'Philosophy, Scholastic Theology, Law, and Medicine', led to 'extravagances and usurpations'; some 'protested against' these at the time, yet, though there were times when the old traditions seemed on the point of failing, somehow it has happened that they have never failed. He draws a parallel between this 'movement against the Classics' of the Middle Ages and what he considers to be happening in his own day. 'The Baconian method' he identifies with the scientific method. 'Now, Bacon himself... would not have needed to be reminded that to advance the useful arts is one thing, and to cultivate the mind another.'

The answer lies in a return to the classics, for the benefits of science to civilization remain unproven:

> The simple question... is, how best to strengthen, refine, and enrich the intellectual powers; the perusal of the poets, historian and philosophers of Greece and Rome will accomplish this purpose, as long experience has shown; but that the study of the experimental sciences will do the like, is proved to us as yet by no experience whatever.[78]

There were plenty who thought it easy to show that the classics set a young man up for anything else he might want to do with his mind. Benjamin Jowett was in favour of the idea that a young man who had had a classical education designed to enrich and stimulate his mind would be able to perform better in any future profession than one who had begun on specialist studies too young.[79] Robert Saundby still endorsed the value of at least a preliminary acquaintance with general liberal studies in his *Introductory address at the opening of the University College Medical School*, Cardiff, in 1898:

> You are associated at the outset of your professional education with a broader culture than that of a purely medical school. On the other hand these students were not offered 'a complete course of medical instruction' but only two years, of 'botany,

> geology, chemistry, physics, anatomy, physiology, materia medica and pharmacy'.[80]

The Welsh students, he felt, benefited from a differently structured grounding from the English ones, whose professional training has grown up 'in connection with hospitals'.[81]

A.E. Houseman (1859–1936), a former undergraduate at St. John's, wrote in a letter of 3 June 1903:

> My trade is that of professor of Latin in this college [University College, London]: I suppose that my classical training has been of some use to me in furnishing good models, and telling me what to leave out.[82]

He had writing in mind, but the principle he was laying down is more extensive. It amounts to a claim that the very intellectual discipline involved in the study of the classics trains the mind better than anything else, for whatever specialized learning might be wanted later.

It seemed to many that a narrow philistinism threatened if the study of classics was abandoned. Matthew Arnold, troubled by the Irish Question, had written a series of 'Irish Essays' (1882), in which he himself looked back a generation, to Charles Dickens, to help him formulate a memorable image in rethinking the balance to be struck between 'culture' and the need to meet the needs of the present commercial situation. He chose Salem House in *David Copperfield*, published in 1849–50 (not Dickens's only portrayal of a dreadful school). Among the masters, Mr. Creakle 'knew nothing himself, but the art of slashing'.[83] To Arnold, and Haldane still found this opinion eminently quotable in 1902, the schoolmaster Creakle and his ally, David Copperfield's tormentor Mr Murdstone, represented the 'commercial gentleman'. 'The English in the Transvaal,' reported Arnold, 'contain a wonderful proportion of attorneys, speculators, land-jobbers, and persons whose antecedents will not bear inspection' but which Arnold was confident were 'middle class'. 'They have almost all, we may be very sure, passed through the halls of a Salem House and the hands of a Mr. Creakle.'[84]

What is wrong with this middle class in Arnold's view is its cultural 'narrowness'. It is a product of a strictly functional education. Arnold recoiled from the intellectual poverty Dickens portrayed. In a speech he gave to the Eton Literary Society apparently in 1882, he put the argument for the continuing study of the classics:

> It seems to me, firstly, that what a man seeks through his education is to get to know himself and the world; next, that for this knowledge it is before all things necessary that he

> acquaint himself with the best which has been thought and said in the world; finally, that of this best the classics of Greece and Rome form a very chief portion, and the portion most entirely satisfactory. With these conclusions lodged safe in one's mind, one is staunch on the side of the humanities.[85]

Arnold did not hesitate to draw upon the classics in seeking to win over his readers, for he could be confident that they would not find it unfamiliar territory. In the preface to his *Irish essays* he writes of the way 'the barren logomachies of Plato's *Theatetus* are relieved by half-a-dozen immortal pages'. 'Among them are those in which is described the helplessness of the philosopher in the ways of the world, the helplessness of the man of the world in a spiritual crisis.' 'Mr. Jowett is uncommonly happy in his translation of the account of the man of the world at such a crisis, "drawn into the upper air."' He has to:

> get himself out of his commonplaces to the consideration of government and of human happiness and misery in general what they are, and how a man is to attain the one and avoid the other. 'Then, indeed,' says Platon, 'when that narrow, vain, little practical mind is called to account about all this, he gives the philosopher his revenge'.[86]

He is laughed at, by every man who has been brought up as a true freeman.

Dickens was far from disparaging the intellectual efforts of those who did not get their 'culture' at Oxford and who would not have engaged with ease with Arnold's way of presenting the case for culture by way of the citation of the classics. Dickens's dislike for middle-class narrowness did not involve spurning self education by the disadvantaged. But he liked it to be authentic, curious, hungry, an honest search for knowledge. Among the records of the many public speaking engagements he accepted, he was enthusiastic about mechanics' institutes. In December 1847 he spoke at Leeds at the soirée of the Mechanics' Institution there. Towns like Leeds are 'full of busy men', and 'there is ignorance, dense and dark'. 'In that town, education – the best of education: that which the grown man from day to day and from year to year furnishes for himself and maintains for himself, and in right of which his education goes on all his life.'[87] In Lancashire and Cheshire he found an Association of 114 such Institutions and Mutual Improvement Societies, who were 'keeping their best aims steadily before them', and circulating books, which were 'constantly being read with inexpressible relish by thousands upon thousands of toiling people' (and never being defaced or damaged). Dickens made a speech about all this in December 1858 (stressing the importance of the local character of such arrangements).[88]

The defenders of a classical education believed that intellectual excitement, the heights and depths of Dickens's 'inexpressible relish', or of Arnold's 'large and instructive results', the stretching of human capacities, is an exercise of value in itself even if it does not make for better or more compliant employees.

Matthew Arnold:

> As Goethe says of life: 'Strike into it anywhere, lay hold of it anywhere, it is always powerful and interesting' – so one may almost say of classical literature. Strike into it where you like, lay hold of it where you like, you can nearly always find a thread which will lead you, if you follow it, to large and instructive results.'[89]

Arnold's vision was of the clear practical benefits of including 'cultural' elements in the work of universities: it is in the public interest for them to produce graduates who can think clearly and write well; who are sufficiently aware of ethical considerations to perceive that greed for profit can interfere with propriety of conduct; who can offer the population something to satisfy needs which go beyond the consumption of goods; who are knowledgeable enough to be vigilant about the protection of liberties; who can think and write in a bigger frame of reference than the short-term and local and travel the world in thought.

New subjects as substitutes for the classics?

Nineteenth-century Oxford saw the emergence of new 'Arts' subjects, such as 'History' which had previously not been thought suitable for undergraduate study but which were developed to meet the needs formerly met by the study of the classics. History, for example, was found to be good for forming citizens and public servants.

A plan to found a Society for the study of Antiquity and History had been put forward in 1602, on the understanding that it would not be in competition with what Oxford or Cambridge did, since History was not a 'university' subject:

> This Society will not be hurtful to either of the universities, for it shall not meddle with the arts, philosophy or other final studies there professed, for this society tendeth to the preservation of history and antiquity of which the universities being busied in the arts take little regard.[90]

The urge to study 'history' had subsequently been satisfied for most undergraduates through the study of classical literature. The study of Modern History (particularly political and constitutional aspects of the subject) began to be regarded as an appropriate training for the Civil Service, particularly with the introduction of Civil Service examinations in the middle of the nineteenth century. History was first added to other subjects, in Oxford to Law and in Cambridge to Moral Sciences. In 1850 new Examination Statutes in Oxford introduced a School of Law and Modern History as one of the options which could be taken after completing the preliminary classical papers, colloquially known as 'Lit Hum'.[91] After 1864 this requirement was dropped and the dimmer 'passmen' who did not need to attempt a profession but were just going to go home and be country gentlemen took Modern History on its own, with a simplified examination paper and set books.

'Pass degrees' were introduced to allow the less able student to leave with a degree even if he could not attain the standard expected for an 'honours degree'. The difference of expectations may be noted in the contrasting style of the printed examination papers of the 1870s. Those for passmen have space for name and college and two-inch gaps between the questions to allow the candidate to write in short answers. So standards might be extremely modest,[92] as we see in examples of the examination papers such candidates took, reduced from the level of the testing essay questions honours candidates answered, to a series of simple questions which could be answered in the small blank spaces provided for a short answer. A three-hour Logic paper of 1879 contains eleven questions (mixing traditional and modern, inductive and deductive logic), for example, 'Explain with instances the chief divisions of Terms and Propositions'. In another such paper, a faint air of kindly whimsy is detectable, as the examiners temper the winds to these dim-witted lambs:

> Examine the following arguments...
> (3) It is safer to take in logic in Moderations, for more men are plucked in Algebra.[93]

It is in this context and against this background that the questions on (for instance) the Oxford examination papers of the 1870s need to be set. They are still concerned with the sort of physics-with-metaphysics which characterized Johnson's Cambridge list of questions of 1735.

> **Moral and Political Philosophy**
> 1. In what respects has modern ethical sentiment departed from the Greek views on the four cardinal virtues?...

3. Discuss and illustrate the likeness and difference of moral and aesthetic approbation...
5. Is the Freedom of the Will a necessary postulate of Ethics?...
10. Propose a classification of the various functions of Government...
11. Discuss the expediency of the compulsory relief of the poor.
12. On what circumstances does the price of a commodity depend?[94]

In the case of the History papers, here was an early test of the question how far the study of a subject can be 'dumbed down' without its ceasing to be degree-worthy.

The quality of the course and the standard expected rose under the pressure of demand from those who saw it as a preparation for a political career and for the training of future public servants. This aspirational approach to the value of the study of History is visible in 1872 in the Inaugural Presidential Address of Earl Russell to the Royal Historical Society, which had been founded in 1868. It is summed up in the delightful:

> Mr. Grote[95] was too enlightened a lover of freedom and civilisation not to appreciate the importance of the battle of Marathon.

'It has been,' he continues, 'the task and the glory of eminent authors to describe the causes which have led to the decline and fall of great States'. He cites Montesquieu and Gibbon. His point is that there are lessons, applicable to the modern world:

> It becomes a curious and interesting subject of inquiry, What is to be the fate of the civilized nations of the world?[96]

One of the beneficiaries of these new options, the Geography student O.G.S. Crawford, a future archaeologist, commented that:

> Going from Greats [Classics] to Geography was like leaving the parlour for the basement; one lost caste but one did see life. Geography was then a new subject, struggling to gain recognition...I immediately felt at home in the new environment of maps and things of this world, so refreshingly different from the musty speculations about unreal problems that had hitherto been my fare. ...We were being taught how modern communities were influenced by [the geographical]

environment, and I argued quite correctly, that ancient ones must have been as much or more influenced.[97]

Oxford studies the sciences

Establishing expertise

Both the ancient Universities had had their Professors of the sciences for a couple of centuries, but it was only with the nineteenth century as the subjects began to define their parameters that the holders of the Chairs began to feel any obligation to make themselves expert in the subjects they 'professed'. In a letter of November 1853, George Eliot mentions T.H. Huxley (1825–95) as 'a scientific man who is becoming celebrated in London'.[98] Huxley, an autodidact, had been, like Darwin, a voyager on oceanic field-trips and a strong supporter of Darwin's theory; he was becoming a noted public speaker. Such activities made his name. Did they make him an 'expert'? Where was such a reputation to be established without benefit of the possession of a degree and a post in a University?

In *Reliquiae Diluvianae: or observations on the organic remains contained in caves, fissures, and diluvial gravel, and on other geological phenomena attesting the action of a universal deluge,* which he published in 1823, William Buckland (1784–1856) gives a long list of his credentials. He is Bachelor of Divinity (BD), Fellow of the Royal Society (FRS), Fellow of the Linnean Society (FLS). He claims membership of the Geological Society of London and of the Imperial Societies of Mineralogy and Natural History at Petersburg and Moscow and the Natural History Society at Halle. He is an honorary member of the American Geological Society and a correspondent of the Museum of Natural History in Paris, as well holding posts in Mineralogy and Geology in Oxford. In his dedicatory letter to the Bishop of Durham, he speaks of his 'endeavours to call the attention of the University to the subject of geology, a combine with those braches of study which are more strictly academical this new and interesting science'. Only a few years earlier he had been consciously at the beginning of his researches but now he felt the need to establish a range of claims to be taken seriously in the study of his subject.

Settling the boundaries of a subject

In 1818, William Buckland moved from the Oxford Readership in Mineralogy he had held from 1813 to the Readership in Geology. Feeling his way from one subject to another, from the study of lumps of rock to the study of rocks in the landscape, he gave an inaugural lecture in 1819, leaning heavily on information provided by William Conybeare of Christ Church relating to the geology of the Oxford area. He had another dimension to accommodate too. His idea was to give his audience every confidence that Genesis and geology agreed that there must have been a great flood (Genesis 6.11–8.14). Buckland's lectures, which he used to give in the Ashmolean Museum in its old building were, and continued to be, popular.

Buckland's *Reliquiae Diluvianae* of 1823 was written at a time when he was still expecting the evidence to confirm the literal truth of the story of Noah's flood as it is told in Genesis. His exploratory 'scientific' method is to describe what has been found in detail, not merely geologically but archaeologically, bones as well as rocks. The style of the description has the air of a Sherlock Holmes enquiry, with inferences drawn or hinted at as possible to be drawn from the collected evidences. For example, in the course of his 'general remarks on the German caves', he notes that 'the mud and pebbles were not introduced at a period anterior to that at which the caves were inhabited; for in this case they would have found a separate bed at the bottom, beneath the bones'.[99]

It was this sort of approach, like that of the collectors and classifiers who were striving to let their discoveries help to determine the structure of the way they could best be studied, that began to present a challenge to academic complacency and to all sorts of things previously considered settled. In the study of the natural world, geology and mineralogy became exciting and dangerous when it was realized that this hobby of scientifically-inclined early modern gentlemen amateurs[100] was beginning to throw up questions about the historical truth of Genesis which were hard to answer.

Buckland showed himself a true scientist in the modern sense by his willingness to revise his ideas and rethink his position. He won the Copley Medal of the Royal Society for his analysis of the evidence found in a newly-discovered cave in Kirkdale in Yorkshire.[101] A collection of bones of animals no longer seen in England was found, including elephants, rhinoceros and hippopotamus, as well as hyenas. Those who wanted to support the historicity of the Flood claimed that these must all have been swept into the cave in the Deluge. But Buckland noticed that the bones had been chewed and he conducted experiments which established that bones chewed by modern hyenas looked much the same. So he concluded that this had merely been a hyena den and was not evidence for the Flood at all.

By the 1830s two schools of thought were emerging. Some, such as the younger Charles Lyell, contended that the surface of the earth had been shaped by a steady progression of minor causes.[102] Others favoured the view that major catastrophes must have occurred.[103] Charles Lyell was drawn from the legal career his father had intended for him, to an interest in geology, particularly the study of stratification, in 1821, after he met Gideon Mantell. Mantell had been studying geological formations in Sussex and Lyell began to compare his explanations with formations further west to see if they fitted. There was plentiful exchange on such matters among the gentleman amateurs who were turning themselves into specialist professionals. Lyell was aware that Thomas Webster had perceived similarities between formations on the Isle of Wight and those that Georges Cuvier (1769–1832) and Alexandre Brongniart (1770–1847) had identified in the Paris area. Lyell was working here on the kind of geology (later termed stratigraphy) on which the leading members of the Geological Society were then engaged. In 1823 he was elected secretary to the Geological Society of London, founded in 1807,[104] and the same year he went to Paris to meet Cuvier and Brongniart and study the Paris area himself under the guidance of one of Brongniart's former students. In return he unfolded for the French scholars the arguments for change by sudden deluge which Buckland had been proposing in England. Lyell was persuaded by the Frenchmen.

Boundaries of subjects and the taxonomy of knowledge

The new science which was throwing up so many discomfiting questions did not confine itself to mineralogy, geology and religion. Buckland had been involved in the discovery and scientific discussion of the first dinosaur which was found in England, in 1824 and wrote a paper on the '*Megalosaurus* or Great Fossil Lizard of Stonesfield'.[105] Richard Owen (1804–92), an instigator of comparative anatomical studies, was the first to call the newly-discovered giant reptiles 'dinosaurs' (1842), classifying them on the basis of observable common anatomical features which appeared to distinguish them from lizards. So the emerging geological evidence held lessons for zoology and botany and it raised questions in cognate fields, such as anatomy and physiology, which tempted students of human medicine and encouraged an awareness that human beings are animals too. Yet it was a huge change to study human beings as merely members of the animal kingdom.

Buckland came to believe that Geology had rather lagged behind in the process of becoming a science in the new academic sense:

> Its elements have been long accumulating, and in the accurate but limited observations of a few strong-minded individuals

> its seeds have been scattered irregularly on the field of knowledge.[106]

He begins his *Vindiciae Geologicae* by setting out the claims of geology to be not only a science but one which ought now to be considered an essential part of the syllabus:

> from the general favour and approbation with which it is now regarded, from its intimate alliance with Physical Geography, and its national importance as connected with Statistics and Political Economy, we may henceforward consider Geology as exalted to the rank of the sciences the teaching of which forms a part of our established system of education.[107]

It was important to his claim at that date that geology seemed to overlap with, or share a boundary with, so many other sciences:

> It is now admitted on all hands, that no man can be qualified to enter any of the highest walks of science, who is acquainted only with one branch of natural knowledge.[108]

Undergraduates and non-specialists find out about science

Ordinary students in Oxford might become aware of some of what was happening in these early ventures into modern academic science. John Henry Newman mentions attending Buckland's lectures in Hilary Term 1821.[109] He wrote to his mother to say:

> Buckland's lectures...I had intended to have taken down, as I did last term, but several things prevented me – the time it takes, and the very desultory way in which he imparts his information: for, to tell the truth, the science is so in its infancy that no regular system is formed. Hence the lectures are rather an enumeration of facts from which probabilities are deduced, than a consistent and luminous theory of certainties, illustrated by occasional examples. It is, however, most entertaining, and opens an amazing field to imagination and to poetry.[110]

John Ruskin had also developed a youthful interest in mineralogy, making a collection of drawings as a boy and even publishing articles in the *Magazine of Natural History* in 1834, before he went to Oxford. He was 'taken up' by Buckland and did drawings for him to use in his lectures. He understood the value of accurate observation and exact reproduction in such drawings, but he also wanted to see the essence of the thing captured. (He respected Turner especially because of the way he drew a stone or a tree, 'no other man ever having learned their organization, or possessed himself of their spirit'.[111]) John Ruskin exclaims in his *Deucalion* (1875–83) how 'in preparing for the arrangement' of his 'Sheffield Museum' he was disconcerted to find to his 'no small consternation' that 'the assertions' he had 'supposed beyond dispute' as 'made by geologists of forty years back' 'are now all brought again into question'.[112] The work he was doing had begun in connection with lectures he proposed to give in Oxford to members of the University in 1874.

The debate about the *Origin of species* held in the University Museum

The furore caused by Charles Darwin's *Origin of species* posed a challenge to human self-image as well as to acceptance of the literal truth of Scripture. A debate about Charles Darwin's *On the origin of species* was held in June 1860, in the University Museum in Oxford, a new building with a self-conscious message, with its stone and metal trees and foliage. The protagonists were Samuel Wilberforce, then Bishop of Oxford, and T.H. Huxley, a Darwin supporter. This was intended to be merely a session in the annual conference of the British Association for the Advancement of Science (BAAS), which had had its beginnings in 1831 partly at the instigation of Cambridge scientists. The BAAS always had a popular appeal and its annual meetings attracted good attendances. The 1860 debate was triggered by J.W. Draper who gave a paper 'On the intellectual development of Europe, considered with reference to the views of Mr. Darwin and others, that the progression of organisms is determined by law'.[113] Wilberforce rose to comment eloquently on the paper and took the opportunity to attack Huxley for supporting Darwin. An eye-witness account by Mrs Isabella Sidgwick was published in *MacMillan's Magazine* in 1898:

> I was happy enough to be present on the memorable occasion at Oxford when Mr Huxley bearded Bishop Wilberforce. There were so many of us that were eager to hear that we had to adjourn to the great library of the Museum. I can still hear the American accents of Dr Draper's opening address, when he asked 'Are we a fortuitous concourse of atoms?' and his discourse I seem to remember somewhat dry. Then the Bishop rose, and in a light scoffing tone... he assured us there was nothing in the idea of evolution; rock-pigeons were what rock-pigeons had always been. Then, turning to his antagonist with a smiling insolence, he begged to know, was it through his grandfather or his grandmother that he claimed his descent from a monkey? On this Mr Huxley

> slowly and deliberately arose. A slight tall figure stern and pale, very quiet and very grave, he stood before us, and spoke those tremendous words – words which no one seems sure of now, nor I think, could remember just after they were spoken, for their meaning took away our breath, though it left us in no doubt as to what it was. He was not ashamed to have a monkey for his ancestor; but he would be ashamed to be connected with a man who used great gifts to obscure the truth. No one doubted his meaning and the effect was tremendous. One lady fainted and had to be carried out: I, for one, jumped out of my seat; and when in the evening we met at Dr Daubeney's, every one was eager to congratulate the hero of the day. I remember that some naive person wished it could come over again; and Mr Huxley, with the look on his face of the victor who feels the cost of victory, put us aside saying, 'Once in a life-time is enough, if not too much'.[114]

Vivisection and animal rights

Vivisection became the controversy of the moment a decade later. Charles Dodgson set out to 'formulate and classify some of the many fallacies' which had appeared in the arguments about vivisection, 'at a time when this painful subject is engrossing so large a share of public attention':

> 'No greater service can be rendered to the cause of truth, in this fiercely contested field, that to reduce these shadowy, impalpable phantoms into definite forms, which can be seen, which can be grappled with', once and for all, he optimistically believes.[115]

This theme was developed in Lecture VIII (delivered on March 2) of a series given by John Ruskin as Slade Professor in 1872. Ruskin had begun cautiously in early 1870 with a series of *Lectures on art.* They became more ambitious and began to present Ruskin's own views on matters which were particular preoccupations with him, including *Ten lectures on the relation of natural science to art* in early 1872. The lecture touching on the vivisection controversy was entitled, 'The relation to art of the sciences of organic form' and it took the form of a diatribe against the study of the internal structure:

> Man has to think of [living things] essentially with their skins on them, and with their souls in them. He is to know how they are spotted, wrinkled, furred, and feathered: and what the look of them is, in the eyes; and what grasp, or cling, or

> trot, or pat, in their paws and claws. ...He is never to think of them as bones and meat.

To do that 'is more of a hindrance than a help' and in the case of 'the human form, such knowledge is a degradation as well as a hindrance; and even the study of the nude is injurious, beyond the limits of honour and decency in daily life'.[116] Ruskin became deeply hostile to anatomical studies.[117]

Science proves dangerous ground

So the rapid emergence of science as an area of serious study proved unsettling. In *The storm cloud of the nineteenth century*, Ruskin defined 'blasphemy' as 'Harmful speaking', 'not against God only, but against Man, and against all the good works and purposes of Nature'.[118] He particularly castigates science, the '*deliberate* blasphemy of science', for 'the assertion of its own virtue and dignity against the always implied, and often asserted, vileness of all men and – Gods – heretofore'.[119] 'Within the last few years we have had the laws of natural science opened to us with a rapidity which has been blinding by its brightness,'[120] he said in his *Lectures on art* in Oxford in 1870.

But science is expensive: museums and laboratories

More than two centuries before Francis Bacon had seen the need for equipment even with this forewarning, it seems to have come as something of:

> And if Alexander made... a liberal assignation to Aristotle of treasure for the allowance of hunters, fowlers, fishers, and the like, that he might compile a history of nature, much better do they deserve it that travail in arts of nature.[121]

He also saw that it was going to be expensive:

> we see spheres, globes, astrolabes, maps, and the like, have been provided as appurtenances to astronomy and cosmography, as well as books. We see likewise that some places instituted for physic have annexed the commodity of gardens for simples of all sorts, and do likewise command the use of dead bodies for anatomies. But these do respect but a few things. In general, there will hardly be any main proficience in the disclosing of nature, except there be some allowance for expenses about experiments; whether they be experiments appertaining to Vulcanus or Daedalus, furnace or engine, or any other kind.[122]

It seems to have come as something of an unwelcome surprise to Oxford that science, in moving out of the gentleman's study, the Royal Society and eventually the BAAS and into the universities, was going to demand organization and large-scale investment:

> It is ignorance, and not ill-will, that directs the popular discussions on the subject of the highest education. Men in general cannot imagine what they have seen no example of. When the British Association [for the Advancement of Science] was first formed, it had to encounter a storm of vulgar raillery from our middle classes, not because they were against science, but because they were unable to conceive the use of organization and concert in science...science had been the work of individual enterprise....A permanent organization of science, a home where the cultivation of knowledge for its own sake shall be a profession, a life-business, will be also a new idea which a vast number of Englishmen will be loth to believe in at first.[123]

Oxford, like Cambridge, had museums before it had laboratories. Its scientists made collections before they made experiments. The Ashmolean Museum, the oldest purpose-built museum building still in use as a museum,[124] was first opened in 1683 beside the Sheldonian Theatre, to display the collection which Elias Ashmole (1617–92) gave to the University in 1677. Ashmole's collection was nothing if not comprehensive. It included objects of scientific interest and objets d'art with a generous inclusive sweep. The building had laboratory space only in its basement.

The Ashmolean Museum moved to its present site in Beaumont Street in 1845 and underwent a change of philosophy. The modern Ashmolean seems to have begun with the Randolph Gallery built with a £1000 benefaction left by the Principal of St. Albans Hall, Francis Randolph (c.1713–97),[125] though he did not give enough for building actually to begin until the middle of the next century. Put together with money from the Taylor fund, however, the gift made possible the purchase of land in Beaumont St., which belonged to Worcester College; bids were invited for the building and design of the two buildings which became the Taylorian Institute and the Ashmolean Museum. The gallery was to have a basement, ground floor space for sculptures and an upper floor for paintings. Randolph's hope was that if there was a gallery important works of art would come; an immediate objective was to house the recent Pomfret gift of some statues. So the Ashmolean moved in the direction of art and sculpture and objects of archaeological interest.

John William Burgon's 'Some remarks on art with reference to the studies of the University, in a letter addressed to The Rev Richard Greswell' (Oxford, 1846) was a bid to get the University to take art seriously as one of its proper activities. Here was another example of the disagreements which could arise about the taxonomy of knowledge. Greswell had written a paper in 1843 'On education in the principles of art', apparently for the Ashmolean Society. Burgon's argument is that not enough has been done since Ashmole's time. Thanks to Ashmole, Oxford had the first museum in England. But little had been added to it since, he complains. His museum is now of interest chiefly as a curiosity because it remains so unchanged. It is a mere 'collection of curiosities' still (pp.4–5):

> With all respect for the portraits of the Tradescant family on the stairs and that of the Dodo in the entrance hall, it must be allowed that it contains very little deserving the name of Art. (p.5)

If one wants to see great art in Oxford, where is one to go? The Bodleian picture gallery (now the Upper Reading Room) is 'a charming place to lounge in' but it has little of note, 'Stiff portraits of cadaverous scholars, and portentous Founders, and quaint old worthies of all sorts', but again these are really mere curiosities (p.5). He takes his reader on a tour of the remarkable objects of Oxford, such as the 'twelve astonishing heads that encircle the [Sheldonian] Theatre' (p.6). He goes on to argue that while in Oxford 'everything is done for the education of the Heart and of the Understanding, nothing seems to be done for the education of the Eye' (p.12). In calling for this to be put right he is thinking strictly of amending educational practice, not of encouraging tourism. He looks with longing towards the possibility of lectures on art, which Ruskin was soon to demonstrate was not such a remote contingency as he feared (p.67).

Meanwhile objects and specimens for scientists seemed to need a different sort of collection. When the University Museum was built just before Darwin and the Bishop debated in it, it was to house some of Ashmole's objects of scientific interest, including the last stuffed Dodo known to exist in Europe. That did not turn out to end the matter, for the 'collector' instinct was not dead. The objects which now form the foundation collection of the Pitt Rivers Museum behind the University Museum in Oxford were brought together by Augustus Pitt Rivers (1827–1900). Pitt Rivers had been not to Oxford, but to the Royal Military College at Sandhurst and thence into the Grenadier Guards. He used the postings in his career to develop a 'hobby' interest in archaeology and made collections of objects and artefacts. When Charles Darwin's *On the origin of species* was published in 1859, he began to think differently about his collection of weapons and tools and to conceive of a principle of arrangement to illustrate the 'evolution' of the patterns of human life, an early ethnography. He won recognition. He became vice-president of the Society of Antiquaries in 1871 and was elected to the Royal Society in 1876. He became an Inspector of Ancient Monuments. He began to set up displays of his collections in Farnham, to educate the public.

The collection he left to Oxford and which now forms the Pitt Rivers Museum, would now be designated 'anthropological', containing as it does preponderantly objects which reveal the differences in the way human societies behave. But 'anthropology' was developing other directions of study; other sorts of collection were being amassed, and other principles of classification were emerging, by field study and reading the speculative literature. George Eliot's Mr. Casaubon was sketched with a knowledgeable eye. Among the definitions of the period listed in the *Oxford English dictionary*, one of 1834 sees it as something close to a political science and having 'nothing properly to do with the varieties of the human race'.[126] Another, of 1861, says the opposite, making anthropology the natural history of 'the principal characters of our species, its perfection, its accidental degradations, its unity, its races, and the manner in which it has been classified'.[127] The 'classification of man' is proposed as the chief task for the anthropologist again in 1881.[128] By such definitions Mr. Casaubon is only on the fringe of modern scientific anthropology because he is studying comparative religious practices within a 'branch' of anthropology in which the 'behaviour' of different portions of humanity is the object of analysis and comparison, not putative physical differences among races. At this end of anthropology it is closer to theology and political science; at the other end it treats people like animals for the purposes of study.

The radical reappraisal of the conspectus of knowledge and which parts of it were proper for study in universities opened up a period of extreme richness of intellectual possibility especially in these shifting 'sciences', in which many felt free to participate, even ladies on visits (though perhaps only famous lady novelists could expect quite such a feast of privileged glimpses as George Eliot describes). It is possible to glimpse in George Eliot's letters a certain bright-eyed curiosity and openness to the question how the new knowledge was to be divided for study, even well into the second half of the nineteenth century. On 25–28 May 1870, George Eliot recorded a visit to Oxford in her journal. She and her husband went to stay with Mark Pattison, then

Rector of Lincoln College, and his wife. As they walked about the city they met a string of well-known dons. The next day they went twice to the University Museum, where the Linacre Professor of Anatomy and Physiology obligingly dissected a brain for them in the morning, and in the afternoon they visited Sir Benjamin Brodie in his 'laboratories' there, 'seeing various objects', 'amongst others the method by which weighing has been superseded in delicate matters by *measuring* in a graduated glass tube'.[129] The day after, they were able to go to a meeting in the Sheldonian Theatre 'apropos of Palestine Exploration':

> Captain Warren [1840–1927], conductor of the Exploration at Jerusalem read a paper, and then Mr. Deutsch gave an account of the interpretation, as hitherto arrived at, of the Moabite Stone. I saw 'squeezes' of this stone for the first time with photographs taken of the squeezes.

At dinner that evening the Pattisons assembled a company which included Benjamin Jowett (1817–93) and Walter Pater (1839–94).

George Eliot was working on *Middlemarch* at the end of the 1860s until it was finally published in 1873 after she had made this visit. The result is especially interesting with reference to the development of anthropology. Will makes Dorothea realize the limitations of her new husband's scholarship as he works obsessively on his *Key to all mythologies*:

> what you said about the necessity of knowing German ... it seems to me that with Mr. Casaubon's learning he must have before him the same materials as German scholars – has he not?[130]

she asks anxiously. Will answers that:

> The subject Mr. Casaubon has chosen is as changing as chemistry: new discoveries are constantly making new points of view.[131]

He is trying to make her realize that all Mr. Casaubon is doing is 'crawling a little way after men of the last century'. Later in the novel, in a growing and painful awareness, Mr. Casaubon's own failure to keep up with current developments becomes clear even to himself. The 'result' of his 'hard intellectual labours' has been:

> not the Key to all Mythologies, but a morbid consciousness that others did not give him the place which he had not demonstrably merited – a perpetual suspicious conjecture that the views entertained of him were not to his advantage ... and

> a passionate resistance to the confession that he has achieved nothing.[132]

E.B. Tylor was first Reader in Anthropology at Oxford, after the Readership was established as a condition of the bequest of the contents of the Pitt-Rivers Museum. In his *Primitive culture* (London, 1871, 2 volumes), Tylor expressed in his preface (p.vi) his 'general acknowledgement of obligations to writers on ethnography and kindred sciences, as well as to historians ... and missionaries'. He was concerned from the outset to establish his subject as a science, with its 'phenomena related according to definite laws', and lift it above the level of travellers' tales.

But what kind of science is this? It is a historical science, in which the scientist must seek to show 'not merely succession, but connexion':

> 'One event is always the son of another, and we must never forget the parentage,' was a remark made by Bechuana chief to Casalis the African missionary.[133]

Tyler narrows it, however, to those aspects of history which relate to 'culture' ('knowledge, religion, art, culture and the like') and postulates that 'the character and habit of mankind display' such a 'similarity and consistency of phenomena' that it is possible to generalize without bothering about date or place.[134] 'There is found to be such regularity in the composition of societies of men, that we can drop individual differences out of sight.'[135] So anthropology is different from archaeology, where dating is important.

He also, like Pitt Rivers, thought classification important. 'A first step in the study of civilization is to dissect it into details, and to classify these in their proper groups.'[136] This he does with impartial unconcern for the differences between objects and concepts. Weapons 'are to be classed under spear, club, sling, bow and arrow and so forth' and myths 'under such headings as myths of sunrise and sunset, eclipse-myths, earthquake myths, local myths which account for the names of places'. 'To the ethnographer, the bow and arrow is a species, the habit of flattening children's skulls is a species, the practice of reckoning numbers by tens is a species.'[137] It is all one.

He then looks at 'connection', or rather 'development', contrasting the confidence with which the ethnographer can determine that there has been development, for example in the implements used, by tracing the sequence of inventions, with the uncertainty the naturalist faces:

> among naturalists it is an open question whether a theory of development from species to species is a record of transitions

> which actually took place, or a mere ideal scheme serviceable in the classification of species whose origin was really independent.[138]

From this area of endeavour emerged James Frazer's *Golden Bough,* first published in two volumes in 1890.[139] Sir James George Frazer (1854–1941), son of an industrial chemist and a merchant's daughter, graduated from Glasgow University in 1874 and then went to Cambridge, where he met William Robert Smith, later author of *Lectures on the religion of the Semites* (1889), who asked him to write articles for the *Encyclopaedia Britannica* on 'taboo' and 'totemism'. Among the ways in which Frazer broke new ground was his willingness to set the familiar classical mythologies alongside the information which was being brought back by contemporary travellers about the religious ideas and practices of tribes all over the worlds. This had been a contentious matter in Tyler's Oxford. Tylor had met opposition from the classicists, who were no happier to have the legends discussed in the literature of Greece and Rome treated as mere anthropology than the natural scientists were to be persuaded that anthropology was truly a 'science'. Anthropology won its place as a degree subject only later, when it was successfully argued that it was going to be of practical usefulness to those who were to go out to govern the Empire and would need to understand the peoples they would be dealing with.[140]

Hanging back or taking the plunge

It was partly because the investment was going to be too great that the Oxford and Cambridge colleges did not take a lead in the move to the sciences, because it needed too much equipment and was beyond their purses. And as autonomous bodies it would be difficult for them to work together in a cooperative endeavour.

Obscure academic study is expensive to fund, and tax-payers will not willingly pay for it if they cannot see the point, warned Mark Pattison:

> M. Rénan, who takes the most flattering view of democracy, confesses some misgiving as to how it might be possible to preserve a chair of the higher mathematics, e.g., supposing it to be necessary to its preservations that the tax-payers should comprehend the bearing and utility of the science.[141]

Convocation was not keen to pay for it either. The Clarendon Laboratory was completed in 1872, with money made available by the Clarendon Trustees. Convocation remained unconvinced that there was much future for science and refused to spend money on setting up an electricity laboratory at the Clarendon Laboratory in 1887, partly because it was argued that only three undergraduates were reading Physics. The Clarendon Laboratory was not connected to the mains electricity supply when the Museum was connected in 1902 because it had its own generator and it was thought that would save money.[142]

At the end of the nineteenth century, the urge to go on expeditions to find things was still in process of moving from the sphere of the curious gentleman traveller to that of the scholar and scientist. The Anglo-Saxon scholar W.W. Skeat (1835–1912) wrote to Sir Edward Burnett Tylor, 26 January 1899, to ask whether there is a possibility of a grant from the Oxford University Museum to support an expedition he was going on to Malaya. He would be happy with a contribution of £50. Three days later another letter was sent with a warning that any specimens found on this expedition must first go to Cambridge. Edward Burnett Tylor replied offering the money on conditions. Skeat wrote on 6 February to say that in view of the imminence of the departure of the expedition it might not be possible to get formal agreement to the conditions. The money was offered informally, to be used if projected expenses were exceeded.[143] No one seems to have been concerned about the appropriateness of sending an Anglo-Saxon specialist to Malaya on the available funding.

Examinations reformed

Matriculation

Modern concerns about the educationally damaging effects of 'teaching to the examination' were the subject of active discussion in mid-nineteenth-century Oxford. Mark Pattison ran an eye over the history of somewhat unsatisfactory attempts to introduce matriculation requirements in Oxford. He cited a letter written recently (1863) to the Vice-Chancellor by Mr. O. Ogle. Ogle writes of what he found in the candidates as an examiner:

> An ignorance of the easiest principles and rudiments of language, an inextricable confusion of thought, a perfect inability to do more than guess at the meaning of a question asked, an absence of ordinary facility in English. ...Their hope and the hope of their friends is ... that in time the standard will be low enough ... and that ... they will so get through.[144]

Pattison shares his gloom. 'The examinations have destroyed teaching ... the student is not taught the things in which he is examined.

He is prepared to pass an examination in them.'[145] He foresees a world in which this leads to the efficient production of graduates, with no room for idlers, and every teacher delivering the course as he should, but the destruction of the essence of the university:

> We should have a varied staff of masters, under whom every sort of accomplishment might be acquired in little time, or at little cost, and youth prepared to pass unnumbered competitive examinations in every subject... the drones would be driven out. ...Before this catastrophe overtakes us, can we do anything towards averting it?[146]

It was not only the new style of preparation for matriculation which was thought to have had this damaging effect. Degree examinations had also been 'reformed' and some thought the effects were regrettable.

The revolution in the conduct of examinations: from disputation to question paper

A note of 1790, extracted from the *Gentleman's Magazine*, describes the set-piece character of examinations at Oxford at the end of the eighteenth century:

> Every Undergraduate has in his possession certain papers, which have been handed down from generation to generation and are denominated strings. ...These consist of two or three arguments, fairly transcribed in that syllogistical form which is alone admitted. The two disputants having procured a sufficient number of them and learned them by heart, proceed with confidence to the place appointed. From one o'clock until three, they must remain seated opposite each other, and if any proctor should come in, who is appointed to preside over these exercises, they begin to rehearse what they have learned, frequently without the least knowledge of what is meant. ...'Four times must this farce be performed before the student is qualified for the degree of Bachelor of Arts.'... 'It is true, he is examined in three classical authors, but as these are his own choice, and he has 3 or 4 years in which he may prepare himself, he will certainly take care to run no risque on this point'.[147]

The Oxford Statute of 1800, *Of examining candidates for degrees,* Tit. IX, sec. 2, makes it plain that the degree examination is still thought of as above all a *viva voce* examination requiring a candidate to show his mettle in a live performance:

> It is…incumbent on the examiners to inquire what facility each individual possesses of giving utterance to his thoughts in Latin.

The 1807 Statute makes the same assumption.[148]

It was held in some quarters that the changes to the examination system had introduced a salutary new seriousness among students. A Letter of Reginald Heber to E.D. Davenport, 27 November 1818, says as much:

> The general story is, that [the young men] were never so diligent and so orderly as at present; all which is put down to the account of the system of examination.[149]

Edward Copleston, in one of his ripostes to the series of criticisms of Oxford which were being published in the *Edinburgh Review*, discusses how well the changes Oxford had made at the beginning of the century to its 'course of studies' was working out. After two years the student takes a public examination, 'which still retains its old title of *Sophista Generalis*. The old exercise was a logical disputation in the public Schools on three philosophical questions'. Now under the new arrangements, the student must construe in Greek and Latin and he is examined in Logic and Euclid, and he must translate from English into Latin, all in public.[150]

The Examination moved slowly from oral to written, with the questions ('problems') to be solved on paper. At first these were not handed out as an examination paper but dictated to the candidates. As a candidate finished each question, another one would be dictated to him by the examiners. The move to printed examination papers from 1830 is mentioned by Newman in a letter of May 1831 to Henry Wilberforce, who was anxious to know the results:[151]

> You must digest your impatience some days as you may, for the Class List will not be published till next week. ...The Classmen were had in all together, and given the same (printed) questions, which are to be printed (I suppose published!) all together by Parker when the Examination is ended.

The written papers, lasting five days for those seeking Honours, became the thing that counted after 1830, though the viva persisted as requirement.[152] In a loose counterpart to the public 'practising' of the debating of *quaestiones* in Cambridge in the third year, Oxford candidates had formerly been required to have attended the *vivas* as spectators before attempting the live examination themselves, as a practical method of ensuring that they were not taken by surprise by the procedure, but this was not required after 1849.

The viva survives

Oscar Wilde describes his Oxford Moderations Viva in a letter of 5 July 1876 to Reginald Harding:

> I came down Monday night to read for viva voce, but yesterday morning at ten o'clock was woke up by the Clerk of the Schools, and found I was in already. I…got a delightful exam from a delightful man…I was up for about an hour and was quite sorry when it was over. In Divinity I was ploughed of course.[153]

In a Letter a few days later to William Ward he describes the result (a First) and gives more detail of the Viva:

> 'first in the Odyssey, where we discussed epic poetry in general, dogs, and women. Then in Aeschylus, where we talked of Shakespeare, Walt Whitman and the Poetics. He had a long discussion about my essay on Poetry in the Aristotle paper and altogether was delightful'.[154]

By March 1877 he was finding dining in Hall 'horrid' and entertaining in his rooms 'rather a bore and that one gains nothing from the conversation of anyone', but he was noting the good looks of some of the Demies arriving as Freshmen.[155] In April he wrote to his tutor to apologize that he will be ten days late for the beginning of term because he is on an educational journey in Greece with his old tutor from Trinity College, Dublin.[156]

Wilde got his First in Greats in 1878. He wrote to William Ward about 'this display of fireworks at the end of my career'. 'I got a very complimentary *viva voce*':

> The dons are "astonied" beyond words…they made me stay up for the Gaudy and said nice things about me…Then I rowed to Pangbourne with Frank Miles in a birchbark canoe! And shot rapids and did wonders everywhere.[157]

The debate about competitive examinations

There had always been a competitive edge in competitions for scholarships and for prizes and Fellowships in Oxford and that was heightened with the introduction of the classification of degrees into Firsts and Seconds and so on at the beginning of the nineteenth century. Arthur Hugh Clough mentions both in a single letter:

> The examinations are coming to an end: Congreve, I am glad to say, has got a first, pretty certainly. Our Scholarship Examinations are just beginning – who are to get them, no one can guess at all. There are two candidates from Rugby, one of them Dr. Arnold's son and he of the two has the best chance.[158]

He claimed unconvincingly that he did not really care about his disappointing result:

> You must really not trouble yourself about my class. I do not care a straw for it myself, and was much more glad to have it over than I was disappointed at hearing of the result. I suppose a good many whom I ought to wish to gratify are disappointed a good deal, and it will perhaps leave me without an adequate supply of pupils this summer. ...I did my papers not a quarter as well as my reading would naturally have enabled me to do and if I get a 2d with my little finger it would not have taken two hands to get a double first.[159]

Of the English Verse prize, Clough writes, 'I have but little hope of proving a prize gooseberry'.[160] Here, too, he had to face disappointment:

> The English Verse disappointment, as you suppose, was no heavy burden to learn and if Burbidge has sent you the specimen line he threatened to do, you will say it should have been no disappointment at all.[161]

But competitiveness in examinations was here to stay. Civil Service Examinations were introduced from the mid-nineteenth century for the home civil service and after the passing of the India Act in 1853, for the Indian Civil Service too. There were concerns. Macaulay wrote in 1855 to complain that the decision to require candidates to attempt the examination by the age of 22 would 'tell greatly against Oxford and Cambridge, which, much as they need reform, are still the first schools in the empire, and in favour of the London University, the Scotch Universities, and the Queen's Colleges in Ireland.' He says others agree with him that the change will, 'as respects the English universities, have a very pernicious effect'.[162] Gladstone's Order in Council of 4 June 1870 directed that there should be competitive examinations for entry to permanent posts in the Civil Service.

The first consequence noticed was the deplored shift in the student attitude towards a hard-headed concentration upon preparing for the examinations in their studies and away from the more relaxed following up of their interests wherever those interests led. College examinations were used to keep a check on students during their courses,[163] with intentions which could be seen as helpful and pastoral, but which might have quite other results:

> It is not to be expected that young men, who suppose their success in life to depend on success in these Examinations, will bestow or (as they think) waste time in attending lectures which are in no way likely to promote their main object. Students have had no motive whatever supplied by the University to induce them to study Physiology, Chemistry, and other Natural Sciences. ...Under such circumstances, the teaching of the ablest Professors would be unable to secure a permanent audience.[164]

In the House of Commons debates of 23 April 1850 on the English and Irish Universities, Sir R.H. Inglis (cols.716–17):

> It is ... impossible to compel young men to attend a lecture in the same way in which a boy is compelled to attend a class in school; and I am quite willing to admit, that the lectures of the most eminent professors in Oxford are quite scantily supplied with pupils; and that the same fact is, perhaps, not less apparent at Cambridge also.

This he puts down to the fact that the demands on students are 'almost every year advancing'. They have to cover more and to a higher standard. Perhaps a sixth of those who seek honours fail:

> Before the increased rigours of the University examination, many more had leisure to attend the lectures of professors in those subjects which are not directly connected with that examination.

He gives the example of the experience of one professor who has seen attendance at his lectures drop by a quarter since the Little-Go was introduced.[165]

'Cram'

Matthew Arnold wrote down a jotting from Lyon Playfair's 'On teaching universities and examining boards', his address to the Philosophical Institution of Edinburgh, 31 January 1872 (Edinburgh, 1872), in his *Notebook*:

> the mode of getting and keeping true knowledge is by a process of natural sequence and development; its indiscriminate acquirement is cram.[166]

Arnold wrote to the *Pall Mall Magazine* in October 1870 on the subject of the pros and cons of appointment on merit, which was being discussed with reference to the civil service. The discussion which he was contributing included consideration of the question whether it would be in the public interest to require an objective test before admitting the ambitious to coveted (including civil service) posts or to enter upon careers:

> One main advantage of opening a career to merit – such merit, at all events, as can be tested in an examination – is supposed to be the stimulus which it will supply to schools and colleges. Throw open all appointments, from the highest to the lowest, and learners of all ages, from the university student to the national school boy, will have an additional inducement to industry.[167]

He argues later in this letter that it is a mistake to assume that a system of competitive examination 'is identical with appointment by merit'.[168]

Against this argument, Arnold suggests, 'is to be set the consideration... that we are already suffering from an excessive development of the competitive system':

> Education, instead of consisting in a careful and systematic development of all the faculties, is in danger of reducing itself to preparing children for a series of spasmodic efforts.[169]

This has a diffusive effect:

> Not only is cram in more or less virulent shape becoming more and more rampant even at early ages, but the whole theory of education becomes disturbed.[170]

Arnold sums up this effect, contrasting general care of a child's health with training him as an athlete with the sharp observation, 'We substitute the trainer for the physician'.

Arnold protests in this letter that 'the rivalry for Fellowships is already the animating principle of our university education'. To extend this to a competition for entry into the Civil Service or university would be to offer 'a similar incentive to schools of the lower grades'. His idea is that a simple proficiency requirement would be better, set at a series of appropriate levels:

> It should be made a necessary qualification for candidates that they should have gone through a certain defined course at a school or university and attained a certain degree of

> proficiency. For some offices we may suppose, by way of illustration, that it would be necessary to obtain a degree at one of the universities ... such a plan ... would give a considerable additional value to the certificate to be gained at the place of education. A degree, for example, would have a recognized and definite value ... it would be a strong motive for many youths to enter the universities who now cut short their education at an earlier period; and the stimulus thus created would not, as a present, be confined to the few who compete, but would have a direct influence upon the whole education system. If certain recognized certificates, to be obtained by a given course of instruction, implied eligibility to certain public offices, the instruction would, of course, gain in commercial value.[171]

Arnold's scheme had, he recognizes, the difficulty that it could not be put into operation while 'there is no general or uniform system of instruction'. He has specifically in mind the difficulty of being sure of the comparability of qualifications obtained in different places. 'A degree at Oxford or Cambridge may mean (I do not say that it does mean) a very different thing from a degree at London or Dublin.' There would need to be 'some general scheme of examinations such as is imperfectly supplied at present by the Oxford and Cambridge middle-class examinations'. To motivate schools to cooperate he suggests that 'only those schools which were officially inspected could give the necessary certificate to public offices'. So he was not envisaging 'examining boards' external to the schools but allowing those schools which were approved to grant their own certificates.[172]

Oxford does its bit for social mobility

> And once, in winter, on the causeway chill
> Where home through flooded fields foot-travellers go,
> Have I not passed thee on the wooden bridge,
> Wrapt in thy cloak and battling with the snow,
> Thy face towards Hinksey and its wintry ridge?
> And thou hast climb'd the hill,
> And gained the white brow of the Cumnor range;
> Turned once to watch, while thick the snowflakes fall,
> The line of festal light in Christ-Church hall –
> Then sought thy straw in some sequesterd grange
> But what – I dream! Two hundred years are flown
> Since first thy story ran through Oxford halls[173]

The notion of Oxford's exclusiveness has a long history. This story was originally related by Joseph Glanvill (1636–80), one of the founders of the Royal Society. Glanvill tells of a poor scholar who could not afford to become a student, the 'scholar gypsy', whose ghost forever wanders Oxford and its surrounding countryside, a paradise from which he is shut out. Matthew Arnold (1822–88), John Keble's godson and a scholar at Balliol from 1841 before becoming a Fellow of Oriel in 1845, here retells the story in *The Scholar Gypsy*.

More than half a century later, Thomas Hardy (1840–1928) takes his character Jude to Oxford (called Christminster in *Jude the obscure*). Jude is an intelligent artisan eager to become a student. As he arrives, he imagines those who have studied there, 'the scholar, the speaker, the plodder; the man whose mind grew with his growth in years, and the man whose mind contracted with the same'. 'The scientists and philologists followed on in his mind-sight ... men of meditative faces, strained foreheads, and weak-eyed as bats with constant research.'[174] He 'hears' in the air quotations from John Henry Newman's *Apologia*.[175]

Jude sets off the next morning to find work so that he can earn his living while he prepares to be a student. He seeks it in the stone-mason's yard where repair work on college buildings is going on:

> there fell on Jude a true illumination; that here in the stone yard was a centre of effort as worthy as that dignified by the name of scholarly study within the noblest of colleges.[176]

He works all day and reads all night. He believes fervently that the colleges 'are for such ones'[177] as he; if he can only prepare himself by reading and support himself he will have 'a seat in the paradise of the learned'.[178] But he begins to realize that he will need to discover how to get in.

He systematically observes the Heads of Colleges on their walks about the city, selects five whose faces look encouraging, and writes and posts a letter of enquiry to each of them. None of them replies. It is this lack of response to his ardent wish to be a student which ultimately breaks his spirit. He realizes that to win a scholarship 'reading on his own system, however, widely and thoroughly', is going to be all but impossible when he will be competing with those prepared by experienced teachers. Looking out from the top of the dome of the Sheldonian 'Jude's eyes swept all the views in succession ... those views were not for him'.[179] 'This hovering outside the walls of the colleges, as if expecting some arm to be stretched out from them to lift one inside, won't do.'[180] The acceptance that he cannot 'go to Oxford' except as one of the supporting cast is one of the most poignant moments in the novel:[181]

> He saw that his destiny lay not with these, but among the manual toilers in the shabby purlieu which he himself occupied, unrecognized as part of the city at all by its visitors and panegyrists, yet without whose denizens the hard readers could not read nor the high thinkers live.[182]

In this opinion he is soon confirmed by a letter from the Master of 'Biblioll College' who advises him to remain in his 'own sphere'.[183]

This fictional account has a loose parallel in Hardy's own life. Hardy's parents were country people of no social pretensions and limited education. They did the best they could for their son and apprenticed him to an architect. In the 'biography' *The early life of Thomas Hardy,* published in the name of his second wife, Florence Emily Hardy, is mentioned his 'visionary' scheme of 'combining poetry and the Church'. When he was 25, feeling on his birthday that 'he had lived a long time, and done very little',[184] he 'wrote to a friend in Cambridge for particulars as to matriculation at that university',[185] confident that his father would provide the money he needed for the required period of residence, and aspiring eventually to a curacy in a country parish. He wrote to his sister Mary Hardy in 1866, to say that he had received the information but when he added up what it would cost 'and the time I should have to wait', 'it seems absurd to live on now with such a remote object in view', and he 'gave the scheme up'.[186]

His reasons for abandoning the idea of taking a degree were not quite the same as Jude's but he had done much as Jude had done in striving to make up the defects in his educational opportunities. During his time doing his articles in the architect's office in Dorchester in the late 1850s, he read classical authors with another pupil[187] often using night-time and early morning hours and going without sleep as Jude does. While in London in his early twenties he 'entered himself at King's College for the French classes' and went to readings by Dickens, the National Gallery and Shakespeare productions at Drury Lane. So he got some 'culture', but not an Oxford or Cambridge degree. There is room for striking comparison here with the opportunities for independent study we saw young men enjoying in the seventeenth and eighteenth centuries, without damage to their future acceptability among the pioneers in the advancement of knowledge.

Vocational education for Oxford?

Many of the leaders of nineteenth-century opinion about the social purposes of a university education were Oxford graduates or had active links with the University during their careers. Some argued that what was needed was an upgrading of the status of what would now be called 'vocational' learning. William Morris (1834–96), who had a considerable influence on the visual appearance of late nineteenth-century Oxford, offered a definition of a 'liberal education' which reflected his own preoccupation at the time. He wanted to promote the reputation of the 'useful arts' and get them taken seriously. He observes that human beings not only have different capacities but also different bents, some practical some intellectual, and he argues that the available educational opportunities ought to reflect that:

> Now the next thing I claim is education ... liberal education; opportunity, that is, to have my share of whatever knowledge there is in the world according to my capacity or bent of mind, historical or scientific; and also to have my share of skill of hand that is about in the world, either in the industrial handicrafts or in the fine arts ... I claim to be taught, if I can be taught, more than one craft to exercise for the benefit of the community.

He believes it is beneficial to the community as well as to the individual if practical skills are taken seriously and taught to a high standard:

> You may think this a large claim, but I am clear it is not too large a claim if the community is to have any gain out of my special capacities, if we are not all to be beaten down to a dull level of mediocrity as we are now, all but the very strongest and toughest of us.

And this, he confidently asserts, any 'reasonable' community ought to provide for, in its own interests:

> But also I know that this claim for education involves one for public advantages in the shape of public libraries, schools, and the like ... but these I claim very confidently, being sure that no reasonable community could bear to be without such helps to a decent life.[188]

'Culture ... the study and pursuit of perfection ... does not try to teach down to the level of inferior classes ... it seeks to do away with classes,' urged Matthew Arnold (1822–88) in his last lecture as Professor of Poetry at Oxford.[189]

'Happier as a carpenter'?

How realistic was this vision of gentlemen reaching over to grasp the hands of upwardly toiling artisans to form a classless society?

John Ruskin became the first Slade Professor of Fine Art at Oxford from 1869 to 1879. He published *Fors Clavigera, Letters to the Workmen and Labourers of Great Britain*, in a monthly series from 1871. Letter 1, 8, argues that it is a mistake to think that learning will improve earning-power:

> I am convinced their present eagerness for instruction in painting and astronomy proceeds from an impression in their minds that, somehow, they may paint or star-gaze themselves into clothes and victuals.[190]

In 1877, Ruskin, after staying with 'the good Mayor of Birmingham' as his guest, discoursed on:

> the modern idea that the master and his men should belong to two entirely different classes ... the one supported in its dishonourable condition by the hope of labouring through into the higher one – the others honourably distinguished by their success, and rejoicing in their escape from a life which must nevertheless be always (as they suppose) led by a thousand to one of the British people.[191]

So leaders of radical thought in and out of Oxford were also calling for a revaluation of honest physical labour and a recognition of its dignity, but sometimes in a clumsily patronizing way. In 1874, Ruskin gathered together a party of Oxford undergraduates to clean up a lane near Ferry Hinksey which had fallen into disrepair:

> My chief object is to let my pupils feel the pleasure of useful muscular work, and especially of the various and amusing work involved in getting a Human Pathway rightly made through lovely country and rightly adorned.[192]

Some of these ventures 'worked'; some were felt by the intended beneficiaries to be patronizing:

> Humphry was a very bright schoolboy, and the masters at his Quaker school persuaded [his father] to send him to Oxford. ... Humphry graduated in 1877 ... full of excitement, gravitated naturally to the East End. ... He gave classes in all sorts of places on all sorts of things: the English, the Ideals of Democracy, Sanitation, Henry V, the Gold Standard, and English Literature. ...In 1879 he put on A Midsummer Night's Dream in a church hall in Whitechapel.

The audience was 'a daring mixture of real workers and idealistic visitors'.[193]

Following the founding of the Workers Educational Association in 1903, a conference held in Oxford in 1907 concluded that

> the nation needs the services not only of the professor, the lawyer, the doctor, the civil servant, but of the miner, the bricklayer, the engineer, and an unnumbered army of labourers. The eleven millions who weave our clothes, build our houses, and carry us safely on our journey, demand University education.[194]

The 'task of educationalists in the future' must, accordingly be 'to ennoble the status of every class'. One aspect of the call to accord labour a proper dignity must be the encouragement to consider one's position in life a happy one as it was, rather than something to be 'bettered'.

The Christian Socialist Movement, in which J.M. Ludlow, Thomas Hughes, E.V. Neale and F.D. Maurice were prominent, pressed for the creation of cooperative workshops to provide less oppressive working conditions for tradesmen, such as tailors. While nineteenth-century gentlemen formed 'learned associations',[195] the upwardly-mobile skilled workmen were forming 'associations' of another sort, the beginnings of the trade union movement, to work for better conditions and social acceptance and respect.[196] A 'Parson Lot' piece in the *Journal of Association* (1852) speaks of even the best employer as a 'benevolent despot'. 'I build them schools and churches,' he says:

> I found mechanics' institutes and singing classes; I speak to them as brothers, I visit them in sickness, I send my wife and daughters to teach them, I pray to God night and day to enable me to make every one of them better and wiser men than they are.

This is no better than feudalism is the contention. 'If the *most* intelligent and highly-educated workmen (such as the working engineers in particular) fail, *a fortiori* the inferior ones will.' 'We must impress on the Engineers' Associations, that they are the very crucial experiment of English Association.'[197] Part of the problem lay in the existence of a gulf of understanding. Those whose families had no tradition of going to university were ill-placed to envisage what it would mean. The upper classes did not really understand how the 'other half' thought:

> Is there no feeling of aristocracy among skilled workmen, and the members of trade-societies? ... I fear that aristocracy ... runs through all society, from the peer to the costermonger, or the

> dustman who refused to allow his daughter to ally herself with a sweep, on the ground 'that the connexion was so low'. This is a feeling which I trust the operation of the Working Association will correct, which am sure it must correct, if men act in the spirit of Association.[198]

F.D. Maurice gave a lecture on 31 March 1851 in Southampton Town Hall, on the occasion of 'the opening of the Working Tailors Association'. This had the air of a high-minded 'call', as much a sermon as a political lecture (harking back, had he known it, to the style of some of the medieval university lecture-sermons). He took as his title 'The Reformation of Society'. His was a lengthy and wide-ranging treatment of a large subject. Among other matters, he explored the question what makes for sound learning and whether there should be any room for competitiveness in the process, comparing the obtaining of a professional qualification with learning a trade. 'A man may prepare himself to be a physician, a lawyer, a divine.' His hours of study

> are the most profitable when he most feels that he is connected with a set of men who are engaged in the same task with himself, when he most feels that he is profiting by what they have done before him, and when he most remembers that all which he and they have done, is not for themselves, but that they may find out what is true, and that they may bring their truths to bear upon the condition and wants of human beings. And the moment that any students begin to think of those who are working for the same object as themselves as mere competitors who may distance them in the race ... those who feel they have strength and quickness for the race determine to sacrifice real study and with it the chance of conferring any blessings on their fellow men.

He invites the Southampton tailors to respond with fellow-feeling:

> Is it otherwise with the merchant or the tradesman? Do you find from your own experience that the man whose whole soul is set upon underselling his neighbour, upon driving him out of the market, is the one who has in the plain commonsense meaning of the words, most enterprise and spirit. He has the semblance of these qualities I know. ... But do you not find that the energy and enterprise consist mainly in producing goods which have a fair outside and no substance?

He asks them to consider the grand public good:

> And I ask whether the kind of cleverness and diligence which has been cultivated in him by the feeling that everyone is his rival ... is that kind of energy which established the trade and merchandize of England.[199]

This, it seems, went straight over the heads of the Southampton Working Tailors:

> After the Lecture a gentleman in the room asked for some more detailed account of the objects and plans of the Southampton Working Tailors.[200]

The London Working Men's College was the creation of Christian Socialists, with F.D. Maurice as its first principal. Ruskin was connected with the London Working Men's College, mainly in the 1850s when he gave classes himself. Ruskin gave evidence to the National Gallery Site Commission on 6 April 1857, and at the end of the session Professor Faraday asked him about his own 'attempts to instruct the public' and 'whether the course taken had produced improvement or not'. Ruskin admitted that it was hard to say. His class of about forty workmen, to whom he had been teaching elementary and landscape drawing at the Working Men's College in Great Ormond Street, came and went and he had been doing it for only 'a couple of years'. He has, however, 'the greatest delight in the progress these men have made' and he concluded with a statement that his 'efforts are directed not to making a carpenter an artist, but to making him happier as a carpenter'.[201] The linked modern debates about higher education and social mobility, and the need for 'parity of esteem' between academic and vocational education are already going on here.[202]

Poverty and exclusion: Oxford tries to do something

E.V. Arnold wrote on *College expenses* in 1883,[203] concerned about those who 'have been either totally debarred from a University career, or who, having passed through it, have found themselves starting hurriedly on an ill-paid professional career with a heavy weight of debt'. He reckons the costs to an ordinary student (yearly average £260, of which fees are about £40 a year) against those to a student with a 'bursary', the Sizar (£150 of which fees are about £12 a year). Being short of money was a problem which affected would-be students in all sorts of institution:

> I fear from what I hear that it is unlikely that the Council will grant you a free place at the Birkbeck College, but I shall of

> course do what little I can in the matter,

> writes the Principal of Birkbeck on 9 October 1906.[204]

Part-time study for an undergraduate degree was one method, a method which now seems obvious, of enabling students to work for their livings while they studied. Yet its development as a formally recognized route awaited the next century.

In a climate where 'widening access' was already turning out to be not at all straightforward, some of the great public schools developed a conscience and a sense that they ought to be sharing their privileges. This was especially marked at Rugby, with its strong links with Oxford in this period. There was discussion of ways and means, with Matthew Arnold considering that the

> plan of a scholarship at Oxford for all boys from all schools ... to be held like a University Scholarship seems preferable to any other I have heard.[205]

'The complaint of the costliness of a university education is one of the oldest and most urgent complaints which has been standing against us.'[206] Subsidies to education are discussed in Part IV of Mark Pattison's *Suggestions on academical organization* (Edinburgh, 1868). Pattison (1813–84), Rector of Lincoln College from 1861 and an active contributor to debate on the purposes of a University, describes the changes Oxford had made to its scholarships to ensure that it would be possible for the able to study there, and turning its back on a proposal of 1846 'for the foundation of exhibitions, to be conferred, not upon grounds of literary merit, but of poverty, character, and economical habits'.[207] Oxford has begun to admit a wider section of the population, he claims. 'The increase of the matriculations proves that a poorer class have reaped some of the benefit of the creation of scholarships.'[208] His belief is that it is important to provide enough opportunities to promote hope and encourage boys to try for admission. 'The supply must precede the demand.'[209] But there is a danger that this will attract boys 'who have no vocation for science or literature' but who may 'come here as a commercial speculation' since a degree will increase their earning power.[210] He distinguishes between the objective of increasing the numbers of students and the objective of 'the admission to its benefits of a class which has been hitherto excluded by position or income'.[211] It is important not to create a provision which will not have the latter effect, and it was even suggested that the old Sizarships and servitorships should be reinstated.

Pattison conjures with the notion of University Extension,[212] a quite different idea, which would involve providing a different sort of education, 'better adapted to the wants of the class intended to benefit by it'. This was a proposal he had himself put to the Commissioners who had visited Oxford in 1852, with due reservations about not being 'rash'. He suggested trying the experiment and finding out whether the university can 'attract here, and can usefully deal with, that larger circle of youth'.[213] The University Extension movement evolved in the end into 'Continuing Education' and then in the later twentieth century 'Lifelong Learning' and 'Executive Education' provision. There should be no need to say more about the strength of the thread of concern for 'widening access' which has run through the nineteenth century and on into the contemporary world, but which brought in able and ambitious young persons from the beginning.

CONCLUSION

> One day when I was eight years old curiosity moved me to take down a little black book lettered on its spine 'Kant's Theory of Ethics'...and as I began reading it, my small form wedged between the bookcase and the table I was attacked by a strange succession of emotions. First came an intense excitement. I felt that things of the utmost importance were being said about matters of the utmost urgency: things which at all costs I must understand...I felt that the contents of this book, although I could not understand it, were somehow my business...felt as if a veil had been lifted and my destiny revealed.[1]

This 8-year-old, R.G. Collingwood (1889–1943), eventually became the Waynflete Professor of Metaphysical Philosophy in the University of Oxford. Oxford evidently gave him an education which extended his natural capacities in the spirit of John Stuart Mill's:

> Whatever helps to shape the human being; to make the individual what he is, or hinder him from being what he is not – is part of his education.[2]

In the generation before Collingwood, it seemed to Hastings Rashdall (1828–1924) that human knowledge was expanding at such a rate that even the brightest young mind needed a steer:

> The bewildering accumulation of literature and the rapidity with which it is diffused have only emphasized the necessity for personal guidance and interpretation.[3]

One of the achievements of Oxford over more than 800 years has been to provide a community in which interested persons could engage with one another, student and teacher, colleague and colleague, in the delightful task of 'understanding'. It is above all a society, a community of free speech and independent opinion:

It is a community with the highest intellectual and educational aspirations and a sense that it is important that to protect the traditions which have made it so. Max Beerbohm at the beginning of *Zuleika*

Dobson gives us the Warden of Judas, 'aloof and venerable.... An ebon pillar of tradition seemed he, in his garb of old-fashioned cleric'. Much is perceived to be at stake in preserving what is good. 'Whether a particular institution should or should not be called a university may seem by itself to be a very small thing,' said Rashdall:

> But the name has got to be associated with education of the very highest type: to degrade the name of a university is therefore to degrade our highest educational ideal.[4]

It has its flaws and its failures too. In Thomas Hardy's *Jude the obscure*, published in 1895, Sue says to Arabella:

> Of course Christminster is a sort of fixed vision with him, which I suppose he'll never be cured of believing in. He still thinks it is a great centre of high and fearless thought, instead of what it is, a nest of commonplace schoolmasters whose characteristic is timid obsequiousness to tradition.[5]

Academic Oxford has suffered onslaught many times in its nine centuries, sometimes literally, in the town-gown battles of the Middle Ages and after, and during the Civil War in the seventeenth century. The State and the Church have repeatedly intruded upon its activities in ways short of violence. 'Visitations' and 'purgations' succeeded each other throughout this book, and although they make a good read from the safe distance of centuries, each was a dark moment in its time. John Fell (1625–86), Dean of Christ Church, was distressed by what he described as the 'endeavors', 'used by the Papists, fanatics, travaild fops, witts, virtuosi & Atheists... to disparage... university educations, and afright all persons from sending their children hither'.[6] In more modern times, that is from the eighteenth century, it has faced allegations such as that of 'Sue' it is not all it is cracked up to be.

How should a resilient institution deal with such enemies? Oxford's defenders and apologists have often been masters of the amused self-mockery a great institution can afford when it can see that it makes its enemies nervous. Oxford was described as 'the Treasury of Refractory obstinacy, and the storehouse of our Mischiefes' in *Oxford besieged,* a satire by John Taylor (Oxford, 1646), who was far from wishing to see this change. The problem, generation after generation, was that to the eyes of a vulnerable state, and a sometimes embattled Church, dons were dangerous, and particularly when they collectively set themselves against current fashions of opinion, as those of Oxford frequently did, and do.[7] John Henry Newman was only one of many down the centuries to remark on the adroitness with which Oxford could adapt to changing times. Conservative?[8] Complacent? It read the newspapers, he pointed out, and it responded proactively:

> A place like Oxford, it need scarcely be said, alters very much year by year in the outward characteristics of its society; and more so, in a time like this, when alterations and developments of a serious nature are taking place in the structure of society in general.[9]

A university needs an ability to laugh at itself. Oxford is still outstanding at confident amused deprecation of its own achievements, as displayed each year at Encaenia when the University orator makes his speech:

> The subject of sex at Oxford is greatly discussed in the outside world and in Oxford itself. Indeed, except for politics, it is about the most popular subject, even more popular than dialectical materialism.[10]

NOTES

Preface

1. *John Betjeman's Oxford*, first published as *An Oxford University Chest*, illustrated L. Moholy-Nagy, Osbert Lancaster and Edward Bradley ("Cuthbert Bede") (Oxford, 1938 and 1979), pp.13ff.
2. Jan Morris, *Oxford* (Oxford, 1965, 1978, 2001), p.15.
3. R. Lane Poole, *A lecture on the history of the University Archive* (Oxford, 1912), p.6.
4. Fellows of colleges are 'corporator' members of the college as a 'corporation'. This is a legal relationship.
5. Hastings Rashdall, *Medieval universities* (Oxford, 1895), revised Powicke and Emden (Oxford, 1936), 3 vols.
6. Hastings Rashdall, *The universities of Europe in the Middle Ages* (Oxford, 1895), vol. III, revised Powicke and Emden (Oxford, 1936), p.461.
7. http://www.ox.ac.uk/gazette/1998-9/supps/2_4486.htm.b.
8. *The history of the University of Oxford* (Oxford, 1984–94), 8 vols.
9. John Dryden, in Samuel Johnson, *Lives of the poets*, ed. Roger Lonsdale (Oxford, 2006), vol. ii, p.119.

Introduction

1. Elizabeth Goudge, *Towers in the mist, the cathedral trilogy* (London, 1964), p.9.
2. Evelyn Waugh, *Brideshead revisited* (Originally published 1945; Everyman, 1993), p.17.
3. 'Thomas Baskerville's account of Oxford c. 1670–1700', ed. Humphrey Baskerville, *Collectanea*, IV, OHS, 47 (1905), p.187.
4. Iris Murdoch, *The Book and the Brotherhood* (London, 1987).
5. Philip Larkin, *Jill* (London, 1946 edition of 1975), p.42.
6. Ibid.
7. Ibid., p.43.
8. http://www.ox.ac.uk/gazette/1997-8/weekly/290198/news/story_2.htm.
9. Ruskin, 'The eagles' nest: ten lectures on the relation of natural science to art', *Works*, XXII, p.205.
10. Ibid., p.192.
11. Dorothy Sayers, *Gaudy Night* (Hodder, 2003), pp.5–6.
12. Ruskin, 'Val d'Arno: ten lectures on Tuscan art', *Works*, XXIII, p.25.
13. Penelope Lively, *The house in Norham Gardens* (London, 1974, repr. 2004), p.1.
14. Lewis Carroll, 'The deserted parks', *Complete works* (1994), pp.823–5.
15. Lively, *The house in Norham Gardens*, pp.58–9.
16. Ibid., p.59.
17. On Convocation and Congregation, see pp.86–7.
18. Lively, *The house in Norham Gardens*, pp.58–9.
19. Lewis Carroll, *The New Belfrey of Christ Church*, (1872), pp.1026–36.
20. Lewis Carroll; 'Maggie's visit to Oxford' (1994), p.848.
21. Ruskin, *Works*, XXIII, pp.219–22.
22. Ibid., XXXIII, p.91.
23. John Ruskin, *Fors Clavigera*, VI, Letter 66 (June 1876), Works, XXVIII, p.618.

24. *John Betjeman's Oxford*, first published as *An Oxford University Chest*, illustrated L. Moholy-Nagy, Osbert Lancaster and Edward Bradley ("Cuthbert Bede") (Oxford, 1938 and 1979), p.2.
25. Ibid., p.6.
26. Ibid., p.3.
27. Ibid., p.4.
28. By convention the punt-pole is wielded by someone who stands at the opposite end of the punt in Oxford from the end favoured in Cambridge.
29. J.I.M. Stewart, *The Madonna of the Astrolabe* (London, 1977), pp.170–1.

1 Towards Oxford today

1. C.S. Lewis, *The last battle* (London, 1956), p.176.
2. J.C. Masterman, *To teach the Senators wisdom or an Oxford guide-book* (London, 1952), p.10.
3. 1861–1922, Professor of English Literature and Fellow of Magdalen.
4. The live (*viva voce*) examination taken after the written papers have been marked, which was a remnant of the medieval system of examining.
5. *Letters of J.R.R. Tolkien*, 83, ed. Humphrey Carpenter and Christopher Tolkien (Boston, 1981), p.95.
6. Owen Barfield, *Romanticism comes of age* (1966), p.9.
7. *Letters of J.R.R. Tolkien*, 304, p.391.
8. Ibid., 3, p.8.
9. Ibid., 4, p.8.
10. Ibid., 66, p.78.
11. Ibid., 45, p.55.
12. *War in Heaven* (1930), *Many dimensions* (1931), *The place of the lion* (1931), *The greater trumps* (1932), *Shadows of ecstasy* (1933), *Descent into Hell* (1937), and *All Hallows' Eve* (1945).
13. Ibid., 298, pp.387–8.
14. Colin Duriez, *J.R.R. Tolkien and C.S. Lewis: the story of a friendship* (Paulist Press, 2003, Sutton, 2005).
15. C.S. Lewis, *The four loves*, Friendship (London, 1960), p.82.
16. *Letters of J.R.R. Tolkien*, 83, p.95.
17. Lewis, *The four loves*, pp.90–1.
18. Ibid., pp.86–7.
19. http://www.keble.ox.ac.uk/about/past/letters-home-eve-of-first-world-war, accessed 14 November 2009, with the note: These letters are reproduced with permission from the biography by Simon Harris, *RBK. A Very Parfit Gentil Knight* (Clenchwarton, 2004). Copies are available from Rooke Publishing, Porch Farm, Clenchwarton, King's Lynn, Norfolk, PE34 4AG.
20. Ibid.
21. Ibid.
22. Ibid.
23. See p.101.
24. *Collected papers of the conference*, Bodleian Library G.A. Oxon c.130,131.
25. *The Oxford Magazine*, 28 November 1957, p.150. The Oxford Greyfriars was closed as a Permanent Private Hall in 2008.
26. *Why we are at war: Great Britain's case, by the members of the Oxford Faculty of History* (third edition, Oxford, 1914).
27. *Letters of T.S. Eliot*, ed. Valerie Eliot (London, 1988), vol. I, pp.74–5.
28. Ibid., vol. I, pp.60–2.
29. Max Beerbohm, *Zuleika Dobson*, VIII, pp.105–6.
30. *Oxhist*, VIII, pp.3ff.
31. *Oxhist*, VIII, pp.3ff.
32. Robert Sangster Rait, *The Universities Commission: a review* (Banff, January 1898), p.16.
33. Robert Graves, *Goodbye to all that* (London, 1929, 4th edition, 1966), p.247.

34. A version of the next section was published as 'Reminders' in the *Oxford Magazine* of Noughth Week, Trinity Term, 2009.
35. *Oxford University Gazette* (1918–19), pp.471ff.
36. Oxford's Vice-Chancellorship rotated among the Heads of Colleges until very recently and no one held the office for long.
37. See *Oxhist*, VII, pp.459–60.
38. *Oxhist*, VII, p.474.
39. Ibid., p.475.
40. Ibid., p.478.
41. *St. Anne's College, a history: retrospects and recollections*, ed. R.F. Butler and MH. Prichard (Oxford, 1930), vol. I (1879–1921), pp.108 ff. On Bertha Johnson, see pp. 25, 27, 32.
42. Ibid., p.19.
43. Ibid., pp.210–16.
44. Ibid., p.435.
45. J.C. Masterman, *To teach the Senators wisdom or an Oxford guide-book* (London, 1952), p.143.
46. *St. Anne's College, a history*, vol. I , pp.9–10.
47. Cf. *Gazette*, 1918–19, pp.471ff.
48. *St. Anne's College, a history*, vol. I, p.11.
49. *The letters of Lewis Carroll*, ed. Morton N. Cohen (London, 1979), vol. I, pp.564–5.
50. Ibid., p.565.
51. Ibid.
52. Ibid.
53. Ibid.
54. Ibid., p.566.
55. Ibid., p.567.
56. Ibid.
57. 'The beginning of women's ministry: the revival of the deaconess in the nineteenth-century Church of England', *Church of England Record Society*, 14 (Boydell, 2007).
58. *Gazette*, 22 October 1919, p.108.
59. Ibid., p.109.
60. Ibid., p.111.
61. Ibid., p.108.
62. Vera Brittain, *Testament of youth* (London, 1978), p.471.
63. Vera Brittain, *Testament of friendship* (London, 1997) vol. VI, p.73.
64. Ibid., p.88.
65. *St. Anne's College, a history*, vol. I, p.19.
66. Ibid.
67. Ibid., pp.16–17.
68. Brittain, *Testament of friendship*, vol. VI, p.91.
69. Winifred Holtby, *Land of Green Ginger* (Virago, 1983), pp.21–3.
70. *John Betjeman's Oxford*, pp.56–7.
71. Pauline Adams, *Somerville for women: an Oxford College, 1873–1993* (Oxford, 1996), p.188, and see B. Reynolds, *Dorothy Sayers: her life and soul* (London, 1993), p.252.
72. Nina Bawden, *In my own time: almost an autobiography* (London, 1994), p.74.
73. Adams, *Somerville for women*, pp.167ff.
74. Jenifer Hart, *Ask me no more, autobiography* (London,1998).
75. Peter Wright, *Spycatcher* (London, 1987).
76. Adams, *Somerville for women: an Oxford College, 1873–1993* (Oxford, 1996), p.191.
77. Ibid., p.193.
78. Ibid.
79. *St. Anne's College, a history*, vol. I, p.99.
80. Barbara Pym, *Jane and Prudence* (London, 1953, repr. Virago, 2007), p.1.
81. Ibid.
82. *John Betjeman's Oxford*, pp.43ff.

83. Ibid., pp.54–5.
84. Ibid.
85. Ibid., p.56.
86. Waugh, *Brideshead revisited*, p.34.
87. Ibid., p.35.
88. http://www.keble.ox.ac.uk/about/past/letters-home-1930s.
89. http://www.keble.ox.ac.uk/about/past/letters-home-1930s.
90. *Gazette*, 17 November 1937, p.164.
91. Fellows of Christ Church are known as Students.
92. J.I.M. Stewart, *The Madonna of the Astrolabe* (1977), p.52.
93. See *The University of Cambridge: a new history*, pp.79–80.
94. *Gazette*, 28 May 1931, p.577.
95. Danielle Besomi, 'Roy Harrod and the Commission of Inquiry into the Bodleian Question, 1930–1', *Bodleian Library Record*, 17(2000–2), 36–44.
96. Bawden, *In my own time*, p.67.
97. *Gazette*, 8 September 1939, p.4.
98. Bawden, *In my own time*, p.67.
99. Ibid., p.70.
100. Ibid., pp.67–8.
101. Ibid., pp.68–9.
102. Ibid., p.69.
103. Ibid., p.71.
104. Philip Larkin, *Jill*, Introduction of 1963 (London, 1946, edition of 1975), pp.12–13.
105. Ibid., p.42.
106. Ibid., p.45.
107. Leslie Mitchell, *Maurice Bowra: a life* (Oxford, 2009).
108. Noel Annan, *The dons* (London, 1999), p.140.
109. Hugh Lloyd-Jones, *Maurice Bowra* (London, 1974), p.46.
110. Mitchell, *Maurice Bowra: a life* (Oxford, 2009), p.178.
111. See also Mitchell, pp.179–81, for other examples.
112. *Gazette*, 1940–1, pp.246 and 248.
113. http://www.soue.org.uk/souenews/issue3/eng1930s.html.
114. Nancy Arms, 'A prophet in two countries, the life of F. E. Simon', *American Journal of Physics*, 35.3 (1967), pp.290–1.
115. *Oxhist*, VIII, pp.252–3.
116. *The Oxford Magazine* died in 1970, was revived briefly in 1972–3, and was re-established 15 years later, arguably as distinct publications.
117. Ibid., 5 December 1957, p.174.
118. Adams, *Somerville for women*, pp.252ff.
119. Masterman, *To teach the Senators wisdom.*
120. See p.12.
121. Stephen Potter, *The theory and practice of gamesmanship* (London, 1947).
122. J.C. Masterman, *The double cross system in the war of 1939–45* (London, 1972).
123. Masterman, *To teach the Senators wisdom or an Oxford guide-book*, pp.88–9.
124. Ibid., pp.138–9.
125. Ibid., pp.88–9.
126. *Oxford Magazine* (5 November 1953), p.57, has a note ahead of its time on what is to be done 'with undergraduates whose mental health is the occasion of anxiety'.
127. http://www.keble.ox.ac.uk/about/past/student-attitudes-survey-early-1950s.
128. *Oxford Magazine*, 28 November 1957, p.146.
129. 'A brief guide to the undergraduate press', *Oxford Magazine*, 13 March 1958, pp.377–9.
130. *Gazette*, March 1961, pp.873–5.
131. Ibid., p.874.
132. Ibid.

133. Ibid., 1961–2, pp.873–5.
134. *Oxford Magazine*, 12 November 1953, p.74.
135. *Gazette*, March 1961, p.874.
136. *Oxhist*, VIII, pp.403, 706, 726, 744–5.
137. Masterman, *To teach the Senators wisdom or an Oxford guide-book*, p.147.
138. See p.254 on the attitude of *The Times* in the nineteenth century.
139. *Oxford Magazine*, 3 June 1954, p.368.
140. Ibid., 15 May 1958, pp.434–5.
141. See *Oxhist*, VIII, p.702 on Congregation's size and attendance rates at this period.
142. *Oxford Magazine*, 5 November 1953, p.58.
143. *Isis*, 12 June 1968, p.17.
144. *The Oxford Magazine*, 5 December 1957, p.169.
145. Ibid. The *Magazine* served a purpose for Oxford which sometimes seemed more analogous to the regular Discussions of the Senate in Cambridge than to the *Cambridge Review*. But there was at this time still a *Cambridge Review*.
146. *The Oxford Magazine*, 13 March 1958, p.362.
147. Ibid.
148. Ibid., January 1957, p.194.
149. *Gazette*, 1973–4, p.105.
150. Clyde and co. to Major Hailey, 10 December 1958, Survey of College Property, Box B6, Quoted in C.S. Nicholls, *The history of St. Anthony's College, Oxford, 1950–2000* (Basingstoke, 2000), p.1.
151. Ibid., pp.2–4.
152. Ibid.
153. *The Oxford Magazine*, 6 March 1958, p.334.
154. Adams, *Somerville for women*, pp.298 ff.
155. On 7 June 2006, the Governing Body voted to change the Statutes and Charter in order to be able to admit men to the College. A supplemental charter was granted in October 2007.
156. *Oxhist*, VIII, p.746.
157. Clare Hopkins, *Trinity: 450 years of an Oxford College community* (Oxford, 2005), pp.436–8, quoting Report (1995), 87, 'Women's Group', JCR C/WG/1/.
158. In the 1970s more students were doing multi- and dual-Honours courses but colleges were slow to adjust the balance of their teaching provision through new specialist Fellowships. See too comments in J.I.M. Stewart, *A memorial service* (1976), pp.179–80.
159. A summary for the Cabinet, October 1963, C(63) 173, is available at http://filestore.nationalarchives.gov.uk/pdfs/small/cab-129-114-c-173.pdf.
160. *Report of the Commission of Inquiry*, vol. I, p.535, http://www.oua.ox.ac.uk/enquiries/congandconvsix.html.
161. Bawden, *In my own time*, pp.76–7.
162. http://news.bbc.co.uk/onthisday/hi/dates/stories/january/29/newsid_2506000/2506019.stm.
163. Richard Dawkins, 'Evolution in biology tutoring', *The Oxford Tutorial*, ed. David Palfreyman (Oxford, 2001), p.62.
164. 'Islam, Empire and the Left', Conversation with Tariq Ali, Editor, *New Left Review*, 8 May 2003, http://globetrotter.berkeley.edu/Elberg/Ali/ali-con2.html.
165. Bernard Wassersten remarks about Nuffield College, in Robert Taylor, *Nuffield College memories: a personal history* (Oxford, 2008), p.137.
166. A Robbins-like summary of the essentials constitutive of academic freedom was quoted from the University of Capetown in the Standing Committee's discussion of the drafting of the Education Reform Act 1988. It comprised 'the right to determine, on academic grounds, who may teach, who may be taught, what may be taught and how it should be taught', Standing Committee J, col.1654.
167. Hansard HL, vol. 488, col.163.
168. Hansard, 123 (1987–8), HC Debates of 1 December 1987, col. 781.
169. http://www.ox.ac.uk/gazette/backissues/supps/9394/1_4301; http://www.ox.ac.uk/gazette/back issues/supps/9394/1_4301, cf. http://www.ox.ac.uk/gazette/1998-9/supps/2_4486.htm.

170. 'Dr. P.A. Slack' (Exeter College; Chairman of the General Board), *Verbatim report of proceedings in Congregation*, Supplement 1 to *Gazette* No. 4391, Monday, 19 February 1996, http://www.ox.ac.uk/gazette/1995-6/supps/1_4391.htm.
171. Report of the Committee on University Libraries.
172. Committee of Inquiry into the Future of Library Services.
173. 'After the publication of the Thomas Report, the *Oxford Magazine* (Fourth-Week issue, Michaelmas Term 1995) published a letter from seven of the library staff of the Taylorian, who include five members of the faculty, expressing their anxiety about the changes proposed in the Thomas Report and pointing out that all the advantages of the present system, as listed in the report, concern the library's readers, while all the advantages claimed for the proposed new system are of a managerial nature', Dr. P.A. Mackridge (St Cross College; Chairman of the Modern Languages Faculty) in the same debate.
174. Mr. D.L.L. Howells (Jesus College).
175. Report of Council's Working Party to review the initial period of library integration, http://www.ox.ac.uk/gazette/2002-3/supps/1_4650.pdf.
176. In the *Gazette* of 28 April 2005, the OULS Curators published a statement that it was 'no part of the Curators' intention to support any proposals to Council that would involve the Radcliffe Camera no longer serving the academic purposes of the University', though a Minute of the OULS Executive of 13 January 2005 proposed that the Camera become a 'central public relations display space'.
177. http://www.development.ox.ac.uk/webimages/osneymead.pdf, OUTLINE 205 (20 January 2005). Cf. Curators' statement, *Gazette*, 28 April 2005.
178. 'A University Library for the twenty-first century', http://www.ox.ac.uk/gazette/2005-6/supps/1_4743.htm.
179. http://www.ox.ac.uk/gazette/backissues/supps/9394/1_4301.
180. www.isis-innovation.com/enterprise.
181. The speeches in this debate were not published but indignation ensured that the practice was changed and in future speeches were to be published even when the matter under discussion did not go to a postal vote.
182. Oxford used the term 'Discussion', not Debate, to distinguish this sort of airing of views from the Debate which traditionally preceded a vote about a legislative proposal. On promotions in 1990s, see http://www.ox.ac.uk/gazette/backissues/supps/9495/.
183. Colin Lucas, Congregation Debate 17 June 1997, http://www.ox.ac.uk/gazette/1996-7/supps/2_4442.htm.
184. R. Lane Poole, *A lecture on the history of the University archive* (Oxford, 1912), p.6.
185. http://www.princeton.edu/international/partnerships/linkages/oxford/.
186. http://www.admin.ox.ac.uk/coi/.
187. http://www.ox.ac.uk/gazette/1996-7/supps/1_4418.htm.
188. A *White Paper on University governance* of Trinity Term, 2006, sought to clarify the sequence of events: 'The North Report was published in November 1997, just five months after the publication of the report of the National Committee of Inquiry into Higher Education (the Dearing Committee) ... almost all the deliberation and the formulation of proposals in the North Report took place before the publication of the Dearing Committee report', http://www.ox.ac.uk/gazette/2002-3/supps/1_4660.htm, http://www.admin.ox.ac.uk/gwp/whitepaper.pdf.
189. http://www.admin.ox.ac.uk/coi/main.shtml#_Toc157564559 and http://www.admin.ox.ac.uk/coi/govrep.shtml#_Toc157240611.
190. http://www.ox.ac.uk/gazette/1997-8/weekly/290198/news/story_1.htm.
191. http://www.admin.ox.ac.uk/coi/govrep.shtml#_Toc157240611.
192. http://www.admin.ox.ac.uk/coi/govrep.shtml#_Toc157240611.
193. http://www.admin.ox.ac.uk/coi/govrep.shtml#_Toc157240611.
194. http://www.ox.ac.uk/gazette/1997-8/weekly/050298/news/story_2.htm.
195. http://www.ox.ac.uk/gazette/1997-8/supps/2_4471.htm.
196. Supplement 1 to *Gazette*, 25 March 2004.
197. http://www.ox.ac.uk/gazette/2004-5/weekly/230904/agen.htm#9Ref.
198. http://www.ox.ac.uk/gazette/2004-5/weekly/050505/agen.htm#6Ref.

199. http://www.ox.ac.uk/gazette/2004-5/weekly/050505/agen.htm#6Ref.
200. http://www.ox.ac.uk/gazette/2006-7/supps/1_4788.htm.
201. Debate, 28 November 2006, http://www.ox.ac.uk/gazette/2006-7/supps/1_4791.htm.
202. From the outset, he was a most active Chancellor: in his Romanes Lecture for 1996, entitled *The Chancellorship of Oxford: a contemporary view with a little history* (though in reality as so often the case with him, there was rather a lot of history).

2 Oxford's Middle Ages

1. The points which follow are taken from Geoffrey Tyack, *Oxford, an architectural guide* (Oxford, 1998).
2. Anthony Wood, 'A survey of the antiquities of the City of Oxford', ed. Andrew Clark, OHS, xv (1899), p.60.
3. Ibid., pp.64–6.
4. *A fifteenth century school book*, ed. W. Nelson (Oxford, 1956), p.10, quoted in *Oxhist* I, p.151.
5. Letter 72, *Patrologia Latina*, 207.221.
6. No. 62 in *Patrologia Latina*, 207.185.
7. See p.89.
8. Edmund of Abingdon, *Speculum Ecclesie*, ed. Helen O. Forshaw (London, 1973).
9. *Apud Oxoniam, ubi clerus in Anglia magis vigebat et clericatu praecellebat, opus suum in tanta audentia recitare disposuit*, Giraldus Cambrensis, *De rebus a se gestis, xvi, Opera*, vol. I., ed. D.S. Brewer, Rolls Series, 21 (1861), pp.72–3.
10. *Doctores diversarum facultatum omnes et discipulos famae majoris et notitiae.*
11. Abbot Samson, Chronicle of Jocelin of Brakelond, ed and tr. H.E. Butler (London, 1949), pp.94–5.
12. *The letters of Pope Innocent III (1196–1216) concerning England and Wales*, ed. C.R. and M.G. Cheney (Oxford, 1967), p.279.
13. The Cambridge exodus was a quarrel which was also a crisis for Oxford – the University could have ended there. *Oxhist*, I, p.26, note 1.
14. Salter, *Medieval Archives*, I, 2-10 and 16-7, for the legatine settlement when the scholars returned.
15. Edward Gibbon, *Memoirs of my life*, ed. Georges A. Bonnard (London, 1966), p.29.
16. Mark Pattison, *Suggestions on academical organization* (Edinburgh, 1868), p.128.
17. *Oxhist*, I, pp.83ff.
18. J.C. Masterman, *To teach the Senators wisdom or an Oxford guide-book* (London, 1952), p.96.
19. *Annales Sex Regum Angliae*, ed. T. Hog (London, 1845), p.209.
20. The DNB entry for Grosseteste lists Walcher of Malvern, Petrus Alfonsi, and Adelard of Bath in the early years of the twelfth century, and Daniel of Morley, Robert of Ketton, Robert of Chester, Roger Infans of Hereford, and Alfred of Shareshill later.
21. See pp.91, 111.
22. Johannes Blund, *Tractatus de anima*; ed. D.A. Callus and R.W. Hunt (London, 1970).
23. Richard Rufus of Cornwall, *In Physicam Aristotelis*, ed. Rega Wood (Oxford/London, 2003).
24. Ibid., p.7.
25. Robert Grosseteste, *Hexameron, Proemium*, Part II, Chapters i–xi, Chapter iv () , ed. Richard C. Dales and Servis Gieben (London, 1982), tr. C.J.F. Martin (London, 1996), pp.87–8.
26. On inception, see pp.94–5, 100, 137
27. Adam Marsh, *Epistolae*, ed. J.S. Brewer, Rolls Society, IV (London, 1858), 346–9.
28. W.A. Hinnebusch, 'The pre-reformation sites of the Oxford Blackfriars', *Oxoniensia*, iii (1938), 57–82.
29. Reginald Pecocke, Early English Text Society, EETs volume plus *Cambhist* vol.1 index on him.
30. Robert Kilwardby, *De ortu scientiarum*, ed. Albert Judy (London and Toronto, 1976).
31. Robert Kilwardby (c.1215–79), studied Arts at Paris after 1231, and Bonaventure may have been one of his students there while he was lecturing in arts in the 1240s.
32. John Jones, *Balliol College, a history* (second edition revised, Oxford, 2006), p.320, from H.E. Salter, *Oxford Balliol Deeds* (London, 1913), p.277.

33. It has been suggested that the 1204 Capture of Constantinople may have heightened interest.
34. See p.111.
35. Bradwardine, *Tractatus de proportionibus*, ed. and tr. H. Lamar Crosby (Wisconsin, 1955).
36. God's 'cause' is a legal notion.
37. Bacon was later thought ahead of his time when it came to 'experimental science' (to which he gave the title *scientia experimentalis*), and it was on the basis of this claim that he was given his place in the Oxford Museum, though it is not certain what he meant by the expression.
38. Falconer Madan on 'Some interesting features in the Past History of Science in Oxford' (G.A. Oxon c.130, item 6).
39. *Oxhist*, II, pp.44, 47, 68.
40. Roger Bacon, *Opus tertium*, ed. J.S. Brewer (repr. London, 1965), p.1.
41. W.A. Pantin, 'Tackley's Inn, Oxford', *Oxoniensia*, 7 (1942), 80–92.
42. A.B. Emden, *An account of the Chapel and Library Building, St. Edmund Hall, Oxford* (Oxford, 1932).
43. Robin Darwall-Smith, *A history of University College, Oxford* (Oxford, 2008), p.516.
44. Virgina Davis, 'The making of English Collegiate Statutes in the Later Middle Ages', *History of Universities*, XII (1993), 1–24, p.5.
45. Ibid., pp.4–5.
46. G.H. Martin and J.R.L. Highfield, *A history of Merton College* (Oxford, 1997), pp.22–3.
47. *Oxhist*, II, p.753.
48. Ibid., p.763.
49. E.A. Gee, 'Oxford carpenters 1370–1530', *Oxoniensia*, 17–18 (1954), 112–184, pp.113–14.
50. *Oxhist*, II, p.764.
51. Ibid., p.749.
52. E.A. Gee, 'Oxford masons 1370–1530', *Archaeological Journal*, 109 (1953) and Gee, 'Oxford carpenters 1370-1530', pp.112–84.
53. *Oxhist*, II, p.750.
54. Ibid., p.751.
55. Gee, 'Oxford carpenters 1370-1530', p.114.
56. Lane Poole, *A lecture on the history of the University archive*, p.9.
57. *Oxhist*, I, pp.117ff.
58. Ibid., pp.116–17.
59. *Oxford City Documents, financial and judicial, 1268–1665*, ed. J.E. Thorold Rogers, OHS, XVIII (Oxford, 1891), pp.245ff.
60. 'Thomas Baskerville's account of Oxford c. 1670–1700', *Collectanea*, III, OHS, 32 (1896), p.162.
61. Chaucer, 'The Clerks' prologue', *The Canterbury Tales*, Riverside Chaucer (Oxford, 1988).
62. Thomas Bradwardine, *De Causa Dei* (London, 1618), p.308.
63. Chaucer, *Nun's Priest's Tale*, l.422, Riverside Chaucer (Oxford, 1988).
64. John Wyclif, *De civili dominio*, ed. J. Loserth (London, 1900), II, pp.1–3.
65. *Fasciculi zizaniorum*, ed. Walter Waddington Shirley, Rolls Series, 87 (London 1858), pp.110–13.
66. Wyclif, *Trialogus*, ed. G. Lechler (Oxford, 1869), p.375.
67. Wyclif, *Polemical works*, ed. R. Buddensieg (London, 1883), vol. II, p.556.
68. Roger Bacon was a notable Oxford author on the subject. His *Antidotarium* includes discussion of how to slow down the aging process; see *Oxhist*, II, p.378. Oxford gave degrees in music in the fifteenth century, *Oxhist*, II, p.367, but they were rare. Oxford gave one before 1479, one in 1501, one in 1505, *Oxhist*, II, p.369.

3 Oxford and the interfering Tudors

1. John Baker, *The Oxford history of the laws of England* (Oxford, 2003), vol. VI, p.447.
2. Ibid., p.448.
3. On benchers and barristers, see J.H. Baker, *The third university of England*, Selden Society (1990), pp.16–17.

4. On the earlier study of Greek in Oxford, see pp.125–8.
5. See *Cambridge History,* p.135 on Erasmus' disappointment when his Cambridge lectures were not well attended.
6. More does not mention Lorenzo Valla's revelation that the author of the *Celestial Hierarchy* and the *Ecclesiastical Hierarchy* was the individual mentioned in Acts 17:31. This was not yet widely-known in northern Europe though he seems to have learned of it while he was lecturing.
7. *Cambridge History,* p.135.
8. Polydore Vergil says that he lectured on St. Paul in London.
9. *Oxhist,* II, p.378.
10. Letter 4, *The correspondence of Sir Thomas More,* ed. Elizabeth Frances Rogers (Princeton, 1947), pp.9–10.
11. *Collected works of Erasmus* (Toronto, 1974–), II, pp.147–8.
12. Thomas More, *Utopia,* ed. Edward Surtz and J.H. Hexter (Yale, 1965), p.52.
13. Particularly in 'the affair of the Indies', which was debated in 1504 and in 1512–13.
14. Anthony Pagden, 'The "School of Salamanca" and the "affair of the Indies"', *History of Universities,* 1 (1981), 71–112, p.71.
15. See Lewis Hanke, *The Spanish struggle for justice in the conquest of America* (Boston, 1965).
16. Thomas More, *History of Richard III.*
17. *Letter to Oxford,* 1518, ed. Daniel Kinney, *Works,* 15 (Yale, 1986), pp.130–49, p.139, the spoiling of the Egyptians was a theme familiar from Augustine, deriving originally from Origen, *Commentaries of Origen,* in *Original supplement to the American Edition* in Ante Nicene Fathers, ed. Alexander Roberts and James Donaldson (repr. Grand Rapids, MI: Wm. B. Eerdmans, 1955), X, 295–7.
18. *The correspondence of Sir Thomas More,* Letters 151, 157, 158, 167, 177, 181, 60, 133, 150, p.304.
19. *Cobbett's Parliamentary history of England, 1066–1803* (London, 1806), vol. I, col.487.
20. *The correspondence of Sir Thomas More,* Letter 114, p.273.
21. Thomas More, *Diatribe against Luther, Responsio ad Lutherum* 1523, *Complete Works* (Yale, 1969), vol. 5.
22. Ibid., p.9.
23. Thomas More, *A dialogue concerning heresies,* 1531, *Complete Works* (Yale, 1981), vol. 6, and his *Confutation of Tyndale's answer, complete works* (Yale, 1973), vol. 8.
24. Cicero.
25. Thomas More, *'Utopia' and 'A dialogue of comfort',* ed. John Warrington (London, 1951).
26. *Oxhist,* III, pp.122ff.
27. Letters 98–100, 102, 106, 110–11. *Epistolae Academicae, 1508–96,* ed. W.T. Mitchell, OHS, NS xxvi (1980).
28. *Sed etiam Oxoniam vestram- et merito quidem vestram, quippe cui tantum debet quantum alii nemini-tamquam unicus sol illustrabit,* Letter 125, 26 April 1524, *Epistolae Academicae, 1508-96,* ed. W.T. Mitchell, OHS, NS xxvi (1980), p.167.
29. Letter 129, 4 August 1524, *Epistolae Academicae,* pp.171–4.
30. *Nam cum fere omnia statuta unversitatis aut in seipsis aut respective concernant usum bonum litterarum studiique scolastici, si omnis auctoritas quoad talia statuta transferatur in alium ab universitate – hoc est a cancellario congregationeque regentium et non regentium – non video quid auctoritatis restabit apud eosdem, eritque universitatis auctoritas inane nomen.* [For since almost all the statutes of the University either in themselves or by reference, concern sound use of letters and of learned study, if all the authority over such statutes is transferred away from the University, that is from the Chancellor and the Congregation of Regents and Non-Regents, I do not see how authority is to be restored to them and the authority of the University will become a meaningless term.]
31. Letter 64, *Epistolae Academicae, 1508–96,* ed. W.T. Mitchell, OHS, NS xxvi (1980), pp.74–7.
32. Letter 130, p.75. John Cottisford (d.1540) became the Chancellor's commissary.
33. *Epistolae Academicae, 1508–96,* ed. W.T. Mitchell, OHS, NS xxvi (1980), pp. 3–4.
34. Ibid., pp.11–12.
35. *Oxhist,* 3, p.119.
36. *Epistolae Academicae, 1508–96,* pp.4–6.
37. 'Register of Congregations, 1505–17', ed. W.T. Mitchell, OHS NS XXXVII, XXXVIII (1998), 2 vols.

38. Ibid., vol. I, p.1.
39. Ibid., p.11.
40. Ibid., p.13.
41. Ibid., p.4.
42. *Statuta Antiqua*, pp.xxi–xxxix, lxxiv
43. *Epistolae Academicae, 1508–96.*
44. Ibid., p.xii. Registers of Congregation and Convocation also survive.
45. *Oxford City Documents, financial and judicial*, p.268.
46. Ibid., pp.270–1.
47. Ibid., p.272.
48. Ibid., p.277.
49. Ibid., p.272.
50. Letters 153, 155, 157–60, 165, 184, 187b. *Epistolae Academicae, 1508–96*, ed. W.T. Mitchell, OHS, NS xxvi (1980).
51. Letter 153, p.218.
52. Ibid.
53. Letter 155, p.221.
54. Letter 157, p.223.
55. Letter 158, p.225.
56. James Ingram, *Memorials of Pembroke College, Oxford* (Oxford, 1841), pp.2–3.
57. Letter 187b, p.262.
58. Letter 194, p.270.
59. Letter 195, p.272.
60. The history of this document is confusing. In a letter of June 1515, the University thanked Wolsey for procuring the restoration of its liberties (Letter 49, p.53). The actual date is 1523 though Wolsey's seems not to have given the actual charter for five years, perhaps because he was waiting to complete the revision of the statutes.
61. Letter 210, p.339.
62. Wood, *Annals*, II, p.53.
63. *History of the University of Oxford*, ed. James McConica (Oxford, 1986), vol.3, p.365.
64. *Oxhist*, III, pp.128 and 365.
65. Ibid., p.128.
66. See ibid., pp.342–3ff. on the King's Readers.
67. Inception was both the final stage of receiving the degree and a 'licence to practise' as a teacher.
68. 'Register of Congregations, 1505–17', OHS, NS XXXVII, XXXVIII (1998), 2 vols, vol. I, p.59.
69. Ibid., pp.60–1.
70. Quoted in William Holden Hutten, *St. John Baptist College* (1898–1903, repr. London, 1998), pp.36–7.
71. Ibid., p.38.
72. Ibid., p.35.
73. Ibid., p.38.
74. Ibid., p.35.
75. Quoted in William Holden Hutten, *St. John Baptist College* (1898–1903, repr. London, 1998), p.37.
76. Peter Denley, 'The collegiate movement in Italian universities in the late Middle Ages', *History of Universities*, 10 (1991), 29–91.
77. Similarly with King's Cambridge and Eton.
78. *Oxhist*, III, pp.521ff.
79. Chantries and Colleges Act, Hen VIII c.4, sec. 6.
80. Stat. 37 Henry VIII. c.4, s.6.
81. C.H. Cooper, *Annals of Cambridge* (1842), vol. I, pp.429ff.
82. *Chantry Certificates*, ed. Rose Graham, *Oxfordshire Record Society*, 1 (1919), pp.viii–x.
83. J.H. Baker, *The third university of England*, Selden Society Lecture, 1990 (London, 1990), pp.16–18.

84. Ibid., p.9. Different forms of Fellowship, chivalric fraternities, such as the order of the Garter (1348); academic communities, including a law college at Cambridge (1350) where the Fellowship were enjoined by the statutes to conduct regular disputations on legal questions.
85. J. Mordaunt Crook, Brasenose, *The biography of an Oxford College* (Oxford, 2008), p.16.
86. Thomas Fowler, *Corpus Christi* (London, 1898), p.18.
87. J.G. Milne, *The early history of Corpus Christi College, Oxford* (Oxford, 1946), p.39.
88. Wood, *Annals*, II, p.96.
89. Ibid., p.87.
90. Ibid.
91. M.W. Anderson, *Peter Martyr, a reformer in exile (1542–1562)* (Niewekoop, 1975).
92. *Original letters relative to the English Reformation*, ed. Hastings Robinson, Parker Society (Cambridge, 1846), p.419.
93. Ibid., p.476.
94. Ibid., pp.173, 360–1, 377–468, 481, 719–27.
95. Wood, *Annals*, II, pp.86ff.
96. *Original letters relative to the English Reformation*, pp.377–8.
97. Wood, *Annals*, II, p.95.
98. Ibid.
99. Ibid., p.99.
100. Marvin W. Anderson, '*Vista Tigurina*: Peter Martyr and European Reform (1556–1562)', *Harvard Theological Review*, 83.2 (April 1990), pp.181–206, pp.191–2, http://www.jstor.org/stable/1509942.
101. *Original letters relative to the English Reformation*, p.469.
102. *Oxhist*, III, p.373.
103. John Jewel, *Works*, ed. Ayre, IV, pp.1232, 1213.
104. Wood, *Annals*, II, p.89.
105. Ibid., p.90.
106. Ibid., p.91.
107. Ibid., p.92.
108. *Original letters relative to the English Reformation*, p.391.
109. Ibid.
110. Wood, *Annals*, II, p.100.
111. Ibid., pp.100–1.
112. Ibid., p.107.
113. Ibid.
114. Ibid.
115. Jennifer Summit, *Memory's Library* (Chicago, 2008), p.101, quoting Matthew Parker, 'A preface unto the Byble', *The Holie Bible* (1568), sig. iir.
116. Ibid., p.102.
117. Ibid.
118. *Statuta antiqua,* pp.341–55, pp.355–60.
119. Ibid.
120. Oxford, *Statuta antique,* pp.343ff. Statuta, pp.341–55, 355–60.
121. *Original letters relative to the English Reformation*, p.481.
122. Ibid., p.488.
123. Ibid., p.494. Martyr to Bullinger on Richard Smith's attack on Martyr from his exile at Louvain, on celibacy and justification.
124. *New College, Oxford, 1379–1979*, ed. W.J.M. Buxton and P.H Williams (Oxford, 1979), p.47.
125. Wood, *Annals*, II, pp.110–11.
126. *Oxhist*, III, p.374.
127. *Original letters relative to the English Reformation*, p.505.
128. *Works*, ed. Ayre, 1.61.
129. *Works*, ed. Ayre, 4.1193.
130. Eamon Duffy, *Fires of faith: Catholic England under Mary Tudor* (Yale, 2009), p.97.

131. Anthony à Wood, *The history and antiquities of the University of Oxford* (Oxford, 1796), II, pp.124–5.
132. Wood, *Annals*, II, pp.124–6.
133. (1 & 2 Ph. & M. c.6) the letters patent of 1382 of King Richard II, an Act of 1401 of King Henry IV, and an Act of 1414 of King Henry V, all repealed under Henry VIII.
134. Wood, *Annals*, II, p.126.
135. Ibid.
136. Ibid., pp.131ff.
137. Ibid., p.134.
138. *Statuta Antiqua*, pp.363ff.
139. *Finitis lectionibus professores aliquantisper in scholis commorentur, et si aliquis scholaris voluerit arguere contra ea que fuerunt ab illis dicta in lectione, vel alias de aliquo dubitet, illum benigne audiant, difficultatibusque et dubiis sibi motis respondeant.*
140. Wood, *Annals*, II, p.133.
141. Ibid., p.135.
142. John Jewel, *Works*, ed. Ayre (1850), 4.1211, 1213. Also in *Zurich letters*, ed. Hastings Robinson, Parker Society (1842), 1, p.33.
143. Wood, *Annals*, II, pp.138ff.
144. Formerly Bishop of Chichester.
145. One of the exiles during Mary's reign.
146. Later bishop of Rochester.
147. *Works*, ed. Ayre, 4.1204.
148. John Jewel to Peter Martyr, 20 March 1559, *Zurich letters*, ed. Hastings Robinson, Parker Society (1842), vol. 1, p.16.
149. Ibid., pp.10–11; *Original letters relative to the Reformation*, ed. Hastings Robinson, Parker Society (1847), pp.360–1, 377–468, 719–27, 419, 173, 481.
150. John Jewel, *Works*, ed. Ayre (1850), 4.1232, 1233. Also in *Zurich letters*, ed. Hastings Robinson, Parker Society (1842), vol. 1, p.77.
151. *Works*, ed. Ayre, 4.1221.
152. An English translation first appeared in 1562. Ann, Lady Bacon, published another in 1564 as entitled *Apologie or Answere in Defence of the Churche of Englande*, with a preface written by Matthew Parker.
153. *History of the University of Oxford*, ed. James McConica (Oxford, 1986), vol. 3, pp.313–14.
154. L. Jones, *The discovery of Hebrew in Tudor England* (Manchester, 1983).
155. Richard Hooker, *Ecclesiastical Polity*, http://www.luminarium.org/renlit/hookbio.htm, http://anglicanhistory.org/hooker/preface/125-131.pdf, p.128.
156. *Magdalen College, Oxford, a history*, ed. L.W.B. Brockliss (Oxford, 2008), pp.159, 259.
157. *The Epistles of Erasmus*, ed. Francis Morgan Nichols (London, 1901–8), II.12,13.
158. C.M. Dent, Protestant reformers in Elizabethan Oxford (Oxford, 1983), pp.74–5.
159. *Zurich letters*, ed. Hastings Robinson, Parker Society (1842), pp.201–5.
160. Jewel's address to Oxford in Humphrey's *Life* (London, 1573), pp.35ff.
161. Anthony Wood, *The history and antiquities of the colleges and halls in the University of Oxford* (Oxford, 1786), II.154–6.
162. *Elizabeth I, Translations, 1544–1589*, ed. J. Mueller and J. Scodel (Chicago, 2009), p.7.
163. *Elizabethan Oxford*, ed. C. Plummer, OHS, VIII (1886), pp.180–1.
164. *The sententiae* include extracts *de regno, de iustitia, de misericordia, de consilio, de pace, de bello.*
165. *Elizabethan Oxford*, pp.197ff.
166. *Oxhist*, III, p.398.
167. Brigid Allen, 'The early history of Jesus College, Oxford, 1571–1603', *Oxoniensia*, 62 (1997), 105–24.
168. Alexander Nowell, *Catechism*, with translation by Thomas Norton (Cambridge, 1853).
169. 13 Eliz. c. 29.
170. *Oxhist*, III, p.400.

171. *Elizabeth I, Translations, 1544-1589*, p.1.
172. Humphrey Gilbert, *Queene Elizabethe's Achademy (The erection of an achademy in London for educacion of her maiestes wardes, and others the youth of nobility and gentlemen)*, ed. F.J. Furnivall Early English Text Society, extra series, viii (London, 1869), p.9.
173. Izaak Walton, *Lives*, in *The Compleat Walton*, ed. Geoffrey Keynes (London, 1929), p.340.
174. J.M. Fletcher, 'Change and resistance to change: a consideration of the development of English and German universities during the sixteenth century', *History of Universities*, 1 (1981), 1–36.
175. Richard Hooker, *Ecclesiastical Polity*, Preface 5.1, http://anglicanhistory.org/hooker/preface/162-171.pdf.
176. On this see the introduction to Eleonore Stump, *Boethius 'De differentiis topicis'* (Cornell, 1978).
177. In his second book of *Dialecticae partitiones*, Ramus seems deliberately to move away from the familiar distinction of the demonstrative method from merely 'probable' arguments by using the term *axioma* for the first proposition in a syllogism. These are divided into universal (*axiomata generalia*) and particular statements (*axiomata particularia*). The second proposition becomes the *assumptio* and the conclusion is labelled the *quaestio*.
178. Robert Sanderson, *Logicae Artis Compendium*, ed. E.J. Ashworth, *Instrumenta rationis*, II (Bologna, 1985), pp.XIII–XVI.
179. A 'supposition' is not the same as a 'signification,' Sanderson explains, touching on a matter of great late-medieval importance, which often confused students then and later. A 'supposition' identifies one of the range of significations of a term but distinguishing a number of different ways or levels of substituting for a word or a thing, depending on how the word is being used in its context. In '"Man" is a word of two syllables', and '"He runs" is a verb', the supposition is material. In 'Man is an animal' the supposition is formal. Robert Sanderson, *Logicae Artis Compendium*, ed. E.J. Ashworth, *Instrumenta rationis*, II (Bologna, 1985).
180. *The Compleat Walton*, ed. Geoffrey Keynes (London, 1929), pp.524–6.

4 Oxford keeps up with the times

1. Douglas Macleane, *A history of Pembroke College anciently Broadgates Hall* (Oxford, 1897), p.241.
2. *Conference between William Laud and Mr. Fisher the Jesuit 1622*, ed. C.H. Simpkinson (London 1901).
3. C. Wren, *Parentali* (1750), p.46.
4. *An Historical Account of all material transactions relating to the University of Oxford, from Archbishop Laud's being elected Chancellor to his resignation of that Office, written by himself, Works of the Most Reverend Father in God, William Laud*, vol. VI (Oxford, 1853), p.120.
5. Ibid., p.292.
6. Ibid., vol. V, p.13.
7. Ibid., vol. VI, p.294.
8. Ibid., vol. V, p.15, and see Wood, *Annals*, p.370.
9. *An Historical Account of all material transactions relating to the University of Oxford*, vol. V, pp.16–17.
10. Ibid., p.24.
11. Ibid.
12. Ibid., pp.12–3.
13. Bodleian Library, Oxford, Bodleian Antiq.e.E.77, and see Aubrey's *Lives*, pp.104–5. p.105. After the surrender of Oxford, he was putt out of his Fellowship by the Visitors, and was faine to shift for himself as well as he could.' He left all his copies in his will to the Archbishop's library.
14. *Statutes of the University of Oxford*, ed. John Griffith (Oxford, 1888), p.viii.
15. *An Historical Account of all material transactions relating to the University of Oxford*, vol. VI, p.294.
16. Ibid., vol. V, p.13.

17. Ibid., p.14.
18. Quoted in Trevor Royle, *Civil War: the wars of the three kingdoms, 1638–1660* (London, 2004), p.204.
19. 'Thomas Baskerville's account of Oxford c. 1670–1700', *Collectanea*, IV, OHS, 47 (1905).
20. Ibid., p.201.
21. Printed in William Holden Hutten, *St. John Baptist College* (1898–1903, repr. London, 1998), p.150.
22. R.T. Lattey, E.J.S. Parsons and I.G. Philip, 'A contemporary map of the defences of Oxford in 1644', *Oxoniensia*, I (1936), 161–72.
23. A.H. Burne and P. Young, *The Great Civil War, a military history* (London, 1959), S.R. Gardiner, *History of the great Civil War*, vol. 1 (London, 1888), P.R. Newman, *Atlas of the English Civil War* (London, 1985).
24. See Trevor Royle, *Civil War: the wars of the three kingdoms, 1638–1660* (London, 2004), p.210.
25. *The papers of Captain Henry Stevens, Waggon-Master-General to King Charles I*, ed. Margarent Toynbee, *Oxfordshire Record Society*, 42 (1962).
26. Ibid., p.19.
27. *The Royalist Ordnance Papers, 1642–46*, ed. Ian Roy, *Oxfordshire Record Society*, 43 (1963–4), pp.26–9.
28. Aubrey's *Lives*, p.89.
29. See *Cambridge History*, p.190.
30. See p.188.
31. John Aubrey, *Brief Lives*, ed. Andrew Clark (Oxford, 1898), 2 vols, vol. I, p.37.
32. On Hobbes, see p.206.
33. Bodleian Library, Oxford, Bodleian Antiq e E.77.
34. Thomas Hobbes, *English Works*, ed. William Molesworth (1840), vol. VI, p.347.
35. Ibid., p.348.
36. Thomas Hobbes, *Correspondence*, ed. Noel Malcolm (Oxford, 1944), vol. I, pp.379–80.
37. Bodleian Library, Oxford, Bodleian Antiq.e.E.77.
38. E.F.A. Shuttle 'Henry Aldrich, Dean of Christ Church', *Oxoniensia*, 5 (1940), 115–16.
39. Bodleian Library, Oxford, Bodleian Antiq.e.E.77.
40. Martial, *Epigrams*, ed. and tr. D.R. Shackleton-Bailer (Loeb, 1993).
41. Fellowship.
42. Wood, *Life and Times*, II, pp.421–2.
43. Ibid., p.422.
44. Ibid., p.424.
45. Ibid., p.449.
46. *Robert T. Gunther and the Old Ashmolean*, ed. A.V. Simcock (Oxford, 1985), p.5.
47. Wood, *Life and Times*, II, pp.529–34.
48. Ibid., pp.530–1.
49. Ibid., pp.532–3.
50. H.G. Rawlinson, 'Three letters of Dr. Richard Traffles', *Oxoniensia*, 7 (1942), p.96.
51. Ibid., p.97.
52. Ibid., p.99.
53. *Oxhist*, V, pp.20ff.
54. *The Flemings in Oxford 1650–1680*, ed. John Richard Magrath, OHS, 44 (1903), II, 248.
55. Gilbert Burnet, History of his own time (London, 1724).
56. J.A.W. Bennett, 'Oxford in 1699', *Oxoniensia*, 3 (1939), 148–9.
57. 12 June 1729, *Remarks and collections of Thomas Hearne*, ed. H.E. Salter, OHS 67 (1915), pp.144–5.
58. *Hearne's Collections*, IV, OHS 34 (1897), p.181.
59. Ibid., vol. V, pp.32–3.
60. See p.241.
61. W.R. Ward, *Georgian Oxford: University Politics in the Eighteenth Century* (Oxford, 1958), pp.59–6, 70, and N. Amhurst, *'Terrae Filius', Reminiscences of Oxford by Oxford men, 1559–1850*, ed. Lilian M. Quiller Couch, OHS, 22 (1892), pp.70–1.

62. W.R. Ward, *Georgian Oxford*: University politics in the eighteenth century (Oxford, 1958), p.70
63. *Hearne, Remains* IV, 409, V, 95.
64. Francis Atterbury, *Epistolary correspondence, miscellaneous works* (London, 1783–87), 1.15–16.
65. On the Bentley affair in which he was involved, see *Cambridge History*, pp.226–7.
66. *Oxhist*, V, p.104.
67. B. Williams, *Stanhope* (Oxford, 1932), pp.456–7.
68. In this speech, printed in 1749 as *Oratio in Theatro Sheldoniano habita idibus Aprilis, MDCCXLIX: die dedicationis Bibliothecae Radclivianae* and reprinted in 1750.
69. T. Warton, *The triumph of Isis* (London, 1750).
70. 'Gaudy' or 'gaudie', from *gaudium*, 'rejoicing', refers to commemorative college feasts.
71. Aubrey, *Brief lives*, vol. I, p.27.
72. Clare Hopkins, *Trinity: 450 years of an Oxford College Community* (Oxford, 2005), pp.70ff.
73. Hopkins, *Trinity*, pp.72–3.
74. Aubrey's *Lives*, p.120.
75. Ibid., p.121.
76. *A letter of advice to young gentleman at the University to which are subjoined, directions for young students* (London, 1701, repr. 1721), pp.24–5.
77. The student of divinity is to spend four years reading philosophy and the classics as well as theological works. The book-list included the contemporary Tillotson as well as the ancients.
78. *A letter of advice to young gentleman*, p.7.
79. See p.231.
80. *Oxhist*, IV, pp.293–5.
81. G.A. Oxon, b.19, 152.
82. Embodied in statutes and other domestic legislation, and see pp.188, 191, 235 on the dissenting academies.
83. Luther came to the conclusion that the Bible teaches a form of good citizenship which consists in obeying the secular authority as something God-given. This idea was embodied in the Lutheran decision to replace 'papal' authority in ecclesiastical affairs with a supervisory jurisdiction by the 'Magistrate'.
84. Robert Ascham's *The Scholemaster*, published posthumously in 1570, and dedicated to Queen Elizabeth, reminded her that it is a Prince's duty to lead 'scholars and learners' and the Prince ought therefore to attend to his own education so as to be effective in his office and an example to his or her people.
85. Macleane, *A history of Pembroke College*, p.255.
86. Robert Boyle, *The Christian Virtuoso, I (1690–1), Works*, ed. Michael Hunter and Edward B. Davis (London, 2000), vol. XI, p.365. Cf. 'It may seem to some Readers, that I have too much enlarged the notion of Experience, and too much insisted on the proofs deducible from that Topick', Robert Boyle, *The Christian Virtuoso* (1690–1), *The Works of Robert Boyle*, ed. Michael Hunter and Edward B. Davis (London, 2000), vol. 11, p.283.
87. Michael Hunter, *Robert Boyle (1627–91): scrupulosity and science* (Woodbridge, 2000), pp.18–19.
88. Ibid., p.19.
89. Boyle, *The Christian Virtuoso*, vol. 11, p.283.
90. *The Spectator*, 634, 17 December 1714, ed. Donald F. Bond (Oxford, 1965), V, pp.638–9.
91. Amhurst, *'Terrae Filius'*, pp.68–9.
92. *Reminiscences of Oxford*, selected by L.M. Quiller Couch, OHS, xxii (1892), pp.4–5. See *Collectanea* I, OHS 5, 1885, pp.272–7 and 284–5 on 'riding the great horse'.
93. Richard Tuck, *Natural rights theories: their origin and development* (Cambridge, 1979), p.174.
94. *Letter* 109, 23 December 1656, *The correspondence of Thomas Hobbes*, ed. Noel Malcolm (Oxford 1994), 2 vols, p.420.
95. Jonathan Swift, *Irish Tracts, 1728–1733*, ed. Herbert Davis (Oxford, 1955), pp.50–3.
96. Ibid.
97. 'But these schools ... deposit in the hands of a disciple the keys of two valuable chests' [the Latin and Greek languages]. Gibbon, *Memoirs of my life*, p.38.
98. Jacques Paquet, 'Coût des etudes, pauvreté et labeur: fonctions et métiers d'étudiants au moyen âge', *History of Universities*, 2 (1982), 15–52.

99. *The Flemings in Oxford 1650–1680*, vol. I, p.13.
100. Ibid., p.17.
101. Ibid., p.17.
102. *Boswell's Life of Johnson*, ed. George Birkbeck Hill, revised L.F. Powell (Oxford, 1934), pp.59–61.
103. Though numbers of students at Magdalen dropped severely while other colleges had healthy numbers. *Magdalen College, Oxford, a history*, ed. L.W.B. Brockliss (Oxford, 2008), pp.159, 259.
104. Gibbon, *Memoirs of my life*, chapter III, p.53.
105. 'Thomas Baskerville's account of Oxford c. 1670–1700', ed. Humphrey Baskerville, *Collectanea*, IV, OHS 47 (1905), p.197.
106. Gibbon, *Memoirs of my life*, chapter III, p.48.
107. Ibid., pp.46–7, 49.
108. Vivian Green, *The commonwealth of Lincoln College, 1427–1977* (Oxford, 1979), p.325ff.
109. John Richard Green and George Roberson Roberson, 'Oxford during the eighteenth century', ed. C.L. Stainer *Studies in Oxford History*, OHS, 41 (1901), 46–7.
110. Ibid., pp.50–1.
111. Ibid., and see Thomas Baskerville's account of Oxford, *Collectanea* IV, OHS, 47 (1905), pp.192–3 on St. John's.
112. *Letters of Richard Radcliffe and John James of Queen's College, Oxford, 1755–83*, ed. Margaret Evans, OHS, ix (Oxford, 1888), pp.2–3.
113. William Hazlitt, 'On the ignorance of the learned', Essay VIII, *Table Talk* (London, 1952), pp.71–3.
114. Jane Austen, *Sense and sensibility* (Basingstoke, 1987), Chapter I, p.19.
115. Oliver Goldsmith, *An enquiry into the present state of polite learning in Europe* (000) vol. 1, p.331.
116. John Evelyn, *The diary of John Evelyn*, ed. E.S. de Beer (London, 1959), p.341.
117. John Evelyn, *Kalendarium* for July 1675, vol. IV, p.68.
118. *Letters of Sir Robert Moray to the Earl of Kincardine, 1657–73*, ed. David Stevenson (Ashgate, 2007), p.43.
119. Ibid., p.102.
120. Gert Vanpaemel, 'Experimental Physics and the Natural Science curriculum in eighteenth century Louvan', *History of Universities, 7* (1988), 175–196, p.183.
121. Ibid., p.181.
122. Ibid.
123. Ibid., p.177.
124. *The remains of Thomas Hearne*, ed. John Bliss and John Buchanan Brown (London, 1966), p.387.
125. Robert Boyle, *Works*, ed. Michael Hunter and Edward B. Davis (London, 2000), vol. III, pp.115–20.
126. Francis Bacon, Aubrey's *Lives*, pp.70–1.
127. Francis Bacon, *The advancement of learning*, ed. Michael Kiernan (Oxford, 2000), C4v and p.15.
128. Francis Bacon, *Novum Organum*, Preface, based on the standard translation of James Spedding, Robert Leslie Ellis and Douglas Denon Heath in *The Works*, vol. VIII, published in Boston by Taggard and Thompson in 1863.
129. Bacon, *The advancement of learning*, 2C4v and pp:67–8.
130. Ibid., p.xxxiii.
131. Alan Ford, *James Ussher: theology, history and politics in early modern Ireland and England* (Oxford, 2007), pp.32ff.
132. John Morgan, *Godly learning: Puritan attitudes towards reason, learning and education, 1560–1640* (Cambridge, 1986), p.109.
133. 1589 NASHE *Pref. Greene's Menaphon* (Arb.) 16–17 '[T. Atchelow] hath more than once or twise manifested his deepe witted schollership in places of credit'.
134. 1784 COWPER *Tiroc.* 280 'Ye once were justly fam'd for bringing forth Undoubted scholarship and genuine worth'.
135. John Milton, *On education* (1673), 2, modern edition, *The works of John Milton*, ed. F.A. Patterson (1931), vol. IV, pp.275–91.

136. Milton, *Divorce,* Intro, 5, cited in the *Oxford English Dictionary.*
137. HOBBES, *Leviath.* IV, xlvii, 383.
138. Sermon 4, *The sermons of John Donne*, ed. G.R. Potter and Evelyn M. Simpson (Berkeley, 1953–1962), 10 vols, vol. I, p.224.
139. Sermon 2, *The sermons of John Donne*, vol. IV, p.85.
140. Sermon 4, *The sermons of John Donne*, vol. III, p.327.
141. Sermon 3, *The sermons of John Donne*, vol. V, p.91.
142. Sermon 15, *The sermons of John Donne*, vol. III, p.327.
143. Sermon 17, *The sermons of John Donne*, vol. III, p.355.
144. Sermon 4, *The sermons of John Donne*, vol. III, p.117.
145. (*Reliquiae Baxterianae*, 1.126). DNB.
146. John Friesen, 'Christ Church, Oxford, the Ancients-Moderns controversy, and the Promotion of Newton in Post-Revolutionary England', *History of Universities,* XXIII (2008), 33–66.
147. Sir William Temple, 'Thoughts upon reviewing the essay of ancient and modern learning', *The works of Sir William Temple, Bart. In four volumes. To which is prefixed, The life and character of the author* (Edinburgh, 1754), 489pp., 4 vols, vol. 2, pp.430ff.
148. Ibid., p.448–9.
149. Ibid., p.448. 'the ancient authors ... must be acknowledged to have been the foundation of all modern learning, whatever the superstructures may have been (p.430). ... Descartes was the next that would be thought to excel the ancients by a new scheme or body of philosophy ... [it is as distressing to see] "young scholars possessed with all his notions" as to see them taking "the for true stories".'
150. OED STEELE *Tatler* No. 244 2.
151. OED BURKE *Pres. Discont.* Wks. II. 340.
152. Hume Equ. Prin. Morals vi.120.
153. Jonathan Swift, *A tale of a tub*, ed. D. Nichol Smith and A.C. Guthkelch (Oxford, 1958), p.223, quoted in Jesse M. Lander, *Inventing Polemic: religion, print and literary culture in early modern England* (Cambridge, 2006), p.2.
154. OED GOLDSM. *Polite Learn.* xi. Wks. (Globe) *Ibid.* 444/1.
155. OED HUME *Ess. Mor. & Polit.* (ed. 3) 223.
156. OED GOLDSM. *Polite Learn.* xi. Wks. (Globe) 443/2.
157. OED J. Wharton Ess. Pope (ed.4) I.vi.313.
158. John Dryden, *The life of St. Francis Xavier* (1688), *The works of John Dryden*, ed. Alan Roper and H.T. Swedenberg (Berkeley, 1979), XIX, p.14.
159. James Yates, *Thoughts on the advancement of academical education in England* (London, 1826), pp.71–2.
160. Coleridge, *Biographia Literaria*, Chapter V, ed. G. Watson (London, 1906), p.55. William T. Costello, *The scholastic curriculum in early seventeenth-century Cambridge* (Cambridge, MA, 1958).
161. Matthew Arnold, *Schools and Universities on the Continent, first written as a report to the Schools Inquiry Commission* (1865–7), ed. R.H. Super (Ann Arbor, 1964), p.144.
162. Peter Searby, *The history of the University of Cambridge*, vol. III (1750–1850) (Cambridge, 1997), pp.152–3.
163. *The Spectator*, vol. 518, 16 October 1711, ed. Donald F. Bond (Oxford, 1965), IV, p.346.
164. Ibid., V, p.20.
165. *The Spectator*, 16 October 1711.
166. Ibid.
167. James Binns, 'The decline of Latin in eighteenth century England', *Britannia Latina: Latin in the culture of Great Britain from the Middle Ages to the twentieth century*, ed. Charles Burnett and Nicholas Mann, Warburg Institute Colloquia, 8 (London/Turin, 2005), pp.170–7.
168. John Locke, *Essay concerning human understanding*, ed. Peter H. Nidditch (Oxford, 1975).
169. Ibid., book 3, chapter 1, sec. 4.
170. *Ex quo manifestum est legem Macometi multominus legem esse vel posse dici, quae multo pauciora naturalis continet honestatis; de gratuita vero apud utrumque nihil. ... Macometus vero pauca de honestate, multa vero de inhonestate, et vitiorum foeditate deliramentis suis immiscuit*, William of Auvergne, *De legibus*, 1, *Opera Omnia* (Paris, 1674, repr. Frankfurt-am-Main,

1963), p.22. Chapter XVIII contains a hostile life of Mahommed with the usual accusations. Chapter XIX criticizes his idea of paradise with its fleshly pleasures. Chapter XX compares the Judaic law (*lex fortunae*) with the Moslem (*lex naturae*) and the Christian (*lex gratiae*).

171. Mordechai Feingold, 'Oriental studies', *Oxhist,* vol. IV, ed. Nicolas Tyacke (Oxford, 1997), pp.449–503.
172. Hunter, *Robert Boyle, 1627–1691*, pp.53–5.
173. Robert Boyle, *Style of the Scriptures, works*, ed. Michael Hunter and Edward B. Davis (London, 1999), vol. II, pp.381–488, p.449.
174. Ibid., p.453.
175. Feingold, 'Oriental studies', *Oxhist,* vol. IV, pp.451–2.
176. Boyle, *Style of the Scriptures, works*, p.450.
177. Robert Boyle, 'On the diversity of religions', *The works of Robert Boyle*, ed. Michael Hunter and Edward B. Davis, vol. 14, pp.250–1.
178. *History of the University of Oxford*, V, ed. L.S. Sutherland and L.G. Mitchell (Oxford, 1986), p.538.
179. Lorenzo Valla, *De linguae latinae elegantia*, I, ed. Santiago López Moreda (Extremadura, 1999), 2 vols, vol. I, p.58.
180. Augustine, *De Doctrina Christiana*, II.xi.16.34, ed. and tr. R.P.H. Green (Oxford, 1995), pp.72–3.
181. John Locke, *Correspondence*, ed. E.S. de Beer (Oxford, 1976), vol. I, p.57.
182. Aubrey, *Lives*, pp.171, 173.
183. Ibid., p.64.
184. Ibid.
185. Amhurst, *'Terrae Filius'*, pp.72–4.
186. *History of the University of Oxford* V, ed. L.S. Sutherland and L.G. Mitchell (Oxford, 1986), pp.565ff. and 571.
187. At para. 10 he comes to the *seculum scholasticum in quo Logica et Philosophia Peripatetica a plurimis illustrata; stylo quidem ineleganti, nec elaborato, sed quem abunde compensavit admirabilis iudicii profunditas, et in rebus perscrutandis omnino felix subtilitas.*
188. On tutorial duties, and the new tutor–student relation, Victor Morgan and Christopher Brooke, *A history of the University of Cambridge*, II (Cambridge, 2004), pp.314–42.
189. J. Bateman, *Daniel Wilson* (1860), 2 vols, vol. I, p.113.
190. *Artis Logicae Plenior Institutio ad Petri Rami Methodum concinnata* (1672), ed. and tr. Allan H. Gilbert, *The works of John Milton*, vol. 11 (New York, 1935). See W. and M. Kneale, *The development of logic* (Oxford, 1962), p.305, for the probable date of composition.
191. *Complete prose works of John Milton*, ed. and tr. Walter J. Ong and Charles J. Ermatinger (New Haven and London, 1972), vol. VIII, pp.144ff.
192. See A.P. Davis, *Isaac Watts: his life and works* (1948), pp.86ff., on the logic. He suggests this drew on Locke as well as Aristotle. Dr. Johnson said that its 'radical principles' may 'indeed be found in Locke's Conduct of the Understanding, but they are so expanded and ramified by Watts, as to confer upon him the merit of a work in the highest degree useful and pleasing'. Johnson's *Works*, XI, p.48.
193. Isaac Watts, *Logic; or, the right use of reason in the inquiry after truth with a variety of rules to guard against error, in the affairs of religion and human life, as well as in the sciences* (published 1724, London, 1845).
194. Ibid., general Rule II, vol. IV, pp.316–17.
195. Ibid., vol. IV, p.317.
196. Ibid., p.314
197. Ibid., p.315.
198. Ibid.
199. Ibid., p.316.
200. Ibid., III, ii.2, p.188.
201. Ibid., III, i.5, p.187.
202. Edward Copleston, 'Three replies to the calumnies of the *Edinburgh Review* against Oxford', *Edinburgh Review*, xvi (1810), pp.158 ff. (repr. Bristol, 2001), pp.15–16.
203. Robert Southey, *The Life of Wesley*, ed. Maurice H. Fitzgerald (Oxford, 1925), 2 vols, vol. I, p.30.
204. Jones, *Balliol College, a history*, p.320, from H.E. Salter, Oxford Balliol Deeds (1913), p.277.

205. Locke, *Correspondence*, vol. I, pp.25ff.
206. Boyle, *Style of the Scriptures, works*, vol. II, pp.381–488, p.454.
207. Wilbur Samuel Howell, *Logic and rhetoric in England 1500–1700* (Princeton, 1956).
208. Boyle, *Style of the Scriptures, works*, p.390.
209. *Rhetorica ad Herennium*, ed. F. Marx (Leipzig, 1923).
210. *De Schematibus et Tropis. Rhetores Latini Minores*, ed. C. Halm (Leipzig, 1863).
211. Boyle, *Style of the Scriptures, works*, pp.456–7.
212. Ibid., p.417.
213. Ibid., p.416.
214. Ibid., p.418.
215. James Boswell, *Life of Johnson: an edition of the original manuscript*, ed. Marshall Waingrow (Edinburgh/Yale, 1750/1994), vol. I, p.149.
216. Ibid., p.150.
217. Ibid., p.149.
218. Aubrey, *Lives*, p.298.
219. Ibid., p.299.
220. Eric Fletcher, *John Selden, 1584–1654,* Selden Society (London, 1969).
221. French, German, Spanish, Italian, Latin, Greek, Old English, Hebrew, Chaldean, Samaritan, Aramaic, Arabic, Persian and Ethiopic were all cited in his published works.
222. The project of comparative legal history also informed Selden's notes to Sir John Fortescue's *De laudibus legum Angliae* in an edition published in 1616. He worked with Edward Coke (1552–1634), whose constitutional achievement lay in taking a firm line with Charles I.
223. J.H. Baker, *Legal education in London, 1250–1850*, Selden Society (London, 2007), p.24. On the origins of solicitors, see Tom Harper, 'From Laissez-faire to discipline, The Society of Gentleman Practisers', *Then and Now*, 1799–1974, foreword by Peter Allsop (London, 1974), pp.191–200, p.193.
224. G.A. Oxon b.19, 137, cf. *Oxhist*, vol. V, pp.601–3 and G.A. Oxon b.19, p.118.
225. Wood, *Annals*, II, pp.322–4. *The life and times of Anthony Wood, Antiquary, of Oxford*, 1632–95, collected by Andrew Clark, OHS, 26 (1894), (Oxford, 1894), vol. III.
226. 30 September 1717, *Works*, 1.332.
227. *The life and times of Anthony Wood*, vol. III, p.21.
228. I.G. Philip, 'A proposed refounation of St. Mary Hall', *Oxoniensia*, 22 (1957), 92–6. The proposed founding of a puritan college in Durham in the late 1650s had Cromwell's approval as a potential source of 'godly' preachers for the north of England.
229. R.A. Beddard, 'A projected Cromwellian Foundation at Oxford and the "True Reformed Protestant" interest, c.1657–8', *History of Universities*, 15 (1997–9), 155–191, p.156.
230. Text in ibid., pp.178–9.
231. Ibid., p.157.
232. Ibid., p.161.
233. E.D. Tappe, 'The Greek College at Oxford, 1699–1705', *Oxoniensia*, 19 (1954), 92–3.
234. Masterman, *To teach the Senators wisdom or an Oxford guide-book* (London, 1952), p.98.
235. Irene Parker, *Dissenting academies in England: their rise and progress and their place among the educational systems of the country* (Cambridge, 1914), Appendix I.
236. Oliver Goldsmith, *An enquiry into the present state of polite learning in Europe*, ed. Arthur Friedman, *Collected Works* (Oxford, 1966), vol. 1, p.332.
237. Ibid., p.333.
238. Francis Bacon, *The advancement of learning*, Book II.
239. On Webster see too Rhodri Lewis, 'A Babel off Broad Street: artificial language planning in 1650s Oxford', *History of Universities*, XX (2005), 108–45.
240. See p.201.
241. Thomas Hobbes, *Leviathan*, ed. G.A. Rogers and Karl Schuhmann (London, 2005).
242. *The Spectator*, 575, 16 October 1711 [Addison], ed. Donald F. Bond (Oxford, 1965), IV, p.566.
243. *The remains of Thomas Hearne*, p.453.
244. The debate concerns the case for external interference with the running of colleges and the University and with the appointment of Heads of House.

245. John Milton, *Of education, complete prose works*, ed. D. Bush et al. (Yale, 1959), vol. II, p.364.
246. Gilbert Burnet, *A dialogue concerning education, a collection of several tracts of the right honourable Edward, Earl of Clarendon, published from his Lordship's original manuscripts* (London, 1727) pp.324–5.
247. Ibid., p.326.
248. Goldsmith, *An enquiry into the present state of polite learning in Europe*, vol. I, pp.334 and 333.
249. Cf. p.234 on the eighteenth-century call for reform.
250. Philip Pullman, *The Amber Spyglass* (London, 2000), p.543.
251. *From the life of Sir Thomas Bodley, written by himselfe (Oxford, 1647), Reminiscences of Oxford by Oxford men, 1559–1850*, ed. Lilian M. Quiller Couch, OHS, 22 (1892), p.2.
252. It has been argued that the sixteenth century observed the rise of 'intellectuals' as a distinctive class; Mark Curtis, 'The alienated intellectuals of Early Stuart England', *Past and Present*, 23 (1962), 25–41.
253. *Letter of Thomas Bodley, printed in Bodleian Quarterly Record*, II (1919), p.287.
254. Thomas Bodley, Letter to the Vice-Chancellor, 27 March 1602, *Letters of Thomas Bodley to the University of Oxford*, 1598–1611 (Oxford, 1927), p.12.
255. R.E. Beddard, 'The Bodleian Library's First Foreign Reader', *Bodleian Library Record*, XVIII.2 (2003), 151–73.
256. Beddard, 'A projected Cromwellian Foundation at Oxford', pp.155–91, p.167. Bodl. Library Records e.533, 158–175v, on the *Extranei nobiles et generosi* from all over Protestant Europe, including Scandinavia, who were allowed to use the Public Library in Oxford with the permission of Congregation. See too, G.W. Wheeler, 'Sir Thomas Bodley's "Heads of Statutes"', *Bodleian Quarterly Record*, iii (1293), 119–21. Joseph Addison, *Miscellaneous works* ((London, 1914), p.157.
257. J. Levine, *The battle of the books: history and literature in the Augustan Age* (Ithaca and London, 1991).
258. Paul Nelles, 'The uses of orthodoxy and Jacobean Erudition: Thomas James and the Bodleian Library', *History of Universities*, 22 (2007), 21–70, p.22.
259. Ibid., p.28.
260. Ibid., pp.53–9.
261. *Life records*, ed. J. Milton French (New Jersey, 1958), vol. V, pp.262–3, and see W.R. Parker, *Milton a biography* (Oxford, 1968), vol. I, p.661.
262. See p.255.
263. *Oxhist*, IV, pp.201ff
264. Ibid., p.420.
265. Ibid., p.421.
266. See *Oxhist*, IV, p.424, on the rejection of Locke in Oxford.
267. Locke, *Correspondence*, vol. VII, Letter 3248, pp.743–4; 3261, p.755; 3270, p.764; and vol. VIII, 3569, p.334, cf. John Locke, *An essay concerning toleration*, ed. J.R. Milton and Philip Milton (Oxford, 2006), p.113.
268. *Editorial notions* (1788). G.A. Oxon, b.19, 262, proposal by Robert Holmes.
269. Marginal note by Thomas Hearne in Bodleian copy of *Commentarii de Scriptoribus Britannicis auctore Joanne Lelando*, ed. Anthony Hall (Oxford, 1709).
270. *The building accounts of the Radcliffe Camera*, ed. S.G. Gillam, OHS (NS), 13 (1958), p.xxv and Bodl, MS Rawl Lett.13, fol.30.
271. Ibid., pp.xxxiv–v.
272. Mick Belson, *On the press: through the eyes of the craftsmen of Oxford University Press* (Witney, 2003).
273. See p.259.

5 The nineteenth-century transformation

1. *Correspondence of Arthur Hugh Clough*, Balliol, December 31, 1839, to J.N. Simpkinson, ed. F.L. Mulhauser (Oxford, 1957), vol. I, p.98.

2. Ibid., Balliol, 27 August 1840, vol. I, p.102.
3. Lewis Carroll, *Diaries*, vol. 8, p.73.
4. *Letters and correspondence of John Henry Newman*, ed. Anne Mozeley (London, 1891), vol. I, pp.31–4. In the autobiographical memoir, written in the third person which is interwoven with illustrative material from the letters in the *Letters and correspondence of John Henry Newman*, ed. Anne Mozeley (London, 1891).
5. *Letters and correspondence of John Henry Newman*, ed. Anne Mozeley (London, 1891), vol. I, p.39.
6. On classing degrees, see p.294.
7. He wrote a long letter to H.P. Liddon, intended to help in the writing of the *Life of Pusey*, which is quoted at length in David Watson Rannie, *Oriel College* (London, 1900), pp.170ff.
8. David Watson Rannie, *Oriel College* (London, 1900), p.171, quoting Church.
9. Ibid., pp.172–3.
10. Mordechai Feingold, 'The humanities', *Oxhist*, IV, pp.212–13.
11. 'There ran in the common-room, when the century was in its teens, a spirit of inquiry – an almost skeptical leaven. When the High Church revival began to stir and to move the minds of able men at Oxford [Oriel elected Edward Hawkins rather than John Keble as Provost] and so it did not carry the movement forward as an Oriel movement even though so many of the leading lights were Oriel men', Rannie, *Oriel College*, pp.157–8,
12. John Henry Newman, *Letters and diaries*, vol. I, 21 March 1826, pp.280–1.
13. Caution money was a deposit of money required of a student by way of security in case he did not pay his bills.
14. Newman, *Letters and diaries*, vol. I, pp.282, Memorandum.
15. Ibid., II, pp.22ff, 25 July 1827.
16. Ibid., II, pp.39ff.
17. S.L. Ollard, *The six students of St Edmund Hall expelled from the University of oxford in 1768* (Oxford, 1911).
18. Hannah More compared Oxford and Cambridge piety, see *Oxhist*, VI, p.200, note 20.
19. Newman, *Apologia*, p.39.
20. *Letters and correspondence of John Henry Newman*, ed. Anne Mozeley (London, 1891), vol. I, pp.104–7.
21. Newman, *Apologia*.
22. John Henry Newman, *The Arians of the fourth century* (1833).
23. Newman, *Apologia*, p.39.
24. See pp.245–6.
25. Letter 45, 15 January 1838, Arthur Hugh Clough, *The Correspondence*, ed. Mulhauser (Oxford, 1957), vol. I, p.67.
26. Letter 115, 21 September 1845, ibid., p.153.
27. http://www.newmanreader.org/works/historical/volume3/oxford.html.
28. See Cambridge book, pp.259–65 of the Tauris History of Cambridge.
29. No author, *The history of the times: "The Thunderer" in the making, 1785–1841* (London, 1935), p.405.
30. Hansard, 3rd series, vol. 110, pp.691–765.
31. Pattison, *Suggestions on academical organization*, p.147.
32. *Educational documents: 1816 to the present day* (8), ed. J. Stuart MacClure, pp.63ff. http://books.google.com/books?id=n7yLL47MUKQC&dq=educaitonal+documents:+1816&printsec=frontcover&source=bl&ots=7Vy-3YqP5Z&sig=C-S1o9n3TZJVHTBqnLlII9CWF0M&hl=en&ei=ZxEkSvXVCMLH-Aboz_y3CQ&sa=X&oi=book_result&ct=result&resnum=3#PPA64,M1 *The University Commission, or John Russell's Postbag* (1850), written by Sewell of Exeter.
33. p.68 (from pp.54–6 of the Report). http://books.google.com/books?id=n7yLL47MUKQC&dq=educaitonal+documents:+1816&printsec=frontcover&source=bl&ots=7Vy-3YqP5Z&sig=C-S1o9n3TZJVHTBqnLlII9CWF0M&hl=en&ei=ZxEkSvXVCMLH-Aboz_y3CQ&sa=X&oi=book_result&ct=result&resnum=3#PPA64,M1.
34. pp.65, 67. http://books.google.com/books?id=n7yLL47MUKQC&dq=educaitonal+documents:+1816&printsec=frontcover&source=bl&ots=7Vy-3YqP5Z&sig=C-S1o9n3TZJVHTBqnLlII9CWF0

M&hl=en&ei=ZxEkSvXVCMLH-Aboz_y3CQ&sa=X&oi=book_result&ct=result&resnum=3#PPA64,M1.

35. See W.E. Gladstone *On books and the housing of them* (London, 1898) and E.W. Nicholson, *Mr. Gladstone and the Bodleian* (Oxford, 1898).
36. Charles Edward Mallet, *A history of the University of Oxford* (London, 1927), vol. III, pp.333 and 339.
37. John Ruskin, *Works*, XXII, p.xlii.
38. Elizabeth Gaskell, *Wives and daughters* (London, 1866), p.253.
39. Parliamentary Papers, 1852, xxii, pp.93–4, cited in *The Cambridge history of the book in Britain*, VI (1830–1914), ed. D. McKitterick (Cambridge, 2009), p.501.
40. Martin Maw, foreword to Mick Belson, *On the press: through the eyes of the Craftsmen of Oxford University Press* (Witney, 2003), p.viii.
41. Belson, *On the press*, p.ix.
42. Ibid.
43. R.M. Ritter, *The Oxford guide to style* (Oxford, 2002).
44. Belson, *On the press*, p.ix.
45. Ibid., p.x.
46. Ibid., p.xi.
47. Ibid., p.x.
48. Ibid., pp.62–3.
49. Ibid., p.86.
50. Bateman, *Daniel Wilson*, vol. 1, p.113.
51. Lewis Carroll, *Alice through the looking glass*
52. Medieval logicians of the twelfth century onwards.
53. Richard Whateley, *Logic* (1827), p.63, explains that it is not every word that is categorematic, that is, capable of being employed by itself as a term.
54. Whateley, ibid., edition of 1843, I. ii. §2, p.347. Syncategorematic words are such as cannot singly express a term, but only a part of a term.
55. Quoted in Carroll's *Diaries*, vol. VII, pp.167–9, note 316.
56. (Letter, pp.11–12). G.A. Oxon, b.19 (356), pp.383 ff. *A letter to the Rector of Lincoln College*, by Philalethes (1807).
57. Bodleian Library, Bod 2626 b. 1, 2.
58. *Edinburgh Review*, xvi (1809), pp.158–97, pp.162–3, 'The Scottish universities...have not retained [the] pernicious structure [of the English ones]...they are without any of those artificial impediments which, in the south, have so effectually resisted the progress of improvement'.
59. The reviewers in question are thought to have been John Playfair, Richard Payne Knight and Sydney Smith.
60. Copleston, 'Three replies to the calumnies of the *Edinburgh Review*', p.21.
61. Ibid., p.22.
62. *A reply to the Calumnies of the* Edinburgh Review *against Oxford; containing an account of studies pursued in that University, Edinburgh Review*, 16.31(April 1810) p.159.
63. De Quincey's review of general educational handbooks. 'Excepting only a little treatise of Erasmus, *de Ratione Studii*, all the essays in this subject by eminent Continental writers appeared in the 17th century; and of these, a large majority before the year 1640. They were universally written in Latin....About the year 1645, Lewis Elzevir published a corpus of these essays, amounting in all to four-and-twenty.' *Letters to a young man whose education has been neglected*, II, first published in *London Magazine*, VII (February 1823), pp.189–94, *The works of Thomas de Quincey*, ed. Frederick Burwick (London, 2000), vol. III, pp.50–8, p.53.
64. Ibid., p.56.
65. F. Oakley, *Remarks upon Aristotelian and Platonic ethics, as a branch of the studies pursued in the University of Oxford* (Oxford, 1837), p.25.
66. Ibid., p.11.
67. John Henry Newman, *University sketches*, ed. George Sampson (Scott Library, London and Newcastle, 1902), p.xiii, quoting Newman.

68. *Letters to a College Friend*, III, 1 September 1840, John Ruskin, *Works*, vol. I, pp.418–19.
69. John Ruskin, *The stones of Venice*, II, Chapter VIII, 51, *Works*, vol. X, pp.374–5.
70. Quoted in footnote, ibid., p.374.
71. Coleridge and Watts are not mentioned in W. and M. Kneale, *The development of logic* (Oxford, 1962), but ibid p.298. describes Aldrich's book.
72. Coleridge, *Logic*, ed. J.R. de J. Jackson, *Collected works*, 13 (London, 1981), p.51.
73. Copleston, 'Three replies to the calumnies of the *Edinburgh Review*', pp.15–16.
74. Bodleian Library, Oxford, Bod 2626 b. 1,2.
75. John Stuart Mill, Inaugural address delivered to the University of St. Andrews, 1867, *Essays on equality, law and education,* ed. John M. Robson (Toronto, 1984), pp.217–57, p.223.
76. Ibid., p.224.
77. John Henry Newman, *Lectures and essays on University subjects* (Longman, 1859), pp.1–28.
78. Ibid.
79. Evelyn Abbot and Lewis Campbell, *The life and letters of Benjamin Jowett* (London, 1897), vol. I, pp.185–6.
80. Robert Saundby, *Introductory address at the opening of the University College Medical School, Cardiff* (Birmingham, 1898), pp.4–5.
81. Ibid.
82. A.E. Houseman, *Letters*, ed. Henry Maas (London, 1971), p.65.
83. Charles Dickens, *David Copperfield*, ed. Nina Burgis (Oxford, 1981), p.74.
84. Matthew Arnold, *Education and empire*, pp.3–4, quoting Arnold's *Irish essays*, p.75.
85. Matthew Arnold, *English literature and Irish politics*, ed. R.H. Super (Ann Arbor, 1973), pp.21–2.
86. Ibid., p.315.
87. *The speeches of Charles Dickens*, ed. K.J. Fielding (Oxford, 1960), pp.81–2.
88. Ibid., pp.279–81. See, too, Matthew Arnold, *Culture and anarchy*, 1869, *Prose works*, 5.165.
89. Arnold, *English literature and Irish politics*, p.23.
90. Kevin Sharpe, 'The foundation of the Chairs of History at Oxford and Cambridge: an episode in Jacobean politics', *History of Universities,* II (1982), 127–53, p.127, quoting BL Cottonian MS Faustina E V, ff.89–90v.
91. *Oxhist*, VII, p.362.
92. Ibid., p.423, on low standards for pass degree examinations in French. An examination in German was available from 1872.
93. First Public Examination, MT 1879, Bodleian Library, Bod 2626 b. 1, 2.
94. Bodleian Library, Bod 2626 b. 1,2 Trinity Term, 1879.
95. George Grote (1794–1871) was the author of a lengthy *History of Greece* (London, 1846–56).
96. *Transactions of the Royal Historical Society*, 2 (1873), 9–10.
97. O.G.S. Crawford, *Said and done: the autobiography of an archaeologist* (London, 1955), pp.44–5.
98. George Eliot, *Letters*, vol. VIII, p.89.
99. William Buckland, *Reliquiae Diluvianae: or observations on the organic remains contained in caves, fissures, and diluvial gravel, and on other geological phenomena attesting the action of a universal deluge* (London, 1823), p.143.
100. Amateurs, connoisseurs, entrepreneurs, *Enlightenment: discovering the world in the eighteenth century*, ed. Kim Sloan (London, 2004), p.85.
101. *Monographs by the very Rev. Dr. Buckland* (Oxford, Bodleian Library, Bod.18811 d.31), includes a series of publications on this matter and some manuscript letters bound in with them.
102. Charles Lyell, *Principles of Geometry* (1830–3), ed. Martin J.S. Rudwick (Chicago, 1990).
103. The botanist Charles Lyell (1769–1849) became a fellow of the Linnean Society in 1813. He was the father of the Geologist Charles Lyell (1797–1875).
104. The Geological Survey (a project which also fell outside the universities) was instituted in 1837.
105. See p.281.
106. *Monographs by the very Rev. Dr. Buckland Bod.18811 d.31 including Vindiciae Geologicae* (Oxford, 1820), p.2.

107. Ibid.
108. Ibid., p.10.
109. As did Arnold, Hampden, Keble, Newman, Pusey, Whately, Wilberforce and, notably, Charles Lyell.
110. John Henry Newman, *Letters and diaries*.
111. John Ruskin, *Modern painters*, 3.252. *The works of John Ruskin*, ed. E.T. Cook and Alexander Wedderburn, vols. 2–5, vol. 3, p.252.
112. *The works of John Ruskin*, ed. E.T. Cook and Alexander Wedderburn (London, 1906), vol. XXVI, p.197.
113. *Oxhist*, VI, p.658 describes the scene.
114. Mrs. Isabella Sidgwick, *Macmillan's Magazine*, LXXVIII, no. 468 (October 1898), 'A Grandmother's tales', pp.433–4, taken from J.R. Lucas, 'Wilberforce and Huxley: A legendary encounter', J.R. Lucas says that he 'owes the identification to Mr Christopher Chessun, of University College, Oxford', http://users.ox.ac.uk/~jrlucas/legend.html.
115. Lewis Carroll, *Some popular fallacies about vivisection, complete works* (1994), p.1071.
116. John Ruskin, *Works*, XX, pp.222–3.
117. Although life-drawing remains central to the syllabus of the Ruskin School in Oxford.
118. *The Storm Cloud*, Lecture II, *Works* 34, p.72.
119. Ibid., p.73.
120. John Ruskin, *Lectures on art, delivered before the University of Oxford in Hilary term, 1870, Works* XX (1870), p.41.
121. Francis Bacon, *The advancement of learning*, Book II, 11.
122. Ibid., 10.
123. Pattison, *Suggestions on academical organization*, p.146.
124. The buildings became the present Museum of the History of Science in 1935.
125. After whom the Randolph Hotel is named.
126. 1834 *Penny Cycl.* II. 97 Anthropology considers man as a citizen of the world, and has nothing properly to do with the varieties of the human race.
127. 1861 HULME *Moquin-Tandon* Pref. 8 Natural History, or Anthropology the principal characters of our species, its perfection, its accidental degradations, its unity, its races, and the manner in which it has been classified, cited in the *Oxford English Dictionary*.
128. 1881 FLOWER in *Nature* No. 619. 437, cited in the *Oxford English Dictionary*. The aim of zoological anthropology is to discover a natural classification of man.
129. George Eliot, *Letters*, ed. Gordon S. Height (Yale, 1956), pp.99–101.
130. George Eliot, *Middlemarch* (Oxford 1986), p.216.
131. Ibid., p.217.
132. Ibid., p.409.
133. E.B. Tylor, *Primitive culture* (London, 1871), 2 vols, vol. I, p.4.
134. Ibid., p.5.
135. Ibid., p.10.
136. Ibid., p.5.
137. Ibid.
138. Ibid., p.13.
139. R. Angus Downie, *Frazer and the Golden Bough* (London, 1970).
140. *Oxhist*, VII, pp.703–4.
141. Pattison, *Suggestions on academical organization*, p.141.
142. Quoted in *Oxhist*, VII, p.460.
143. Pitt Rivers Museum Archives, Correspondence of Sir Edward Burnett Tylor.
144. Pattison, *Suggestions on academical organization*, p.232.
145. Ibid., p.234.
146. Ibid., p.138.
147. *Collectanea*, II, ed. Montagu Burrows, *Oxford Historical Society*, xvi (1890) pp.428–30.
148. *Oxford University Statutes, translated to 1843*, tr. G.R.M. Ward and James Heywood (London, 1851), vol. II, p.33. 1807 Statute of examining candidates for degrees Tit. IX, sec. 2, also requires live examination, ibid., pp.62–3.

149. *181 in Reminiscences of Oxford by Oxford Men*, ed. L.M. Quiller Couch, *Oxford Historical Society*, xxii (1892), p.241.
150. Copleston, 'Three replies to the calumnies of the *Edinburgh Review*', p.138.
151. Letter to Henry Wilberforce, 13 May 1831, *Letters and diaries*, vol. II, p.330.
152. See *The history of the University of Oxford*, ed. M.G. Brock and M.C. Curthoys (Oxford, 1997), vol. VI, p.347, for the changeover, and *Oxford University Magazine*, I (1834), 99.
153. *The letters of Oscar Wilde*, ed. Rupert Hart-Davis (London, 1962), p.14. *Oscar Wilde's Oxford notebooks*, ed. Philip E. Smith and Michael S. Helfand (Oxford, 1989).
154. *The letters of Oscar Wilde*, p.15.
155. Ibid., p.33.
156. Ibid., p.35.
157. Ibid., p.53.
158. *Correspondence of Arthur Hugh Clough*, Balliol, 16 November 1840, to Anne Clough, ed. F.L. Mulhauser (Oxford, 1957), vol. I, p.73.
159. Ibid., 6 June 1841, to Anne Clough, to J.N. Simpkinson, ed. F.L. Mulhauser, p.109.
160. Ibid., Balliol, 19 May 1839, to J.P. Gell, ed. F.L. Mulhauser (Oxford, 1957), vol. I, p.90.
161. Ibid., Balliol, 19 May 1839, to J.N. Simpkinson, 27 August 1840, ed. F.L. Mulhauser (Oxford, 1957), vol. I, p.102.
162. Macaulay, *Letters*, 19 January 1855, p.438.
163. Several examples in Christopher Stray, 'From oral to written examinations: Cambridge, Oxford and Dublin 1700–1914, *History of Universities*, XX/2 (2005), 76–130, p.78.
164. Report of Her Majesty's Commissioners…University and Colleges at Oxford (1852), printed in Michael Sanderson, *The universities in the nineteenth century*, p.95.
165. Hansard, 3rd series, vol. 110, pp.691–765.
166. Lyon Playfair's 'On teaching Universities and Examining Boards' (Edinburgh, 1872), p.28, quoted in *The note-books of Matthew Arnold*, ed. Howard Foster Lowry, Karl Young and Waldo Hilary Dunn (Oxford, 1952), p.189.
167. *The letters of Matthew Arnold*, October 1870, ed. Cecil Y. Lang (Virginia, 1996–2001), vol. III, p.440.
168. Ibid., p.442.
169. Ibid., p.440.
170. Ibid.
171. Ibid., pp.440–1.
172. Ibid., pp.441.
173. Matthew Arnold, *The scholar gypsy: The poems of Matthew Arnold*, ed., Kenneth Allott (London, 1965), pp.331–343.
174. Thomas Hardy, *Jude the obscure* (London, 1912), p.93.
175. Ibid., p.95.
176. Ibid., p.98.
177. Ibid., p.133.
178. Ibid.
179. Ibid., p.137.
180. Ibid., p.134.
181. Ibid., p.137.
182. Ibid.
183. Ibid., p.138.
184. *The life and work of Thomas Hardy, by Thomas Hardy*, ed. Michael Millgate (London, 1984), p.52.
185. Florence Emily Hardy's *The early life of Thomas Hardy* (London, 1928), 2 vols, vol. II, p.66.
186. *The collected letters of Thomas Hardy*, ed. Richard Little Purdy and Michael Millgate (Oxford, 1978), vol. I, p.7
187. *The life and work of Thomas Hardy, by Thomas Hardy*, p.32.
188. 'Signs of change', in William Morris, *Hopes and fears for art and signs of change*, introduced by Peter Faulkner (Thoemmes Press, Chippenham, 1994), p.18.

189. Quoted in Veronica Franklin Gould, *G.F. Watts: the last great Victorian* (Yale, 2004).
190. *Fors Clavigera*, Letter I, 8, John Ruskin, *Works*, XXVII, pp.18–9. Cf. Kingsley's *Cheap clothes and nasty* (London, 1850).
191. *Fors Clavigera*, Letter 80, August 1877, *Works*, XXIX, pp.170–1.
192. Mark Girouard, *The return to Camelot: chivalry and the English gentleman* (Yale, 1981), pp.222–3.
193. A.S. Byatt, *The children's book* (London, 2009), pp.29–30.
194. *Oxford and working-class education, being the Report of a joint committee of University and working class representatives on the relation of the University to the higher education of workpeople* (Oxford, 1908), p.86.
195. See p.282.
196. *Politics for the people* was launched on 6 May 1848.
197. *Journal of Association* (1852), p.211.
198. Ibid., p.162.
199. *Democratic Socialism in Britain: classic texts in economic and political thought, 1825–1952*, ed. David Reisman, vol. 2, Frederick Denison Maurice, Charles Kinglsey and John Malcolm Ludlow: The Christian Socialists (London, 1996), paginated as facsimiles, p.42, of this lecture. Christian Socialism produced 'Tracts'.
200. Ibid., pp.18–20.
201. *Works*, 13.553.
202. Gentlemen were still not supposed to be interested in making money. If higher education gives entry to particular professions or activities, are those who are allowed to become professionals also allowed to earn without loss of class? (There was controversy in the 1890s about the amateur–professional 'divide' in sport.) Girouard, *The return to Camelot*, p.248.
203. E.V. Arnold, *College expenses* (Cambridge, 1883), p.3.
204. Institute of Education Archive, *Principal's letter book*, June–December 1906, 2 October.
205. *The letters of Matthew Arnold*, January 1843, vol. I, p.50.
206. Pattison, *Suggestions on academical organization*, p.57.
207. Ibid.
208. Ibid., p.59.
209. Ibid., p.81.
210. Ibid., p.62.
211. Ibid., p.68.
212. Ibid., p.80.
213. Ibid., p.83.

Conclusion

1. R.G. Collingwood, *An autobiography* (Oxford, 1939), pp.3–4.
2. Mill, Inaugural address delivered to the University of St. Andrews, pp.217–57, p.217.
3. Hastings Rashdall, *The Universities of Europe in the Middle Ages* (Oxford, 1895), vol. III, revised Powicke and Emden (Oxford, 1936), p.463.
4. Ibid., pp.460–2.
5. Hardy, Thomas, *Jude the obscure* (London, 1912).
6. Nicholas Keene, 'John Fell: education, erudition and the English Church in late seventeenth century Oxford', *History of Universities,* XVIII (2003), 62–102, p.65.
7. Elizabethanne Boran, 'Malignancy and the reform of the University of Oxford in the mid-seventeenth century', *History of Universities,* XXVII (2001–2), 19–46.
8. *Oxhist*, III, p.395
9. John Henry Newman, *The British Critic* (July 1838).
10. *John Betjeman's Oxford*, p.41.

SELECT BIBLIOGRAPHY

Abbot, Evelyn and Lewis Campbell, *The life and letters of Benjamin Jowett* (London, 1897).

Abelard, Peter, *Collationes*, vol. II, ed. and tr. John Marenbon and Giovanni Orlandi (Oxford, 2001), pp.78ff.

Abelard, Peter, *Ethics (Scito te ipsum)*, ed. David Luscombe (Oxford, 1971).

Adams, Pauline, *Somerville for women: an Oxford College*, 1873–1993 (Oxford, 1996).

Addison, Joseph, *Miscellaneous works* (London, 1914).

Address by the Vice-Chancellor at the Memorial Service for Lord Jenkins of Hillhead, OM, *At the University Church of St Mary the Virgin, Oxford*, 1 March 2003, http://www.ox.ac.uk/gazette/2002-3/supps/1_4651.htm. Accessed 7 December 2009.

Ali, Tariq, 'Islam, empire and the left', Conversation with Tariq Ali, Editor, *New Left Review*, 8 May 2003, http://globetrotter.berkeley.edu/Elberg/Ali/ali-con2.html. Accessed 7 December 2009.

Allen, Brigid, 'The early history of Jesus College, Oxford, 1571–1603', *Oxoniensia*, 62(1997), 105–24.

Anderson, M.W., *Peter Martyr, a reformer in exile (1542–62)* (Niewekoop, 1975).

Anderson, Marvin W.,'*Vista Tigurina: Peter Martyr and European reform* (1556–62)', *The Harvard Theological Review*, 83.2(1990), 181–206.

Annales Sex Regum Angliae, ed. T. Hog (London, 1845).

Anon, *The history of the times: 'The thunderer' in the making, 1785–1841* (London, 1935).

Anon, *A letter of advice to young gentleman at the University to which are subjoined, Directions for young students* (London, 1701, repr. 1721).

Arms, Nancy, 'A prophet in two countries, The life of F.E. Simon', *American Journal of Physics*, 35.3(1967), 290–1.

Arnold, E.V., *College expenses* (Cambridge, 1883).

Arnold, Matthew, *Culture and anarchy* (1869), (New York, 1983).

Arnold, Matthew, *English literature and Irish politics*, ed. R.H. Super (Ann Arbor, 1973).

Arnold, Matthew, *The letters of Matthew Arnold*, October 1870, ed. Cecily Y. Lang (Virginia, 1996–2001).

Arnold, Matthew, *The note-books of Matthew Arnold*, ed. Howard Foster Lowry, Karl Young and Waldo Hilary Dunn (Oxford, 1952).

Arnold, Matthew, *Schools and Universities on the Continent, first written as a Report to the Schools Inquiry Commission* (1865–7), ed. R.H. Super (Ann Arbor, 1964), p.144.

Ascham, Roger, *The Scholemaster* (London, 1570).

Ashworth, E.J., 'The Libelli Sophistarum and the use of medieval logic texts at Oxford and Cambridge in the early sixteenth century', *Vivarium*, 17(1979), 134–58.

Aubrey, John, *Brief lives*, ed. Oliver Lawson Dick (Michigan, 1957).

Augustine, *De Doctrina Christiana*, ed. and tr. R.P.H. Green (Oxford, 1995).

Austen, Jane, *Sense and sensibility* (Basingstoke, 1987).

Bacon, Francis, *The advancement of learning*, ed. Michael Kiernan (Oxford, 2000).

Bacon, *Works* (1957–).

Bacon, Francis, *Novum Organum*, ed. James Spedding, Robert Leslie Ellis and Douglas Denon Heath, *The works*, vol. VIII (Boston, 1863).

Bacon, Roger, *Opus tertium*, ed. J.S. Brewer (repr. London, 1965).

Baker, J.H., *Legal education in London, 1250–1850*, Selden Society (London, 2007).

Baker, J.H., *The third University of England*, Selden Society Lecture (London, 1990).

Baker, John, *The Oxford history of the laws of England* VI (Oxford, 2003).

Bateman, J., *Daniel Wilson* (London, 1860), 2 vols.

Bawden, Nina, *In my own time: almost an autobiography* (London, 1994).

Beddard, R.A., 'A projected Cromwellian Foundation at Oxford and the "True reformed Protestant" interest, c.1657–8', *History of Universities*, 15(1997–99), 155–91.

Beddard, R.E., 'The Bodleian library's first foreign reader', Bodleian Library Record, XVIII, 2(2003), 151–73.

Beerbohm, Max, *Zuleika Dobson* (London, 1947).

Bennett, J.A.W., 'Oxford in 1699', *Oxoniensia*, 3(1939), 148–9.

Belson, Mike, *On the press: through the eyes of the craftsmen of Oxford University Press* (Witney, 2003).

Besomi, Danielle, 'Roy Harrod and the Commission of Inquiry into the Bodleian Question, 1930–1', *Bodleian Library Record*, 17(2000–2), 36–44.

Betjeman, John, *John Betjeman's Oxford*, first published as *An Oxford University chest*, illustrated by L. Moholy-Nagy, Osbert Lancaster and Edward Bradley ('Cuthbert Bede') (Oxford, 1938 and 1979).

Binns, James, 'The decline of Latin in eighteenth century England', *Britannia Latina: Latin in the culture of Great Britain from the middle ages to the twentieth century*, ed. Charles Burnett and Nicholas Mann, Warburg Institute Colloquia, 8 (London/Turin, 2005), pp.170–7.

Blund, Johannes, *Tractatus de anima*, ed. D.A. Callus and R.W. Hunt (London, 1970).

Bodley, Thomas, *Letter of Thomas Bodley, printed in Bodleian Quarterly Record*, II(1919), 287.

Bodley, Thomas, *Letters of Thomas Bodley to the University of Oxford*, 1598–1611 (Oxford, 1927).

Boran, Elizabethanne 'Malignancy and the reform of the University of Oxford in the mid-seventeenth century', *History of Universities*, XXVII(2001–2), 19–46.

Bossuet, Jacques-Bénigne, *Politics drawn from the very words of Holy Scripture*, Introduction, tr. and ed. Patrick Riley, Cambridge texts in the history of political thought (Cambridge, 1990), p.2.

Boswell, James, *Boswell's life of Johnson*, ed. George Birkbeck Hill, revised L.F. Powell (Oxford, 1934), pp.59–61.

Boswell, James, *Life of Johnson: an edition of the original manuscript*, ed. Marshall Waingrow (Edinburgh/Yale, 1994).

Bowyer, William, *Literary anecdotes of the eighteenth century: an incidental view of the progress and advancement of literature in this kingdom during the last century*, vol. I, ed. John Nichols (1782, second edition, London, 1812), 6 vols.

Boyle, Robert, *The Christian virtuoso* (1690–1), *The works of Robert Boyle*, vol. 11, ed. Michael Hunter and Edward B. Davis (London, 2000).

Boyle, Robert, *Style of the scriptures, works*, vol. II, ed. Michael Hunter and Edward B. Davis (London, 1999), pp.381–488.

Bradwardine, Thomas, *De Causa Dei* (London, 1618).
Bradwardine, Thomas, *Tractatus de proportionibus,* ed. and tr. H. Lamar Crosby (Wisconsin, 1955).
Brewer, Sarah, ed., *The early letters of Bishop Richard Hurd (1739–62), Church of England Record Society,* 3(1995), pp.70–1.
Brittain, Vera, *Testament of friendship* (London, 1997).
Brockliss, L.W.B., ed., *Magdalen College, Oxford, a history* (Oxford, 2008).
Buckland, William, *Monographs by the very Rev. Dr. Buckland Bod.18811 d.31 including Vindiciae Geologicae* (Oxford, 1820).
Buckland, William, *Reliquiae Diluvianae: or observations on the organic remains contained in caves, fissures, and diluvial gravel, and on other geological phenomena attesting the action of a universal deluge* (London, 1823).
Burnet, Gilbert, *A dialogue concerning education, a collection of several tracts of the right honourable Edward, Earl of Clarendon, published from his Lordship's original manuscripts* (London, 1727).
Burrows, Montagu, ed., *Collectanea,* II, *Oxford Historical Society,* xvi(1890), 428–30.
Burton, Robert, *The anatomy of melancholy,* ed. Thomas C. Faulkner (Oxford, 1989).
Burton, Robert, *Philosophaster,* tr. Paul Jordan-Smith (Stanford, 1931).
Butler, R.F. and M.H. Prichard, *St. Anne's College, a history: retrospects and recollections,* vol. I, 1879–1921 (Oxford, 1930).
Buxton, W.J.M. and P.H. Williams, eds., *New College, Oxford, 1379–1979* (Oxford, 1979).
Byatt, A.S., *The children's book* (London, 2009).
Cambrensis, Giraldus, *De rebus a se gestis, opera,* vol. I, ed. D.S. Brewer, Rolls Series, 21(1861), pp.72–3.
Carroll, Lewis, *Complete works* (London, 1994).
Carroll, Lewis, *The letters of Lewis Carroll,* ed. Morton N. Cohen (London, 1979).
Chaucer, Geoffrey, *The Canterbury tales,* Riverside Chaucer (Oxford, 1988).
Clough, Arthur Hugh, *Correspondence of Arthur Hugh Clough,* ed. F.L. Mulhauser (Oxford, 1957).
Cobbett, William, *Cobbett's parliamentary history of England, 1066–1803,* vol. I (London, 1806).
Coleridge, S.T., *Logic,* ed. J.R. de J. Jackson, *Collected works,* vol. 13 (London, 1981).
Coleridge, Samuel Taylor, *Biographia Literaria,* ed. G. Watson (London, 1906), p.55.
Collingwood, R.G., *An autobiography* (Oxford, 1939).
Cooper, C.H., *Annals of Cambridge,* vol. I (1842).
Copleston, Edward, *Three replies to the calumnies of the* Edinburgh Review *against Oxford* (*Edinburgh Review,* xvi(1810), 158ff.) (repr. Bristol, 2001).
Costello, William T., *The scholastic curriculum in early seventeenth-century Cambridge* (Cambridge, 1958).
Crawford, O.G.S., *Said and done: the autobiography of an archaeologist* (London, 1955).
Curtis, Mark, 'The alienated intellectuals of early Stuart England', *Past and present,* 23(1962), 25–41.
Darwall-Smith, Robin, *A history of University College, Oxford* (Oxford, 2008).
Davis, A.P., *Isaac Watts: his life and works* (1948).
Davis, Virginia, 'The making of English collegiate statutes in the later middle ages, *History of Universities,* XII(1993), 1–24.
Dawkins, Richard, 'Evolution in biology tutoring', *The Oxford tutorial,* ed. David Palfreyman (Oxford, 2001), p.62.

de Quincey, Thomas, *Letters to a young man whose education has been neglected*, II, first published in *London Magazine*, VII(February 1823), 189–94.

The works of Thomas de Quincey, ed. Frederick Burwick III (London, 2000), pp.50–8.

Delaney, Patrick, *Fifteen sermons upon social duties* (London, 1744).

Delhaye, P., '"Grammatica" et "ethica" au xiie siécle', *Recherches de théologie ancienne et médievale*, 25(1958), 59–110.

Denley, Peter, 'The collegiate movement in Italian universities in the late middle ages', *History of Universities*, 10(1991), 29–91.

Dent, C.M., *Protestant reformers in Elizabethan Oxford* (Oxford, 1983).

Department of Education and Skills (DES) NEWS 232/87, 23 July 1987.

Dickens, Charles, *David Copperfield*, ed. Nina Burgis (Oxford, 1981), p.74.

Dickens, Charles, *The speeches of Charles Dickens*, ed. K.J. Fielding (Oxford, 1960).

Dodgson, Charles, *see* Lewis Carroll.

Donne, John, *The sermons of John Donne*, 10 vols, ed. G.R. Potter and E.M. Simpson (Berkeley, 1953).

Downie, R. Angus, *Frazer and the golden bough* (London, 1970).

Dryden, John, *The life of St. Francis Xavier* (1688), *The works of John Dryden*, ed. Alan Roper and P.H. Swedenberg (Berkeley, 1979).

Duffy, Eamon, *Fires of faith: Catholic England under Mary Tudor* (Yale, 2009).

Edinburgh Review, xvi(1809), 158–97.

Edmund of Abingdon, *Speculum Ecclesie*, ed. Helen O. Forshaw (London, 1973).

Eliot, George, *Middlemarch* (Oxford, 1986).

Eliot, T.S., *Letters of T.S. Eliot*, ed. Valerie Eliot I (London, 1988), pp.60–2.

Elizabeth I, Translations, 1544–89, ed. J. Mueller and J. Scodel (Chicago, 2009), pp.1, 7.

Emden, A.B., *An account of the Chapel and library building, St. Edmund Hall* (Oxford, 1932).

Epistolae Academicae, 1508–96, ed. W.T. Mitchell, OHS, NS, xxvi(1980), 3–4.

Erasmus, *Collected works* (Toronto, 1974).

Erasmus, *The epistles of Erasmus*, ed. Francis Morgan Nichols (London, 1901–8).

Evans, Margaret, ed., *Letters of Richard Radcliffe and John James of Queen's College, Oxford, 1755–83*, vol. ix, OHS (Oxford, 1888).

Evelyn, John, *The diary of John Evelyn*, ed. E.S. de Beer (London, 1959).

Faculty of History, Oxford, *Why we are at war: Great Britain's case, by the members of the Oxford Faculty of History* (third edition, Oxford, 1914).

Feingold, Mordechai, 'Oriental studies', *Oxhist*, vol. IV, ed. Nicolas Tyacke (Oxford, 1997), pp.449–503.

Fletcher, Eric, *John Selden, 1584–1654*, Selden Society (London, 1969).

Fletcher, J.M., 'Change and resistance to change: a consideration of the development of English and German universities during the sixteenth century', *History of Universities*, 1(1981), 1–36.

Ford, Alan, *James Ussher: theology, history and politics in early modern Ireland and England* (Oxford, 2007).

Fowler, Thomas, *Corpus Christi* (London, 1898).

Franklin Gould, Veronica, *G.F. Watts: the last Great Victorian* (Yale, 2004).

Franks Commission, *Report of the Commission of Inquiry* (Oxford, 1970).

Friesen, John, 'Christ Church, Oxford, the ancients-moderns controversy, and the promotion of Newton in post-revolutionary England', *History of Universities*, XXIII(2008), 33–66.

Froude, James Anthony, *Short studies on great subjects* (1867–82) (London and Glasgow, 1909).

Galileo, *Galileo on the world systems*, tr. Maurice Finochiaro (Berkeley, 1977).

Gee, E.A., 'Oxford carpenters 1370–1530', *Oxoniensia,* 17–18(1954), 112–84.

Gibbon, Edward, *Memoirs of my life,* ed. Georges A. Bonnard (London, 1966).

Gibson, Strickland, ed., *Statuta Antiqua* (Oxford, 1931).

Gilbert, Humphrey, *Queene Elizabethe's Achademy (The erection of an achademy in London for educacion of her maiestes wardes, and others the youth of nobility and gentlemen*), vol. viii, ed. F.J. Furnivall, Early English Text Society, extra series (London, 1869).

Gillam, S.G., ed., *The building accounts of the Radcliffe camera,* OHS, 13(1958).

Girouard, Mark, *The return to Camelot: chivalry and the English gentleman* (Yale, 1981).

Gladstone, William Ewart, *On books and the housing of them* (London, 1898).

Goldsmith, Oliver, *An enquiry into the present state of polite learning in Europe,* ed. Arthur Friedman, *Collected works* (Oxford, 1966).

Goudge, Elizabeth, *The cathedral trilogy* (London, 1964).

Graham, Rose, ed., *Chantry certificates, Oxfordshire Record Society,* 1(1919), viii–x.

Graves, Robert, *Goodbye to all that* (London, 1929, fourth edition, 1966).

Green, John Richard and George Roberson Roberson, 'Oxford during the eighteenth century', ed. C.L. Stainer, *Studies in Oxford History,* OHS, 41(1901), 46–7.

Green, Vivian, *The commonwealth of Lincoln College, 1427–1977* (Oxford, 1979).

Grosseteste, Robert, *Hexameron,* ed. C.F.J. Martin (Oxford, 1996).

Grote, George, *History of Greece* (London, 1846–56).

Hanke, Lewis, *The Spanish struggle for justice in the conquest of America* (Boston, 1965).

Hansard, http://www.publications.parliament.uk/pa/pahansard.htm. Accessed 7 December 2009.

Hardy, Florence Emily, *The early life of Thomas Hardy* (London, 1928), 2 vols.

Hardy, Thomas, *The collected letters of Thomas Hardy,* ed. Richard Little Purdy and Michael Millgate (Oxford, 1978).

Hardy, Thomas, *Jude the obscure* (London, 1912).

Hardy, Thomas, *The life and work of Thomas Hardy, by Thomas Hardy,* ed. Michael Millgate (London, 1984).

Harper, Tom, 'From Laissez-faire to discipline', The Society of Gentleman Practisers, *Then and now,* 1799–1974, foreword by Peter Allsop (London, 1974), pp.191–200.

Harris, Simon, *RBK, a very Parfit Gentil Knight* (Clenchwarton, 2004).

Hart, Jenifer, *Ask me no more, autobiography* (London, 1998).

Hazlitt, William, 'On the ignorance of the learned', Essay VIII, *Table talk* (London, 1952).

Head, Edmund Walker, *A few words on the Bodleian library* (Oxford, 1833).

Hill, R.H., ed., *Shelley correspondence in the Bodleian library* (Oxford, 1926).

Hinnebusch, W.A., 'The pre-reformation sites of the Oxford Blackfriars', *Oxoniensia,* iii(1938), 57–82.

Hobbes, Thomas, *The correspondence of Thomas Hobbes,* ed. Noel Malcolm (Oxford 1994), 2 vols.

Hobbes, Thomas, *English works,* vol. VI, ed. William Molesworth (1840), p. 347.

Holtby, Winifred, *Land of green ginger* (Virago, 1983).

Hooker, Richard, *Ecclesiastical polity* (London, 1830).

Hopkins, Clare, *Trinity: 450 years of an Oxford College community* (Oxford, 2005).

Houseman, A.E., *Letters,* ed. Henry Maas (London, 1971).

Howell, Wilbur Samuel, *Logic and rhetoric in England 1500–1700* (Princeton, 1956).

http://anglicanhistory.org/hooker/preface/162-171.pdf

http://www.keble.ox.ac.uk/about/past/letters-home-eve-of-first-world-war, with the note: These letters are reproduced with permission from the biography by Simon Harris, *RBK. a very Parfit Gentil Knight* (Clenchwarton, 2004). Accessed 7 December 2009.

Hunter, Michael, *Robert Boyle (1627–91): scrupulosity and science* (Woodbridge, 2000).

Innocent III, Pope, *The letters of Pope Innocent III (1196–1216) concerning England and Wales,* ed. C.R. and M.G. Cheney (Oxford, 1967).

Institute of Education Archive, *Principal's letter book*, June–December 1906, 2 October.

Jewel, John, *Works*, ed. Ayre, Parker Society (Cambridge, 1850).

Jocelin of Brakelond, *Chronicle,* ed. and tr. H.E. Butler (London, 1949), pp.94–5.

Johnson, Samuel, *Lives of the poets*, ed. Roger Lonsdale (Oxford, 2006).

Jones, L., *The discovery of Hebrew in Tudor England* (Manchester, 1983).

Keene, Nicholas, 'John Fell: education, erudition and the English Church in late seventeenth century Oxford', *History of Universities* XVIII(2003), 62–102.

Kilwardby, Robert, *De ortu scientiarum,* ed. Albert Judy (London and Toronto, 1976).

Kingsley, Charles, *Cheap clothes and nasty* (London, 1850).

Kneale, W., M. and W.C., *The development of logic* (Oxford, 1962).

Lander, Jesse M., *Inventing polemic: religion, print and literary culture in early modern England* (Cambridge, 2006).

Lane Poole, R., *A lecture on the history of the University Archive* (Oxford, 1912).

Lang, Cecil, Y., ed., *The letters of Matthew Arnold* (Virginia, 1996–2001).

Lattey, R.T., E.J.S. Parsons and I.G. Philip, 'A contemporary map of the defences of Oxford in 1644', *Oxoniensia*, I(1936), 161–72.

Laud, William, *Conference between William Laud and Mr. Fisher the Jesuit 1622*, ed. C.H. Simpkinson (London, 1901).

Laud, William, *An historical account of all material transactions relating to the University of Oxford, from Archbishop Laud's being elected Chancellor to his resignation of that Office, written by himself, works of the most reverend Father in God, William Laud*, vol. V (Oxford, 1853), p.120.

Levine, J., *The battle of the books: history and literature in the Augustan age* (Ithaca and London, 1991).

Lewis, Rhodri, 'A Babel off Broad Street: artificial language planning in 1650s Oxford', *History of Universities,* XX(2005), 108–45.

Lively, Penelope, *The house in Norham Gardens* (London, 1974, repr. 2004).

Locke, John, *Correspondence,* ed. E.S. De Beer (Oxford, 1976, 1982, 1989).

Lyell, Charles, *Principles of geology,* ed. Martin J.S. Rudwick (Chicago, 1990).

Macleane, Douglas, *A history of Pembroke College anciently Broadgates Hall* (Oxford, 1897).

Madan, Falconer, 'Some interesting features in the past history of science in Oxford', Bodleian Library, G.A. Oxon, c.130, item 6.

Mallet, Charles Edward, *A history of the University of Oxford* (London, 1927).

Marsh, Adam, *Epistolae,* vol. IV, ed. J.S. Brewer, Rolls Society (London, 1858).

Martial, *Epigrams,* ed. and tr. D.R. Shackleton-Bailer (Loeb, 1993).

McKitterick, D., ed., *The Cambridge history of the book in Britain, (1830–1914)*, vol. VI (Cambridge, 2009).

McKitterick, David, *Printing and the book trade in Cambridge, 1534–1698, History of Cambridge University Press*, vol. I (Cambridge, 1992).

Medwin, T., *The life of Percy Bysshe Shelley* (London, 1847).

Mill, John Stuart, Inaugural address delivered to the University of St. Andrews, 1867, *Essays on equality, law and education,*, ed. John M. Robson (Toronto, 1984), pp.217–57.

Millgate, Michael, ed., *The life and work of Thomas Hardy, by Thomas Hardy* (London, 1984), p.32.

Milne, J.G., *The early history of Corpus Christi College, Oxford* (Oxford, 1946).

Milton, John, *Artis Logicae Plenior Institutio ad Petri Rami Methodum concinnata* (1672), ed. and tr. Allan H. Gilbert *The works of John Milton*, vol. 11 (New York, 1935).

Milton, John, *Of education, complete prose works,* ed. D. Bush et al. (Yale, 1959).

Mitchell, W.T., ed., 'Register of congregations, 1505–17', OHS, NS, XXXVII, XXXVIII(1998), 2 vols.

Mordaunt Crook, J., *Brasenose, The biography of an Oxford College* (Oxford, 2008).

More, Thomas, *Confutation of Tyndale's answer, complete works,* vol. 8 (Yale, 1973).

More, Thomas, *The correspondence of Sir Thomas More,* ed. Elizabeth Frances Rogers (Princeton, 1947).

More, Thomas, *A dialogue concerning heresies*, 1531, *Complete works,* vol. 6 (Yale, 1981).

More, Thomas, *Diatribe against Luther, Responsio ad Lutherum* 1523, *complete works*, vol. 5 (Yale, 1969).

More, Thomas, *Letter to Oxford*, 1518, ed. Daniel Kinney, *Works,* vol. 15 (Yale, 1986), pp.130–49.

More, Thomas, *Utopia,* ed. Edward Surtz and J.H. Hexter (Yale, 1965).

Morgan, John, *Godly learning: Puritan attitudes towards reason, learning and education, 1560–1640* (Cambridge, 1986).

Morris, Jan, *Oxford* (Oxford, 1965, 1978, 2001).

Morris, William, *Hopes and fears for art and signs of change*, introduced by Peter Faulkner (Chippenham, 1994), p.18.

MS Bodley 282.

Newman, John Henry, *Lectures and essays on University subjects* (Longman, 1859).

Newman, John Henry, *Letters and correspondence of John Henry Newman,* ed. Anne Mozeley (London, 1891), 2 vols.

Newman, John Henry, *Letters and diaries*, ed. I.T. Ker et al. (London, 1961–2008), 32 vols.

Newman, John Henry, *University sketches,* ed. George Sampson (Scott Library, London and Newcastle, 1902).

Nicholls, C.S., *The history of St. Anthony's College, Oxford, 1950–2000* (Basingstoke, 2000).

Nicholson, E.W., *Mr. Gladstone and the Bodleian* (Oxford, 1898).

Nina Bawden, *In my own time: almost an autobiography* (London, 1994).

Nowell, Alexander, *Catechism,* tr. Thomas Norton (Cambridge, 1853).

Oakeley, F., *Remarks on the study of Aristotelian and Platonic ethics, as a branch of the Oxford system of education* (Oxford, 1837).

Ollard, S.L., *The six students of St Edmund Hall expelled from the University of Oxford in 1768* (Oxford, 1911).

OUTLINE, staff newsletter Oxford University Library Services.

Oxford and working-class education, being the Report of a joint committee of University and working class representatives on the relation of the University to the higher education of workpeople (Oxford, 1908).

Oxford University Gazette (Oxford, 1870).

Oxford University Statutes, tr. G.R.M. Ward and James Heywood (London, 1851).

Oxhist, III, pp.257ff., the King's Reader.

Pagden, Anthony, 'The "School of Salamanca" and the "Affair of the Indies"', *History of Universities*, 1(1981), 71–112.

Paley, William, *A view of the evidences of Christianity* (London, 1796).

Pantin, W.A., 'Tackley's inn, Oxford', *Oxoniensia,* 7(1942), 80–92.

Paquet, Jacques, 'Coût des etudes, pauvreté et labeur: fonctions et métiers d'étudiants au moyen âge', *History of Universities,* 2(1982), 15–52.

Parker, Irene, *Dissenting academies in England: their rise and progress and their place among the educational systems of the country* (Cambridge, 1914).

Parker, Matthew, 'A preface unto the Byble', *The Holie Bible* (London, 1568).

Parker, W.R., *Milton a biography*, vol. I (Oxford, 1968).

Pattison, Mark, *Suggestions on academical organization* (Edinburgh, 1868).

Philalethes, *A letter to the Rector of Lincoln College, by Philalethes* (1807), G.A. Oxon, b.19(356), pp.383ff.

Philip, I.G., 'A proposed refoundation of St. Mary Hall', *Oxoniensia,* 22(1957), 92–6.

Pitt Rivers Museum Archives, Correspondence of Sir Edward Burnett Tylor.

Playfair, Lyon, *On teaching Universities and examining Boards* (Edinburgh, 1872).

Plummer, C., ed., *Elizabethan Oxford,* OHS, VIII(1886), 180–1.

Prest, John, ed., *The illustrated history of Oxford University,* ed. John Prest (Oxford, 1993).

Pullman, Philip, *The amber spyglass* (London, 2000).

Pym, Barbara, *Jane and Prudence* (London, 1953, repr. Virago, 2007).

Quiller-Couch, L.M., ed., 'Reminiscences of Oxford by Oxford men', *Oxford Historical Society,* xxii(1892), 241.

Rait, Robert Sangster, *The Universities Commission: a review* (Banff, 1898).

Rannie, David Watson, *Oriel College* (London, 1900).

Rashdall, Hastings, *The Universities of Europe in the middle ages,* vol. III (Oxford, 1895), revised Powicke and Emden (Oxford, 1936).

Rawlinson, H.G., 'Three letters of Dr. Richard Traffles', *Oxoniensia,* 7(1942), 93–101.

Reid, David A., 'A science for polite society: British dissent and the teaching of natural philosophy in the seventeenth and eighteenth centuries', *History of Universities,* 21(2006), 117–58.

Reisman, David, ed., *Democratic socialism in Britain: classic texts in economic and political thought, 1825–1952,* Frederick Denison Maurice, Charles Kingsley and John Malcolm Ludlow: The Christian Socialists (London, 1996).

Reminiscences of Oxford, selected by L.M. Quiller Couch, OHS, xxii(1892).

Report of Her Majesty's Commissioners. University and Colleges at Oxford (1852), printed in Michael Sanderson, *The Universities in the nineteenth century.*

Reynolds, B., *Dorothy Sayers: her life and soul* (London, 1993).

Robinson, Hastings, ed., *Original letters relative to the English reformation,* Parker Society (Cambridge, 1846).

Roy, Ian, *The Royalist ordnance papers, 1642–1646,* ed. Ian Roy, *Oxfordshire Record Society,* 43(1963–4), 26–9.

Rufus of Cornwall, Richard, *In Physicam Aristotelis,* ed. Rega Wood (Oxford and London, 2003).

Ruskin, John, *The works of John Ruskin* (London, 1871–1880), vols 1–39, 1903–12.

Ruskin, John, *The works of John Ruskin,* ed. E.T. Cook and Alexander Wedderburn (London, 1906).

Salter, H.E., *Medieval archives of the University of Oxford,* 2 vols (Oxford, 1920–1).

Salter, H.E., *Oxford balliol deeds* (Oxford, 1913).

Salter, H.E., ed., *Remarks and collections of Thomas Hearne,* OHS, 67(1915).

Sanderson, Robert, *Logicae Artis Compendium,* ed. E.J. Ashworth, *Instrumenta rationis,* vol. II (Bologna, 1985).

Saundby, Robert, *Introductory address at the opening of the University College Medical School*, Cardiff (Birmingham, 1898).

Sayers, Dorothy, *Gaudy Night* (Hodder, 2003).

Searby, Peter, *The history of the University of Cambridge,* vol. III (1750–1850) (Cambridge, 1997), pp.152–3.

Shaw, Bernard, *Pen portraits and reviews*, *works*, 29(1931), 156–7.

Shirley, Walter Waddington, ed., *Fasciculi zizaniorum*, Rolls Series, 87 (London, 1858).

Shuttle, E.F.A., 'Henry Aldrich, Dean of Christ Church', *Oxoniensia,* 5(1940), 115–16.

Simcock, A.V., ed., *Robert T. Gunther and the Old Ashmolean* (Oxford, 1985).

Sloan, Kim, ed., *Enlightenment: discovering the world in the eighteenth century,* ed. Kim Sloan (London, 2004).

Smalley, Beryl, *The study of the Bible in the middle ages* (third edition, Oxford, 1983).

Smith, Jonathan, *Charles Darwin and Victorian visual culture* (Cambridge, 2006).

Southey, Robert, *Journals of a residence in Portugal 1800–1 and a visit to France 1838*, ed. Adolfo Cabral (Oxford, 1960).

Southey, Robert, *The life of Wesley*, 2 vols, ed. Maurice H. Fitzgerald (Oxford, 1925).

Statuta Antiqua universitatis Oxoniensis, ed. Strickland Gibson (Oxford, 1931).

Statutes of the University of Oxford, ed. John Griffith (Oxford, 1888).

Stevenson, David, ed., *Letters of Sir Robert Moray to the Earl of Kincardine, 1657–73* (Ashgate, 2007).

Stewart, J.I.M., *The Madonna of the Astrolabe* (London, 1977).

Stray, Christopher, 'From oral to written examinations: Cambridge, Oxford and Dublin 1700–1914, *History of Universities,* XX/2(2005), 76–130.

Stump, Eleonore, *Boethius 'De differentiis topicis'* (Cornell, 1978).

Summerson, Henry, *The Lucys of Charlecote and their library,* National Trust Studies 1979 (London, 1978), pp.149–60.

Summit, Jennifer, *Memory's library* (Chicago, 2008).

Swift, Jonathan, *Irish tracts, 1728–33*, ed. Herbert Davis (Oxford, 1955).

Swift, Jonathan, *A tale of a tub,* ed. D. Nichol Smith and A.C. Guthkelch (Oxford, 1958).

Tappan, Henry P., *University education* (New York, 1851).

Tappe, E.D., 'The Greek College at Oxford, 1699–1705', *Oxoniensia,* 19(1954), 92–3.

Taylor, Robert, *Nuffield College memories: a personal history* (Oxford, 2008).

Temple, William, Sir. 'Thoughts upon reviewing the essay of ancient and modern learning *'The works of Sir William Temple, Bart. In four volumes... to which is prefixed, the life and character of the author,* vol. 2 (Edinburgh, 1754), 4 vols, p.489.

Testament of youth (London, 1978).

'The beginning of women's ministry: the revival of the deaconess in the nineteenth-century Church of England', *Church of England Record Society,* 14 (Boydell, 2007).

The Chancellorship of Oxford: a contemporary view with a little history, Romanes Lecture (1966).

The history of the University of Oxford, general editor T.H. Aston (Oxford, 1984–94), 8 vols.

The Oxford Magazine (1958), p.232.

The Spectator, ed. Donald F. Bond V (Oxford, 1965).

The University Commission, or John Russell's Postbag (Oxford, 1850).

Thorne, S.E., *Essays in English legal history* (London, 1985).

Toynbee, Margaret, ed., *The papers of Captain Henry Stevens, Waggon-Master-General to King Charles I,* Oxfordshire Record Society, 42(1962).

Trinity College, *Report* (1995), 87, 'Women's Group', JCR C/WG/1/.

Tuck, Richard, *Natural rights theories: their origin and development* (Cambridge, 1979).
Tyack, Geoffrey, *Oxford, an architectural guide* (Oxford, 1998).
Tylor, E.B., *Primitive culture* (London, 1871), 2 vols.
Valla, Lorenzo, *De linguae latinae elegantia*, vol. 1, ed. Santiago López Moreda (Extremadura, 1999), 2 vols.
Vanpaemel, Gert, 'Experimental physics and the natural science curriculum in eighteenth century Louvan', *History of Universities,* 7(1988), 175–96.
Vericour, Professor de, *Transactions of the Royal Historical Society,* 1 (second edition 1975), p.9.
Vickers, Ilse, *Defoe and the new sciences* (Cambridge, 1996).
Walton, Izaak, *The Compleat Walton,* ed. Geoffrey Keynes (London, 1929), pp.524–6.
Walton, Izaak, *Lives,* in *The Compleat Walton,* ed. Geoffrey Keynes (London, 1929).
Ward, W.R., *Georgian Oxford: University politics in the eighteenth century* (Oxford, 1958).
Warton, T., *The triumph of Isis* (London, 1750).
Watts, Isaac, *Logic; or, the right use of reason in the inquiry after truth with a variety of rules to guard against error, in the affairs of religion and human life, as well as in the sciences* (published 1724, London, 1845).
Waugh, Evelyn, *Brideshead revisited* (1945) (Everyman, 1993).
Whateley, Richard, *Logic* (1827) (edition of 1843).
Wheeler, G.W., 'Sir Thomas Bodley's "Heads of Statutes",' *Bodleian Quarterly Record,* iii(1923), 119–21.
Whewell, William, *On the principles of English University education* (London, 1837).
Wilde, Oscar, *The letters of Oscar Wilde,* ed. Rupert Hart-Davis (London, 1962).
William of Auvergne, *De legibus,* 1, *Opera Omnia* (Paris, 1674, repr. Frankfurt-am-Main, 1963), p.22.
Williams, B., *Stanhope* (Oxford, 1932).
Wood, Anthony, *Athenae Oxonienses* (London, 1691).
Wood, Anthony, *The history and antiquities of the colleges and halls in the University of Oxford* (Oxford, 1786).
Wren, C., *Parentali* (1750), p.46.
Wright, Peter, *Spycatcher* (London, 1987).
Wyclif, John, *Trialogus,* ed. G. Lechler (Oxford, 1869).
Wyclif, John, *Polemical works,* ed. R. Buddensieg II (London, 1883), p.556.

INDEX